The Men Who Flew the Vought F4U Corsair

In Memoriam
For Colonel J. Hunter Reinburg USMC, 5 May 1918 to 23 June 1997,
and Roy D. 'Eric' Erickson USNRC and to all
former Corsair pilots throughout the world.

The Men Who Flew the Vought F4U Corsair

Martin W. Bowman

Pen & Sword
AVIATION

First published in Great Britain in 2021 by
Pen & Sword Aviation
An imprint of
Pen & Sword Books Ltd
Yorkshire – Philadelphia

ISBN 978 1 52670 580 8

A CIP catalogue record for this book is
available from the British Library.

Typeset by Mac Style
Printed and bound by CPI Group (UK) Ltd, Croydon CR0 4YY

MIX
Paper from
responsible sources
FSC® C013604

Pen & Sword Books Limited incorporates the imprints of Atlas,
Archaeology, Aviation, Discovery, Family History, Fiction, History,
Maritime, Military, Military Classics, Politics, Select, Transport,
True Crime, Air World, Frontline Publishing, Leo Cooper, Remember
When, Seaforth Publishing, The Praetorian Press, Wharncliffe
Local History, Wharncliffe Transport, Wharncliffe True Crime
and White Owl.

For a complete list of Pen & Sword titles please contact

PEN & SWORD BOOKS LIMITED
47 Church Street, Barnsley, South Yorkshire, S70 2AS, England
E-mail: enquiries@pen-and-sword.co.uk
Website: www.pen-and-sword.co.uk

Or

PEN AND SWORD BOOKS
1950 Lawrence Rd, Havertown, PA 19083, USA
E-mail: Uspen-and-sword@casematepublishers.com
Website: www.penandswordbooks.com

Contents

Acknowledgements

Alan Armstrong; Mike Bailey; Fred 'Crash' Blechman; Howard Cook; Lee Cook, author of *The Skull & Cross Bones Squadron; VF-17 in World War 2 (Schiffer, 1998)* Graham Dinsdale; the late Robert Dorr; Owen W. Dykema, who kindly gave permission to quote freely from "*From The Bird Barge* (Dykema Publishing Co. 1997); the late Roy D. 'Eric' Erickson; Andy Height; Nigel McTeer; the late Colonel J. Hunter Reinburg USMC, who kindly gave permission to quote freely from *Combat Aerial Escapades* (1966) and *Aerial Combat Escapades* (1988); Gareth Simons; Peter C. Smith; Tom Smith; Andy Thomas; Wallace Bruce Thomson; Terry C. Treadwell.

Chapter 1

A Dream is Born

The Corsair was a rugged machine which could take any amount of punishment on the flight-deck and appeared to make light of it. Everything about it was high-class and great attention to detail proclaimed itself wherever one looked. The cockpit was meticulously arranged with all dials readily visible and every lever and switch comfortably and conveniently to hand, without any need to search or grope. (Infinitely superior, I may say, to the cockpits of British aircraft of that time which suggested, by comparison, that they had been designed by the administrative office charwoman) … Somehow or other the Royal Navy would see to it that the Corsair could be deck-landed.

Carrier Pilot: An Unforgettable True Story of Wartime Flying
by Norman Hanson, by kind permission of Patrick Stephens (PSL) 1979

In 1938 the US Navy had decided that the time was long overdue to bring carrier-based aviation up to the same performance level as land-based aircraft. On 30 June 1938, the US Navy ordered the Grumman XF5F-1 and the Vought XF4U-1, while a third aircraft, the Bell XFL-1, was ordered later, on 8 November. The XF5F-1 was the first twin-engine, single-seat aircraft to be built for the navy, while the Bell XFL-1 was a carrier-based version of the P-39 Airacobra. The XFL-1 differed in some respects to the P-39, including the installation of a tail wheel in place of the tricycle arrangement. As it turned out, the twin-tailed Grumman machine was delayed by cooling problems to its Wright R-1820-40 Cyclone engines and the prototype did not complete tests until February 1941. After this setback, more problems were experienced with the aircraft. After just over 200 flights the XF5F-1 project was abandoned in favour of the XF7F-1, which later became the Tigercat. Equally, the Bell machine, first flown on 13 May 1940, was not proceeded with either.

At Vought the F4U-I project came under the wing of C.J. McCarthy who, in March 1940, had been appointed general manager of the Chance Vought Division. Early in 1938 McCarthy, who had worked with the late Chance Vought on the original Corsair, directed Rex B. Beisel and his team, who were already committed to the Vindicator and Kingfisher company projects, to turn their thoughts to the new carrier-borne fighter project. V-166A, Beisel's first proposal, incorporated the Pratt & Whitney R-1340 radial engine, but this was not proceeded with. V-166B, his second proposal, designed around the new 1,800hp experimental Pratt & Whitney XR-2800-2 Double Wasp air-cooled radial with a two-stage, two-speed supercharger, was submitted to the Bureau of Aeronautics on 8 April 1938. At the time the huge XR-2800-2 engine promised to be the most powerful powerplant available. Its take-off power alone was rated at 1,850hp at 2,600rpm (navy 'pursuits or fighters, of the day were rated at about 840hp to 1,200hp at best) and it could develop 1,500hp at 2,400rpm at 17,500 feet. The Pratt & Whitney experimental engine had the potential to make the XF4U-1 the navy's first 2,000hp fighter.

Beisel and his team had to design the smallest possible fuselage around the mighty Double Wasp. Everything possible that could be done to limit drag would have to be incorporated in the design, so use of spot-welding and flush-riveting was made throughout the external surfaces and a completely faired-in landing gear greatly reduced the drag penalties. Three gear-doors, one on the forward strut and two doors attached to the wing on either side of the wheel well ensured that not one part of the main landing gear or tail wheel protruded into the slipstream. Then there was the seemingly insurmountable problem posed by the massive 13 feet 4 inch diameter three-bladed propeller, which had to be used if the XR-2800-4 engine (which would power the prototype) was to enable the Corsair to attain its optimum design speed.

Meanwhile, the US Army Air Corps tried in vain to influence Pratt & Whitney to get them to develop a liquid-cooled inline engine instead of the air-cooled radial. Beisel and his team, however, were committed to the XR-2800 but they realised that unless they came up with a fairly radical design to accommodate the massive engine's 13-feet-4-inch-diameter three-bladed propeller, then its arc would give insufficient ground clearance on both take-off and landing. They could have opted for a much longer landing gear but that would have been too stilted and too heavy. The solution lay in the XF4U-1 wing design, which was gulled downwards, a feature that would also result in less aerodynamic drag at the juncture of wing and fuselage. The gulled wing was achieved by dropping the stub wings at an angle as they left the fuselage, with the outer-wing panels canted upwards again at a dihedral of 8 degrees for 30 minutes in the outer sections. The stub wings included open vents in their leading edges to allow cooling air for engine oil and air for supercharger intercooler equipment.

Inverted gull wing design was not new. But, in January 1941 Giuseppe M. Bellanca, chairman of the board of directors of the Bellanca Aircraft Corporation, New Castle, Delaware, which had been issued a US patent for an inverted gull wing on 17 September 1935, considered that Vought might have infringed his company's patent. The matter remained unresolved until United Aircraft Corporation successfully pointed out several British patents to the gull design, which dated back to the late 1920s. Bellanca, who were anxious not to be seen rocking the boat in time of war when everyone should be 'pulling together', and the Bureau of Aeronautics, which, at the behest of Vought, carried out its own investigation, fully exonerated the company from any patent infringements.

Using the gull wing instead of a straight wing made possible the use of a shorter, lighter landing gear than would ordinarily have been possible. Also, the main wheels could easily be retracted backwards (as they did on the SB2U-1 Kingfisher scout-bomber then in production) and swivelled through 87 degrees flat into the wing, which folded upwards for stowage aboard carriers. The wing arc joined the fuselage at 90-degree angles to allow the air to flow smoothly over the wing root/fuselage joint, eliminating the need for a wing fillet. The wings were of all-metal construction, built as an integral part of the fuselage centre section. The outer wings were metal forward of the spar, and fabric-covered plywood to the trailing edges. They folded upward over the cockpit canopy, hinging at the elbow of the gull wing. Fabric-covered plywood flaps spanned the width of the stub wings and one-half the distance of the outer-wing panels. Ailerons formed the balance of the outer-wing panel's trailing edge.

Small bomb cells featured in the outer-wing panels which, in theory, would be used to drop twenty 5.2lb bombs (four in each of five compartments) on formations of enemy bombers, the pilot sighting the bomb drop through a glass 'teardrop-shaped' panel in the cockpit floor. This feature was never implemented on production models. Fuel was carried in four integral tanks located in the wing centre sections and outer-panel leading edges with total capacity of 273 gallons. The carburettor, air supercharger intercooler and oil-cooler air inlet ducts were situated at the leading edge of the wings to remove the need for a drag-inducing scoop for each. In flight this layout created a curious high-pitched whistling sound as air was sucked into the ducts. Its effect later would not be lost on the Japanese who called the Corsair the 'Whistling Death' after the bloodcurdling scream emitted during high-speed dives on their positions. To American troops, particularly the USMC 'grunts' fighting in the Pacific Islands campaign, the 'Bent Winged Bird' was their saviour and the marines finally dubbed the Corsair the 'Sweetheart of Okinawa'.

A .30 calibre and a .50 calibre machine gun were mounted above the massive engine, firing through the upper propeller arc, and a .50 calibre machine gun outward of each wing-fold mechanism. The upper fuselage guns had 750 rounds of ammunition each and each wing gun had 300 rounds of ammunition. Provision was made to replace the wing guns with 23mm Madsen cannon, if available. On 28 November 1940, the navy asked for a production configuration with increased firepower and fuel capacity. Everything about the new fighter was massive. It weighed 9,357lb empty and measured 31 feet 11 inches with a 41 feet 11 inch wing spread – the largest American fighter yet built.

The Bureau of Aeronautics awarded Vought contract number 61544 for a single prototype on 11 June 1938 and the XF4U-1 was assigned Bureau Number (BuNo.) 1443. Beginning in January 1939, United Aircraft Corporation moved Chance Vought Aircraft into a plant shared with the Sikorsky Aircraft Division to become the Vought-Sikorsky Aircraft Division, United Aircraft Corporation. The XF4U-1 full-scale engineering mock-up, which would be used in wind-tunnel tests, was inspected by the Bureau of Aeronautics during 8 to 10 February 1939 and, shortly afterwards, construction of the prototype was given the go-ahead. New manufacturing techniques, such as spot welding of aluminium, developed by the Naval Aircraft Factory, would be employed in the construction. Spot welding hastened mass production because it enabled a structure of heavy aluminium skin and supports to be built up to form a very strong fuselage and wing framework. By 1 July that year the basic XF4U-1 design was 95 per cent complete. It was powered by the XR-2800-4, which was an improvement over the earlier -2.

After several hours of taxi tests and days of ground engine runs, the yellow-and-silver-painted XF4U-1 was ready for its first flight, at the Bridgeport Municipal Airport, Stratford, Connecticut on 29 May 1940.

Lyman A. Bullard, the Chief of Flight Test at Vought-Sikorsky Aircraft, would be at the controls. Bullard took the fledgling fighter up to 10,000 feet while executing some very basic standard manoeuvres such as turns, and he cycled the gear and flaps a few times. He then headed away from the airfield to carry out a couple of stalls and to test the cruise power ability. The flight lasted 38 minutes and went mainly without a hitch, although flutter had briefly attacked the elevators and the spring trim tabs had shimmied off in flight. This had made the aircraft vibrate badly but had not prevented Bullard returning safely to the airport in full control. These problems were indicative of the usual niggling little problems associated with most new aircraft and other problems began to manifest themselves during the two-month flight-test programme.

The XF4U-1 had sticky brakes, bouncy landing gear and aileron spin and the experimental fighter was so sleek aerodynamically that it would accelerate to the edge of compressibility, making recovery from extremely steep dives almost impossible. Spinning such a heavy aircraft made recovery exacting and, later, during final acceptance tests, the US Navy eliminated the two-turn spin requirement and required that the Corsair be spun only once. Another main concern was engine cooling. Poor fuel distribution from the carburettor caused hot and cold cylinder-head temperatures and became a chief concern for Pratt & Whitney chief test pilot A. Lewis MacLain who flew the development programme on the experimental versions of the R-2800 engine. After its first flight a second test pilot at Vought Sikorsky, Boone T. Guyton, took over the test flying of the XF4U-1.

All went well during his first four test flights but on the fifth, while performing a series of low altitude cabin pressurization and high-speed cruise tests, low on fuel, the XF4U-1 crashed on the Norwich Golf Course far to the north-east of the airfield at Stratford. Guyton was not helped by the weather, which produced heavy rainfalls in the test area. He attempted a short carrier-type landing on the fairway, nose high with full flaps and power on, in order to maintain the slowest possible landing approach speed. All was fine and dandy until he chopped the throttle and allowed the XF4U-1 to float onto the fairway. The aircraft touched down at the relatively high landing speed of around 80 knots and skidded on the wet grass. The brakes proved ineffective on the slippery surface and the smooth tyres were unable to get a firm grip. In desperation, Guyton tried to ground loop the aircraft to prevent it crashing off the edge of the fairway, but his efforts were in vain. The XF4U-1 crashed into a wood and the prototype was catapulted upwards by trees, flipped over onto its back and slid along rudder first until it hit a tree stump, before finally coming to rest midway down a shallow ravine. Incredibly, Guyton emerged unhurt and was able to scramble out of the crumpled wreckage. Damage to the aircraft was severe and it looked for a time as if it might have to be written off. One wing had been sheared off, the empennage had been torn from the fuselage and the propeller was smashed, but the main fuselage, engine and undercarriage were relatively unharmed and Vought worked night and day and were able to completely rebuild the Corsair. Within two months the XF4U-1 was airworthy once again.

Lyman Bullard demonstrated the XF4U-1 for USN officials on 1 October 1940. He flew from Stratford to Hartford, Connecticut, at a speed of 405mph, making the Corsair the first single-engine single-seat navy fighter to fly over 400mph. The effects of the achievement were not lost on the Army Air Corps, especially its chief, Major General Henry H. 'Hap' Arnold, who now re-evaluated his stance on the air-cooled radial powerplant. He gave Pratt & Whitney permission to cease development on liquid-cooled inline engines and forge ahead instead with radial engine development.

On 24 October 1940, the XF4U-1 was delivered to NAS Anacostia for US Navy evaluations. Final US Navy demonstrations were carried out by Boone Guyton at Anacostia during 24/25 February 1941. Much to the delight of the navy, already pleased with the top speed of the new aircraft, their evaluations revealed that the XF4U-1, despite its size and weight, had an excellent all-round performance too. A new Hamilton Standard Hydromatic airscrew, which was fitted, increased efficiency over the previous propeller arrangement and power was further boosted by using a 'jet thrust' exhaust system. This, and very high ram pressure recovery by the wing leading-edge carburettor air intakes, contributed greatly to the excellent overall performance of the aircraft. At a normal fighter weight of 9,374lb, the Corsair's sea level rate of climb was 2,600 feet per minute and its service ceiling was 35,500 feet. Take-off distance in calm conditions was 362 feet and, with a 25-knot headwind, just 150 feet. It had a range of 1,040 miles at 3,500 feet altitude.

On 3 March 1941 Vought received a letter of intent from the Bureau of Aeronautics inviting them to propose a production version of the Corsair. On 2 April 1941 Vought submitted Proposal VS-317, which would become the F4U-1. On 14 June, the XF4U-1 was flown to the National Advisory Committee for Aeronautics (NACA) facility at Langley Field, Virginia. Less than a month later, the XF4U-1 returned to Anacostia only to be transferred to the Naval Aircraft Factory (NAF) in Philadelphia on 1 August 1941. The XF4U-1 returned to Vought later in August where it remained with periodic postings to Anacostia and to the NAF. Meanwhile, on 30 June, the Bureau of Aeronautics awarded Vought Contract 82811 for 584 F4U-1 production aircraft for the navy, with initial deliveries to begin in February 1942 (the first production model was actually delivered to the USN on 31 July 1942). Mass production of all types of combat aircraft in America became critical with the Japanese attack on Pearl Harbor, 7 December 1941, the action that finally forced the USA into the start of a global war. The Corsair became one of the first combat aircraft to have its production programme expanded and the VGB programme, consisting of Vought, Goodyear and Brewster, was formed to mass produce the F4U-1. The Brewster Aeronautical Corporation was designated as an associate contractor for Corsair production on 1 November 1941. Brewster's Johnsville Pennsylvania factory would build only 735 F4U-1s, designated F3A-1s, which finally began delivery in April 1943, before the US Navy put it out of business in July 1944. (More than half of Brewster's production was delivered to the Royal Navy.) Goodyear Aircraft, a division of the Goodyear Tyre and Rubber Company, joined the programme in December 1941 and their Akron, Ohio, facility built 3,941 FG-1 versions, 35 per cent of all Corsairs built.

The production model would differ from the prototype in several respects, not least in having an increased length, to more than 33 feet 4⅔ inches. At first two more .50 calibre M-2 machine guns were installed in the wings, while the two machine guns mounted atop the engine cowling were permanently deleted. Later, the four wing-guns were increased to six. Each inboard and intermediate .50 machine gun was fed with 400 rounds of ammunition and the two outboard guns were supplied with 375 rounds apiece. Anti-aircraft bombs and wing-mounted flotation bags were deleted and two Mark 41-2 bomb racks and two mounts for 100lb bombs were installed beneath the wings.

The increases in wing armament resulted in the leading-edge fuel tanks being removed, although the two outer-wing-panel leading-edge fuel tanks, each with a capacity of 63 gallons, were retained. Experience gained by the Royal Air Force in combat led to the tanks being fitted with a carbon-dioxide vapour-dilution system which made the atmosphere above the fuel inert to prevent the petrol being ignited by gunfire in combat. F4U-1 fuel capacity was replaced with a 237 US-gallon self-sealing tank, which included a standpipe reserve of fifty gallons, in the fuselage between the engine and the pilot. Mounting this tank ahead of the cockpit and near the aircraft's centre of gravity obviated the need for attitude changes as the fuel was used, but the fuselage had to be extended to make room for the fuel tank. The cockpit was therefore moved about three feet further back than on the prototype which, in turn made the forward view worse for the pilot, especially during the nose-high landings which were a characteristic of deck operations. Improvements designed to increase pilot visibility over the new 'hose-nose' were rudimentary at best. The number of metal ribs in the jettisonable canopy, nicknamed the 'squirrel-cage' or 'bird-cage' canopy, so called for the number of reinforcing bars in the sliding cockpit canopy, was reduced and fuselage cut-outs were introduced behind teardrop-shaped windows as a further aid to vision.

After the removal of the wing tanks to make room for the additional guns, new wing fuel cells were installed which added a further 62 US gallons to each wing. Some 155lb of armour plate was added to the area around the cockpit and oil tank, while the pilot was protected by the addition of half-inch-thick laminated bulletproof glass behind the forward windshield. Identification, Friend or Foe (IFF) radar transponder equipment was installed. The wings still retained the use of fabric-covered panels but, by slightly reducing the span of the landing flaps, it was possible to increase aileron size to greater than on the prototype. This prompted a faster rate of roll than had been possible on the XF4U-1. Complicated deflector plate type flaps, which had been used on the prototype, were replaced with NACA slotted flaps which were lighter and had fewer moving parts as well as giving a higher maximum lift coefficient. Maximum flap deflection was decreased from 60 to 50 degrees to decrease drag in the landing configuration. Modifications were made to the arrestor hook and tail landing gear systems. All of these changes increased the F4U-1's all-up fighting weight to 12,061lb.

The uprated Pratt & Whitney R-2800-8 Double Wasp, which used a manual Eclipse starter cartridge system, was chosen as the powerplant for the production model of the Corsair. The -8 produced 2,000hp at 2,700rpm at sea level and 1,550hp at 2,550rpm at 22,000 feet. This high-altitude power would give the Corsair a top speed of 417mph at 19,000 feet and 397mph at 23,000 feet. The F4U-1 had a sea level rate of climb of 3,000 feet per minute and a service ceiling of 37,000 feet.

Meanwhile, in January 1942, the XF4U-1 was fitted with the XR-2800-4 engine rated at 1,850hp at 2,600rpm at take off. Later that month the aircraft was flown to the Naval Aircraft Factory, Philadelphia, Pennsylvania, for field carrier-landing tests on the airfield runways. For five days navy pilots had the chance to fly the XF4U-1 before the aircraft was returned to the factory. On 12 May 1942 the XF4U-1 left for a 29-day test at NAS Anacostia and the aircraft was used to test future modifications on the production Corsair models. The XF4U-1 left the Vought factory on 3 December 1942 and, by 30 June 1943, had relocated to the new Flight Test Center at NAS Patuxent River, Maryland. The XF4U-1 spent the remainder of its career at the technical training centre at Norman, Oklahoma, before being struck from the US Navy's inventory on 22 December 1943. Meanwhile, at the Stratford, Connecticut, plant during the early summer of 1942, the production lines began turning out the first of the F4U-1 models. Boone T. Guyton carried out the maiden flight of an F4U-1 when he piloted BuNo02153, the fourth production F4U-1, on 25 June 1942. The new Corsair notched a maximum speed of 415mph, a sea level rate of climb of 3,120 feet per minute and a service ceiling of 37,000 feet.

BuNo02156, the seventh production Corsair, became the first to be delivered to the US Navy at NAS New York on 15 August 1942. This aircraft was flown aboard the escort carrier USS *Sangamon* in Chesapeake Bay by Lieutenant Commander Sam Porter on 25 September 1942 for carrier qualifications. Porter carried out four landings and four take offs to determine the Corsair's suitability for carrier-borne operations. Unfortunately, it became immediately obvious to the navy observers that the Corsair had still to gain its sea legs. Serious doubts were raised as to the aircraft's ability to be used as a future shipboard fighter when a series of landing problems manifested themselves. It was quickly apparent that in the three-point landing attitude the pilot's visibility was impaired by the long round-nosed engine installation.

The pilot's poor visibility was not helped either by his location well aft of the aircraft fuselage, or by oil from the hydraulically-actuated upper engine cowl flaps and engine valve push-rods, which deposited a fine film of oil to coat the windscreen. The individual actuators of each cowl flap and the early magnesium rocker-box covers, which tended to warp, leaked oil badly. The cowl flap problem was finally solved by a modification in December 1942 by using one actuator and a cable-and-roller mechanism while the magnesium rocker-box covers were replaced by aluminium ones, many of them borrowed from F4F Wildcats and PB4Y-1 Liberators. During the slow speed approach to the carrier, when the pilot was given the cut over the deck the Corsair descended almost stalling onto the flight-deck in an attempt to grab an arresting wire, but the F4U-1's 'stiff' main landing gear caused the aircraft to bounce very badly after landing. On touchdown the landing-gear oleos would compress and then extend quickly back to full travel, bouncing the fighter into the air again.

Other serious problems were caused by the Corsair's unhappy stall characteristics. The huge flaps and low-set tail wheel created a directional stability problem, which would only later be corrected on the production line with the use of an inflatable tail wheel and with the fitting of a stilted tail wheel leg. A sharp fall in the F4U-1's lift curve scope near the stall, combined with the high power and torque of the huge propeller, caused the aircraft to stall suddenly and drop its left wing before the right wing, especially during deceleration. The port wing tended to stall first because of the upwash from the propeller. True, a highly skilled pilot could pre-empt this problem, but it would be beyond the range of most newly trained carrier pilots. If the inexperienced pilot tried to regain control after bouncing on the first landing, touching down again with the brakes on could put the aircraft over on its back with disastrous results. Another annoying malfunction was the 'rudder kick,' something which had already occurred during testing of the XF4U-1. It was evident to Vought and the navy that all these serious problems would have to be solved and solved fast, if the Corsair was to go to sea.

Vought flight-test and engineering departments went quickly to work to try to remedy the situation and a series of design changes were suggested and later instituted during production. Vought suggested to the navy that the top three cowl flaps be permanently sealed to prevent oil from coating the windscreen and the individual hydraulic cowl flap actuators be replaced with a single hydraulic cowl flap master actuator and mechanical linkage to the remaining cowl flaps. (Later, pilots would learn to look for rain clouds to give their windscreens a quick wash.) Before agreeing to these modifications, the navy requested that a test aircraft be flown at military power with both the top three cowl flaps opened and sealed to compare engine-cooling data. As expected, sealing the top three cowl flaps did not significantly increase cylinder-head temperatures, but it did complicate engine maintenance. It now became necessary for mechanics to remove a pair of the mechanical cowl flap pulleys to gain access to the spark plugs of the top rear cylinder.

To cure the stall problems a small, six-inch wooden spoiler, or stall strip, was added to the leading edge of the right wing panel just outboard of the machine-gun ports. This refinement effectively spoiled the airflow over the area of the wing immediately behind it and caused both wings to stall at the same time. BuNo02510 became the first F4U-1 to be fitted with the 'stall improvement device' and it was delivered to NAS Anacostia and then to the Naval Aircraft factory for testing. The addition of the spoiler was incorporated continuously from the 943rd Corsair onward to solve a potentially dangerous flight characteristic. Equally, the 'rudder kick' problem was easily solved, by increasing the length of the tail-wheel strut, which effectively reduced the aircraft's ground clearance angle from 13.5 to 11.5 degrees. This reduced the percentage of maximum lift coefficient used for landing and the downwash angle over the tail.

Other problems were not so easily solved. During flight testing, a number of F4U-1s were found to have a wing heaviness, which required aileron trim tab deflection of from 8 to 10 degrees out of the 15 degrees available to achieve level flight at cruising speed. A number of corrective measures were tried until Vought concluded that the problem was the result of manufacturing irregularities in the ailerons which were too small to positively detect. Replacing the ailerons could alleviate wing heaviness but Vought had to try a number of different pairs before the problem was solved. Beginning with the F4U-4 the company used ailerons fitted with balance tabs. In the meantime, Vought engineers corrected the wing heaviness problem by gluing a 1/8 inch by 18-inch strip of wood to the bottom of the aileron on the wing that rode high.

Altering the Corsair's landing characteristics proved more difficult and 'Programme Dog' was instituted to modify the landing gear quickly and get the Corsair carrier-qualified. The programme ran a whole year before the problem was finally solved. Then it was a case of simply replacing the landing-gear oleo's Schrader valve with a Chance Vought valve and increasing the strut's air pressure, something which took just ten days, although it took much longer to implement. This changeover was incorporated on all production line aircraft and was performed on Corsairs during major overhauls. A side benefit of this modification was a reduction of twenty feet in the F4U-1's take-off distance in a 25-knot head wind. Meanwhile, Vought was requested by the navy to redesign the tail-wheel yoke, so that it raised the Corsair's tail six inches and improved pilot visibility on the ground. At the same time, the arresting hook-down angle was changed from 75 to 65 degrees to prevent the Corsair from 'sitting on the hook in a full stall landing'.

BuNo02557, the 404th F4U-1, became the first Corsair with the extended tail wheel and it was delivered to NAS Patuxent River, Maryland on 8 September 1944. BuNo02161, the ninth F4U-1 built, was delivered to the NACA full-scale wind tunnel at Langley, Virginia to find ways of reducing the drag. NACA recommended the installation of smooth-surface wing walkways and smoother wing surfaces, plus smoother, tighter fitting wing access doors, and the addition of aileron gap seals and an arrestor-hook cut-out fairing. The navy soon carried out all of NACA's drag-reducing recommendations except for the aileron gap seals. The tail hook was partially faired over with the extension of the tail-wheel gear door, enclosing the hook up to the last six inches.

Meanwhile, the Bureau of Aeronautics wanted the pilot's seating position raised to increase visibility and, on 27 February 1943, Vought requested that a different model designation be given to Corsairs with the raised-seating modification. This was duly carried out by the Bureau of Aeronautics and what become known as the F4U-1A featured a semi-bubble canopy with only two reinforcing bars in the upper surface of the blown glass structure, replacing the F4U-1's 'squirrel cage' or 'bird cage' canopy. However, there was a war on and the Bureau of Aeronautics requested that the -1A modifications 'be incorporated in the earliest airplanes in which it can be made without seriously affecting production'. BuNo02557, the 689th F4U-1, served as the prototype aircraft with the seating raised nine inches and a semi-bubble canopy. The new seat raised the pilot's line of sight five inches. BuNo17647 was the first F4U-1A production model to have the raised cabin. In all, forty-two significant changes were made on the F4U-1A production run, many of the major ones being made to the cockpit. The new pilot's seat that could be raised and lowered approximately nine inches incorporated an armoured pilot's headrest. The control stick was lengthened and the rudder/brake pedals were revised. There was a new instrument panel, gunsight and turtle deck and cockpit armour plating; and the overturn structure was reinforced.

Despite all the last-minute changes, the navy had decided that the Corsair was not suitable for carrier operations and it would be the US Marine Corps that would introduce the F4U-1 to combat. A Corsair modification centre was formed at San Diego as Air Base Group Two, Fleet Marine Force West Coast, commanded by Colonel Stanley Ridderhoff. Vought Field Service Manager Jack Hospers supervised the incorporation of 159 changes that went on right around the clock to get the Corsair combat ready in time. And time was short. The changes went from the sublime, such as having to add a rear-view mirror to the canopy, to the extreme. Other pressing problems centred on the master brake cylinders, which had to be modified and the engine ignition harness had to be improved for operation at altitude. The horizontal stabilizer in the tail needed to be reinforced and the rudder control horn attachments needed to be strengthened.

Changes too had to be made to improve the belt feed of the .50 calibre machine guns. The duct seals between the engine and intercoolers and to the carburettor had to be improved and the attachments fastening the fuselage fuel tank to the bulkheads had to be reinforced. Also, the hydraulic engine cowl flap controls had to be replaced with mechanical controls. The ignition harness problems and problems with the radios were not rectified by the time VMF-124 left for the South Pacific and kits to correct both had to be fitted in the field at Espíritu Santo in the New Hebrides. Most of the other myriad problems, however, were alleviated, if not solved completely.

Marine squadron VMF-124, commanded by Major William Gise, at Camp Kearney, California, received its first Corsair on 7 September 1942, but was not declared fully operational until three months later. In October VF-12, commanded by Lieutenant Commander Joseph C. 'Jumping Joe' Clifton, became the first USN Corsair squadron to be formed, at NAS North Island, California. However, after navalized Corsairs had been declared unserviceable for use aboard carriers, the intended Corsairs were soon replaced by F6F Hellcats. The USMC – the 'Flying Leathernecks' – would take the Corsair to war. VMF-124, which had priority for Corsairs, departed for the South Pacific in January 1943, arriving on Guadalcanal on 12 February 1943.

Chapter 2

Land and Sea

Suddenly Zeros were all around us. Their big red meat balls flashed angrily in the sun. If they fired, I didn't see any tracers. We knew Zero's couldn't dive with the Corsairs, especially if they feared that other American planes were down there. Their attack ended as quickly as it had started. The Zero's disappeared for good.

(USMC Corsair pilot, Wallace B. Thompson, VMF-211. Born, 31 January 1924, on a dairy farm in Collinsville. He died on 26 June 2013. Credit passages "correspondence with the author")

VMF-124 'Checkerboards' had received its first Corsair on 26 October and was hurriedly brought up to strength. On 28 December 1942, though its twenty-two F4U-1s were not strictly combat-ready and none of its pilots were combat-experienced, VMF-124 was declared operational. Such was the urgency of the situation in the South Pacific that the marines, with or without their Corsairs, were shipping out in January and if the F4Us had to be picked up at Pearl Harbor en route, then that was how it would be. As at 31 December 1942 the US Navy had a grand total of just 178 Corsairs, having accepted fifty five aircraft in November and sixty eight F4U-1s in December. Early in January 1943 VMF-124, commanded by Major William E. Gise, sailed from San Diego, California, for New Caledonia in the Loyalty Islands aboard an unescorted passenger ship. Its Corsairs, meanwhile, were freighted and shipped via Espíritu Santo, to Guadalcanal, a hilly, tropical jungle-covered island in the Solomon Group, where, in July, the Japanese had started building an airfield on the Lunga Plain. When Lunga airfield was complete the Japanese could send land-based bombers on raids on the New Hebrides for a thrust southward.

The small islands of Tulagi, Gavutu and Tanambogo enclose Guadalcanal. As early as April 1942 Tulagi had been deemed the number one American objective in the Solomons. The deep and spacious harbour with air cover from Guadalcanal presented the Japanese with an excellent naval base to threaten the lifeline to Australia. Guadalcanal was captured by US Marines in August 1942 and the captured airstrip was renamed Henderson Field after the commander of the USMC dive-bombers at Midway and, gradually, the 'Cactus Air Force' as it was known, took shape. Further Japanese and USMC reinforcements arrived on Guadalcanal in September and October 1942 and the fierce fighting carried on into November 1942 with air attacks on Guadalcanal and the neighbouring islands of Tulagi, Gavutu and Tanambogo. One of the most frequent American aerial missions was against the 'Tokyo Express', the Japanese transport and combat ship task force that plied the 'Slot' (the channel between New Georgia and Santa Isabel Islands north-west of Guadalcanal) almost nightly to reinforce their hard-pressed ground troops on the embattled island. The enemy then built a new airfield at Ondonga in a coconut grove at Munda on the New Georgia Islands. In the local language, Ondonga meant the 'Place of Death'. Army Air Force bombers and fighters made many air raids on these enemy bases and others in the Solomons area, at Rabaul, Bougainville and the Russell Islands. On 4 January 1943, the Japanese Imperial Staff finally issued orders for the evacuation of Guadalcanal to begin.

On 9 January 1943 VF-12 (Fighting Squadron 12) was commissioned at San Diego under the command of Lieutenant Commander 'Jumping Joe' Clifton, with Commander H.H. Caldwell as CAG (Commander, Air Group). Five days later VF-12 received its first ten F4U-1s and the unit was declared operational. By 25 January, the navy squadron had twenty-two Corsairs on strength. Fighting Squadron 12 moved to Hawaii preparatory to moving to New Caledonia for, unlike VMF-124, VF-12 not only had to convert to the Corsair, it had also to practise carrier landings, even thought it was destined as a land-based Corsair squadron. VF-12 lost seven pilots while training on the Corsair, four of them in an early morning storm. At the same time Vought engineers were still wrestling with the myriad problems which were still troubling Corsair operation aboard carriers. Pilots disliked the Eclipse 'shotgun' starters (later replaced with electric starters) and the flap blow-up feature and the battery installation were proving unpopular. Leaking cowl flap cylinders also added to the general mistrust.

To improve landing stability larger tail-wheel bearings were used on F4U-1s and two Corsairs were fitted with pneumatic tail wheels on longer struts and tested by VF-12 on the escort carrier USS *Core*. There was some improvement on carrier landings, but the tail wheels tended to blow out. VF-12 considered the Corsair tricky to fly, with a bad stalling characteristic and the aircraft was soon dubbed the 'Hog', because it was about as co-operative as a 'hog on ice'. An F4U-1 was written off aboard the *Core* and another crashed trying to land onboard the USS *Enterprise* near Hawaii. Inflatable tail wheels, which were supposed to aid Corsair stability on landing, proved more of a hindrance when several began bursting during hard landings. These and the other well-documented carrier landing problems hardly won over the Corsair pilots but the overriding problem, one which would prevent VF-12 taking the Corsair to sea, was the lack of a supply of spare parts onboard the carriers. By the time VF-12 sailed aboard the USS *Saratoga* from Hawaii in July 1943, F6F Hellcats had replaced the Corsairs for combat sea duty.

VF-17 became the second navy squadron to operate the Corsair and, in February 1943, began receiving their first F4U-1s for training, at NAS Norfolk, Virginia. Its CO, Lieutenant Commander John Thomas 'Tommy' Blackburn, born 24 January 1912 in Washington DC, had graduated from Western High School. His father and brother were naval officers. Blackburn graduated from the United States Naval Academy in 1933, became a naval aviator and was a flight instructor in 1941 when the United States entered the Second World War. He was anxious to get into combat but was relegated to flying the Brewster F2A Buffalo at Opa Locka Naval Air Station near Miami where he had been a flight instructor. After several requests for a combat assignment, he received orders in July 1942 to organize VGF-29 as commanding officer and report aboard the new escort carrier USS *Santee*. VGF-29 was equipped with the Grumman F4F-4 Wildcat. Blackburn assembled a ready room of mainly brand-new ensigns fresh from winning their wings at advanced flying school at Naval Air Station Corpus Christi. Luckily, he had the assistance of a combat veteran from the recent Battle of the Coral Sea, Lieutenant (j.g.) Harry 'Brink' Bass who received the Navy Cross for his attack on the Japanese aircraft carrier *Shōhō*. Blackburn set up operations at a remote field at Pungo, well away from the brass and traffic at NAS Norfolk, and was soon promoted to lieutenant commander. Pungo suited Blackburn fine as he wanted an undisturbed environment to get the squadron acquainted with the Wildcat and ready for deployment and the combat likely to follow. The squadron embarked aboard the USS *Santee* in October 1942 to participate in Operation Torch, the Allied invasion of French North West Africa. Arriving in the waters off Morocco on 6 November VGF-

29 flew its first combat mission on 8 November but could not find the target and poor weather and damaged homing equipment aboard *Santee* forced the pilots to ditch or force-land their Wildcats. Blackburn floated adrift in a life-raft for three days before he was spotted by a destroyer and rescued. Thus ended VGF-29's inauspicious debut and Blackburn's first combat deployment. Shortly thereafter, Blackburn was ordered to stand up a new squadron, VF-17. When Blackburn assumed command, he recruited fellow instructor Lieutenant Commander Roger R. Hedrick, born 2 September 1914 in Pasadena, California, as his executive officer. VF-17 was to become fully operational on the improved F4U-1As and take them to sea aboard the new Essex-class escort carrier, USS *Bunker Hill*, which would make its shake-down cruise in July. The pilots of VF-17 were high-spirited, rugged individuals with little or no combat experience. They were thrilled with their new hot planes and flew them under bridges and skimmed the waters near the fleet at every opportunity. 'Flat-hatting', or low-level flying and other the hell-raising escapades, however, soon earned them the nickname, 'Blackburn's Irregulars'.

Ensign Howard McClain 'Teeth' Burriss, born 28 March 1921 in Washington DC, ran a truck off a highway while playing 'chicken' in an inverted Corsair, while Ensign Ira 'Ike' Cassius Kepford upset the good people of Norfolk when he and an army P-51 Mustang pilot entered into a low-level dogfight overhead. Kepford, born on 29 May 1919 in Harvey, Illinois, came from a poor family and grew up in Muskegon, Michigan. He was a star right halfback for the Northwestern University 'Wildcats' in Evanston, Illinois, and was described as 'weighing 185lbs he hit you as though he were 250. On defence he was a rough, tough player who wouldn't give you an inch. He was a great inspiration to the team'. He enlisted in the US Naval Reserve in a halftime ceremony during the final game of the season on 22 November 1941, fifteen days before the Japanese attack on Pearl Harbor. On 26 April 1941 *The Muskegon Chronicle* said: '"Ike" Kepford of Muskegon, outstanding halfback at Northwestern University, won't be unprepared when an expected draft call comes in June or early summer. "Ike", son of Mr and Mrs George R. Kepford, 191 W. Forest, has enrolled in a Civil Aeronautics Administration course at Northwestern and now has more than twelve hours of solo flying to his credit. The Muskegon halfback had been counted on for heavy duty with Coach Lynn Waldorf's Wildcat 11 next fall as a senior but he has been advised by draft board officials to expect a call in June, or shortly after. He expects to apply for service in the Marine Air Corps. Flying, Ike is finding, is no simple matter of toting a pig skin around each end and falling to earth when tackled. When you're a few thousand feet aloft at the pilot's controls, you need more than good blocking to get through. "Ike" experienced a thrill recently when the motor on his training plane sputtered and stopped on a practice flight south of Milwaukee, his family disclosed today. Forced to make a landing, "Ike" successfully put the plane down in the first handy location – a Wisconsin farmer's wheat field. Uninjured, he repaired the plane motor, took off and returned to his home airport near Chicago.'

By Christmas 1941, five months before he officially became an aviation cadet, Kepford had already logged twenty-five hours flying Piper Cubs at Chicago's Sky Harbor Airport in Northwestern's Civil Aeronautics Administration pilot training programme. 'I had no reason to think I wasn't doing pretty good,' Kepford told *Chicago Daily News* reporter John P. Carmichael in 1944. 'But along came Christmas vacation and I got lonesome for my folks and went home without telling anybody. When I got back they told me I didn't have the right attitude for a flier and washed me out. They said I could continue ground school if I wanted to. I'd like to see some of those guys now.'

On 29 April 1942 Kepford accepted an appointment as a naval aviation cadet and he earned his wings at Corpus Christi, Texas, and Miami, Florida, on 5 November 1942 and was assigned to VF-17 the following January. After the incident at Norfolk, Kepford was confined to quarters for ten days. In March 1943 VF-17 were ordered to leave town and 'Blackburn's Irregulars' relocated to NAAS (Naval Auxiliary Air Station) Manteo on the coast near Kitty Hawk, North Carolina, where they completed their pre-carrier training. During training at Manteo VF-17 lost six pilots, including two who collided in mid-air during gunnery practice.

Blackburn's Irregulars worked hard to break in their wild Corsairs, and they helped improve some of the F4U-1's more alarming traits. They softened the shock of landing by changing the fluid-air mixture in the oleo-compression cylinders. Lieutenant (j.g.) Merl W. 'Butch' Davenport, VF-17's Engineering Officer, partly developed the new wing anti-stall device and pilots tried to overcome the restricted view out of the 'birdcage' canopy by sitting on two and even three parachute cushions. In combat they knew they would not be able to see 'diddly-squat' from the birdcage and the situation only really improved when VF-17 received the F4U-1A with the semi-bubble canopy. VF-17's free-spirited aviators were prepared to forgive the Corsair its faults because more than anything else they wanted to fly them in combat as soon as possible.

Operating from land bases, Blackburn's Irregulars had broken in the Corsair but on 1 May there was a portent of things to come. Tom Blackburn, with the skilled LSO, Shailer 'Catwalk' Cummings, made the first real carrier landing on a simulated carrier landing area marked off on a concrete runway. VF-17's CO approached at 90 knots, chopped the throttle, hit the deck and bounced about twenty feet into the air. Blackburn made further operational tests in Chesapeake Bay using the jeep carrier *Charger*, a converted merchantman.[1] When his pilots had sufficient flight time in the Corsair they began their initial carrier landing qualifications (carquals) on *Charger*. It proved difficult landing a Corsair on the jeep carrier's 50-feet deck and there were mishaps along the way, but they mastered it, safe in the knowledge that the larger Essex-class deck of the *Bunker Hill* beckoned. During their land-based training, formation loops involving eight to twelve F4U-1s at a time was not uncommon – but Blackburn had one grand finale in mind. While en route to Boston for the *Bunker Hill* commissioning on 23 May 1943, Blackburn led his formation of twenty-five F4Us over New York and they all dropped down and flew under the Brooklyn Bridge.

Bunker Hill cleared the ways at Quincy, Massachusetts, in June and shortly arrived off Norfolk where VF-17's Corsairs welcomed the carrier in style, three eight-plane flights buzzing her from three different directions. On 7 July 1943 VF-17, now part of CAG-17 (Carrier Air Group 17), embarked aboard the *Bunker Hill* for her shake-down cruise to Trinidad's thirty- by seventy-mile Gulf of Paria Bay. (CAG-17 also included the Avengers of VT-17 and the troublesome SB2C Helldivers of VB-17 and VS-17.) Carrier operations concentrated minds wonderfully and bouncing over the barrier wire and flipping over or crashing into the parked aircraft ahead became commonplace. On final approach the

---

1. An escort carrier or escort aircraft carrier (CVE), also called a 'jeep carrier' or 'baby flattop' in the USN or 'Woolworth Carrier' by the Royal Navy, was a small and slow type of aircraft carrier typically half the length and a third the displacement of larger fleet carriers.

Corsair's elongated nose made it difficult for pilots to see the landing signal officer. If a pilot opened his fourteen cowl flaps they cut down forward visibility to almost zero but, if he left them closed, the engine would soon overheat. Soon, F4U performance was judged in some circles to be 'too hot' for deck operations and on occasion so, too, were the pilots. One VF-17 pilot was grounded for a few days after making a barrel roll over the flight deck.

Other problems manifested themselves on the voyage. Engines and propellers were changed frequently. It was found that the Corsair's arrestor hook simply snapped when it came into contact with the steel drain channels on landing. When the hook caught a barrier wire the F4U-1's tail was lifted clear of the deck. If the pilot missed the arresting wire the hook caught a drain channel and snapped. This problem was solved with a redesigned hook.

Though many of the Corsair's other faults had also been overcome by a combination of squadron ingenuity and Vought adaptability, in the final analysis the navy brass would decide that the Corsair had not gained its sea legs. VF-17's valiant quest to become the first USN unit to go to war at sea with the Corsair would be in vain.

At first the omens had appeared to be good. On 10 August VF-17 returned to Norfolk aboard the *Bunker Hill* and CAG 17 returned to shore bases while the carrier and the squadrons were brought up to combat readiness. By 26 August VF-17 had received thirty-six new, raised-cockpit F4U-1As, which embodied many of the modifications recommended and carried out as a result of the shakedown cruise to the Caribbean. In deference to the Corsair's 'Hog' nickname, Tom Blackburn's call sign became 'Big Hog' and he had the name painted on the tail of his personal F4U-1, BuNo17649 'White 1'. On 10 September when VF-17 and the rest of CAG-17 left Norfolk for the SW Pacific aboard the *Bunker Hill*, each of the Corsairs had a small skull and crossbones motif painted on its engine cowling. VF-17 was going to war, or so they thought!

The carrier sailed south off the east coast of the USA and on through the Panama Canal to San Diego, California, before heading westwards to Hawaii on 28 September. A few days out, however, orders were received detaching VF-17 from CAG-17 and their beloved Corsairs were to be put ashore upon arrival at Pearl Harbor on Oahu. The 'Jolly Rogers' could remain aboard the *Bunker Hill* and fly F6F Hellcats but, to a man,

VF-17's dejected pilots voted to retain their F4U-1As. When *Bunker Hill* docked at Pearl Harbor on 2 October their beloved Corsairs were flown ashore to Ford Island, next to which, on 7 December 1941, the Japanese had decimated 'Battleship Row', to await onward transportation to the Solomon Islands. VF-17 was replaced aboard the *Bunker Hill* by VF-18, equipped with the F6F. (*Bunker Hill* and CAG 17 first went into action on 11 November with a strike on Rabaul.)

A perceived shortage of spares in the fleet supply line (which was full of parts for the hundreds of Grumman fleet fighters but not for one squadron of thirty-six fighters of a different type) was further justification that the Corsair was not yet ready for combat operations aboard US carriers. Though they were short of one or two important items, the USMC Corsairs had all the spares they needed.

VMF-124 arrived on Guadalcanal on 12 February 1943 with twelve Corsairs. The most experienced of VMF-124's pilots had accumulated just twenty hours on the new fighter. An hour after landing at their airstrip, called 'Cactus', the dozen Corsairs were tasked to fly CAP (Combat Air Patrol) over the island and escort a PBY Catalina on a 230-mile flight to Sandfly Bay on Vella Lavella to rescue two rescue two downed F4F pilots. The following day, 13 February, the Marine Corps Corsairs were plunged into action when the short range of the Navy F4F Wildcats saw the Corsairs used as long-range escorts for US Navy PB4Y-1 Liberators making the 300-mile trip to bomb shipping in Buin Harbour. No enemy fighters appeared.

Next day, 14 February, VMF-124's Corsairs saw action for the first time when they joined P-40 Warhawks and P-38 Lightnings in an escort for PB4Y-1 Liberators raiding Kahili airfield on Bougainville Island. It was hardly an auspicious debut. In what became known as the 'Saint Valentine's Day Massacre', the force encountered fifty Mitsubishi A6M Zero fighters, which shot down two of VMF-124's Corsairs, flying middle-level escort cover, all four P-38s, flying top cover and two P-40s flying low cover. Two of the PB4Y-1s were also shot down. Only three Zeros were shot down, a fourth collided with one of the downed Corsairs and one of the American pilots was strafed in the water after he had ditched. Despite this setback, the signs were that the Corsair could more than hold its own. It soon became obvious in combat with Zeros that if the American pilots had altitude advantage the Corsair largely had the upper hand. The

Zeros could not out-turn the F4U-1, nor out-dive it or out-climb the American fighter. However, VMF-124 was encountering problems with their Corsairs. There was limited visibility out of the 'birdcage' canopies, there were engine ignition faults and the nose-high attitude on landing with the short tail-wheel strut caused more difficulties.

On 1 April 1943, the Japanese Operation I-Go Sakusen[2] started and the first big battle between the Corsairs and Japanese aircraft occurred during attempts by Seabee construction battalions to build a landing strip at Banika. The Corsairs, together with some Wildcats and P-38 Lightnings, fought a series of dogfights with fifty-eight Zeros and 'Val' dive-bombers. Eighteen enemy aircraft were shot down for the loss of six American fighters. Second Lieutenant Kenneth Ambrose Walsh of VMF-124 shot down a Zero and an Aichi D3A Val dive-bomber over the aptly named Ouch, to begin his score which would result in him becoming the first of the Corsair aces. Born in Brooklyn, New York, on 24 November 1916, Ken Walsh enlisted in the Marine Corps on 15 December 1933, serving as an aircraft mechanic and radioman before being accepted for Naval Flight Training in March 1935, where he graduated in April 1937.

Walsh, who would rack up a total of twenty-one kills during the war remembered: 'I learned quickly that altitude was paramount. Whoever had altitude dictated the terms of the battle and there was nothing a Zero pilot could do to change that – we had him. The F4U could outperform a Zero in every aspect except slow speed manoeuvrability and slow speed rate of climb. Therefore you avoided getting slow when combating a Zero. It took time but eventually we developed tactics and deployed them very

---

2. An aerial counter-offensive launched by Imperial Japanese forces during the Solomon Islands and New Guinea Campaigns from 1-16 April 1943. The aim of the operation was to halt the Allied offensives in New Guinea and the Solomons and to give Japan time to prepare a new set of defences in response to recent defeats to the Allies in the Battle of Guadalcanal and in New Guinea at Buna-Gona, Wau and the Bismarck Sea. The operation consisted of several massed aerial attacks by Japanese bomber and fighter aircraft based at Rabaul, Bougainville and the Shortland Islands against Allied targets on and around Guadalcanal and the Russell Islands in the Solomons and Port Moresby, Oro Bay and Milne Bay in New Guinea. Although the Japanese sank several Allied transports and warships, the attack failed to inflict serious damage on Allied forces. Yamamoto halted the attacks on 16 April, believing the operation to be a success. The operation, however, did not significantly delay Allied preparations for further offensives in the South Pacific area.

effectively.... There were times, however, that I tangled with a Zero at slow speed, one on one. In these instances I considered myself fortunate to survive a battle. Of my 21 victories, 17 were against "Zeros" and I lost five aircraft in combat. I was shot down three times and I crashed one that ploughed into the line back at base and wiped out another F4U.'

In three tours in the Solomons VMF-124 'Checkerboards' would destroy sixty-nine Japanese aircraft in the air for the loss of eleven Corsairs and just three pilots. On 4 April VMF-213 'Hellhawks', commanded by Major Wade H. Britt, became the second USMC F4U-1 squadron in the Southwest Pacific when it arrived on Guadalcanal. Britt was killed in take-off accident on 13 April and was replaced by Major Greg Weissenberger. On 15 April VMF-121, which was equipped with Wildcats, was taken out of the front line for a short while to change to Corsairs and received between ten and fifteen hours' training on the F4Us before becoming the third Corsair squadron to go into combat. VMF-213 'Hellhawks' went into action on 25 April when four of its Corsairs engaged sixteen Japanese dive-bombers and more than twenty Zeros. Five of the Zekes were shot down for the loss of two of the F4Us and one of its pilots.

Just after noon on 13 May upwards of twenty-five Zeros escorted a reconnaissance plane down the 'Slot' towards Guadalcanal. Intercepted near the Russell and Florida Islands by fifteen Corsairs of VMF-112 and VMF-124 led by Major Gise, the VMF-124 commanding officer, fifteen of the Zekes were shot down by the F4Us; a sixteenth was downed by an AAC P-38. Three Corsairs were lost and one of the pilots killed was Major Gise. Second Lieutenant Ken Walsh downed three enemy aircraft fifteen miles east of the Russells to take his score to six and make him the first of the Corsair aces. Walsh would eventually notch twenty-one victories flying with VMF-124 and he scored his twenty-second and final kill of the Pacific War flying with VMF-222. His tally led to the award of the Medal of Honor on 8 February 1944. Captain Archie G. Donahue of VMF-112 shot down four of the Zekes west of Florida Island to add to his two previous F4F victories in November 1942 and he also attained ace status. A fifth, which almost certainly fell to Donahue's guns, was credited as a 'probable'.

In late March and early April the Japanese built up a large aerial strike force at Bougainville, transferring many carrier-based planes for the purpose. On 7 April sixty-seven 'Judy' dive bombers, supported by 110 Zero fighters struck at Tulagi harbour in the Solomon Islands area. As division leader of VMF-221 'The 'Fighting Falcons', which, on 19 May started flying Corsairs after operating the F4F-4 Wildcat, First Lieutenant James Elms Swett, born on 15 June 1920 in Seattle, Washington, was awarded the Medal of Honor. Swett unhesitatingly hurled his four-plane division into action against a formation of fifteen bombers and personally exploded three in mid-air with accurate and deadly fire during his dive. Although separated from his division while clearing the heavy concentration of anti-aircraft fire, he boldly attacked six enemy bombers, engaged the first four in turn and, unaided, shot down all in flames. Exhausting his ammunition as he closed the fifth Japanese bomber, he relentlessly drove his attack against terrific opposition which partially disabled his engine, shattered the windscreen and slashed his face. In spite of this, he brought his battered plane down with skilful precision in the water off Tulagi without further injury. First Lieutenant Swett was credited with the destruction of seven enemy bombers and a probable in a single flight. When the day was over, the Americans claimed fifty-eight destroyed enemy aircraft, including ten by F4Fs of VMF-214 'Swashbucklers', their highest single day in their two combat tours.

After a short rest in Australia, Swett checked out in the F4U to which VMF-221 was converting and moved to a new base in the Russells. Promoted to captain, Swett covered the Rendova landings on 30 June, adding two Mitsubishi G4M 'Betty' twin-engined medium bombers to his score and sharing the destruction of a Zero. Eleven days later, near the island of New Georgia, Swett downed two more Bettys. Seeing his wingman's Corsair under attack, he also shot down a Zero. However, he failed to see a second Zero and was himself shot down. He was rescued by indigenous tribal members in a canoe and travelled by ten-man canoe for several hours to an Australian coastwatcher's location. A PBY flying boat returned Swett to the Russells. On 18 October 1943 over the major Japanese airbase at Kahili, Bougainville, Swett added one confirmed Zero and one probable, but lost his wingman. On 2 November he added to his list of kills two more Vals and a possible Kawasaki Ki-61 'Tony'. On 11 December Swett returned to the United States on a Dutch motor ship, arriving in San Francisco on New Year's Eve. After less than twenty-four hours he shipped out to San Diego where he was granted thirty days' leave and married Lois Anderson, his longtime sweetheart. Swett was then transferred to NAS Santa Barbara, California, where he worked up a newly manned VMF-221 in the Corsair.[3]

Meanwhile, in the United States on 1 April 1943, two F4U-2 night-fighter squadrons, VF(N)-75 at NAS Quonset Point, Rhode Island, and VMF(N)-532 at MCAS Cherry Point, North Carolina, were commissioned. In June VMF-122, an F4F-4 Wildcat unit, re-equipped with Corsairs and they completed a tour on Guadalcanal, returning to the United States on 23 July. VMF-214 'Swashbucklers' also converted to F4U-s from the F4F-4 during June and flew a tour at the Russell Islands and Munda from 21 July to September 1943.

On 5 June the Corsairs of VMF-112 and VMF-124 escorted fifteen SBD Dauntless and a dozen Avengers on a raid on Japanese shipping off Buin. Second Lieutenant Ken Walsh downed a Zeke and a Mitsubishi 'Pete' float biplane. In all, the Corsairs destroyed fifteen of the enemy aircraft. Two days later, on 7 June, Corsairs were among US fighters which intercepted 112 Japanese aircraft on a raid to Guadalcanal and the Marine Corps pilots claimed twenty-three enemy aircraft shot down. VMF-112 destroyed seven of the enemy but four Corsairs and an RNZAF P-40 were lost. All the downed US pilots were rescued, although Lieutenant Sam Logan of VMF-112 was picked up minus most of one leg after a Zero pilot had shot at him dangling helplessly in his chute and, having missed, decided to try and chop him in half with his propeller. On 16 June about 120 Zekes and Vals made a final daylight raid on Guadalcanal, attacking shipping between the island and Tulagi. Corsairs of VMF-121, VMF-122 and VMF-124 claimed eight enemy aircraft destroyed. Altogether, 107 Japanese aircraft were shot down, eighty by defending fighters and the remainder by anti-aircraft fire. Six US aircraft and five pilots were lost.

---

3. Now carrier-qualified and assigned to the *Bunker Hill* Swett flew two strikes over Japan and then supported the landings at Iwo Jima and the operations on Okinawa. On 11 May 1945 he shot down a 'Jill' kamikaze, which he described as a 'sitting duck'. Swett watched from the air as the *Bunker Hill* was struck by two kamikazes, causing such damage that he was forced to land on another carrier. Swett later returned to the States and was assigned to MCAS El Toro, California where he began to train for Operation Olympic, the invasion of Japan. At war's end VMF-221 was second in aerial victories among Marine Corps squadrons with 185 enemy planes downed. Swett's combat record includes 103 combat missions, 15.5 confirmed victories and four probables.

On 30 June the USMC squadrons supported the US landings at Rendova and Vangunu in the New Georgia Island group. Four Corsair squadrons numbering thirty-two F4Us, though heavily outnumbered, claimed fifty-eight Japanese aircraft shot down in three determined enemy attacks on the landing beaches. VF-21 claimed thirty aircraft while P-40 Warhawks destroyed another eleven enemy planes. Fourteen US fighters were shot down with seven of the pilots lost.

On 2 July VMF-123 'Eight-Balls' flew its first mission after converting to Corsairs, bringing the number of USMC Corsair squadrons in the Solomon Islands to eight. Five days later, on 7 July, twelve Japanese bombers escorted by sixty Zeros attempted to sink the US invasion ships off Rendova Island. Intercepted by the Corsairs of VMF-122, VMF-121 and VMF-221, sixteen Zekes and Betty attack bombers were claimed shot down and the raid was broken up. Meanwhile, seventy-eight US bombers escorted by forty-four Corsairs and sixty-nine P-38s, P-40s and F4F-4s, bombed shipping in the Kahili area at Bougainville in a surprise raid. During three Japanese raids, on 11, 14 and 15 July, VMF-213 added to their score of enemy fighters destroyed. On the 15th the Corsairs of the newly-formed ComAir New Georgia, claimed forty-four Japanese aircraft destroyed, fourteen of them by VMF-122 in a fifteen-minute air battle. Not to be outdone, eight Corsairs of VMF-213 claimed another sixteen victims. On 17 July, the four Corsair squadrons, part of the escort covering almost eighty SBDs, TBFs and PB4Y-1s against enemy shipping at Kahili, claimed forty-one of the fifty-two enemy aircraft reported destroyed during the raid. On 26 July ten PB4Y-1s bombed Kahili airfield after twenty-one Marine Corsairs had strafed the area with their machine guns. Four days later, nine of the Navy Liberators, escorted by sixty-two fighters including F4U-1s, bombed Ballale Island a few miles south of Kahili.

On 14 August, nine days after it was captured by US forces, the Corsairs of VMF-123 and VMF-124, newly returned after R&R in Australia, began operations from the former Japanese airstrip of Munda on New Georgia Island. (Normally, a squadron would remain in the forward combat zone for four to six weeks before being sent on leave in Australia or New Zealand. This would then be followed by a two- to four-week sojourn in a back area such as Espíritu Santo or Efate in the New Hebrides before returning to action on Guadalcanal, New Georgia,

Vella Lavella or Bougainville.) Next day, 15 August, the 'Eight-Balls' and the 'Checkerboards' provided the escort cover for the US invasion of Vella Lavella Island, beating off heavy enemy attacks and shooting down seventeen Japanese aircraft, three of them falling to the guns of First Lieutenant Ken Walsh of VMF-124.

On 28 August Lieutenant Alvin J. Jensen of VMF-214, an enlisted man who won his wings under the Naval Aviation Pilot (NAP) programme, made a spectacular solo strafing attack on Kahili airfield after becoming separated from the rest of his flight in a tropical storm. 'Al' Jensen earned a Navy Cross for his one-man shoot-up of Kahili. The dawn strafing mission was planned as a joint operation of VMF-214 and -215, but darkness, engine troubles, radio problems and stormy weather messed up the whole operation, a real *snafu*. Jensen emerged from the storm near Fauro Island, twenty miles from Kahili. Alone, he roared over Tonolei Harbour and set up his gunnery run over the airfield. He flew in low and fast, blasting away, then swung around for another pass. Total damage was uncertain, but the squadron war diary credited him with about fifteen ground kills. Japanese records indicate only five were burned but a photo-reconnaissance mission the next day showed eight Zeros, four Vals and a dozen Betty bombers burning; possibly First Lieutenant Charles Cobb Lanphier who was missing, also contributed to the destruction.

'Charlie' Lanphier was born in Omaha, Nebraska, and then moved to Detroit, Michigan. Son of First World War veteran Lieutenant Colonel Thomas G. Lanphier, his brother was Thomas G. Lanphier Jr, the P-38 Lightning pilot who, on 18 April 1943, claimed credit for shooting down the G4M1 Betty with Admiral Isoroku Yamamoto aboard. That evening Tom Lanphier had visited the VMF-214 camp and told his brother and other pilots about the Yamamoto mission. 'Charlie' Lanphier baled out over southern Bougainville and landed unhurt. Later, he was captured by the Japanese and became a prisoner of war. He was transported to Rabaul and imprisoned in the PoW camp. On 15 May 1944 he died of disease and neglect in captivity.

On 7 September VMF-124 completed its first deployment in the Solomon Islands and returned to the United States. It had scored sixty-eight aerial victories over the past seven months for the loss of seven pilots killed, three to enemy action and four in operational accidents, and nine seriously injured. Altogether, VMF-124 had written off thirty-two Corsairs, although only eleven were caused by enemy action. By the time of VMF-124's withdrawal from the combat zone, First Lieutenant Ken Walsh, who on 30 August had survived being shot down near Vella Lavella, had taken his score to twenty confirmed victories, two probables and one damaged. VMF-124 had written off thirty-two F4U-1s and F4U-1As, only eleven of them to enemy action. Of the seven pilots killed, four were the result of non-combat accidents. VMF-124 arrived at Miramar, California on 13 October and trained there until 18 September 1944 when it moved to Pearl Harbor before going aboard the USS *Essex* on 28 December 1944 for a second deployment to the Pacific.

On 7 September also, VMF-214 'Swashbucklers' was reorganized at Munda under the command of the legendary thirty-year-old Major Gregory Boyington. 'Pappy' Boyington had been a naval aviator since 1937. He had flown P-40Cs with the American Volunteer Group, the 'Flying Tigers', in Burma, where he was credited with three-and-a-half victories in the air and on the ground, although he reckoned his score was nearer six aerial victories and thirty on the ground. Boyington left the AVG in April 1942 with a dishonourable discharge and, three months later, 'Pappy' had rejoined the US Marine Corps. Early in 1943 he went to the South Pacific and became CO of VMF-122 before relinquishing command of the squadron after breaking his leg in a drunken barracks room wrestling-match. Boyington's new squadron, which took its designation from the squadron returning to the US after their tour of duty in the Solomons, quickly filled up with 'outcasts' from other Marine Corps squadrons. 'Pappy's' pilots wanted to call themselves 'Boyington's Bastards' but this was too risqué even for Boyington and the unit was fittingly retitled 'The Black Sheep Squadron'.

On 16 September Boyington became the first Corsair ace in a day. He led twenty Corsairs on a strike mission against the airfield at Ballale, a small island west of Bougainville, which was to be attacked by three squadrons of SBD Dauntless dive-bombers and two squadrons of Avengers, some 150 aircraft in all. On this momentous mission Boyington shot down four 'Haps' and a Zero while other 'Black Sheep Squadron' pilots were credited with the destruction of six more Zeros and eight probables. After a month of combat the 'Black Sheep Squadron' was credited with forty-seven confirmed aerial victories. By the end of the year Boyington had racked up nineteen more victories on Corsairs and four probables.

At Rabaul Boyington and his 'Black Sheep Squadron' developed the fighter-sweep technique and employed the tactic for the first time on 17 December 1943 when he led seventy-six Corsairs, P-40s and Hellcats over the island and flung down the gauntlet to the enemy fighters. Few appeared, and Boyington decided to reduce the fighter total to a more manageable forty-eight aircraft, mostly Corsairs. This time they destroyed thirty Japanese fighters and more successful sweeps over Rabaul followed.

Meanwhile, on 11 September 1943, VF(N)-75 arrived at Espíritu Santo. Within a fortnight they had moved to Munda with six F4U-2 night-fighting Corsairs which began operational patrols on Munda on 2 October. An F4U-2 of VF(N)-75 made the navy's first successful radar-guided interception over New Georgia Island on 31 October/1 November 1943 when Lieutenant Hugh D. 'Danny' O'Neill shot down a Betty bomber which he spotted by the light of its exhaust flames. VF(N)-75 would be credited with a total of seven night victories flying F4U-2s in the Second World War. VMF(N)-531 Corsairs began their successful night-fighter patrols around Bougainville and made the first successful enemy aircraft interception by a marine Corsair night fighter on 13 November 1943. On the night of 11/12 December Lieutenant Hugh D. 'Danny' O'Neill of VF(N)-75 destroyed another Betty. Operating from Torokina Field on 13 December, Lieutenant John S. Hill was credited with the probable destruction of an enemy floatplane. On successive nights, 15 and 16 December 1943, Hill destroyed two 'Rufe' floatplane fighters and three nights later, on the 19th Lieutenant Ruben L. Johns destroyed a Rufe also. On the night of 1 January 1944 Lieutenant Charles L. Penner destroyed a Val and was credited with probably destroying another. Johns bagged his second night victory on 13 January, when he destroyed a Val.

Meanwhile, VF-17 and its thirty-six new, raised-cockpit F4U-1As in Hawaii awaited their assignment to ComAirsePac Solomon Islands. On 12 October 1943 VF-17 departed Pearl Harbor aboard the jeep carrier USS *Prince William* and, thirteen days later, their Corsairs were catapulted off to Espíritu Santo. VF-17 flew up to Henderson Field on the 26th and, finally, they arrived at the former Japanese airfield carved out of the coconut plantation at Ondonga, on New Georgia. Lieutenant Commander Blackburn described Ondonga as 'clean, virtually bug-less, free of snipers and above all, near the enemy'. By this time most of the central Solomons were in American hands, although Bougainville to the north of New Georgia still had to be taken and occupied. The next objective was the Bismarck Archipelago and the Japanese stronghold at Rabaul on the NE tip of New Britain. The maintenance crew of Marine Squadron VMF-215 adopted the 'Jolly Rogers' from the outset.

VF-17 began their first tour flying from the 4,000-foot white coral runway on 27 October, putting three flights over the Treasury Islands in support of 3rd New Zealand Division which had landed there. On 28 October Corsairs flew forty-four combat sorties on close air support over the Treasury Islands group, part of the Solomon Islands and still no enemy planes showed. (Corsairs elsewhere were in action. On 20 October twenty-four Corsairs raided Kahili and were met by twenty Zeros. The F4Us shot down three of the Zekes for the loss of two Corsairs.) On the 29th VF-17 contented themselves with a sixteen-plane strike on barges and on the 30th twenty-three Corsairs escorted bombers over the Shortlands. That evening Lieutenant James A. Halford led eight F4Us on a 'Dumbo' mission, escorting a PBY Catalina that was to rescue a pilot who had ditched off the enemy-held coast. While VF-17 strafed the enemy shore installations, the PBY landed and the downed pilot was picked up, all within range of the Japanese guns.

VF-17's Corsairs saw action for the first time on 1 November. On this day the US invasion of Bougainville took place at Empress Augusta Bay, at the Cape Torokina Beachhead code-named 'Cherry Blossom'. Eight of Blackburn's Corsairs were among the thirty-two American fighters detailed to cover the Marine landings with staggered eight-plane flights on station until mid-afternoon. Blackburn led off the first flight and, at 0900 hours, they intercepted a formation of eighteen Aichi Vals at 14,000 feet and twelve Zeke escorts flying top cover for the dive-bombers. Both of Blackburn's four-plane divisions went into a long shallow dive, building up their speed to 350 knots before attacking. Lieutenant Shelton R. Beacham, in Lieutenant Thaddeus 'Thad' Bell's second division, drew first blood for the Jolly Roger. Beacham's Corsair was jumped by two Zekes out of the sun who badly shot up his right wing but he managed to nurse the F4U back to Ondonga. Blackburn opened up on a Zeke at 500 yards but although the enemy plane took hits it did not go down when he overhauled a Zeke in a dive and blasted him out of the sky from 200 yards. After the first attack the Corsairs climbed up to 20,000 feet. Blackburn found himself on a Zeke's tail and he fired. The Zeros exploded and Blackburn flew through the burning debris. The Corsairs destroyed three more Zekes and the Jolly Rogers' CO added a second Zeke to his score as they headed for home.

A division led by Lieutenant John M. Kleinman strafed the south shore of Kulitinai Bay after a two-hour patrol over the US invasion fleet failed to find any enemy aircraft. Lieutenant Commander Roger Hedrick and Lieutenant Clement D. 'Timmy' Gile's divisions were also in action and they claimed one Zeke shot down (Hedrick) and three damaged. VF-17 suffered its first casualty of the tour when Lieutenant (j.g.) John H. Keith was shot down by enemy ack-ack over Poporang Island and Faisi Island. Keith successfully ditched about fifteen miles SE of Faisi and was last seen swimming towards land. He was never found. In all, twenty-two enemy aircraft were shot down on 1 November for the loss of four aircraft. Six of the confirmed victories were credited to VF-17, which was also credited with six enemy aircraft damaged.

Wallace B. 'Wally' Thompson entered the service in October 1941 as a naval cadet. He was given the opportunity to switch to the Marine Corps, becoming a second lieutenant in August 1942, mainly because, as he put it, 'I could put holes in the target sleeve and no one else could'. After flying the F4F Wildcat he transitioned to the Corsair in June 1943, training at Pearl Harbor and then going on to serve three combat tours with VMF-211 at places such as Espíritu Santo and the Solomon Islands. He recalled: 'Thirty-eight of us were transferred to a combat area in the Solomons. We were attached to Marine Air Group MAG-21 and later (17 November 1943) MAG-24. This was to the North Strip on the Russell Islands. We were impressed by the beautiful coral runway built by the Seabees through the large coconut palm plantation reputedly owned by the Lever Brothers. The Russell Islands were west of Guadalcanal, about fifty miles from Henderson Field and partway up the Solomons' slot in the direction of New Georgia. The invasion by American forces was started on 21 February 1943 and was conducted by the 3rd Marine Raider Battalion and part of the Army's 43rd Division.

'For the last few days in October 1943 we were told that there would be an invasion of Bougainville Island and that we would supply air cover. From the Russells, Bougainville was beyond our effective range, so we would have to stage through Munda or Vella Lavella refuelling at those airstrips. Bougainville is the most north-western large island of the thousand-mile long Solomon Island chain. It is about 125 miles in length and averages about thirty miles in width. Down its centre runs a spine of very rugged mountains including the smoking, active volcano, Mount Bagana at 10,000 feet in elevation. The heaving ridges and gullies, the dense tangle of jungle vines, the oppressive tropical humidity, the swarms of insects, the torrential tropical rainstorms, the waist-deep swamps and the threat of tropical fevers, all made Bougainville a wretched place to conduct military operations.

'But on 1 November 1943 the Third Marine Division under the command of Marine Major General Turnage invaded the South-west coast of Bougainville at Empress Augusta Bay. The reasons for choosing this location were to construct airstrips close enough (200 miles) to Rabaul so that fighter planes could manage to fly from this bay over to Rabaul and return, to avoid Japanese military forces concentrated at the south and north ends of the island and to locate where the construction of airstrips and radar sites was a feasible project for the Seabees. The Third Division disembarking from a dozen transports assaulted the beaches in the Empress Augusta Bay at Cape Torokina and Puruata Island. The surf ran high; landing craft landed at the wrong beaches, boats broached in the surf and Japanese shellfire killed many marines. By nightfall several beachheads were secured, although many of the troops ended up waist-deep in swamps all night.

'That morning sixteen of us took off for Vella (the airstrip was usually called Barakoma). I was in the last division, my wingman being Lieutenant McCaleb. Normally we would try to use up the gas in the internal wingtip tanks, then purge these two tanks with carbon dioxide so that in combat they would not explode. The gas in these tanks would last roughly a half-hour then we would switch over to the main 230-gallon tank between the pilot and the engine. I had just emptied and purged my wingtip tanks when out of the corner of my eye I saw McCaleb abruptly drop out of formation. My first thought was that he had forgotten to switch tanks. But his engine didn't start and it looked like he would ditch in the water near a small island. I pulled up to the division leader, Major Buck Ireland, and attempted to signal that I was going back to cover McCaleb. Buck nodded, apparently not seeing what had happened to "Mac".

'By the time I caught up with McCaleb he had made a water landing, was floating in his Mae West and was fumbling with his life-raft. I slowly circled and he waved to show that he was OK. I continued to circle, wondering what to do when a PT boat or crash boat appeared in the distance from a direction I judged to be Munda or Ondonga. If McCaleb radioed for help I sure didn't hear him. I checked out the US flag on the boat and could see that it was heading straight for McCaleb. At that point I headed for Barakoma hoping to rejoin the rest of the guys.

'Landing at Barakoma I was able to join them and gas up for our mission to Bougainville. I was startled to realise that the rest of our formation didn't see McCaleb go down, didn't see me go back to help and didn't seem worried that both of us were missing. Our chief mission for that day was still ahead of us. The Third Marine Division was invading Bougainville at Empress Augusta Bay close to a place called Cape Torokina. There were supposed to be about 40,000 Japs on the island. There were several Jap airstrips at each end of Bougainville plus the five airfields at the fortress of Rabaul. For all we knew, the Japs might attack our invading forces with planes coming from all directions.

'The flight from Barakoma up to Torokina took about 45 minutes. We had to circle out to the left then back to the right to avoid the five or six Jap fields at places like Ballale, Shortland, Buin, Kahili and Kara. About twelve of us finally arrived on station. Far below us we could see dozens of landing craft making curving white wakes as they sped toward the shore. From our vantage point up there at 20,000 feet or so things seemed to be going smoothly. In reality (as we later found out) the Marines were having a terrible time. Landing craft landed at the wrong places. Vital supplies were lost, the Japs raked the invaders with 75mm artillery fire, the shore was open to rough seas and troops found themselves waist deep in muck.

'The good news was that the Japs were surprised, not so much that we had invaded, but that we had chosen Torokina – no harbour, no good place for an airfield and all those dismal swamps. Ward Hower, my usual wingman, was back on my wing. We climbed to 25,000 feet to look things over. In a situation like that you don't know whether to fly high or low. If you fly low to protect the troops, the Zeros get a vital altitude advantage. If you fly high, bombers and strafers could get at the landing craft and troops and you never know it. We circled the invasion area for an hour. No Jap planes showed up. We could only guess what was going on down on the ground. We kept circling, surprised that we didn't see any planes at all, friend or foe. Where were all the dozens of Corsairs we had seen at Barakoma? Finally I saw about a dozen P-40s a few thousand feet above us. My first thought was, "Boy, those P-40s sure are flying high, must have those new Rolls Royce engines in them". They also were all strung out in an unfamiliar formation; maybe they were New Zealanders.

'Then the leader waggled his wings and started to dive at us. I went from 1,700rpm to 2,600 and to full throttle just like that. Then I went into a 45-degree dive. Ward followed suit. Suddenly Zeros were all around us. Their big red meat balls flashed angrily in the sun. If they fired, I didn't see any tracers. We knew Zeros couldn't dive with the Corsairs, especially if they feared that other American planes were down there. Their attack ended as quickly as it had started. The Zeros disappeared for good. It was our first contact with the enemy and it was an ignominious retreat for us. But at least we were OK. We finished our patrol at 15,000 feet, nothing happened. Then we returned to Barakoma, gassed up and flew to our base in the Russells. Gulping all that oxygen really made me hungry. I ate enough for three people.

'As I write this I am looking at our squadron "intelligence" record for that day. It says that McCaleb had "engine trouble" and furthermore "none of our pilots had any contact with the enemy". I would guess that McCaleb simply forgot to switch from his wing tanks back to the main tank. Also, Ward and I being jumped by a dozen Zeros certainly would qualify as "contact with the enemy". It is really surprising that there were no more enemy contacts as records show that 104 Jap aircraft attacks were made on the Torokina beachhead during the first 24 hours of the invasion.

'(Within a month the SeaBees had constructed an airstrip at Cape Torokina, complete with a steel-lattice Marston Mat runway. By late December we were based at this new Torokina airstrip living in four-man tents in a forest of huge Banyan trees. It was New Year's Day 1944. Two days earlier our first flight over Rabaul, 200 miles to the west from Torokina, followed by a Dumbo (rescue) flight looking for a downed B-24 Liberator, promised a grim and difficult month of January. On New Year's Day things were easier for me as I was assigned to a routine patrol flight over the Torokina beachhead. It was routine in that no Japanese fighters or bombers showed up.)'[4]

---

4. Correspondence with the author.

On 2 November VF-17 flew forty-seven sorties in response to a Japanese dive-bombing attack on the destroyer *Foote*, but no contact was made. On 3 November more than forty Corsair sorties were flown and again no contact was made, so the 'Jolly Rogers' had to content themselves with strafing enemy positions. Two days later VF-17 flew CAPs over two US carriers as strikes went in against Japanese warships at Rabaul. On 8 November twelve Corsairs of VF-17 were to escort a bombing and strafing strike by nine B-25s on Matchin Bay but only five Corsairs formed up and none of the bombers was sighted. Angered by the debacle, Blackburn, who was leading, decided to head north with his other four F4Us and take on the enemy themselves. They chanced upon a 'Ruth' light transport coming in to land at Buka and Blackburn shot it down. Later in the day a flight of six Corsairs led by Lieutenant Commander Roger Hedrick intercepted twenty-four Zekes and fifteen Vals over Empress Augusta Bay. The Vals turned and ran as soon as the Corsairs were sighted. Three Zekes fell to the Corsairs' guns and Hedrick was credited with three aircraft damaged.

On 9 November some of VF-17's Corsairs had arrestor hooks installed. The reason for this became obvious two days later when, together with VMF-212, VMF-221 and VF-33's Hellcats and a squadron of RNZAF P-40s, VF-17 flew top cover when carrier-borne aircraft from the *Essex*, *Bunker Hill* and *Independence* supported by nine destroyers attacked Rabaul. VF-17's Corsairs were to take off from Ondonga at 0420 hours and fly CAP over the fleet while the strike went in. They were to remain airborne until their fuel reserves were low, at which time the F4U-1As were to land on board the *Essex* and *Bunker Hill* to refuel and re-arm before resuming CAP over the fleet again.

Just before dawn Blackburn led twenty-three Corsairs off from Ondonga and two hours later they were in position, joined by twelve of VF-33's Hellcats from Segi Point. The Corsairs remained on patrol until, at 0830 hours, when, low on fuel and as instructed, Blackburn's twelve Corsairs headed for the *Bunker Hill* and Lieutenant Commander Roger Hedrick's eleven F4Us made for the *Essex*. One of his Corsairs had become lost after leaving Ondonga and was forced to return to base. All the Corsairs landed without one wave off and the Hellcats, meanwhile, landed aboard *Independence*. While the fighters were refuelled and re-armed ready for the next CAP, the Corsairs of VMF-212 from Barakoma and VMF-221 from Munda took over CAP duties overhead. After a late breakfast VF-17's Corsairs took off from the carriers again, although three aborted almost immediately with mechanical problems and had to return to Ondonga. The twenty remaining Corsairs took up station over the invasion fleet as the second strike prepared to go in over Rabaul.

At first the enemy was noticeable by his absence. Lieutenant (j.g.) Fred J. 'Jim' Streig took off in pursuit of a lone Kawasaki Ki-61 Tony and shot it down during a 23,000 feet dive. It was not until just after 1300 hours that the enemy planes appeared in strength and then four waves were picked up on radar heading in the direction of the carriers. The 'Jolly Rogers' sighted sixty-five Zekes at around 24,000 feet, escorting twenty-five Val dive-bombers flying below them at 18,000 feet, with fifteen Nakajima 'Kate' torpedo-bombers behind and below. The Corsairs had height advantage but they had been airborne for three hours so fuel was getting low. However, the enemy had to be stopped and, in any event, VF-17 could not land on the carriers as they were still flying off the strike aircraft. The 'Jolly Rogers' dived on the Zekes and six of the Japanese fighters went down in rapid succession. 'Teeth' Burriss went through the Zekes and shot down one of the Kates. Blackburn damaged a Zeke and followed it down to 2,500 feet, but lost it in the clouds. Then he latched on to a Tony and was gratified to see its port wing catch fire and go down. The rest of the Kates sought cover in the clouds and disappeared from view for a short while. Two more Vals went down in flames and, after searching unsuccessfully for the other Kates, 'Teeth' Burriss spotted a Betty and shot it down. The tenacious pilot was also credited with a half share in a Kate with one of VF-33's Hellcats.

The remaining Kates emerged from the cloud cover and lost height to begin their torpedo attacks on the carriers. Their target was the *Bunker Hill*. Lieutenant John Kleinmann, Lieutenant (j.g.) Robert Hill, Lieutenant 'Timmy' Gile and 'Ike' Kepford saw them and made their attacks amid intense anti-aircraft fire from the carriers. Around them, 20mm and 40mm shells exploded and sent up huge plumes of water as the torpedo-bombers pressed home their attack with grim determination. Hill destroyed one of the Kates before pulling sharply away to avoid being hit by fire from the carrier. (He and Ensign B. W. Baker were forced to ditch en route to Ondonga and both were successfully rescued.) Kleinmann destroyed another before a 'friendly' shell shattered his windshield and peppered his face with broken Plexiglass. He managed to nurse his battered Corsair back to Ondonga where he put down safely. Clement Gile dropped onto the tail of a Kate just after it had launched its torpedo from too high an altitude, causing it to fail, and shot the bomber into the sea after a short chase.

By now the remaining Zekes had appeared and they tried to protect the torpedo-bombers. Undeterred, Ira Kepford saw a Kate which had closed to 1,000 yards of the *Bunker Hill* and blasted it out of the sky just as the Japanese pilot was about to launch his torpedo. A Zeke rounded on Kepford's Corsair but a Hellcat shot him off his tail barely before Kepford had time to notice that the enemy plane was there. The *Bunker Hill's* saviour managed to avoid the flak and he powered up to altitude to take on a flight of six Vals trying to return to Rabaul. Kepford roared in behind them, all his guns blazing. Three of the dive-bombers went down in flames in quick succession but, as he opened fire on the fourth, his guns stuttered to a stop, the last of his ammunition expended.

After almost eleven hours patrolling the skies above a carrier task force in the Solomon Sea, Kepford, low on fuel, dropped down to the deck and was headed back to base when 'all hell broke loose'.

'The sky was black with planes. "Jug" Bell and I got our altitude back as fast as we could and went after them. I went at a dive-bomber, flew over him and blazed away. I pulled up to a wing over and he blew up almost in my face. I got two more. They went up like tissue paper or lanterns at a garden party. Just a flash of flame and boom! The pilots don't even get a chance to jump.'

By the time he'd shot down his third plane, Kepford was so low on fuel that he radioed a nearby carrier that he needed to land immediately. As he neared the ship, a fourth Japanese torpedo bomber glided in for an attack. 'I dipped as quickly as I could and went after him nice and smooth,' Kepford said. 'I touched that stick-trigger just as I went over him and he exploded as the torpedo dropped. The fish hit the water, but the carrier had started to turn aside just enough for it to miss. They told me later this had probably saved the ship.'

Flying on fumes, he landed on the carrier he'd just saved. The grateful crew served up a heaping plate of scrambled eggs for Kepford, who'd eaten only a Spam sandwich all day and the ship's captain personally delivered a steaming mug of navy coffee. By now used to a diet of Spam, dehydrated potatoes and coffee 'morning, noon and night', Kepford savoured every forkful of those scrambled eggs. Between the lousy diet and stress of combat patrols twice a day, Kepford lost 20lb off his playing weight by the time he returned home on leave in the spring of 1944.

One mission stayed with Kepford longer than most. VF-17 was close to the target when Kepford's buddy and wingman 'Jug' Bell broke radio silence with a terse but chilling message: 'Ike … come over … I got eight.' With eight Japanese fighters swarming him, Bell had little chance to survive unless help arrived quickly. Kepford whipped his plane around in a sharp turn, searching for 'Jug'. Kepford shot down a pair of Japanese planes before he spotted 'Jug' in a steep dive with an enemy fighter on his tail. 'I can't tell you how fast we were going, but it was paralyzing,' Kepford said. 'Finally I got close enough to give the [enemy plane] the guns and he blew up like a firecracker. I could see Bell down below and I kept waiting for him to pull out. He never did. He disappeared … straight into the sea. Jug was gone. I wanted to cry out loud. He probably never knew I got the guy.'[5]

The events of 11 November 1943 became to be known as The Battle of the Solomon Sea. The Japanese lost 137 aircraft and VF-17 was credited with eighteen-and-a-half confirmed kills and seven Japanese planes damaged. Ten days later, on the morning of 21 November, the 'Jolly Rogers' followed up their success when four Corsairs, led by Lieutenant Merl William 'Butch' Davenport, born 14 March 1918, in Sterling, Michigan, intercepted a flight of six Zeros in Empress Augusta Bay and all of them were shot down. By 30 November VF-17 had a total of forty-five victories for the loss of five F4U-1As, two of them in combat and three pilots killed. The Battle of the Solomon Sea was a major strategic victory. Never again did the Japanese Navy base its warships in Simpson Harbor and the Japanese gave up all attempts to repel the invasion of Bougainville, resorting only to holding actions in the Solomons while withdrawing their forces to the strongholds of Truk and Rabaul.

In December 1943 VMF-213 completed its SW Pacific tour of duty in the Solomons, having chalked up over 100 victories. Its ranks by now

---

5. Kepford received numerous citations, including two Distinguished Flying Crosses, the Air Medal and the Silver Star. After the war Kepford worked his way up the corporate ladder, retiring in 1960 as president of the Liggett-Rexall drug store chain. He moved to Harbor Springs in 1978 and died at age 68 in 1987. He left a widow, Kraeg and a daughter, Tracy MacDonald; a son, Tim; three grandchildren; a brother, Harry; and three sisters.

included seven aces and the night-fighting Corsair was making quite a name for itself too. During December the F4U-2s, which since the 9th had been based at Torokina on the northern end of Bougainville Island from which to strike the big Japanese base at Rabaul, destroyed two enemy aircraft at night. On 10 December the F4U-2s at Torokina were joined by seventeen F4U-s of VMF-216.

The Corsair was by now one of the most numerous American fighters available to the AirSols (Solomon's Air Forces), with about seventy F4Us, roughly a quarter of the 270 fighters on strength. Apart from the Navy Corsair squadrons (supplemented by fifty-eight Hellcats) five USMC F4U squadrons – VMF-211, 212, 215, 221 and VMF(N)-531 were now based in the Solomons. In the Russell Islands were based twenty-seven Corsairs and thirty-one P-38s, thirty-one Corsairs and P-39 Airacobras were on Munda and 103 Corsairs, P-39s and Royal New Zealand Air Force P-40 Kittyhawks were at Ondonga. While these totals appear impressive on paper, in actuality they were severely reduced by maintenance problems and other operational considerations, which limited the effective total of aircraft available to just over 130 Corsairs, Hellcats and Warhawks, while just 38 per cent of P-38s were normally available. A new command, AirNorSols, carried out its first fighter sweep over Rabaul on 17 December, when the Marine and Navy Corsairs were among the fighters used. The sweep took place using thirty-one F4U-s, along with twenty-two F6Fs and twenty-three RNZAF P-40 Kittyhawks. Only forty-seven of the seventy-one F4Us in theatre were operational.

On 23 December forty-eight Corsairs and forty-four other fighters with a heavy formation of bombers carried out a fighter sweep over Rabaul. This time the Japanese took the bait and about forty Zekes rose to meet the incoming force. The American fighters claimed thirty enemy aircraft destroyed. Over Saint George's Channel in the ensuing air battle Lieutenant John Bolt in VMF-214 shot down two Zekes and Major Henry Miller accounted for one. A Harvard Law School graduate, who had been deemed too old for the US services, Miller had joined the RCAF in 1941. He turned out to be an excellent pilot and, after Pearl Harbor, the US naval services wanted him badly enough to compensate the Canadians with $25,000 for his training. This fighter sweep was flown in conjunction with a bomber strike on the Japanese forces at Rabaul and netted the 'Black Sheep Squadron' a total of eleven Zekes and two Tonys.

The two Zekes claimed by Lieutenant Bolt that day raised his total to five confirmed victories. His final score for the Second World War was six. Bolt went on the fly in the Korean War where he added six MiGs to his tally, making him the only Marine jet ace and the Navy's only two-war ace.[6]

More successes followed on 27 and 28 December when fifty-two enemy aircraft were claimed destroyed, thirty-three of them over Rabaul by the four Marine Corsair squadrons, VMF-214, 216, 223 and 331 staging through Torokina. Despite the Corsair successes throughout 1943 in the Solomons campaign and aboard British carriers, the US Navy still refused to station Corsairs in strength aboard its carriers.

---

6. Colonel Bolt received three DFCs and the Navy Cross. He received the Navy Cross, the second highest award in the Navy for actions on 11 July 1953 when, low on fuel, he lead his flight in an attack on MiG 15s. The flight shot down four MiGs and Bolt shot down two of them.

Chapter 3

Aerial Combat Escapades

All six of my guns needed only to bark for less than a second before he disintegrated. In the next instant, I had to pull back the stick to avoid flying through the debris of the exploding bomber. It was a gruesome and yet rewarding sight. For an instant, several human bodies could be seen among the falling mess.

Hunter J. Reinburg USMC

Twenty-three-year-old Joseph Hunter Reinburg, a Texan from Fort Worth, where he was born on 5 May 1918, joined the Marine Corps and was commissioned a second lieutenant with effect from 14 February 1941. He flew a combat tour with VMF-121 at Guadalcanal after transferring from VMF-111 and was promoted to captain. In January 1943 Captain Reinburg shot down three Zekes flying the F4F-4. He shot the first one down at Vella Lavella Island on the 13th and bagged the other two at Guadalcanal on 27 January. The next day VMF-121 was sent to the back area training base at Turtle Bay on Espíritu Santo. Eight pilots, including Reinburg, who were considered 'healthy enough', were sent to VMF-122 to be checked out in the new F4U-1 Corsair. Many replacement pilots fresh from the United States were being checked out with them. One was Major 'Pappy' Boyington, who became the CO for a short time. Hunter Reinburg recalled that he rarely saw him sober and he was 'continuously flabbergasted at how well he could fly … . Greg never missed a mission assigned to him, thanks mostly to the fact that his plane captain literally poured him into the airplane's cockpit.'

VF-122 was fourth in line to be equipped with the Corsair but there was no time because, on 10 April, with twenty-four Wildcats, they were ordered to Guadalcanal to help defend it against a new Japanese offensive to retake the island. When the enemy offensive failed, VMF-122 was sent to Sydney, Australia, for a week's leave before resuming training on the Corsair at Turtle Bay. On 12 June 1943 VMF-122 returned to

Guadalcanal, this time with Corsairs, but minus 'Pappy' Boyington, who, after recovering from a broken leg sustained in a drunken barracks room wrestling match-cum-brawl, took over VMF-112, before being appointed CO of VMF-124 (214), which became known as the 'Black Sheep' Squadron. Meanwhile, on Boyington's recommendation, Hunter Reinburg, who was promoted to major, was appointed acting CO of VMF-122.

Major Reinburg's Corsair combat career began with mixed emotions when on 30 June 1943, he led his flight of eight F4Us from Fighter Strip No. 1 at Guadalcanal. He recalled later: 'We were assigned to fly combat air patrol over assault landings on Rendova Island, 200 miles to the west. The amphibious attack had commenced at dawn and would be followed in a few days with more landings across the narrow strait on New Georgia Island, with the enemy airfield at Munda Point as the objective. Just under an hour later we were flying over the Rendova area at 10,000 feet. I had just reported to 'Pluto', the Combat Information Center (CIC) on a destroyer warship somewhere below us. Pluto's radarscope was splattered with targets as he transmitted a blanket broadcast: "This is Pluto. Many bogies sixty miles north-west presumed to be very high. All fighters climb to 25,000 feet."

'We always tried to keep our radio conversations to a minimum, transmitting only important messages in concise form. Fortunately, my seven pilots also heard the voice because they anticipated my hand signals to push the mixture control to automatic rich, the propeller to military RPM and the throttle wide open for maximum climb. At the same time, they followed my example of hitching on their oxygen masks, which were necessary for our higher destination.

'After ascending through 22,000 feet, a large formation was visible ten miles to the north-west and considerably higher. I was sure this was the enemy bomber formation because I could also see a covey of smaller planes above them, obviously their fighter escort. My heart action quickened and I radioed to my flight, "This is Red One. Bogies, many bogies, ten o'clock high".

'I continued to climb at full power, hoping we could get to their altitude before the shooting started. There seemed to be no hope of gaining a favourable position up-sun and above them because they were much closer than Pluto's information had indicated. As we approached the Jap-held Munda airfield and were passing through 23,000 feet, my engine quit completely with frightful suddenness. With the sound of my own engine silenced, I could oddly hear the sound of my companion's engines, which only added to my consternation! I instinctively nosed my Corsair over into a glide while frantically glancing at the instruments, hoping to get a clue to the trouble. Much to my surprise, all gauges were normal but the propeller continued to windmill, due to my gliding airspeed.

'In friendly skies such a crisis would not be so bad, but we were deep in enemy territory. The only encouraging thought was that I could glide to water, ditching near our ships supporting the assault landings on Rendova. This fact, however, was outweighed by the realization that enemy fighters could and probably would attack at any moment from above while there was also very active and hostile anti-aircraft fire from Munda, directly below. I was between the proverbial rock and a hard place and virtually helpless with a dead engine. The powerplant was normally rated at 2,000 horsepower, but at the moment it was just so much excess weight contributing only to my high rate of descent.

'The Corsair was our newest type fighter airplane, just completing its fourth month of combat. It soon endeared itself to all of us because it was a match for the Zeros. The engine was new and the most powerful yet built, but in the last few months, we had had a number of mysterious high-altitude engine failures. We felt sure these were caused by unwarranted spark-arcing within the unpressurized magnetos while flying in the rarefied upper air. The obvious cure was pressurized magnetos. These had been ordered from the States but, in the meantime, the war had to go on. Seeing that my instruments were normal, I was quite sure my trouble was arcing-magnetos. The book remedy (which did not seem to work all that often) was to glide to a lower altitude where the denser air would stop the arcing. We already had a history, though, of some pilots never getting their engines started again. This had cost the lives of two pilots so far, so the problem wasn't one of mere inconvenience or lost aircraft.

'The only reason anyone could come up with for the engine's failure to restart was that raw gasoline fouled the spark plugs, thereby drowning out the spark when it returned to normal. The windmilling propeller would keep fuel flowing; the fuel could only be stopped by shutting off the mixture-control level at the throttle quadrant or at the main gas valve alongside the seat.

'Major Herman "Hap" Hansen was the Squadron Commander of VMF-122 by seniority, but because he had just come from a desk job, he had no combat experience. Consequently, I was designated the Acting Squadron Commander. "Hap" was leading my second section this day. I radioed, "Hap, I think I have arcing mag trouble. Take the lead and I'll rejoin you when I get it started." I was either extremely naive or optimistic (I'm still not sure which), considering the imminence of a fight, normal restart difficulties and the enemy airfield located directly below. After 'Hap' acknowledged, I radioed my wingman, "Sims, follow me down and cover me while I get my engine started or I ditch off the Rendova shore." I didn't even want to think that hostile action might intervene.

'While gliding toward Rendova and around the Munda airfield, I checked the propeller control lever and then moved it to the low-pitch position. I moved the throttle back and forth a couple of times, hoping to hear the engine restart, but nothing happened. I pushed the throttle forward to the full-power setting and left it there.

'I imagined that Sanderson Sims was no happier than I was because this would have been his first enemy air contact and I was depriving him of a possible victory. He was easy to see in my rear-view mirror, zigzagging behind me, trying to match speeds with my powerless beast. Remembering that the raw, unburned gas must be prevented from fouling the plugs until a spark returned, I cut off the carburettor mixture control on the throttle quadrant. Since I had no way of knowing when the electricity might be routed through the spark plugs again, I had to guess. I decided to put on the mixture when I felt the timing was right and if the engine started the problem was solved. If not, the mixture control must come off again and more precious seconds wasted until time for the next try.

'While gliding down through 9,000 feet, I began to get really concerned. A water landing was becoming a definite possibility so I jerked off my uncomfortable oxygen mask. By then I had made three tries to revive the dead engine (by moving the mixture control to the auto-rich position), but with no success. While the mixture was off and before my fourth try, I saw a formation of airplanes ahead and slightly below, coming toward us.

'I counted eight aircraft and was then sure, by their silhouettes, that they were Zeros. Christ! What a spot! Japs about to attack and my engine's dead! I was more concerned with starting my engine than warning Sims.

Besides, he also had eyes, he was trained and he was presumably ready for combat. He damn well better cover me or …?

'The Jap pilots did not appear to see us as I unconsciously turned my powerless machine toward them. My actions were purely based on the best means of survival, rather than from heroic intentions. I knew my guns would work so my plan was to get a couple of Japs head-on since I had the altitude advantage, for the moment anyway. Then there would be fewer to bother me in my continued glide toward the water. Moreover, experience had taught us that the enemy would usually scatter in confusion if attacked first.

'While moving my control stick to commence the attack I unconsciously moved the mixture control up to the auto-rich position. I was surprised and elated when my engine roared to life, at full power. Those 2,000 horses made sweet music to my ears and the fight was on. The Zero leader had now seen me and was manoeuvring directly toward me. We were coming at each other, almost head-on, at a terrific closing rate. I was ready for him. I placed my gunsight pipper just in front of him to allow for the proper lead and squeezed the trigger at about 500 yards. An instant later, his leading-edge machine guns spit flame as he exchanged lead with me. My tracers struck his airplane in the engine and since every third bullet fired was a tracer, I knew he was getting hit thrice per tracer flash. My finger released the trigger as he flashed by, close under me. I never felt my Corsair being struck by his bullets and I had no time or cause to give the matter more thought. Before completing a hard left turn, I was in firing position to kill another Zero. I felt this was more important than trying to confirm the leader's destruction. It was almost a no-lead shot and my cone of fire blew him up with a two-second burst.

'There was no time to relax and shout joyous words of victory. Another Zero was looming up in the distance, slightly below and coming head-on, emulating his leader's recent manoeuvre. A forward push on the control stick instantly established the proper lead and my trigger finger flexed. Again I observed my tracers drill into him as he passed beneath me. He did not return my fire and I again turned hard left, hoping to observe him disintegrate. Halfway through the turn, a Corsair passed in front of me, presumably Sims. He was on my level and about 1,000 yards away, passing left to right. Tracers were chasing him and a glance down their path led me to a very unfriendly fellow. The red 'meatball' was very easy to see from the side view.

'You can't do that to my wingman! I reversed my turn to bring my guns to bear on the enemy. The Zero was slightly out of range and both he and Sims were flying a nearly straight and level course. It was imperative that I shoot the Jap quickly because he had already had ample chance to hurt Sims. My rate of closure was slow so I decided to try some long-range shooting. If he could not be fatally hit, my bullets would at least scare him into leaving my wingman alone. Surprise and exhilaration surged through me as the Jap exploded from a three-second burst of my machine guns. I must have hit him at about 1,200 feet, as my tracers crossed before reaching him; they were set to converge at 900 feet.

'While concentrating on Sims' tormentor, I neglected to notice a Jap fighter closing on my tail in much the same manner as I had stalked my now defunct victim. The sudden silence of my own guns revealed that bullets were dancing on and about my machine. My attacker had apparently been shooting at me almost as long as I had been doing the same to his friend. A glance in my rear-view mirror confirmed his presence. I instinctively rammed my stick forward to get below his line of fire, a technique that had served me well in past fights. This caused the subsequent hail to miss me but it was too late. My right wing's internal gas tank was on fire and several large holes were easily discernible. It was obvious he had scored with his cannon because they had an explosive charge when they hit; Zeros had two 20mm cannon, as well as machine guns.

'I thought (and hoped) the fire would go out before it melted the wing off, or the whole works exploded. A cloud was very close by so I ducked into it for greater safety while considering the fire situation. While enshrouded in the mist, I noticed fog beginning to fill the cockpit. The smell of smoke told me I had erred and that the fog was actually smoke!

'It became difficult to breathe and to see the instruments. A glance to the left indicated I was suddenly out of the cloud. Flames were now intermingled with the smoke coming from the top of my engine. Christ, now I've got a fire in the engine! This was it. I was a mass of flames and had to get out – in a hurry! The plane was expendable but I sure as hell was not. I was determined to bale out as fast as possible and avoid being cooked. After many bull sessions with other pilots on how each of us would bale out of a Corsair, my plan was firm. The cockpit canopy slid back in quick response to manual movement. I unsnapped my safety belt and then barrel-rolled the aircraft to the right. This type of roll was intentional: the centrifugal force would hold me in the seat until the Corsair was upside down. Once inverted, a hard push forward on the stick sent the plane in an inverted climb and catapulted me downward into space. My radio connections broke loose easily. It may sound like a complex procedure but it worked great. I felt an instant pleasure to be in the open, breathing clean air again. I enjoyed the quiet fall through space. The silence reminded me of the unwanted stillness I had experienced just a short while ago while trying to coax my dead engine back to life. After counting a short ten seconds, I pulled the ripcord.'

Reinburg landed in the sea and took to his life-raft. Eventually, the destroyer *Woodworth* picked him up and, after three days on board, he was landed back at Guadalcanal. 'After recovering some of my confiscated belongings (no one on 'Canal expected me back), I was happy to be informed that my wingman, Sims, had returned safely in spite of about twenty bullet holes in his Corsair. When I next saw Sims, I asked him, "We jumped eight Zeros. I got four, how many did you get?"

'Sims apologized, "Gosh, I didn't get any because I was getting the hell shot outta me. Then, all of a sudden, it stopped, so I ran for home, plenty scared!"

'This annoyed me so I swore back, "Damn you! The reason you got away is I risked my neck to kill your tormentor. You did a lousy job protecting me when I had engine trouble. You're fired!" The next day, 15 July, I continued my combat sorties, but with a new wingman.

'"Red One from Pluto, I have many bogies approaching from the north-west, high. Climb to Angels 25 over X Ray." This was simply a code for a pre-selected landmark.

'"Roger from Red One." I was transmitting to the destroyer-borne radar station by depressing the microphone button on top of my airplane's throttle lever. I was using a throat microphone, which allowed my hands complete freedom. The seven Corsairs of VMF-122 following me heard the instructions and silently duplicated my climb from 9,000 feet. We were about 120 miles south-east of Kahili, an important Jap airbase on Bougainville Island. Ascending past 22,000 feet, I could see many planes above and quite a distance ahead of us. The sight startled me because I had not expected to see them so soon. An undetermined number of bombers were discernible in close formation. Many flyspecks could be seen above them, which obviously were the enemy fighter escort. I turned my flight slightly to the right to continue our climb perpendicular to the Japs' course. This manoeuvre was calculated to put us a thousand feet above the enemy bombers when close enough to attack.

'The enemy leader apparently did not like what he saw because, a few seconds later, his formation commenced a right turn and at the same time all of the bombers began to hatch eggs. From our location in the sky it was evident the bombs would not fall anywhere near Allied positions. And secondly, it was not normal for big airplanes to bomb from a turn. It seemed obvious that our sudden appearance had caused the enemy to abandon the mission and run for home. The bigger part of our mission was accomplished by scaring the Japs into abandoning their attack. Of course, it was also pleasing to attempt to destroy the twin-engined bombers so they could not return and try again.

'Upon seeing the enemy's change of plans, I altered our climbing course to the left. The bombers had completed 90 degrees of their turn when we were ready to attack from above, on their left side. I knew we had to hurry, as the Zero fighters must have seen us and would soon attack with an altitude advantage.

'It was now easy to see that there were fifteen medium Jap twin-engine bombers arranged in "V" formations. We had given code names to all Japanese planes. Our code name for this particular type was Betty. We were not able to count the exact number of escorting Zeros but my quick guess was twenty. My seven fighters were dropping behind me in a staggered column. As I rolled left and dived on the furthest left "V" of Bettys my flight was supposed to follow in quick succession. From then on, it was individual tactics. We could only hope that our squadron policy of trying to stay in sight of each other would offer us some mutual protection. It was a fond hope to me that each of us might destroy an enemy bomber before we had to protect ourselves from the Zeros. Fighting with Zeros was a greater challenge, but the destruction of bombers was more important to the total war effort.

'Machine guns blinked at me from most of the tail guns in the Betty bombers. I hardly noticed or feared them – the heat of battle was on and the chance for further aerial victories was at hand.

'My Corsair was in a steep dive with the gunsight aligned on the leader of the left-hand "V". My six .50 calibre machine guns had hardly started chattering when the Jap's left engine began to belch black smoke. Upon seeing their leader catch fire, the two wingmen partly broke formation to allow him to fall down and behind them. I quickly shifted my aim to the left wingman and I was able to give him a two-second burst before having to push my stick forward to avoid a collision with him. He, exactly like his leader, began to belch black smoke from his left engine. A flash to my left attracted my gaze. I was exhilarated to see my first target, the leader, disintegrating as the engine fire ignited his gas tanks.

'Wise tactics and a desire to get out of range of enemy tail gunners prompted me to continue my dive below the hostile bomber formation. Two thousand feet below the Bettys, I levelled out parallel to the north-west course they had settled on. My speed was quite a bit faster than the enemy bombers. It was easy to keep track of them above and behind me in the Corsair's rear-view mirror.

'Our radio circuit was squealing unintelligible noises caused by many friendly pilots all trying to get their particular important messages heard simultaneously. I allowed a couple of minutes for my flight to join me at the safer lower level, but none did. I also had expected some Zeros to join me in an attempt to carry out their bomber protection mission. By their absence, I assumed that they and my friends had come to blows back at our original point of contact. Radio chatter substantiated this theory.

'Eagerness for more air victories overshadowed further concern for my fellow fliers. They were supposed to follow me and our number one job was to destroy the bombers. They had chosen another course, I presumed, leaving me to pursue our mission goal alone. Okay suckers, take on the tougher Zeros. I'll get these easy ones all by myself! Hot damn! An exploder and a smoking probable! Maybe one of the fellows can confirm that probable as a sure thing for me. These bombers are duck soup compared to Zeros, who fight back. Gotta get some more!

'One last scan to the rear produced neither good nor bad news. On the good side, I had hoped to see my flight joining me and/or my second target explode obligingly. On the bad side, I expected to see many Zeros coming after me for molesting their charges. I thought I could see what diverted the rest of my companions. Many specks back on the horizon indicated that friendly and enemy fighters were having a grand dogfight.

'My Corsair was now a mile ahead of the Bettys and I commenced a climb, which would put me high on their forward right side. I counted them and looked for their escort. There were thirteen bombers left and no sign of the companion Zeros. The bombers were in a shallow dive and apparently not sparing the engines. They were going very fast for their base at Kahili. Kahili represented a major enemy sea and air base on the southern tip of Bougainville Island; some said it was the biggest Jap airbase in all the Solomons.

'A good fast high-side run and I'll finish off that straggler, there in the left-side formation of three. I suppose I could claim that flaming probable because he's missing from this formation, just like his exploded leader. Oh, what a wonderful opportunity: thirteen sitting ducks and they're mine, all mine.

'I'll use two guns at a time and pick one bomber off on each run. No, that'll take too long! I'll get low on gas and they'll get too near home at the rate they're going. No doubt, right this minute, their new leader is frantically radioing his home base for some fighter help. I'd like to pull in behind their formation and pick them off as fast as I can shoot. No, that's not smart. Their tail gunner crossfire would surely get me. Good sense tells me to use all six guns and accelerate my attacks, pulling out of tail gunner range after getting one or two bombers. Use plenty of speed for each attack and pick off the outside bombers each time. That will expose me the least to tail gunner fire. Come on now, boy, play it smart and you'll have the world's record with eight or more victories on one load of ammunition.

'By this time I had unconsciously attained the high right-side position necessary for a good fast attack. Just before the attack, I took a last look around for other aircraft. Scanning disclosed none, but a quick glance in the mirror revealed a suspicious speck high and about a mile behind me. A few seconds of squinting proved it to be an airplane and on my course, but much too far away for more exact identification. Furthermore, I was too intent upon killing my next victim to worry about the stranger. If he were friendly, I would condescend to share some of this juicy target with him. I really didn't think I had enough ammunition, gas or time to kill them all, anyway.

'The frightened Betty bombers were now passing down through the 19,000-foot level. I was running my Corsair wide open and only seemed to have a fifty-knot speed advantage in my shallow climb for position. Okay, I'm high enough and far enough ahead. My Corsair rotated left and down toward the straggler. When 90 degrees to his course I rolled abruptly to the right and began setting the proper gunsight lead. The Betty was not too near any other planes in the formation, so I would not be able to shoot at two in the same attack. His speed caused me nearly to flatten out behind him before getting close enough to shoot. The tail gunner was already shooting at me. All six of my guns needed only to bark at the bomber for less than a second before he disintegrated. As near as I could tell, the gunner never hit my plane. In the next instant, I had to pull back the stick to avoid flying through the debris of the exploding bomber. It was a gruesome and yet rewarding sight. For an instant, several human bodies could be seen among the falling mess.

'The rest of the bombers were now four hundred yards ahead and it took me long excruciating minutes to gain my attack position again, high on their right side. I realized that it would be impossible to destroy all of the bombers alone. I decided to get on the radio and broadcast the location, course, altitude and speed of the enemy formation. Many flights of friendly fighters were supposed to be in the area and perhaps some of them might be close enough to join and finish what I had started. After transmitting the blanket broadcast twice, I was almost ready for another attack.

'My plane started to roll left for the attack when I realized that tracer bullets were whizzing by me. My first thought was that the tail gunners were responsible. A glance into my rear-view mirror cleared up the mystery. A Zero was there, pumping "arrows" at me. That distant speck I had noticed a short while ago had now grown to a full-sized and very unfriendly airplane. I chopped my throttle while putting the Corsair in a left skid. This decelerating manoeuvre was designed to catch my attacker by surprise, confuse his aim and cause him to scoot by before he could recognize my actions and his mistake. Then, when the nemesis appeared in front of me, I would have him at my mercy. This caper had worked well in practice so I automatically used it.

'My trigger finger itched while I strained my eyes for the first glimpse of the Jap in my gunsight. It was then that I began to suspect that my attacker was no amateur, because he never flew in front of me. My head swivelled on my shoulders as I fearfully tried to relocate my opponent.

There was no sign of him anywhere. I then threw the airplane in a right skid but still could not see him.

'In my frantic search for the Zero, I did happen to notice that the bombers were now a half-mile ahead of me because I had reduced my speed, hoping to trick the Zero. Seeing them again dispelled my fear as I returned my thoughts and efforts toward destroying more of those easy targets. It took several minutes to attain a good attacking position again. But tracers once more began to whizz by and strike my wings. The reappearance of the Zero was confirmed by a glance in the mirror. Without thinking, I executed the same evasive skidding caper. This eliminated the "arrows" like before, but again no Zero appeared in front. An alternate skid to the right still did not reveal the phantom. By now I was getting more angry than frightened. Another search of the sky revealed the Betty bombers, but nothing more. Where was that bastard? But seeing those juicy "sitting-duck" bombers crowded the fears from my mind as I resumed the chase.

'The enemy pilot apparently was an acrobat. He was diving on my tail from higher altitudes and using his excess speed to loop over me when my skidding manoeuvre caused him to overrun my plane before he could aim properly. This would explain his quick disappearing and reappearing. I should have suspected his manoeuvre at the time, as I had already fought with some acrobatic enemy pilots. Amazingly, the whole situation was repeated identically for a third time! However this time the Zero, having more than his share of practice, sent a very hostile bullet into the cockpit. He must have been shooting from slightly on my left side, because the bullet entered just outboard of the armour plate, behind me, on the left, and shattered the altimeter on the instrument panel. The bullet just missed my arm as it passed through the crook of my elbow.

'The real danger from the rear now rudely awakened me. I lost my hero complex and devoted my full thoughts toward getting away from the Jap and giving him no further opportunity to kill me. I recalled that a few seconds before it was hit, the altimeter had registered 17,000 feet. I put the Corsair into a left skid and did a sloppy half-roll. I left the throttle wide open and, when inverted, pointed the airplane straight down. I continued jinking to spoil his aim as I kept the aircraft on its nose.

'Early in the war our intelligence people and engineers had been able to get their hands on a Zero 21 fighter that crash-landed pretty much intact in a bog in the Aleutians. The Zero was scrutinized from stem to stern as well as flown by American pilots (after being rebuilt at North Island Naval Air Station in California). Intelligence reports ascertained that the Zero was prone to lose its wings in a high-speed dive. Furthermore, if it did survive such a dive, I really doubted if it could not hold together in a hard right-turning pull out. With this in mind, I headed for the earth in a full-power, vertical plunge. Of course, I had hoped that he would not try to follow me down, but if he did it was my intention to try to prove or disprove Intelligence's theory.

'My Corsair quickly attained a high rate of descent. Due perhaps to an overpowering urge to go even faster, just the opposite seemed to occur: my plane hardly seemed to be gaining on the earth far below. I could see the island of Kolombangara underneath me, but with no altimeter to tell me when to start my pull out, I knew that I had better judge the moment very carefully or ol' Hunter would grow no older and would become one more MIA.

'Damn! Will my plane hold together? His bullets have struck and could have weakened its structure. Too late now: I'm already in my dive! I was too busy trying to figure out my altitude to be frightened. A glance in my rear-view mirror scared me further. The Zero was right with me in the dive. Gosh! He's still after me and still shooting. He must be their highest ace. I'll have to make this pull out a tough one to finish him … or maybe me. The volcanic peak of Kolombangara was helpful in gauging my altitude. At what I guessed to be 2,000 feet, I commenced easing back on the control stick with both hands. When my eyes began to see more grey than light, I refrained from pulling back on the stick further. I froze it in that position while hoping the recovery would continue. When halfway out of the steep dive, I commenced a right rolling turn and could barely see the island shore line and the sea beyond. Am I going to make it? The island seems to be coming up at me awfully fast! Perspiration stung my eyes. The strain of gravity prevented me from watching the Jap in the Corsair's mirror. Made it!

'I levelled off just above the treetops of the jungle and continued my hard-right turn away from the mountain peak and toward the shore line. As the loads of gravity lessened on my body, I tried to see behind me, hoping to observe the Jap fighter crash. But, if he survived, I wanted to get on his tail and give him some "arrows" in return and show him how he should have hit me.

'After making a complete turn, there was no sign of the slant-eye. I started worrying that he might be close under my tail, in my blind spot and would soon be drilling me again. Several swishes of my tail calmed my fear. Another circle of the area revealed no Zeros. Hey, what's that? Black smoke began to rise out of the jungle at about the place where I would have crashed, if unsuccessful with my pull out. The smoke volume rapidly increased and the blackness was indicative of a petroleum fire.

'Hot damn! That just has to be that Zero, but I'll never know for sure, I guess. I just barely made the recovery so it seemed impossible that he could have. I guess I can't even claim him as a probable even though the evidence is pretty conclusive that he crashed. Anyway, he's not around to bother me. Boy, that fire's really burning fiercely now and only gasoline could make such a blaze.

'One more circle of the area for good measure still did not produce an airborne Zero. I flew low and slow over the fire, but could not see through the thick smoke and foliage. The jungle had swallowed another mystery. A weak thought prodded me to take up the bomber chase again. The Bettys, however, were now out of sight. A glance back into my cockpit revealed a frightening fact: only sixty gallons of gas registered on my fuel gauge. Golly! I'd better scoot for 'Canal. It's well over two hundred nautical miles away and it's going to be close on that little gas. I'd better lean out the mixture and pull the RPMs back.

'After throttling back to an economical cruise setting, I looked the airplane over as well as possible. This was not easy since you can only move around so much in a Corsair cockpit. There were four bullet holes in the right wing, over the wheel well, and three more holes in the same area of the left wing. Aside from the shattered altimeter, I could not see any more holes or damage. Fluid was streaming off the trailing edge of both wings, behind the wheel wells. I knew that it had to be either gasoline or hydraulic fluid. I sure hoped it was the latter!

'Next I figured there might be a little gas left in the wing leading-edge fuel tanks. Without a gauge in the cockpit for these auxiliary tanks, there was no way a pilot could tell when they were empty except to draw fuel from them until the engine quit. A quick switch to a full tank of gas always restored the engine to smooth operation. If the leaking fluid was gasoline, the best practice was to run the engine on the punctured tanks until they were dry. I was happy to get twelve minutes of engine operation from those tanks before I had to switch back to the main.

'Some welcome conversation over my radio convinced me that the Bettys I had been chasing would not get home. A flight of friendly fighters had followed my general broadcast directions and was coaching one another while attacking. It was a consoling thought to know that friends had taken over my unfinished business. Across open ocean from the New Georgia Islands, I rechecked my fuel and airplane condition. The next island group, the Russells, was seventy miles away and not yet visible. It was an uneasy feeling to have to leave land behind me while piloting a wounded airplane. My gas gauge now registered forty-five gallons. I assured myself that it would get me home.

'Fluid had quit dripping from the trailing edges of my wings. The hydraulic gauge now registered zero and the spring-loaded tail wheel and engine-cooling flaps were extended due to this loss of hydraulic pressure. This added drag reduced my airspeed and, in turn, lessened the distance that I could travel on my meagre fuel supply. This also meant that, when ready to land, my main wheels would have to be lowered by the emergency system. Meanwhile, I would have to cruise along in suspense wondering if the long-dormant emergency system would work. There was no back-up system for lowering the wing trailing-edge flaps, but the slightly higher attendant landing speed was only a minor problem.

'The next worry to enter my mind was the embarrassment that always accompanies a wheels-up landing. Everyone immediately accuses the pilot of negligence before considering mitigating circumstances. Furthermore, we needed every airplane and a wheels-up landing would put the machine out of commission for some time. It was not long before the Russell Islands loomed into view. Another gas check convinced me I could barely get home. We had an airstrip in the Russells but I wanted to avoid a landing there if at all possible; I wanted to get back to Guadalcanal. Ten gallons of gas remained upon approaching Henderson Field. With my heart in my mouth, I searched for the emergency system valve, which should extend the wheels. It was hard to reach in its confined position and this prevented me from getting a firm grip. My hand became sorely bruised from the frantic fumbling.

'The small amount of remaining fuel indicated that there was little time to struggle with the valve. One more circle of the field and still the damn valve would not budge! I recalled a cartoon once where the pilot stuck his feet through the bottom of his airplane as a substitute for landing gear. My Corsair was a bit too heavy and fast for such an idea! After lowering my seat to the lowest notch, I made a last try at the valve.

'Damn thing! What a lousy place for leverage. Whoops, there it goes! Yes, the wheels are shown as being down and locked now. Thank God! I'm saved from having to defend myself like a criminal. I massaged my sore hand. Less than a minute later, the crippled Corsair responded to backpressure on the control stick as I stalled it about a foot above the runway. As was common with that early Corsair model, it shook like it was in the throes of death before resigning itself to landing on the pierced-steel matting. I thought I had mastered the airplane's landing peculiarities and so prepared for a normal touchdown in a three-point attitude.

'The wheels had no sooner touched when, much to my surprise, the tail reared up! A thought flashed through my mind: maybe the brakes are locked! But I was sure that my toes were not yet depressing the brake pedals. There was nothing to do but hold the stick all the way back in my stomach and hope there was enough wind across the elevators to prevent the aircraft from nosing over. Just before it seemed certain that the idling propeller would nick the runway, the tail stopped rising and the aircraft teetered like a seesaw. A few seconds later, as the machine slowed almost to walking speed, it settled back on the tail wheel. Knowing other planes were landing behind me, it seemed wise to get the machine off of the runway as fast as possible before investigating the trouble. I forced it along, operating the engine at nearly full power. I turned off on the nearest taxiway before stopping the engine and climbing out to check the trouble. I was happier than usual to once again be home, safe on the ground and among friends.

'My airplane mechanic was running toward me. He slowed to a walk as he reached the plane. "Hey, Major, did you forget to lower your wing flaps? And those two flat tyres look like someone turned machine guns loose on them!"

'Almost every night in the last few weeks, the Japs had used the "Tokyo Express" to reinforce their ground installations in the New Georgia and Kolombangara Island areas. On the night of 12 July 1943 the Express brought 1,200 Jap soldiers to Kolombangara alone; the enemy was still able to land even though allied naval forces had discovered them. Our landings in the area (to capture the airfield at Munda Point on the western end of New Georgia Island) had been going on for three weeks now and the enemy was doing his best to make them unsuccessful. Last winter and spring the Japs had run this same Tokyo Express of fast destroyers to Guadalcanal every night to reinforce their garrisons. From experience gained in the long battle for Guadalcanal, we now had an understanding of the Jap pattern. We had been sending a pre-dawn bomber force out of Guadalcanal every morning to finish off the Tokyo Express stragglers.

'On 20 July the sun was just rising in the east behind us as I led a formation of twelve Corsairs up the "Slot", escorting a similar number of army B-25 Mitchell twin-engine bombers. I gazed to the north-west where Kahili, a Jap harbour with two adjacent airfields, was only forty miles distant, just beyond my view. Kahili was on the south end of Bougainville Island. Choiseul Island was visible about twenty miles to the north. Since early July we had been pounding Bougainville, trying to soften it up for our invasion forces.

'There was a ship off in the distance. It had to be Japanese because we were more than 300 miles up the "Slot" from Guadalcanal. It looked like one of the big destroyers the Japs were using for the Tokyo Express. It appeared dead in the water. There was no wake. I kept my eyes open for Zeros, as the Japs would surely put a fighter cover over this ship. I scanned the sky hoping to increase my seven confirmed air victories. The bombers had led us on a zigzag course up the "Slot" and I knew we could not accompany them much longer or we would not have enough gas to get home. I felt a great obligation to stay with the B-25s and to see them safely home at the end of the mission. Now that they had a target in sight, I figured they would quickly sink the ship and head for home.

'My fighters descended with the bombers to give them the maximum protection if Zeros should appear. I scanned the sky continuously hoping to spot some nervy Jap fighters. Suddenly, I heard my call sign on the radio headset. "Red One, this is Rosebud One. We're getting real low on fuel. We're going home. Over." As 'Rosebud' peeled away with his division of four, I double-checked the other seven Corsairs. Our squadron was now made up of very dependable men as we had eliminated weaklings one way or another. All of my planes were in good combat deployment and the radios were quiet. While scanning the sky for trouble, I noticed that the bombers fell into column and commenced a single-file glide-bombing attack on the ship. The anti-aircraft guns on the ship were blazing away at our Army friends, but it did not seem to be very heavy or effective.

'A count of the bombers indicated all were in good shape after completing one skip-bombing attack. I watched them circle the ship and figured they were going to make another run. The ship did not seem to be further damaged, considering that 6,000lbs of explosive (twelve 500lb bombs) had just been slung at it. The 'Rosebud' division was hardly five minutes away from us when they closed up in a much too close formation for combat cruise. This was foolhardy, as we were a long way from home base and only about forty miles from the operational Jap airfields at Kahili. Consequently, it wasn't surprising that the four 'Rosebuds' were jumped by some Zeros who had been stalking us from a much higher altitude for some time. They had apparently figured that twelve of us were too much for them; our Corsairs had been getting the best of them in recent engagements. However, a mere four were just their meat, especially flying close together.

'Rosebud Three and Four went down in flames before they knew what hit them. By some miracle, although hit by the first attack, Rosebud One and Two were still in flying condition. Rosebud One was able to reach the protection of a nearby cloud and luckily the Japs did not see him when he emerged out the other side. He was then able to scoot for home in his non-fatally hit plane. Rosebud Two managed to get one Zero who carelessly zoomed up in front of him and then he dove away and got home without further incident, unhindered by a few holes through non-vital parts of his Corsair.'

Meanwhile, the bombs dropped by the B-25s had found their mark and in a matter of about a minute the destroyer rose almost in the vertical, before it disappeared beneath the waves. Reinburg noted: 'The ship must have been over 300 feet long' but guessed that '300 feet wasn't deep for the area.

'I had expected to see the bombers rendezvous and head for home down the Slot. Instead, they took up a southerly course. I wondered if the B-25 leader was confused and was mistaking Vella Lavella for New Georgia and thought he was heading down the Slot. Those Mitchells hadn't been out of the States long. As the bombers passed between the islands (which were about thirty miles apart), they were flying low, around 1,500 feet. My fighter formation remained deployed about another thousand feet above them.

'Although the mission seemed to be successfully completed, I searched the sky with some faint hope of an air contact. When my glance routinely returned to the bomber leader, he appeared to be in a shallow dive, so my eyes stayed glued on him. With a little more forward-looking concentration, I could see two "V" marks on the water. I knew such signatures belonged to boats. They were small vessels and by their oversized wakes I quickly guessed they were torpedo boats. For several days now, we had been briefed that our PT boats would be operating in this area. Consequently, we were cautioned not to bother them. In fact, we were told to protect them because there was no evidence of the Japs operating similar vessels.

'I wondered what the B-25 leader planned to do. Us old-timers didn't buzz any vessels unless we considered them to be enemy and then we meant to strafe. Our ships, large and small, were real jumpy. They'd usually shoot at any airplane, which came near them. And those PTs carried a good brace of 20mm and .50 calibre machine guns. I was not kept waiting long for the show as machine-gun tracers began making a two-way path between the PT boat and the friendly bomber converging on it. Recognizing that the boat was a PT and therefore friendly, I made a hasty transmission. "Hey, B-25 leader! Don't shoot at that boat! That's a friendly PT boat!" A call would also have been made to the boats if I had been able to get on their frequency. However, even though we had the newer Corsair fighters, we still had the same old radio system, which did not permit us to change transmitting frequencies while in flight.

'Further alarm shook me, as the second bomber appeared to be ready to join the fray. I again yelled over the radio. "Hey, B-25s! This is your fighter escort. Those are friendly PT boats! Don't strafe or bother them. They're friendly!" My transmission was not answered but I was relieved to see that the second B-25 did not strafe. I double-checked the location of my fighters just to make sure they were not thinking of participating. The attacked boat had stopped dead in the water and the other was pulling up to it. Smoke was beginning to show. If the others attacked, I might have to shoot down some B-25s! Christ, what a mess.

'While busily watching the PT boats and trying to prevent another strafing attack, I had forgotten about the crew who had done the dirty deed. It was easy to locate the misguided airplane because it was now beginning to trail black smoke from its right engine. I watched as the B-25 pilot ditched his airplane in the water about a mile from the burning PT. I was relieved to see the crew climb out and inflate their life rafts. The B-25 formation began to circle their ditched leader, so I postponed thinking about my own miserable night in that ocean. Even though it appeared that they had heard my radio transmission, I was afraid the airborne Mitchells might become angry and sink the burning boat as well as the untouched one.

'"B-25s, your leader seems to be okay. You can't help him now. Let's go home and I'll call the Fighter Direction Station at 'Pluto' and see if they can send a rescue ship. This is the fighter leader. Out." If the bombers were receiving me, they neither answered nor changed their course. A check of my gas gauge warned that I had better get my fighters homeward or some of them might also have to imitate the ditched Mitchell. "B-25s, this is the fighter escort leader. You are heading straight for the Coral Sea where there's nothing but water. We are getting low on gas and must get home. The course for home is 100 degrees! I repeat. The course for home is 100 degrees! We are going to zoom in front of you and then take up the course for home. Follow us. Out." The announced course of retreat was adopted. The mountains of Rendova Island were dead ahead. With such an excellent landmark, there was no excuse to pick the wrong course. It was distressing to look back to my starboard rear and see the bombers in a very loose formation, holding their southerly course.

'The body of water just to the east of Rendova suddenly transfixed my gaze. I momentarily paused in my reminiscing to check navigation, sky and my own iron bird as well as the other airplanes. Twelve of us were about to complete our third tour of air fighting in the Solomons, the first squadron to do so. Some kind of record, I guess. We sure had lost a lot of swell guys. The ones I really missed were Bartel "Ras" Rasmussen and Harold "Fateye" Gardner. It's really strange the way the three of us had our individual bad accidents on the same day, three weeks ago. Luckily, I had only been shot down and forced to spend some time in a raft. "Ras" was fatally burned in his Corsair when he started the engine back there on the Russell Islands airstrip. It was an unusual accident. Apparently, while filling the main tank between the engine and cockpit, the refueller spilled some gas, which dripped into the cockpit. The noonday heat turned the fuel to fumes and a spark from the shotgun starter set it off. 'Ras' was badly burned and died a few hours later. Gosh, how tragic! And "Fateye" Gardner was last seen in a furious dogfight right near where we were flying now. I sure wish he'd have shown up, but there was little chance of that.

My throat contracted momentarily and I yanked myself back to the present. As we approached the Russell Islands, about fifty miles short of Guadalcanal, I double-checked my gas gauge and then radioed, "This is Hunter. I don't think I have enough gas to get home. Any of you other guys in doubt, land here with me, over." Soon after the battle for Guadalcanal had been won last spring, our High Command thought it prudent to build a fighter strip in the Russells. It was now earning its keep in support of the New Georgia campaign. I realized suddenly that if the strip had not been put there several of us would have had to ditch for lack of fuel, no thanks to the B-25 bombers. Three of us made the gas stop and were airborne again within an hour. Soon after take off, I saw some B-25s in formation just ahead of us. Suspecting that they were our recent charges, I counted them and was distressed to tally only nine, when we had started out with a dozen.

'A little later in the day, I learned that the lead B-25 crew was returned safely in a "Dumbo" (PBY) flying boat. I had to assume the other two missing Mitchells had ditched in the Coral Sea and the crews lost. The next day, we learned no one in the PT boat was killed but several were slightly wounded. Their boat sank but all were rescued by their companion craft, which avoided the downed bomber crew like they had the plague. That's why the "Dumbo" had been sent out. Such are the fortunes of war. Incidentally, Munda airfield was finally taken a couple of weeks later (on about 5 August 1943) by American forces after nearly two weeks of ferocious fighting.'

In August 1943 Hunter Reinburg was among the first USMC fighter pilots to complete three combat tours fighting the Japanese. Of those few completing the combat record of three tours while operating out of Guadalcanal, he had been overseas the longest. He went home to the US by ship to San Francisco and enjoyed some greatly overdue liberty, followed by two weeks' leave. Soon after, he became the official CO, charged with rebuilding VMF-122 at MCAS El Centro, California, with a cadre of forty-four second lieutenants. At first Reinburg and his four instructor pilots had to use twenty old F4Fs, as all new Corsair fighters were needed in the Pacific, but about halfway through the combat training curriculum four F4Us arrived. At the end of the first week, VMF-122 was down to three Corsairs, as Reinburg recalled:

'One was wrecked by a student on his very first landing; he hit the brakes too hard and caused the F4U to flip forward, right on over its nose and onto its back. That totalled it. The long snout of the "hosenose" had obstructed the student's forward view as the tail settled on the runway. So, because he could not see forward, he hit the brakes harder than necessary. The student was unhurt, but I sure wanted to clobber him. However, after a long talk, he convinced me that he deserved another chance. He did so well flying the Wildcat for another twelve hours that I decided to let him try the Corsair again. I only agreed to do this after all of the other student pilots had safely checked out in the F4Us. Would you believe it? He did it again, just like the previous accident and it was once more on his very first landing attempt. Now my squadron was down to two hard-to-get F4Us. We also had one less student pilot because the Group Commander quickly transferred the man to another outfit before I had the chance to do him any physical harm. Soon after getting rid of the "Eightball" pilot, my squadron began to receive more Corsairs. At about the same time, we were told not to push the engines any harder than necessary: we were operating on automobile gasoline. This was because all of the higher-octane aviation fuel was needed in the combat zones. We did not "baby" the engines and we never had any of the troubles predicted.

'By the end of 1943 most of my student pilots had completed the training curriculum, but three had been killed in crashes. I informed the Air Group Commander that we were ready for war-zone combat. We five instructors were disappointed and bitter at not being able to return to air combat with such a well-trained squadron of good pilots. The excellent teamwork that we had taught everyone convinced us that we could all get high scores against the enemy with small risk to ourselves. We were told that we would be returning to combat as soon as the new covey of pilots completed the training course. Unfortunately, things got off to a bad start with the new class. One of the new boys, on his very first flight in a Corsair, radioed to the tower operator for landing clearance. He was told to circle east because the duty runway was being changed. The careless man in the tower forgot about the obedient Corsair pilot who silently circled until he ran out of gas. The result was a dead-stick, wheels-up landing in a cornfield and another scarce Corsair was ruined. You can bet that some dumb personnel got a good chewing-out.

'One of the peculiarities of the Corsair was that the landing-gear retraction handle was down by the pilot's left-foot rudder pedal. When the wheels were down, the rod handle pointed downward. There was a knob on the end of the handle, shaped like a tire and wheel, which put a pin in a hole for positive down-lock. To retract the wheels after take off, a pilot had to be comfortably airborne before ducking his head under the instrument panel, momentarily blinding him, to reach the unlocking knob. Then he had to pull the knob out to unlock the handle from the down position and raise it to a horizontal position to be sure it was then locked in the "up" detent.

'If a pilot wore winged shoes [ones with extended soles], the shoe edge could catch under the locking knob and pull it out of the down-lock detent. This occasionally happened if the pilot excessively see-sawed the rudder pedals back and forth while taking off or landing. This inadvertently retracted the landing gear. Result: a bent prop, skinned-up belly, flaps worn off at their trailing edge and a verbal beating from the Commanding Officer. Fortunately, late in 1943 the Chance-Vought factory corrected this potential problem by moving the wheel-actuating handle to a more sensible location up and forward of the throttle quadrant.

'One day I had an unusual test flight to perform which involved a full-power speed run at 30,000 feet. When I pulled back on the Corsair's throttle to reduce power, the engine kept right on running wide open! Jazzing the throttle back and forth made no difference and the ease of movement indicated that the throttle control was disconnected from the engine. A descent with all 2,000 horsepower puffing the airplane downward would result in a fast return to the ground, but what I needed was an ultimate reduction of speed. This would be necessary for a safe landing at home base. I figured that the smartest thing to do would be to stop the engine and glide down. This could be done in one of three ways. One way was to turn off the fuel valve to stop gas flowing from the main tank. Another way was to switch off the magnetos, thus cutting off the ignition. A third way was to keep fuel from entering the engine by cutting off the carburettor mixture control on the throttle quadrant. I selected the third method as the best. So down I came, with an understandably high descent rate. This was because the Corsair was not designed to be a glider; it was more like a gliding brick!

'I was too far away from the field to dead-stick it all the way. After obtaining landing clearance from the tower operator, I put the mixture back on. The engine roared back to full power. When I was in the landing pattern and in position to dead-stick the plane onto the runway, I stopped the engine again by moving the mixture control all the way aft. When I had the plane rolling slow enough to turn onto a taxiway, I brought it to a stop at a spot clear of the duty runway. I considered it too dangerous to taxi into the regular parking area at full power, so I radioed for the tow truck. Back at the hangar on the flight line, investigation revealed a broken throttle rod. It was quickly replaced and the Corsair was ready for flight again.

'In early July 1944 Marine Fighter Squadron (VMF) 122 finally sailed back to SOPAC (South Pacific) aboard the carrier *Hollandia*. Ten days later, we were put ashore on Espíritu Santo Island in the New Hebrides Archipelago. This was the same chunk of land I had departed from some eleven months ago when going home to the States. We were assigned twenty-four new Corsairs on the same old airstrip at Turtle Bay. I immediately started training my squadron on tropical sea/island indoctrination. The Japs no longer had the airpower to launch fighter planes in the Solomon Islands. The next possible action for VMF-122 was the planned invasion of Peleliu Island. Thinking that the Japs would probably defend it fiercely on land and by sea and air we all looked forward to this operation. We were confident of our aerial teamwork system and anxiously figured we could shoot down many enemy planes during combat in the sky. While waiting for the Jap airfield on Peleliu to be captured, we operated off Emirau.

'On 30 September 1944 I led my twenty-four F4Us from Emirau to support the Peleliu invasion. Our first refuelling point was to be a newly-built US Naval airbase on a small island named Owi, in western New Guinea. From there we were to go nonstop to Peleliu. We were forced to fly west-south-west because a typhoon was located just north of our course; the weather also confined us to about 1,000 feet of altitude. The solid overcast above emitted steady drizzle. This made it difficult to see ahead because our planes had no windshield wipers.

'After being aloft for some forty minutes, I switched my fuel selector valve from the main tank to the left-wing leading-edge tank. Then I turned my head to note positions of my other twenty-three Corsairs. My counting was suddenly interrupted by silence as my single engine quit – completely! Automatically, my eyes scanned the instruments along with establishing an appropriate glide angle. With my engine totally silent, I could hear my roaring squadron following me. From years of flying habits, I unconsciously switched the selector valve back to the main tank. My F4U's descending glide speed kept the propeller windmilling so that the oil and fuel-pressure gauges indicated normal just as if the engine was running with power. A moment later, I rammed the throttle, the propeller and the mixture controls to their full-forward positions. This would give me full power if the engine took a notion to fire again. All quick efforts failed. After jettisoning the 150-gallon belly tank, I slid back the canopy. For some inexplicable reason, I ignored good ditching rules and did not jettison the Plexiglass overhead shield.

'The sight of the rough sea below sent a very frightening thought through my mind. Here I was, about to be engulfed by monstrous waves created by the nearby typhoon; the surface wind was at least 35 knots. I aimed my Corsair directly into the wind to attain the slowest possible water contact. I lowered my flaps but kept the wheels retracted. When I had the plane very close to a full-stall attitude, I imagined the seawater was lapping at my Corsair's bottom and new noises seemed to confirm it. But suddenly, I knew that the new noises were in reality coming from my engine, which was roaring up to full power. I slowly breathed a sigh of relief, as I knew I was temporarily saved from Davey Jones's Locker. While nursing the plane and my nerves back to 1,000 feet of altitude, I surmised that my trouble must have been caused by water in the fuel tank. Obviously, I had done the correct thing by going back to the main tank and pushing the three power controls to the full forward positions. The windmilling propeller, induced by my forward airspeed, had kept the fuel pump going. That bit of good mechanical luck had cleared the lines of water.

'The Admiralty Islands were thirty miles south of our present position and I knew that the US Navy had just opened a strip there on Pitelyu Island. I headed straight for it. After landing there with my faithful wingman, Misely, following me, I had my tanks checked. The left-wing leading-edge tank disgorged more water than gas. We fuelled up with fresh gas and were soon on our way and rejoined the squadron at Owi. Later investigation revealed a most plausible cause as to why only the leading-edge gas tank was contaminated. Several weeks back we had ferried our Corsairs to Emirau Island, using all the gas in the leading-edge tanks to get there. These auxiliary tanks were only used for ferry flights. The tanks had not been touched since. While we were on Emirau, there were many rainstorms. My F4U had been parked under trees, which funnelled water onto the leading-edge area. The final piece of the puzzle fell into place when an inspection revealed that the left-wing leading-edge tank cap didn't fit tightly; the right-wing tank cap was fine. When ready to ferry the aircraft to Peleliu on our assigned mission, we requested that all tanks (including the leading-edge ones) be filled. I discovered later that when the gas-truck driver went to fill my left leading-edge tank, he found it full! He assumed the liquid was aviation fuel and replaced the tank cap. Pre-take-off inspections included checking the one water-catcher for all tanks. This is a valve in the engine compartment. If the left wing leading-edge tank had recently fed the engine, the water would have been detected. But such was not the case.'

By November 1944 Hunter Reinburg's war became as routine, 'as the daily commuter in New York', as he recalls: 'We were operating our Corsair fighters from the captured strip on Peleliu Island in the Palau Island group, the last atoll chain in the western Pacific before the Philippines. We had been at the field for two months. Our daily routine was to keep by-passed Jap installations in the area knocked out and provide air defence for our ground forces. We had hoped it would be another Guadalcanal because the enemy-held Philippines was just five hundred miles to the west. Much to our disappointment, however, they did not dispute our invasion and never tried an air raid. Consequently, the day-long combat air patrol over the base and the bombing and strafing of nearby Japs was becoming quite boring.

'Then late in November we started a shuttle bombing service on by-passed Jap bases via a new strip on Ulithi, about 110 miles beyond Yap and almost halfway to Guam further east. We had been raiding Yap for a month now so we knew it well. We were to raid Woleai Island, just over 310 miles south-east of Ulithi. As we passed Yap we were to throw a 500lb GP bomb on the best target we could find and strafe anything which seemed to need it. We were to hit Yap at sundown, so it meant landing at Ulithi after dark. There we were to get the four Corsairs re-armed and refuelled during the night and get off before daylight so we could hit Woleai at the crack of dawn. We were to give it the same pounding as Yap, then return and reload at Ulithi, get airborne and hit Yap again on the way home.

'As the Squadron Commander, I thought it best to take over because these types of raids were much more challenging and interesting than the daily stuff. We wanted to continue to be the chosen squadron for them. This one showed real promise of some dog-fighting.

'At our squadron briefing just before take off on the morning of 27 November, I instructed my pilots not to strafe Yap unless we saw a juicy target, such as an airborne airplane, since Ulithi was not well equipped to re-arm us. We hit Yap right on the button after flying 262 miles over open water. The AA was already spitting in the sky as we rolled over for vertical dives. It was disgustingly easy to ascertain that there were no new targets, so I laid the egg on one of the AA positions and radioed my pilots to do likewise. Recent experience seemed to indicate that we should concentrate on the ever-threatening anti-aircraft emplacements, as they needed punishment for their many hits on us. At times it had seemed to me that we would not have lost so many airplanes and pilots if we had made the AA more of a prime target. My dive-bombing pull out was made over the water.

'The white sand, coral reef and white surf of the Ulithi Atoll was easy to see in the twilight. The airfield was on Falalop Island on the north-east side of the reef, which was a pretty even circle of about ten miles in diameter. I could see many of our ships in the excellent harbour formed by the reef: aircraft carriers, battleships: a complete fleet. The scene had been dubbed 'Murder Row'. Our landing was uneventful. It took several hours to get four more bombs. The island ordnance crew did not take kindly to working after hours, especially at night. The three pilots with me were eager and dependable so we were airborne well before the crack of dawn.

'As the sun rose in our faces, Jim Misely's good eyes won again. He had manoeuvred his airplane close to mine, on my right side and was making pecking motions with his left forefinger, indicating that there was an island dead ahead. As we got closer I compared it to my map and it was definitely our target. Woleai was no bigger than Ulithi. I strained my eyes for airplanes in the sky over the base and squinted into the rising sun. If there were any Japs up, they had the advantage of hiding in the glare. Nope, damn it, there was nothing there. The place looked pretty beat up and deserted, but there was some AA to greet us. I counted about ten puffs of black smoke to our right and slightly above. I told everybody to lay his egg on an anti-aircraft position and see if we could find some low-altitude strafing targets. I told them to keep jinking and not let the AA zero in on them, keep their heads up and keep watching for airborne aircraft. After puffing out from my bombing run, I radioed, "A couple of those planes in the revetments don't look so badly damaged. Let's make a few strafing runs on them and see what happens." After shooting the first one I heard Misely's voice. "Hey, Skipper, the one you strafed is burning."

'I saw four more. They were Betty bombers and three were set on fire. I was pulling up from my third strafing run when "Tabe" said he'd been hit in the tail and his elevators were jammed. We joined up and Tabe seemed to have the wounded Corsair under control. We all made it back to Ulithi and Tabe was able to make a safe landing. Inspection revealed that a bullet had entered the leading edge of the horizontal stabilizer and split the aluminium metal as it went out the rear. The damaged area was not a vital structural member, so I pushed the frayed metal back in place with a screwdriver and the plane was ready to fly again.'

Reinburg planned to waste little time getting back to Peleliu while making the usual pause over Yap. The Corsairs were quickly refuelled, but no ordnance crew could be found to hang bombs and re-arm the guns. While asking the Field Operations Officer to help, the air raid siren went off. It was a bogey coming in high from the north-east and no fighters were assigned to go after him. Reinburg was off like a shot but, as he ran toward the Corsairs, he suddenly remembered that they had not been re-armed. He stopped dead in his tracks and swore out loud, 'Goddamn, we haven't got any ammo! Well, we didn't use it all at Woleai. There ought to be enough to get one bogey. Hell, let's go!' Reinburg resumed his run and all three of his pilots scrambled with him. They got off quickly and climbed at full speed. Passing 25,000 feet they could see nothing. At 30,000 feet above the ocean there was still nothing. The Corsairs stayed at that altitude for about fifteen minutes before Reinburg radioed, '"Hey, Yucca. If you still don't have anything on him, we'll have to come down. We don't have heaters in these crates and we're freezing our fannies off."

I sure hated to give up but I had lost hope. Yucca answered, "We can't pick him up again. Guess he took one quick look and ran. Return to base. Sorry, it was a good try." Back on the ground, there was much profanity while our planes were refuelled and re-armed. It was disheartening to learn a few days later that a rival squadron got the job of defending Ulithi and shot down one of the high-fliers two weeks later. My congratulations to them were tendered with envy.'

On 14 December Hunter Reinburg and Robert 'Lippy' Lepire who was substituting for his regular wingman, Jim Misely, Tom Tulipane and 'Tabe' Tabler took off for a dive-bombing attack on two large enemy ships on either side of an isthmus south of Koror Harbour. The Corsair pilots knew that they had to be aware of anti-aircraft guns on Babelthuap to the north. Two pilots would attack each ship and if their dives were accurate, the 500lb GP bombs fitted with instantaneous nose fuse and a one-second-delay tail-fuse, should do the job. If the nose fuse failed, the tail fuse would cut in a second later. Hunter Reinburg was confident, and he told the lieutenant colonel in charge of operations, 'Don't worry colonel, they're as good as sunk.'

'The four of us took off in quick succession, climbed away from our base on Peleliu and headed north toward the target. It was a beautiful day. There were just enough scattered cumulus clouds to break up the monotony. A large cumulus was over the target, so I immediately planned to use it for cover until ready to dive on my particular ship. The long thin island, which separated the two ships, was visible from ten miles away.

'Soon after entering my dive, I could see my target and noted that it was indeed a fine piece of camouflage work. I'd flown by this location several times lately and not seen the ships. Of course, a few anti-aircraft bursts nearby had caused me to hurry elsewhere. We had quit taking chances since we were apparently winning the war. I concentrated on making an accurate dive. Out of the corner of my eye I could see anti-aircraft gun muzzle flashes and assured myself that they were always inaccurate at first. It was those subsequent passes that were dangerous to us. I was pleased with my dive angle and aim and let the bomb go, pulling out to the west as I passed through 800 feet. As the Gs of the pull out began to strain my body, I instinctively tightened my stomach muscles to prevent blackout.

'My radio came to life. It was Lippy Lepire. "Hey, Hunter, you hit it square in the middle." At this stage of the war we were allowed to use our radios freely since the Japs could do little to bother us. The sky above the target was blotched with many anti-aircraft bursts. Climbing away easily, I glanced back to see Lippy's bomb burst close alongside the same ship that had been my target. I was elated that we had destroyed the larger of the two ships and was now greedy for our squadron to get credit for the second one but Tabe and Tom could not find their target. I told them to follow me down in another dive and I'd spray the target's decks with my guns. Lippy circled and watched. He did not want to go down in that gun hotbed again. Another run did not thrill me either, but I wanted that ship sunk. I cut in front of Tom and rolled over into a dive. This time the muzzle flashes from anti-aircraft guns seemed to spark from everywhere. When passing down through 4,000 feet, the ship was clearly visible to me. Goddamn it! I wished I had another bomb. I'd have gotten this target too. At 2,000 feet I squeezed my gun trigger on the control stick. My tracers were bouncing all over the ship.

'"See them, Tom?" There was no time for further conversation as I hurriedly pulled out to the west, jinking across open sea. In spite of my many past similar missions I cringed behind the plane's armour plating; I always felt uncomfortable until out of gun range. When I was in a position to glance back toward the ship there was no sign of Tom's bomb-burst that I had hoped and expected to see. Tom called. "Sorry, Hunter, I just couldn't see it. And boy is that AA getting thick." A moment later, Tabler's bomb hit about a hundred yards from the objective.

'"This is Hunter. You missed it, Tabe."

'"Well, come on, Tom," I said with disgust. "I'll shoot up the decks again and watch closely this time! Lippy and Tabe, you two watch for gun muzzle flashes and strafe them as we dive in."

'The third time in, Tom still did not see the ship but the strafing by the two wingmen virtually stopped the anti-aircraft firing. Determined to see that Tom found and hit the ship, I led him in three more times. On the last pass, he thought he saw the ship and let his bomb go. Unfortunately, it missed by several hundred feet. In the meantime, some of the ground guns had resumed action, so I would not have made another immediate run under any circumstances. Determined to add the second hidden ship to the squadron scoreboard, I called to my fighters. "This is Hunter, Tom. Take your section on up the coast and shoot something. Lippy and I are going back for some more bombs." I reasoned that if all four of us returned to base for bombs, we would have to check in with Intelligence and then another squadron would get the next crack at the ship. However, if just two of us hurried home, had two more bombs quickly hooked up and got rapidly airborne again, the Group CO likely would not know the difference. Not having to refuel would also save us some time.

'The plan worked and we were airborne again in twelve minutes. In just twelve minutes more, I was pushing over in another dive on the second ship. The enemy anti-aircraft guns came to life again with greater intensity. When I released the bomb, the target was clearly visible to me, because my gunfire in the previous strafing runs had knocked off some of the camouflage. Having already run that AA gauntlet six times in the last hour, I was well aware of the growing danger of each subsequent dive. The Corsair responded properly to my jinking control movements as I dove for the cover of a nearby island to the east. I remembered to make myself as small as possible by cringing behind the armour plate. I threw some caution to the wind and pulled up a little sooner than normal because I was anxious to see the results of my egg laying. Several AA bursts were not far behind me, but I could also see the smoke and debris kicked up by my exploding bomb.

'"You did it again, Skipper! Your bomb hit square on it," Lippy radioed. '"Yours looks right on target also, Lippy!" I replied. "Good work! Join me in a loose column and we'll take a better look." We climbed to 8,000 feet and then I led Lippy in a fast, shallow dive towards the two bombed-ships, jinking constantly. About the time the anti-aircraft gun muzzle flashes became visible, we could see our latest target falling away from the shoreline. It rapidly rolled over on its side and started settling on the bottom. The other ship had already assumed a similar position on the other side of the narrow island ridge. We decided to finish our gun ammunition on the AA emplacement enemy personnel who had failed to keep us from bombing the ships. Our bravado, however, had waned somewhat, so we fired from several thousand feet out. By this time safety was more desirable than accuracy. After joining up with the other section, we returned to base and reported "mission accomplished" without incident, never revealing our chicanery!

'On the morning of 18 December 1944, I led my division off of Peleliu airstrip on one of several daily reconnaissance sweeps of enemy installations just to the north of us. We had fully loaded guns in our four F4U aircraft, but no bombs or other ordnance. Four of the ten enemy aircraft destroyed on the ground by the squadron had been at the Babelthuap airfield. (Babelthuap was by far the largest island in the Palau Islands. It was almost thirty miles long and eight miles wide and the enemy had an airfield on the southern end. We had kept it incapacitated with daily strafing and dive-bombing attacks.) The six others had been acquired on Yap and Woleai. All three airfields were speckled with many wrecked airplanes and it was very difficult to be sure we were not shooting decoys or hulks already claimed by someone else. Our system was "if we can make it burn it must be flyable and therefore claimable".

'The island chain between our base and Babelthuap consisted of many small atolls. Most of them were long and slender-looking, like many worms scattered on the concrete after a rain. The last cluster, just south of the big island, enclosed a magnificent deep harbour at Koror, which averaged about five miles in diameter. The Japanese had developed it into the Pearl Harbor of the western Pacific. When we began operating from Peleliu, forty-five miles to the south, the harbour was on our daily target list, along with the airfield on its north side. All of our squadron pilots had made many strafing and dive-bombing attacks on the enemy's main installations. Several pilots had already been killed in these assignments. We had become quite familiar with the layout and its only remaining means of protection: Jap anti-aircraft guns. These were well camouflaged and seemed to be relocated frequently to foil our counter-attacks. Moreover, the Japanese appeared to have a bottomless pit of ammunition in spite of the fact we had cut them off from surface ship re-supply. We guessed they were getting some replenishment from submarines.

'Since there was a dearth of usable shipping to attack, we considered ourselves lucky to occasionally catch a few small boats in running shape. To get these meagre targets, when we could see them from out of AA range, we had to run the ground-fire gauntlet. We learned that we could generally get away with one fast surprise attack if we kept going while jinking. If we returned immediately, the AA was warmed up and ready, so we seldom took the chance.

'Feeling frisky this day, I led my wingman in a dive down to water level. I planned a fast low-altitude buzz through the harbour, hoping to spot some careless target of opportunity. As we approached the island ridge flanking the south-east side of the harbour I added considerable power to my engine and made sure my six .50 calibre machine guns were ready. A pull back on the stick guided the plane over the sharp ridge. Jim Misely was in the proper position about a hundred yards behind me and offset to the right. It seemed the propeller would nick some foliage from the treetops, but I knew it was just an illusion as my plane made it safely over the other side and into the forbidden harbour.

'My eyes joyously focused on a motor launch putt-putting along, just to the right of my path. It was close to the narrow island, which curved to the left in front of my course. It was apparent that the crew of the twenty-foot boat felt secure hugging the shore line. I rolled my fighter to the right and commenced firing a few seconds after sighting the vessel. The occupants were caught completely by surprise. My low approach had been hidden from sight and sound by the narrow strip of land now behind me. My bullets tore pieces off the craft and many bodies slumped to its bottom. As I passed over my target, it turned toward the shore and several men leaped into the water. I looked back in time to see Misely imitate me and pour a murderous stream of lead into the enemy boat. The converging bullets were interspersed with visible tracers.

'The surprise of our appearance in the harbour was immediately over as the sky above rapidly became cluttered with black flak bursts. These higher explosions which I could see did not worry me but I knew from experience that many unseen smaller guns were surely tuning in on us. I jinked while turning to the right with the expressed intention of getting out of range east of the islands as soon as possible. "Mise" radioed that the launch was burning. He wanted to go back and finish it but I said "Not now. We'll come back later after the AA gunners tire of waiting for us."

'The mountainous island of Babelthuap confronted us as I resumed a northward course. I stayed low on the water, entered a cove and then led us in a gradual climb just above the rising land and jungle. I was trying to see if there was any activity on Babelthuap airfield, which was half a mile to my left. Bomb craters and dispersed wreckage was visible but there were no attractive targets. Misely spotted two camouflaged floatplanes hidden in this cove below. I let him take the lead. Misely acknowledged and I fell in behind him as he cut inside me on a hard right turn. We gained a little altitude over the sea, east of the big island. I watched Mise zoom back into the cove. He concentrated his gunfire on what looked like just a lot of jungle foliage next to the beach. He quit firing and pulled up over the trees as I pressed my gun trigger. My bullets bounced into the same clump of greenery as my wingman's and I still saw nothing unusual. However, black smoke belched upward and, upon zooming over the spot, I could see that our bullets had cut a swath through the area, unveiling glimpses of the floatplanes. They were two-seater Jake biplanes. One more shooting pass finished the job. Both Jakes were burning profusely. We could see men trying to control the fires. We made a third attack, spraying the area generously with 50-calibres, hoping to do all possible additional damage. The two cooking Jakes apparently burned their mooring lines because they began to drift away from the shore. In another minute, they fell apart, scattering their remains on the shallow transparent bottom. Their pontoons were the last to sink.

'Anti-aircraft guns from the airfield and harbour were desperately bursting shells over us, hoping to scare us away. However, this was no bother as we knew they could not depress their aim low enough to score. I then noticed tracer bullets buzzing all around us and was given a momentary scare that an aerial challenge was at hand. However, closer study of the situation revealed that they were coming from several spots flanking the cove. (Misely was killed by one of these same ground guns, on 10 March 1945.)

'We emptied our guns on one more pass, concentrating on spots where the small-arms fire emanated. Then I called Misely to follow me up the east coast of Babelthuap. We radioed congratulations to each other as we capered along the shoreline. Many times we had checked the native villages along the beach but we never bothered them, as there was never any sign of enemy activity. A few natives were usually visible and some of them always waved. After we reached the rendezvous, the other two planes rejoined us. We were all very hot and sweaty from the low altitude tropical heat and from the excitement so I climbed for the higher and cooler heights for the return trip. As we reached 6,000 feet the chilly air felt great. While climbing, I informed the second section of our good fortune in targets. They still had ammunition and requested permission to shoot up the same cove in hopes of finding additional seaplanes. Upon receiving my okay, they dived away as Misely and I continued to climb. Black smoke was still drifting up from the cove and it was not long before we could see the two Corsairs working it over.

'We levelled off at 10,000 feet and noticed that the big guns were active again, with more bursts near the cove. This gave me an idea for more mischief. I decided we would put on an air show to confuse the AA guns and distract them from shooting at the others. Adding combat power, I did a split-S (half-roll to a vertical dive) manoeuvre from 10,000 feet. The airfield was directly below me and in my gunsight. I could see the enemy was ready from the many gun muzzle flashes blinking at us from the field and harbour. Apparently the Japs were extra-angry with us for our better-than-average success, because I never before noticed so many big gun locations. When the first shots burst ten or so seconds later at 10,000 feet, we were passing down through 7,000 feet. Then the enemy must have feared a dive-bombing attack because their bursts suddenly began to clutter the air below us. Having no intention of being so obvious or obliging, I pulled into another loop. Misely and I had a ball putting on an unusual high-altitude airshow over the enemy installations. Our gyrations were an unorthodox collection of every stunt trick I knew. I felt smug because we had caused the enemy to waste precious ammunition while we were just having fun. Then I began to worry that they might just get lucky. I decided to quit while we were ahead. The black anti-aircraft smoke balls cluttered the air around and below us like hundreds of huge ghostly balloons. They slowly dispersed and streaked the sky. A few AA were beginning to explode close to us and I imagined the Japanese were becoming more angry and exasperated at our insolence. However, the rate of fire seemed to diminish, probably because they were getting tired and low on immediately available ammunition. Our last acrobatic stunt was followed by an erratic dive to the east. I radioed rendezvous instructions to my second section. Soon thereafter we rejoined at 1,000 feet above the ocean and headed south for home. Tulipane reluctantly reported that they had not been able to find any more hidden floatplanes.

'As we approached our base on Peleliu I moved my control stick back and forth to indicate close right echelon formation. We clipped along at an indicated airspeed of slightly more than 200 knots. Our squadron took pride in precision flying and I was pleased to see our formation was well dressed. Misely's left wing was inside and behind my right wing and slightly stepped down to just barely miss my slipstream. The other two aircraft held the same excellent position outboard from my wingman. When over the field, I patted my head and pointed to Misely. This hand signal meant we should fall into column for landing. An instant later I made a hard left pull-up into a lopsided loop. The others imitated the manoeuvre at one-second intervals. This wild fan-like breakup was standard squadron procedure and looked most impressive from the ground. Unfortunately, higher-ranking officers had continually cautioned us that the manoeuvre was overly boisterous and therefore dangerous. Privately, we called it the 'bursting fart' breakup.

'We made a snappy landing where our fourth man was just rolling his wheels on the runway as I was turning off at the far end. This landing technique was developed from aircraft carrier operations and was essential for full squadron missions. After parking our Corsairs, the four of us had a jubilant time relating the mission to our ground crews. While chocking my airplane, my crew chief noticed a one-inch hole underneath my right wing where it joined the fuselage. He investigated by removing the fairing plate with the hole in it. He then quickly discovered that a 20mm bullet had done the damage. After entering the aluminium skin the bullet had struck the head of the main bolt, which holds the wing to the fuselage. With the top of the bolt sheared off the metal pin was about to fall out. I broke out in a cold sweat, realizing I had performed the air show with a wing about to break off. I then tried to figure when I had been hit and guessed it was while making the second or third pass at the seaplane cove.

'After nearly two months of flying combat air patrol and fighter-bomber strikes against Japanese-held islands within our combat range (Koror, Babelthuap, Yap, Sonsorol, Pub Anna, Merir, Woleai, etc.), it was getting pretty obvious that the enemy was not going to try any offensives against our captured air base on Peleliu. Morale among my pilots (and me) began to wane.'

Five hundred miles west of Peleliu the Allied invasion of the Philippines began on 20 October 1944, landing on the east coast of Leyte Island near the town of Tacloban. VMF-122, however, remained at Peleliu and it was still operating from there against Babelthuap, Koror and Yap when the war ended. Reinburg, meanwhile, was 'promoted' to be the Air Operations Officer of the Marianas Air Defense Command on Saipan Island. When Admiral Nimitz dissolved the Command he was transferred to the Marine Corps Air Group on Guam on 5 March 1945.

Chapter 4

The 'Black Sheep' and the 'Jolly Rogers' Big Booty

When I was very close, maybe sixty to eighty yards, I opened fire with the six Brownings. He burst into a ball of flame almost at the moment I swept by his left wingtip. I fancied that I could hear the explosion. My Corsair shuddered as I hit the blast and I also felt that something hit my plane.

USMC pilot Wallace B. Thomson, VMF-211. Born, 31 January 1924, on a dairy farm in Collinsville. He died on 26 June 2013

1944 began with mixed fortunes for the Corsair squadrons. In January VF-17, which had recently returned from two weeks R&R in Australia and re-organization on Espíritu Santo, returned to the fight. Eight of its F4U-lAs were now fitted with water-injection equipped engines. By 1 January a total of 147 enemy aircraft had been claimed destroyed since 17 December in fighter sweeps in the Pacific. F4U-2 night-fighters shot down five enemy planes during the month. On the debit side, the Marine Corps suffered a blow when VMF-422, in a flight from Tarawa to Funafuti in the Pacific, became lost over the Pacific. Of the twenty-three F4U-s which started the flight twenty-two Corsairs and six pilots were lost. Thirteen of the F4Us ditched together and their pilots were rescued.

USMC pilot Wallace B. Thomson of VMF-211 recalls: 'On the morning of 3 January 1944 we were awakened in our tents in the jungle at 0500 hours. Our mission that day was to take part in a 48-plane fighter sweep across the Solomon Sea to the vast fortress of Rabaul. We pulled on our flight suits in the semi-darkness. Then we banged our boots on the tent floor to knock out any poisonous centipedes that might have crawled in there during the night. (I never saw any but some guys were bitten.) No shaving, no showers, no brushing of teeth. We shuffled through the giant, towering Banyan trees to the makeshift mess hall fifty yards away. My breakfast consisted of two large cups of coffee and one slice of something that resembled French toast. That was my last meal till evening. Outside on the dank and muddy road some olive-coloured vans that were called "Carry-Alls" were waiting. They bumped all of us on these newly bulldozed paths down to the large command post by the Torokina airstrip. The post was built half underground and had coconut logs for sidewalls. Inside eighty or ninety officers were gathered in the gloom – fighter pilots and Marine Air Group Headquarters brass.

'Two or three colonels gave little talks on the upcoming mission. In the dim light they and their maps were hard to see and their voices hard to hear. Then a chubby yellow-skinned officer arose to complete the briefing. There was a tense silence immediately in the post. The man looked overweight, drawn, humourless, almost suffering. It was Pappy Boyington – to those close to him it was "Gramps". The famous Boyington, who had twenty-five Japanese planes to his credit – two behind [F4F-4 Wildcat ace] Joe Foss [who eventually notched twenty-six victories]. Boyington, who had just four days left before being shipped back to the States. Boyington, whose VMF-214 "Black Sheep" squadron had lost six pilots in the past ten days. Boyington, who had shot down four Japanese planes in the past week in a desperate effort to catch Joe Foss. Boyington, who had to put tobacco grains in his eyes to keep awake and who was covered with a gross tropical skin disease that we all called "the crud".

'"Pappy" was describing our mission. It was a fighter sweep to Rabaul, the deep-water harbour at the north end of the large island of New Britain. Rabaul had been taken over by the Japanese from a small Australian force [on] 23 January 1942 and built into a major naval base with five airfields surrounding it. General MacArthur had strongly advocated taking Rabaul by force. But, probably as a result of Admiral Nimitz's insistence, the strategy of bypassing Japanese strongholds like Rabaul and Truk was adopted. Rabaul, it was decided, would be neutralized by air power – Army, Navy, Marine Corps, Australian and New Zealand. By 1 January 1944 Rabaul was near the peak of its considerable defensive strength. Zeros swarmed around the place from its five airfields. Just four days earlier I had made my first flight over Rabaul. We were escorting Army Air Corps B-25s that had taken off back on Guadalcanal some 600 miles south-east of Rabaul. We wove tightly over the B-25s and kept the Zeros away – but we saw a lot of them out there. The estimate was about sixty Zeros that day.

'Today it would be a forty-eight-plane fighter sweep. Four to twelve planes from each of several Marine Corps' squadrons: VMFs-211, 212, 214, 216 and possibly one or two others. I had friends from flight school in all those squadrons. Our group had three four-plane divisions that were led by Major Ireland, Captain Langenfeld and Major Hopkins. I led a section behind Herb Langenfeld. On my wing, as usual, was my tent-mate, Ward Hower. Flying with Hopkins was my other tent-mate, Adolph Vetter – soon to make Captain, soon to get his first Zeros and soon to die. The mission was a rather simple one. We would fly in toward Rabaul stacked up between 20,000 and 30,000 feet. I was assigned to be in the highest group. The Zeros might rise to attack us or simply stay on the ground. With their good high-altitude performance they might be up in the stratosphere just waiting for us.

'Pappy finished his pilot briefing in about ten minutes. To me he seemed to have physically deteriorated in the past couple of months. Then we all broke up and hurried in the early dawn to our long lines of F4Us strung out along the Torokina strip, wet from last night's rain and streaked with mud. Behind us was the tumultuous Bougainville jungle where, even now, we could hear distant gunfire between the Third Marine Division and the Japanese forces surrounding our little salient. In front of us the grey waters of Empress Augusta Bay. To our right off the western end of the runway was the little island of Purapata.

'With cartridge starters' muffled sounds, the blue and grey Corsairs started one by one. Engines were warmed up, magnetos were checked, wing-flaps tested, cowl-flaps cracked open slightly, seat height adjusted, mixture control set at automatic rich, prop in full low pitch, seat belts snugged up, oxygen masks in place. Then one by one the Corsairs roared down the Marston-Mat-covered Torokina airstrip from east to west. They made a giant, climbing circle to the left over the bay. As we were providing high cover we were the last planes to take off We cut across the circle and gradually closed in on Boyington and the leading planes. Finally in a compact group, we headed for New Britain and the fortress of Rabaul, some 200 miles to the west.

'Most of the time it was business as usual, but occasionally I would look around at the beautiful, yet ominous, planes around me and wonder, "What in God's name are we doing here? Why are we here at the ends of the earth in a death struggle with an enemy that we have never known –

an enemy just as lost as we are in this tropical hell?" Then the smell of the rubber oxygen mask, the maze of gauges in front of me, the vast stretches of sea and clouds and sky would bring me back to reality.

'At first our course took us well away from mountainous Bougainville. For all we knew, Japanese coast-watchers were watching for our missions and could quickly radio on to Rabaul vital information. Then we roughly paralleled the south-west Bougainville coast as we slowly climbed. At about 10,000 feet we augmented the main supercharger with the second supercharger called "Low Blower", which we turned on to push more oxygen into our Pratt & Whitney engines.

'Soon we climbed through a cloud layer, then another, then still another. It became difficult for those of us performing high cover to follow those below. At 18,000 feet or so we turned the supercharger to "High Blower" to feed the maximum amount of air to our eighteen-cylinder engines. At about that time I swung out a little way from the others and fired my six .50 calibre Browning machine guns, giving them a short burst. Some pilots did not take that seemingly essential precaution. The familiar "chug-chug-chug" of the guns and the curving tracers were reassuring. We passed the island of Buka at the north-west end of Bougainville where the Japanese had several airstrips. We couldn't see them because of the several cloud layers. Just ahead of me were Captain Herb Langenfeld and Lieutenant Watson flying a two-plane section. About fifty yards off on my wing was Ward Hower, my faithful wingman with whom I had been flying for the past fourteen months.

'Occasionally we would see some of the other Corsairs below us but the multiple cloud layers made visual contact difficult. Now we were crossing the Solomon Sea aiming for the northern perimeter of Rabaul. We didn't think of it at the time but to the left of us was the yawning New Britain Trench where the ocean reached a depth of 30,000 feet. The multiple cloud layers continued to plague us. Boyington and about half of the forty-eight planes had long since disappeared. Hopkins' four-plane division also was no longer to be seen. We must have been well across the Solomon Sea, but there was no sign of Rabaul on our left, or New Ireland on the right.

'Soon, I heard what must have been Pappy Boyington's voice. "Let's go down, let's go down", he said over and over in a calm and measured tone. So the eight planes I was with nosed down through one cloud layer but still we were well above 20,000 feet. The radio suddenly became full of some sort of frantic, staccato-like yelling that was quite unintelligible to me. Much of it was probably in Japanese. We milled around between various layers of clouds but never went below 12,000 feet.

'Finally we broke through the lowest layer and there was only water below – we hadn't quite reached Rabaul. But there was still action going on as the screaming and yelling over the radio continued. Now I could only see only our own four-plane division headed by Captain Langenfeld. Looking around for the next half-hour we saw no more planes, neither Japanese nor ours.

'It would be nice to say that we found our buddies and rescued them from the Zeros but that's not the way it happened. As I learned in my two years in the Pacific, some missions just get fouled up. Of our twelve guys, Major Ireland and Captain Hopkins each shot down one Zero but the rest of our fellows had no contact with the enemy at all.

'Finally we straggled back to Torokina, not feeling too badly because we all had seen this sort of thing before. The weather and poor communication between squadrons had blunted many a mission. One by one we dropped down to 1,000 feet heading east across Empress Augusta Bay lowered our wheels, circled slowly to the left, received a green light from the newly-built tower and landed on our little Torokina strip. But an hour later when we heard that Pappy Boyington and his wingman, Captain George M. Ashmun had failed to return, it became more than a mission foul-up. We had lost a superb leader in Boyington and a real nice guy in Ashmun. A real shock wave went through the pilots' camp in the jungle above Torokina. Most of us assumed that Pappy and George were dead, although the possibility that they were prisoners was also thought about. The bulk of 214 squadron – the "Black Sheep" – was due to be shipped back to the States in one week. Soon afterwards, fourteen pilots from VMF-214 who had not yet completed their tour of duty were transferred to VMF-211.

It was not until after the end of the war, in September 1945, that we learned that Boyington had become a prisoner of the Japanese and was still alive and that George Ashmun had indeed been killed back on 3 January 1944. [At the time it was believed that the "Black Sheep" leader was dead but, after six weeks on Rabaul, Boyington was put on a transport aircraft and taken to Truk before being made a prisoner in Japan where he sat out the rest of the war. In August 1945 Boyington was one of the American prisoners liberated by the Allies. He was promoted and received the Navy Cross and the Medal of Honor.]

'Then after years of procrastination and, unhappily excessive drinking, Boyington finally came out with his bestselling book, *Baa, Baa Black Sheep* in 1958. I last saw Pappy in 1959 in Cincinnati, Ohio, where he was kind enough to autograph his book for me. We reminisced about his last flight on 3 January 1944. I told him that I always felt that the rest of the flight had not given him sufficient support that ill-fated day. While Boyington did not seem to think there was a lack of support, there are some clues in his book that indicate that he did believe the rest of the Corsairs were slow to follow him down to sea level where he was finally shot down. For example, in his book he talks about the weather that day, "A few hazy clouds and cloud banks were hanging around – not much different from a lot of other days". It is my distinct recollection that there was an unusual number of cloud layers that did tend to disrupt the formations and the visual communication. He may have privately complained that we were slow to follow. In my conversation with Pappy and from the remarkable story in his book this is what happened to him that sad day. Pappy and George Ashmun, being lowest in the formation, spotted about ten Japs just below them. Diving into this group they each shot down one plane. As they started back toward these Zeros, Pappy saw about twenty more planes above him, which he thought, were friendlies but were the enemy.

'Ashmun and Boyington were weaving to cover each other's tail. George was badly shot up, caught on fire and dove into the ocean. Pappy tried to escape but his gas tank erupted in flames. With an amazing effort he baled out, pulled the ripcord and landed in the water in one fell swoop. After floating around for an hour or two, he saw a submarine surface near him. They took him aboard and headed for Rabaul.

'Pappy discovered that he was badly wounded. An ankle was shattered, there was a bullet through one calf, he had almost been scalped and there were shrapnel wounds in his shoulder and groin. His wounds were not treated for ten days. He spent six weeks at Rabaul and six more at the Japanese base at Truk. He was beaten, starved, thirsty and had malaria. He was finally island-hopped to Japan. His weight dropped from 190 to 110lbs. All this is recorded in his book, *Baa, Baa Black Sheep*.

'Pappy writes in his book about how anxious he was to break Joe Foss's record of twenty-six victories as if it was a home run record or something like that and not a matter of life and death. In his book he says several times that he was not interested in records but that it was the news media that kept pushing him. On the other hand, in several chapters of his book written about that period he seems to have been totally preoccupied with breaking Foss's record. It might take a psychologist to perceive what was really driving that gifted, complex man. He certainly was pushing things a bit too far. On that particular mission perhaps his precipitate dive from 20,000 feet down to sea level was ill advised. To us fighter pilots, altitude was always a precious commodity. At that period of time the Marines (to say nothing of the Navy and Air Corps) were pouring an avalanche of fighter pilots into the Pacific. The military situation in the Rabaul area was not critical. So for one pilot to knock down two or three more Japanese planes was not all that urgent.

'Much misinformation has been put out in the media about the 'Black Sheep Squadron'. They were not misfits. They were not always breaking the rules. They were not failures in life. They were more or less just like the other Marine Corps fighter pilots. If you look at the records, you will see that there was a constant transfer of pilots from one squadron to another. The average pilot that entered early in the war probably was in three or four squadrons. They ran the spectrum from hard-drinking, hell-for-leather types like Gregory Boyington to quiet, introspective, professorial types like George Ashmun.

'The following are some cold, hard facts about the "Black Sheep Squadron" as gleaned from the Marine Corps' and National Archive records: "Although VMF-214 had an excellent record in the war by shooting down 127 enemy aircraft, they were only seventh on the list of Marine Corps squadrons. VMF-121 had the great record of 208 planes downed, doing it while flying modest-performing Grumman F4F Wildcats." Having many hours in both the Wildcat and the Corsair, I can tell you the Corsair was vastly superior. VMF-221, which I was in for a short while, compiled a record of 185 victories. I was in VMF-211 for a long time. They knocked down ninety-one planes. Among the best twenty-five Marine Corps aces, the only 'Black Sheep' pilot was Pappy Boyington at the top of everyone with twenty-eight planes. Among the eleven Marine Corps pilots who were awarded the Congressional Medal of Honor, Boyington was the only "Black Sheep" member.

'The "Black Sheep squadron" had an exceptional Intelligence Officer in Colonel Frank E. Walton. During the war his record of the squadron activities was superior to any that I have read – and I have read the records of fifteen to twenty squadrons. Possibly it was his accurate and descriptive writing that caused the newspapers of that day to begin to pay attention to Pappy Boyington and to the Black Sheep.

'In Pappy's chapters concerning the week or two before he was finally shot down, he talks continually about his health, trying to break Foss's record, the media pressing him, but says not a word about the fate of many pilots in his squadron. For example, on 23 December, just eleven days before Boyington's last flight VMF-214 pilots First Lieutenant James Brubaker, First Lieutenant Bruce Ffoulkes (a good friend of mine from our days on Palmyra Island) and Major Pierre Carngey (Pappy's Executive Officer) were killed in action. On that same day Boyington shot down four planes over Rabaul. Then on 28 December, Second Lieutenant Harry Bartl, First Lieutenant Don Moore and Captain Cameron Dustin were also killed in action. Pappy mentioned none of these six tragic deaths. It is easy to read into this that he pushed his men into dangerous situations while seeking fame and fortune for himself and did not care for his men, but probably just the opposite would be nearer the truth. He did care for his men and in his book the sadness of those events very likely led him to ignore the subject.

'Gregory Boyington was a complex and gifted man. He was physically strong, well co-ordinated, had excellent eyesight, had great courage, inspired the pilots that flew with him, intelligent enough to get a degree in aeronautical engineering and developed key friends in the Marine Corps. But on the down side (by his own admission) he was personally irresponsible, always heavily in debt, not a family man, a pronounced alcoholic, involved in countless "barroom brawls", sought personal glory, made many enemies (being politically naive) and seemed to be accident prone. Like many a genius he was loved by many and hated by many. For my part, I know that if I was to meet up with a bunch of enemy planes, I would choose to have a fellow like Pappy with me rather than any other pilot I can think of, with the possible exception of "gentleman Joe Foss". [Boyington died of cancer on 11 January 1988.]

On 8 January VMF-214 completed its tour of duty with ninety-seven enemy aircraft destroyed and thirty-two probably destroyed. Next day, four

F4U-2 night-fighter Corsairs of VF(N)-101 went aboard the *Enterprise*, to become the first Corsairs assigned to a carrier. At the same time, another small detachment joined the *Intrepid*. The Corsair's unhappy landing gear 'bounce' was remedied by a local solution and the leaky wing fuel tanks were not used. After the capture of Roi Island in the Marshalls early in 1944, fourteen F4U-2s of VMF(N)-532 arrived from Tarawa to help defend against night intruders. Later some F4U-2s went to Engebi Island on Eniwetok as a defence force. The F4U-2s' base at Torokina was taken over by USMC Corsairs and, on the 14th, when US fighters claimed to have shot down twenty-nine enemy aircraft in dogfights over Rabaul, nineteen of them were by Corsairs of VMF-215 operating from Torokina. On 21 January 1944 VMF-211 Corsairs from Torokina moved to the south Piva airfield ('Yoke') to begin operations on Bougainville. They were joined by VF-17 and VMF-321 and a New Zealand P-40 squadron and on 24 January, by a new unit, VMF-216 'Wild Hares'.

Equipped with obsolete Curtiss P-40s, Royal New Zealand Air Force (RNZAF) squadrons in the South Pacific performed impressively compared to the American units they operated alongside, in particular in the air-to-air role. The American government accordingly decided to give New Zealand early access to the Corsair, especially as it was not initially being used from carriers. Beginning in late March 1944 the RNZAF received 364 Vought-built Corsairs and sixty FG-1Ds from Goodyear under the terms of Lend-Lease. The F4U-1 and F4U-1Ds were used as fighter-bombers and equipped thirteen squadrons in the Pacific beginning in May 1944 with 20 and 21 Squadrons on Espíritu Santo. By the time the Corsairs arrived, there were very few Japanese aircraft left in New Zealand's allocated sectors of the Southern Pacific and, despite the RNZAF squadrons extending their operations to more northern islands, they were primarily used for close support of American, Australian and New Zealand soldiers fighting the Japanese. The Kiwi Corsairs were the forgotten squadrons of the South Pacific campaign, being used to help mop up considerable enemy forces on islands bypassed during the inexorable advance on Japan. Mostly, the RNZAF Corsairs operated from bases in the Bismarck-Solomons area for strikes on New Ireland, New Britain and Bougainville. They flew numerous bombing and strafing attacks in all weathers from Espíritu Santo, Guadalcanal, Green Island, Emirau in the New Ireland group and Los Negros on Manus in the Admiralty

Islands, attacking targets on New Ireland, New Britain and Bougainville. These were often carried out in support of Australian ground forces and in conjunction with RNZAF Venturas and USAAF B-25 Mitchells.

Wallace B. Thomson USMC recalls: 'On 23 January 1944 on the south-west coast of Bougainville in the Northern Solomon Islands, forty-eight F4U Corsairs, fighter planes attached to Marine Fighter Group Fourteen (MAG-14) coughed and sputtered as they were started one by one. We were poised to fly on a fighter sweep to the major Jap base at Rabaul on the island of New Britain 200 miles to the north-west across the Solomon Sea. Most of us were on Piva airstrip, the second of three runways built by the Seabees (CBs, from Construction Battalions) since the invasion of Bougainville that began on 1 November 1943. Piva was a beautiful coral runway surrounded by coral taxiways, concrete plane revetments and towering jungle Banyan trees. Five miles away the Japs ringed the American invasion salient waiting to pounce if they could. The superb American Third Marine Division had carved out a semi-circle in the swamps, tangled undergrowth, rugged hills, mosquitoes, tropical downpours and strange fevers that came with the Bougainville terrain. By now a US Army division waiting for the inevitable Japanese counter-offensive manned the front lines.

'One by one the Corsairs bumped their way onto the runway, their Pratt & Whitney engines roared and then one by one our blue and white camouflaged craft with the famous inverted gull wings climbed out over the jungle in a gentle curve to the left. At least six Marine fighter squadrons were represented on this mission – each squadron contributing eight planes. All the fighters on this Rabaul fighter sweep were Corsairs. My plane was about in the middle of the pack and was followed by that of my faithful wingman, Ward Hower.

'The flight leaders made a sweeping circle to the left around the Bougainville invasion pocket at Empress Augusta Bay, allowing all the planes to join up in formation by cutting across the circle. Below were the tumultuous, jungle-mountains forming a hundred-mile spine along the length of Bougainville. About fifteen miles inland the active 10,000-foot volcano, Mount Bagana, put out its usual wisp of black smoke. As usual, one or two planes didn't make it, having mechanical, radio or sometimes even 'psychological' problems. We headed north-west along the south coast of Bougainville then swung somewhat left toward Rabaul. There were Jap airstrips at Buka at the extreme north-west end of Bougainville.

We wanted to stay well away from them, especially their coast-watchers, who could and probably did in this case radio an urgent warning to their comrades over at Rabaul.

'Soon we were at 10,000 feet and shifted our super-chargers into low blower. Most of us had been on oxygen right from the start. We were in our standard "Thach Weave" formation – planes flying in pairs, pairs flying in groups of four and so on.[1] The grey-green island of Bougainville with its smoking volcano gradually faded from view. On our left was the slate-blue Solomon Sea with its yawning New Britain Trench, an abyss going down to an incredible depth of 30,000 feet. To us, of course, 30,000 feet was no worse than 30 feet.

'This was a fighter sweep. There were no dive-bombers or torpedo-bombers to escort. That very morning we had escorted SBDs and TBFs to Rabaul and had run into a flock of Zeros. Now we were coming back to challenge the Zeros once again. Only twenty days ago we had lost our controversial and peerless leader, Pappy Boyington, on just such a fighter sweep. On that grim day there were confusing layers of clouds that fouled up the mission, but today there was hardly a cloud in the tropical sky.

'In a few minutes I charged my six .50 calibre Browning machine guns, three in each wing. Then, at a safe moment, I veered a little to the right and gave them a very short burst to see if they were working. The familiar "chug, chug, chug, chug" sound and curving tracers out ahead of me showed that the guns were working OK. I never had any gun trouble at all during the war.

'The Corsairs had auxiliary gas tanks built into each wing near the wingtips, which we all switched to soon after take off. Soon these ran dry and we all switched back to the main gas tank that held 230 gallons of high-octane gas. To avoid a possible explosion in the empty wing-tip tanks during combat, we turned a valve that purged both wingtip tanks with carbon dioxide. These early-model Corsairs had a Plexiglass window at the bottom of the cockpit through which the pilot could (in theory) see downward. This window was usually smeared with oil and dirt so you

---

1. John Smith 'Jimmy' Thach was a Second World War naval aviator, air combat tactician and US Navy admiral. Thach developed the 'beam defence' tactic later called the 'Thach Weave', a combat flight formation that could counter enemy fighters of superior performance. Later he developed the 'big blue blanket', an aerial defence against kamikaze attacks.

couldn't see much. Today, however, I could see oil trickling back from the engine in a little greater quantity than usual. For the time being, I paid no attention to that.

'At about 18,000 feet we switched to high blower which would allow us to climb up as high as the stratosphere. The entire formation continued to climb until we were a little above 25,000 feet. We headed up St George's Channel having the long and curving island of New Ireland on our right and New Britain with its port of Rabaul on the left. To save fuel we had been cruising at 1,750rpm and about 24 inches of manifold pressure. But now we were up to 2,250rpm and 32 inches. At this point I noticed a little more oil was flowing back from the engine over the window below me.

'The formation was now north-north-west of Rabaul so with the sun in the SW we had a good look at the fortress below. Simpson Harbor glistened in the sun. A few small ships – perhaps barges – were in the harbour. Rabaul had five airfields, the most important one being Lakunai right next to Simpson Harbour and the city proper. Suddenly, huge clouds of dust arising from Lakunai and another field to the south, which I judged to be Vunakanau, alerted me. This was a signal that Zeros were taking off to meet our challenge. This was exactly the purpose of our fighter sweep – to tempt the Zeros into the air and then shoot some of them down. The dust clouds were typical of Japanese air operations as the American coral airstrips and steel Marston mats had (with some notable exceptions) much less dust.

'By now we were up to 2,600rpm and almost at full throttle and probably not much below 400mph. The sky was clear in all directions and at this altitude appeared almost black. While the air temperature outside was probably close to -30°F, I was sweating from the intense sunrays and from tension. At this point I was dismayed to see the oil pouring past the lower window in a thick, twisting river. As our whole fighter formation was making a giant circle (possibly twenty miles in diameter) to the left over Rabaul, I thought that Ward and I would be smart to throttle back a bit, cut across the circle, perhaps run into some climbing Zeros and, hopefully, join up with the rest of our Marines. So I cut back to 2,300rpm, reduced the throttle setting then headed across the circle. Ward followed without hesitation.

'In a few minutes we were above the north-eastern tip of New Britain and almost above the city of Rabaul itself. The river of oil slackened noticeably. Suddenly two planes appeared to the left and a few thousand feet below us. In the brilliant sunshine, the red meatballs on the wings were easily seen – they were two Zeros climbing in close formation, heading eastward. I put my Corsair into a shallow dive and headed for the lead plane. Glancing around to my right, I could see that Ward had also spotted them and was diving with me. The Jap wingman, also on the right, began acting nervously but the leader never budged as we closed in on them. The wingman rocked his wings then shot out a few hundred feet from his leader. Then he moved back in formation, then back out again, then back in again – all this in the space of a few seconds. Then to add to his bizarre display he flipped over on his back and flew in perfect formation.

'All this time I was heading for the leader. When I was very close, maybe sixty to eighty yards, I opened fire with the six Brownings. He burst into a ball of flame almost at the moment I swept by his left wingtip. I fancied that I could hear the explosion. My Corsair shuddered as I hit the blast and I also felt that something hit my plane. I remember being annoyed that most of my tracers went slightly left and that I should have trimmed my ship during the long high-speed dive to avoid being in a skid.

'Looking back I could see that Ward had shot down the wingman. But that Zero never did burn. It just went into a grotesque and jerky spin in the manner of a series of stalls. Ward quickly joined up and we headed east. We had lost a lot of valuable altitude and we knew that Zeros could be all around us. However, as we continued east we saw none. The oil leak still looked bad. Also, looking out at my right wingtip I could see that somehow I had sustained damage out there. So after getting out of the Rabaul area we continued on back to the Piva airstrip at a low cruising power. In about forty-five minutes Empress Augusta Bay and the Torokina base came into view. My engine never gave any trouble from the loss of oil. The two coral runways along with the steel Marston mat of the Torokina strip were easy to spot in the green jungle of Bougainville.

'After landing I found that I had indeed lost about half my oil supply. Years later after studying Marine Corps' records, I noticed that there were quite a few engine failures during high performance combat missions, failures that often appeared to be caused by loss of engine oil. But my Pratt & Whitney functioned OK on that mission in spite of a heavy loss of oil. In four years of flying in World War II, I never had an engine failure.

The yellow and silver XF4U-1 first flew at the Bridgeport Municipal Airport, Stratford, Connecticut on 29 May 1940 with Lyman A. Bullard Jr. at the controls.

Early on the Fleet Air Arm had realized that the Corsair could not be accommodated on the low-ceilinged hangar decks of Royal Navy aircraft carriers. Because of their armoured flight decks, British carriers had only 16 feet of vertical clearance available on the hangar deck, while the F4U-1, with its wings folded, had a height of just over 16 feet 2 inches.

FAA F4U Corsair in
December 1943.

F4U 1A 'White 8' *Dangerous Dan/Eight Ball* of VMF-213 'Hellhawks' at Guadalcanal in July 1943.

1st Lieutenant Kenneth A. Walsh of VMF-124 'Black Sheep', the first Corsair ace, who received the Medal of Honor on 8 February 1944 finished the war with 21 confirmed victories, twenty of them with VMF-124 (F4U-1) and one with VMF-222 'Flying Deuces' (F4U-4) on 22 June 1945.

VMF-124 'Black Sheep' pilots 'scramble' to their Corsairs on Espiritu Santo in the New Hebrides Group, 11 September 1943. L to R: Major Gregory 'Pappy' Boyington; Lieutenant Roland N. Rimbarger; Captain Robert Y. Ewing and Lieutenant Henry M. Bourgeois. (*US Nat Archives*)

Among the eleven Marine Corps pilots who were awarded the Congressional Medal of Honor, the legendary thirty-year old Major Gregory 'Pappy' Boyington was the only VMF-124 member. 'Pappy's' pilots wanted to call themselves 'Boyington's Bastards' but this was too risqué even for Boyington and the unit was fittingly re-titled 'The Black Sheep Squadron'. On 7 September 1943 VMF-214 'Swashbucklers' was re-organized at Munda under his command.

F4U-1 'White 465' of VMF-222 'Flying Deuces' at Barakoma airfield at Vella-Lavella in the Solomon Islands on 15 January 1944.

Lieutenant (later Colonel) John H. Glenn was a distinguished fighter pilot in World War II, China and Korea. He shot down three MiG-15 aircraft and was awarded six Distinguished Flying Crosses and eighteen Air Medals. In 1957 he made the first supersonic transcontinental flight across the United States. His on-board camera took the first continuous, panoramic photograph of the United States. He was one of the Mercury Seven, military test pilots selected in 1959 by NASA as the United States' first astronauts. On 20 February 1962 Glenn flew the Friendship 7 mission, becoming the first American to orbit the Earth and the fifth person and third American in space.

Lieutenant John H. Glenn Jr. USMCR flying a F4U-1 with VMF-155 in 1943. (*John Glenn Archives, The Ohio State University*)

1st Lieutenant Robert M. Hanson of VMF-215, the greatest of all Corsair aces, with 25 victories - all made between August 1943 and February 1944, scoring twenty of these kills in a seventeen day period. He was KIA on 3 February 1944. For his 'conspicuous gallantry and intrepidity' on these occasions, he was posthumously awarded the Medal of Honor.

USMC Corsairs of VMF 214 parked on Bougainville on 19 February 1944.

VF-17's F-4U aces pictured on 21 March 1944 after the 'Jolly Rogers' had left the combat zone. Left to right: Lieutenant Commander Roger R. Hedrick (nine victories, twelve by the war's end); Lieutenant Commander John T. 'Tommy' Blackburn, CO (eleven victories) and Lieutenant Ira 'Ike' C. Kepford (sixteen victories), the then leading Navy ace.

USMC Corsairs of 4th Marine Air Wing carrying 1,000lb bombs on a strike mission over Japanese-held bases in the Marshalls in June 1944. (*USMC*)

Captain Harold L. Spears of VMF-215 'The Fighting Corsairs' who was credited with 15 victories in 1943-44 during three tours on Guadalcanal. He was killed in a crash in a SBD-5 while attached to VMF-462 at El Toro, California on 6 December 1944.

USMC Corsairs of 4th Marine Air Wing (possibly of VMF-111) on 19 September 1944 at Majuro Atoll in the Marshall Islands where the Navy had an Air Depot and a Fleet Anchorage.

The USS *Essex* hit by a kamikaze on 25 November 1944.

F4U-1D of VMF-511 on the USS *Block Island* on 4 February 1945. The Squadron specialized in close air support and during the course of the war were credited with only one aircraft shot down.

Corsairs on the *Bunker Hill*.

Famed pre-war aviator, Charles Lindbergh by a VMF-115 F4U Corsair. In 1944 Lindbergh persuaded United Aircraft to designate him as a technical representative in the Pacific Theatre to study aircraft performances under combat conditions. Among other things, he showed Marine pilots how to take off safely with a bomb load double the Corsair fighter-bomber's rated capacity. On 21 May 1944 Lindbergh flew his first combat mission: a strafing run with VMF-222 near the Japanese garrison of Rabaul. He also flew with VMF-216 from the Marine Air Base at Torokina, Bougainville. In his six months in the Pacific in 1944, Lindbergh took part in fighter bomber raids on Japanese positions, flying 50 combat missions.

F4U-1D F-107 of VMF-224 flown by Captain (later Colonel) Philip C. DeLong, who was credited with 11.166 victories, a 'probable' and two enemy planes damaged.

A Corsair burning on the flight deck of the USS *Bennington* on 14 February 1945.

F4U-1D of VMF-312 'Checkerboards' at Kadena airfield on Okinawa on 9 April 1945.

F4U-1D '88' of VF-83 on the Essex on 25 January 1945. The vortices coming back off the propeller tips are vapour trails, a common phenomenon on the carriers during humid atmospheric conditions.

FG-1D of VMF-512 on the escort carrier USS *Sargent Bay* on 2 June 1945 during support operations for the Okinawa campaign 25 March-20 June.

FG-1Ds of VMF-323 'Death Rattlers' over Okinawa on 10 June 1945. On 9 April 1945 the 'Death Rattlers' flew into Kadena airfield in support of Operation 'Iceberg' during the Battle of Okinawa. Combat operations commenced the following day. Between then and the Japanese surrender in August VMF-323 destroyed 124 Japanese planes without a single loss. Twelve 'Death Rattlers' became aces.

F4U-1Ds of VBF-83 aboard the USS *Essex* as it heads towards Japan in 1945.

F4U-1D 'White 183' of VBF-83 crashes into '180' aboard the USS *Essex* in 1945.

F4U-1D 'White 170' of VBF-83 comes to grief on the USS *Essex* in 1945.

F4U-1D '238' of VBF-83 launches from the flight deck of the USS *Essex* on 9 August 1945. Four months after demobilisation there were 25 Navy and 21 USMC fighter units flying Corsairs.

Equipped with obsolescent Curtiss P-40s, RNZAF squadrons in the South Pacific performed impressively compared to the American units they operated alongside, in particular in the air-to-air role, so the US government gave New Zealand early access to the Corsair, especially as it was not initially being used from carriers. A total of 237 F4U-1s and 127 F4U-1Ds equipped thirteen RNZAF squadrons. Pictured here are F4U-1s of 18 Squadron RNZAF flying off the coast of Guadalcanal in the Solomon's in March 1945.

Looking at the wing-tip damage, we judged that it was from exploding debris from the leading Zero. Sometime later I found out that the plane I flew on the mission was one of the FG-1A Corsairs manufactured by Goodyear. The usual bugs found in a production line that had just started possibly caused the severe oil leak.

'Ward commented on the Zero I had shot down. "That ball of flame could have been seen for a hundred miles." We walked over to the mess hall. After little breakfast, no lunch and two exciting missions to Rabaul, we were ravenous. Somehow being on oxygen all day always made me hungry – hungrier than at any other time in my life.'

'The fighter sweep was a success. As I recall, the Marines lost no Corsairs that afternoon and shot down ten or twelve Zeros. How could the Japanese live with such losses? The pressure we put on Rabaul during the past few weeks had been tremendous. As it turned out, the mighty base of Rabaul was bombed and strafed unmercifully while hundreds of Zero fighters were shot down by the allied forces in late 1943 and early 1944.'

On 26 January thirty-two Corsairs of VF-17 escorted SBD Dauntless dive-bombers on a strike to Rabaul's Lakunai airfield. VF-17 shot down eight enemy aircraft for the loss of two pilots and four Corsairs damaged. One of the Zekes shot down fell to the guns of Tom Blackburn, making him VF-17's first ace. Next day, twenty-four Corsairs of VF-17 escorted B-25s in another raid on Rabaul and about seventy Zekes attacked the formation. The Corsairs were credited with six-and-a-half victories but Lieutenant 'Thad' Bell was shot down and killed, while Teeth Burriss' F4U was badly shot up by one of the Zekes. Burriss ditched successfully 120 miles west of Cape Torokina and was picked-up by a Dumbo an hour later. On 28 January the 'Jolly Rogers' provided fourteen Corsairs to escort seventeen TBF Avengers, which would make a glide-bombing attack on Tobera airfield. After losing three pilots in the previous two days Blackburn had devised a new tactic whereby another six Corsairs would fly high above the main escort and attack any enemy fighters that attempted to interfere with the main formation. Lieutenant Commander Roger Hedrick, flying at 32,000 feet, led the RHC (Roving High Cover). The tactic reaped dividends as Hedrick's half-dozen Corsairs shot down four Zekes and broke up the enemy attack, while Blackburn's main body of Corsairs were credited with ten-and-a-half victories.

On the 29th Lieutenants (j.g.) Ike Kepford and Teeth Burriss each shot down four Zekes, which took the former's score to double figures and the latter's score to seven-and-a-half confirmed kills. On the morning of the 30th Lieutenant Commander Roger Hedrick shot down another Zeke over Rabaul, which took his personal score to six confirmed kills. In the afternoon VF-17 took off en masse in search of a Japanese carrier which had been reported off Rabaul. Although the carrier did not appear, VF-17 more than made up for the disappointment by shooting down ten enemy aircraft, two of them being credited to Ike Kepford and two to 'Butch' Davenport. Losses, however, took some of the shine off the proceedings. One pilot was lost and a second recovered after ditching, while Lieutenant (j.g.) Doug H.C. Gutenkunst, Blackburn's wingman and close friend, collided with a Marine F4U as they came in for a dusk landing at Piva 'Uncle' airfield on Torokina. Next day, 31st January, Teeth Burriss' Corsair was badly damaged by a Zeke east of Kabanga Point, New Britain. Burriss force-landed but he was not recovered. He had seven and a half confirmed victories.

During six days, 26 to 31 January 1944 the 'Jolly Rogers' were credited with the destruction of sixty-and-a-half enemy aircraft in the air for the loss of six pilots killed. Thirteen F4U-1As were destroyed, five of them by enemy action, four in crashes after being shot up by the Japanese, three operational landing crashes and one in the mid-air collision. In February VF-17's score for two tours in the Pacific had risen to 152 enemy aircraft shot down for a loss of twenty Corsairs in combat and four due to accidents. On 6 February Tom Blackburn destroyed three Zekes and a 'Hamp' over Rabaul to take his final score to eleven confirmed victories for the war. On 19 February the 'Jolly Rogers' shot down no fewer than sixteen enemy aircraft at Cape Siar, New Ireland, including two Zekes and a Rufe, which were credited to Ike Kepford, whose final score now stood at sixteen confirmed victories for the war. By the time the 'Jolly Rogers' completed their second tour, on 6 March, they had been credited with the destruction of 106½ enemy aircraft during 1,099 combat sorties. VF-17 lost sixteen Corsairs (eight to enemy aircraft, one to flak, four had force-landed because of combat damage and three in operational accidents) and ten pilots. The grand total for two tours was 154 victories in 2,579 combat sorties for the loss of twenty-four Corsairs and thirteen pilots. Another thirty-one enemy aircraft were probably destroyed and twenty-three more damaged.

The Marine squadrons, meanwhile, went from strength to strength also as the American onslaught shifted to the Marshall Islands. By February 1944 Marine Air Group (MAG) 24 numbered six Corsair squadrons – VMF-211, 212, 215, 218, 222 and 223 – in the Solomons, while Corsairs of MAG-13, 22 and 31, all in the 4th Marine Air Wing were based in the Marshall Islands. On 10 February VMF-215 completed its tour of duty. VMF-215 had ten aces. They included First Lieutenant Robert M. Hanson, the greatest of all Corsair aces, with twenty-five victories – all made between August 1943 and February 1944, scoring twenty of these kills in a seventeen-day period – who had been killed a week earlier during a strafing run returning from a mission, but only fourteen of 'The Fighting Corsairs' original pilots survived to return home. Robert Murray Hanson, the son of missionaries, was born on 4 February 1920 in Lucknow, India. He moved to Newton, Massachusetts, with his family, then returned to India after school to become the heavyweight wrestling champion of the United Provinces. On a bicycle trip in pre-war Europe, he was in Vienna in 1938 when the Nazis took over. He attended Hamline University in St Paul, Minnesota, where he continued wrestling. While attending Hamline, he enlisted in the Marine Corps Reserve from Massachusetts in May 1942. Completing flight training in February 1943, he was designated an aviator and commissioned a second lieutenant. After briefly serving at the Marine Corps Air Base at Kerney Mesa, San Diego, California, he transferred to the First Marine Aircraft Wing and departed in June for combat duty to the Pacific war zone. In September he was promoted to first lieutenant. Hanson started his combat career with the original VMF-214, when the unit was known as the 'Swashbucklers', before Pappy Boyington and the 'Black Sheep' assumed the squadron number. Other pilots noted Hanson as somewhat belligerent, who easily took a dislike to other fliers. But he was an excellent gunner. During November 1943 to January 1944, Hanson served as a fighter pilot attached to VMF-215 in aerial combat against the Japanese over Bougainville Island and New Britain. For his time in the area, he was accountable for downing twenty-five enemy aircraft.

On Hanson's first combat mission on 4 August 1943 he flew wing for First Lieutenant Stanley T. 'Chief' Synar. Returning from a strafing run against the Shortlands the 'Swashbucklers' were jumped by the Japanese. One pounced on Chief, dived and then came up beneath him. His gunfire struck the cockpit and injured Synar. But Hanson got behind Synar's attacker and 'shot his ass off' only to get shot up himself, his Corsair taking 20mm rounds between the guns, in the flap and in the right stabilizer. In a probable case of mistaken identity, Hanson reported his victim as a Zero, although the more experienced Synar described the white spinner, in-line engine and rows of exhaust stacks that almost certainly indicated a Ki-61 Tony. Later that month, in a landing mix-up, he stomped on his brakes, flipping over and destroyed his Corsair. The next day, 26 August, Hanson scored his second victory on a B-24 escort. His supercharger was acting up and he lagged behind his division, permitting him to surprise a lone Zero that rashly attacked the Corsairs. Hanson's first shots had little effect, but he closed in, gave another burst and the Zero flamed from the wing root and went down.

His first combat tour with VMF-215 included the Bougainville landings on 1 November 1943. He achieved ace status that day when he downed a Kate and two Zekes over Empress Augusta Bay at about 1345 hours. He was shot down himself and was shortly picked up unhurt from the water. But during his second combat tour, he really ran up his score, shooting down Japanese planes in clumps of three, four and five. On 14 January 1944 he downed five Zeros; on the 24th he claimed another four, on the 26th three and on the 30th two Zeros and a 'Tojo' (Nakajima Ki-44 Shoki [Demon] fighter). On 3 February, one day before his 24th birthday, Hanson participated in a fighter sweep. On the return flight, he left his flight path to strafe a lighthouse on Cape St George, New Ireland, that had proved troublesome as an enemy flak tower and observation post. His friends watched from above as Hanson's big blue-grey Corsair ran at the tower, its six machine guns peppering the structure. Suddenly, they were horrified to see Hanson's aircraft shudder as its wing disintegrated from flak hits. The young ace tried to ditch, but his aircraft hit the surface, cartwheeled and crashed, leaving only scattered debris. He was posthumously awarded the Medal of Honor. His citation said: 'For conspicuous gallantry and intrepidity at the risk of his life and above and beyond the call of duty [while] attached to VMF-215 in action against enemy Japanese forces at Bougainville Island, 1 November 1943; and New Britain Island, 24 January 1944. Undeterred by fierce opposition and fearless in the face of overwhelming odds, First Lieutenant Hanson fought the Japanese boldly and with daring aggressiveness. On 1 November, while flying cover for our landing operations at Empress Augusta Bay, he dauntlessly attacked six enemy torpedo-bombers, forcing them to jettison their bombs and destroying one Japanese plane in the action. Cut off from his division while deep in enemy territory during a high cover flight over Simpson Harbour on 24 January, First Lieutenant Hanson waged a lone and gallant battle against hostile interceptors as they were orbiting to attack our bombers and, striking with devastating fury, brought down four Zeros and probably a fifth. Handling his plane superbly in both pursuit and attack measures, he was a master of individual air combat, accounting for a total of 25 Japanese aircraft in this theatre of war. His personal valour and invincible fighting spirit were in keeping with the highest traditions of the United States Naval Service.'

At the time of his death, Hanson's score stood at twenty-five confirmed air-to-air victories, twenty of them in six combats. All told, VMF-215, in eighteen weeks of combat, had been credited with the destruction of 135½ enemy aircraft and another thirty-seven probably destroyed. The squadron's ten aces had accounted for all except thirty-and-a-half of the total number of victories. Hanson was the third and last Marine Corsair pilot to receive the Medal of Honor and the youngest. Besides Hanson, VMF-215 also boasted two more high-scoring aces, Captain Donald Nathan Aldrich and Captain Harold Leman Spears, senior flight leaders of the squadron. Aldrich, born on 24 October 1917 in Moline, Illinois, had been turned down by American recruiters before Pearl Harbor because he was married. Undaunted, he enlisted in the Royal Canadian Air Force in February 1941 and got his wings in November 1941. Aldrich served as an instructor pilot in Canada until the United States entered the war when Aldrich was able to return home and eventually he got his wings of gold as a Marine aviator on 14 May 1942.[2] 'Hal' Spears, born in Portsmouth, Ohio, on 31 December 1919 graduated from flight training in August 1942 and went out to the Pacific with VMF-215. He became a triple ace, credited with shooting down fifteen enemy aircraft in aerial

2. Captain Aldrich flew three tours with VMF-215 in the Solomons and was credited with the destruction of twenty enemy aircraft in aerial combat plus six probables between August 1943 and February 1944, all while flying the F4U-1 Corsair. He remained in the Marines after the war and was killed while landing his Corsair at Ashburn Airport in Chicago on 3 May 1947.

combat. He died in a flying accident in a SBD-5 at El Toro, California, on 6 December 1944.

First Lieutenant (later Captain) Arthur Roger Conant, born Chrystal Falls, Michigan, on 21 October 1918 had joined up with VMF-215 with only about 200 hours total flying time. He had been taken out to a Corsair and in about fifteen minutes all the switches and controls were pointed out to him; then he was told that he was on his own. 'I went out a circled a brush fire for a while, came back and landed and the next day I was sent overseas.' Conant felt the Corsair was a tough plane to fly: 'It had poor front visibility with the nose thirteen feet in the air and night take-offs were really hazardous, since until the tail wheel lifted off you couldn't see where you were going. It was a beautiful plane in flight. Once it was airborne you could get it to do anything you wanted.'

He recalled one particular mission where the Corsairs were escorting B-24 Liberators to Bougainville when the fighters' job was to weave back and forth in the midst of the bombers, providing cover from enemy fighters: 'We saw thirty or forty Zeros and Tonys hanging around in the distance and once the B-24s dropped their bombs they flew into the clouds. We told them if they went into the clouds they would have no escort. We took off after the Zeros and Tonys and I saw a Tony on Bob Owen's tail.'

Conant thought that the Tony would get to his leader before he could get to the Tony, but he was able to close faster. 'I shot him up pretty good, hit the fuel tank and he went straight down.' At that point, another Zero took out after him, causing Conant to dive away from trouble. 'That night "Tokyo Rose" said that Corsair pilots turned tail and went home when Zeros showed up and I knew she was taking about me.' The victory that day was just one of Conant's total of six enemy kills on 25 August 1943, when he was credited with two Tonys and two more probably destroyed on 22 January 1944. He was flying the F7F Tigercat when the war ended and flew F6F Hellcats after the war. He went to the airlines for about five years and then was called back into the Marine Corps for Korea, flying the F9F-2B in close air support.

Wallace B. Thomson of VMF-211, the 'Wake Avengers', recalls: 'When I first arrived at "Buttons" or Turtle Bay on the east coast of Espíritu Santo in the New Hebrides islands in October 1943 – that great Marine Corps base that fed Marine aviation power into the brutal campaigns in the Solomon Islands – we would hear all kinds of stories of what the war was like. In one story, a Marine flier, whose name and organization I never learned, was flying in formation over the remote interior of Espíritu. This was incredibly rugged country and supposedly infested with head-hunters. Suddenly, without warning, one wing of this poor fellow's plane folded and he gyrated wildly into the jungle below. Since his death was certain, the difficulty in reaching him was so great and our resources for doing so were so limited at that time, no recovery effort was mounted. After the war ended, I'm sure people went in there to find his remains. Since very many of the planes the Marines flew were designed for aircraft carrier operation, they had wings that could be folded. In rare instances they would fold accidentally. Stay tuned!'

On 15 February eight Marine Corsair squadrons flew cover for 5,800 New Zealand troops protected by Marine Corps fighters invading Green Island, an atoll that lies about halfway between Bougainville and New Ireland – about seventy-five miles from each. After three days the Allies had full control of the area. There were about 100 Japanese on this island of which number thirty were killed. The 33rd, 37th and 93rd Seabees worked hard to construct a base there. By 15 March the airstrip was fully operational.

'On 20 March VMF-211 was based at the new airstrip', continues 'Wally' Thomson: 'About fourteen pilots of the "Black Sheep" squadron were now with the "Wake Avengers". On the next day I was at the squadron ready hut prepared for whatever missions were planned. Our squadron ground crew was in the process of relieving the crew of the previous squadron. I was informed that the plane I would be flying for the next few weeks would be number 027 (F4U-1 BuNo56027). One of the ground crew came up to me to talk about the plane. He said that the plane had been in an accident with the previous squadron and as a consequence the left wing had to be replaced. He said that the previous ground crew had installed the new wing and that the plane should be test hopped before going out on a mission. As I was the Engineering Officer of our squadron and as the plane was one I would be flying regularly, it was only natural that I would be doing the test flight.

'Now the F4U was primarily designed as an aircraft carrier fighter plane and hence had wings that could be folded up to allow the craft to be moved from deck to deck on a carrier elevator as well as to provide room for more planes when placed side by side on any given deck. In this particular instance, the installation of a new wing meant that part of the wing that extended from the joint where the folding occurred out to the wing tip. Whatever damage had occurred, and I never learned what it was, had been in that outer part of the left wing. The Corsair had that famous inverted gull wing. These wings folded at about the lowest point of the curvature. During carrier operations the Corsair wings were spread and folded on every flight. All operations with which I was involved were land-based ones where we never folded the wings. In two-plus years of flying the Corsair I never once folded the wings nor did my fellow pilots. Nevertheless, we all were familiar with wing folding, with the two controls in the cockpit: one that placed the wings in "Spread" or "Neutral" or "Fold" mode and the second which would "Lock" or "Unlock" the wing hinge-pins. When the wings were spread as they always were for us the first lever was always moved aft in the "Spread" position while the second was always placed forward in the "Lock" position.

'The wing hinge-pin that, when in place prevented the wing from folding in flight, was a solid cylinder a little over an inch in diameter and made of hardened steel. To indicate that the hinge pins were in place or "home" as they called it, there were indicator doors at the upper surface of the wing at the wing-joint. These doors, measuring perhaps three inches wide and six inches long, lay flat, flush with the wing surface when the wings were "Spread". If the hinge-pins were not in place and the wing could fold, the little doors stood up on edge and one could see the red paint of their under surface.

'If there was any doubt about whether a wing was safely locked or not there were four things one could do to check things out. So when I went out to Corsair 027 that day, I climbed into the cockpit and checked the wing-folding levers. They were in the correct position but seemed to be stiff rather than resting easily in place. Then I glanced at the indicator doors on both sides: they appeared to be flush with the wing upper surfaces. But afterward I wished I had taken a harder look at them. Going down to the landing gear I located the cables connected to the folding mechanisms. The cables were supposed to be somewhat loose – and they were. Finally, following our pilot's handbook instruction, I went to each wingtip and reaching up shook each one as hard as I could. Both wings seemed to be solid, so as far as these checks went, everything was normal.

'I prepared to go on the test-hop and soon was moving down the coral taxiway. The tower surprised me a little by directing me to take off from the north end of the airstrip. I could clearly see that the various windsocks were pointing south so I would be taking off downwind. For a fighter plane with high performance this was no big deal but it still was unusual. Arriving at the north end I could see the tower's reason for sending me there. Gathered at the extreme south end of the runway, perhaps 3,000 feet away were, about thirty P-40 Warhawks. Each one carried below its fuselage a 500lb cluster of thermite bombs – bombs impregnated with magnesium to start intense fires. They were getting ready to pay Rabaul a hot visit. Their props were turning over and they were only minutes from take off.

'The tower wanted to get me out of the way first, so gave me a green light. So I gave my ship the throttle and headed down the airstrip expecting that I would be several hundred feet above the P-40s by the time I reached them. My Corsair had picked up speed to about 60 or 70 knots, close to take-off speed and was still on the deck when something on the left caught my eye. I was horrified to see that the indicator door at the left wing joint had popped up. The wing was unlocked! An instant later the left wing shot upward so that the wingtip was straight above me. It hit the top position with a bang, went all the way down with another bang, then up with yet another bang – the damned thing was flapping like a wounded bird! I cut the throttle instantly and applied the brakes, but the weird aerodynamic forces on the wing made the Corsair snake violently down the runway. My Corsair raced toward the P-40s and their thermite bombs. With all my frantic braking I was never going to stop in time. If I had any thoughts of a hellish finish I don't recall them now. But as I flapped on down toward the P-40s they saw me coming. Some went right; some went left – parting like the Red Sea in Moses' time. Having no control at all I still missed them all, went off the end of the airstrip and into a swamp filled with tree stumps.

'I was unhurt but livid. Two crash trucks were there at once. An ambulance crew checked me out. Damage to the Corsair? I had knocked the tail wheel off the plane. They got me back to the squadron ready hut. Nobody there had noticed anything unusual. Who had botched the wing installation? The responsible squadron was leaving and couldn't be bothered. I tried to talk to the skipper, Tom Murto, but he was too busy moving into Green Island to worry about a minor accident that none of the fellows had even seen. The flight did not even appear in my logbook for the simple reason that I had never left the ground! I could never figure out, after checking all four items in the Corsair pilot's manual, why the wing could appear to be locked in place but obviously was not. Somehow, the hinge-pin was just slightly in place and the levers in the cockpit were forced.

'What about Corsair No. 027? Well, our ground crew repaired the tail wheel, re-installed the left wing – this time correctly – and the plane was back in the air in a few days. My logbook shows me flying that Corsair six days after the folding wing affair. Within the next few weeks I flew 027 eight times: escorted dive bombers to Rabaul, escorted dive bombers all the way to Kavieng, New Ireland, patrolled Green Island (almost like a day off), covered a naval task force, made a barge sweep to Cape Lambert, escorted B-25s to Rabaul and several similar missions. So old No. 027 wasn't so bad after all. But my mind sometimes goes back to that unfortunate Marine flying over the rugged interior of Espíritu whose wing suddenly folded, plunging him into the remote head-hunter country of that New Hebrides island.'

On 17 February F4U-2 night fighters of VFM(N)-531 flying from Green Island carried out two successful night interceptions and destroyed two enemy aircraft and on the 20th they destroyed a third Japanese aircraft. The day before, 19 February, the last important Japanese opposition on Rabaul was encountered when fifty Zeros and Tojo fighters and Rufe floatplanes met a formation of 145 aircraft comprising fifty-four F4U-s and F6F-3 Hellcats, twenty P-40s and seventy-two SBD Dauntless and TBF Avengers. The American fighters destroyed twenty-three of the enemy aircraft, sixteen of which were shot down by the twenty-six Corsairs of VF-17. Three of these were credited to Lieutenant (j.g.) Ira C. Kepford, who destroyed a Rufe and two Zekes off Cape Siar, New Ireland, to bring his total wartime score to sixteen confirmed victories, making him the highest-scoring Navy fighter pilot. AirSols Intelligence believed that eight weeks of fighting had cost the enemy 730 aircraft, but the figure was nearer 400. There was nothing that could disguise the Japanese defeat, however, and the following day Japan pulled its few remaining aircraft back from Rabaul to Truk.

Primarily the USMC Corsairs would be used in the ground-attack role throughout 1944. Starting on 4 March Marine Corsairs of ten different squadrons in the 4th MAW, together with bombers, began attacks on the Japanese-held bypassed islands of Wotje, Maloelap, Mille and Jaluit in the Marshalls. Many of the Corsairs were hit by anti-aircraft fire but this type of Corsair operation would continue throughout the rest of the war. On 18 March 1944 the Corsair's ground-attack role was greatly enhanced by an additional dive-bombing capability courtesy of VMF-111. This squadron, which was commanded by Major Frank Cole and based on Makin, successfully rigged 1,000lb bomb racks to eight of its Corsairs for a raid on Mille. The Marine pilots lowered their wheels in the diving attacks to reduce their air speed. Later, bomb racks and a special slot for the landing gear handle, which dropped only the main landing gear for air-braking was installed to improve dive-bombing.

Meanwhile, on 26 March, as if to confirm the new role for the F4U, six Corsairs of VMF-113 from Eniwetok, while flying escort for four B-25 Mitchells to Ponape Atoll in the Carolines, shot down eight of twelve intercepting Zekes. It brought to an end Japanese resistance in the air in the Carolines and it was the last real dogfight in the Central Pacific area. Two of the victories on 26 March went to the VMF-113 CO, Major (later Colonel) Loren Dale 'Doc' Everton, which took his score to twelve. His previous ten victories had been achieved while flying F4F Wildcats at Guadalcanal, from August to October 1942. Born in Crofton, Nebraska, on 14 July 1915, Everton had been flying for twelve years, since the age of 17. He acquired his nickname when squadron mates learned of his pharmacy major at the University of Nebraska. While covering landings at Ulejang Atoll Everton's Corsairs set an F4U record, remaining airborne for nine hours forty minutes.

Armed with six heavy machine guns and capable of diving on targets from angles as steep as 85 degrees or in shallow glides, the Corsair brought terror to even the most stoical of Japanese anti-aircraft crews. The attacks of course were accompanied by the characteristic 'Whistling Death' sound as air was sucked into the inlet ducts in the wing roots. Bombing and strafing strikes though were not without loss. During September 1944 the 4th Marine Air Wing in the Marshalls lost thirty-six F4Us to enemy anti-aircraft fire while dive-bombing enemy-held atolls.

Another reason for the Corsair's great success in the ground support role can be attributed to 41-year-old aviation pioneer Charles A. Lindbergh who, in May 1944, began flying missions in the Corsair with USMC

MAG-14 pilots at Green Island and Emirau. He had joined United Aircraft as an engineering consultant early in the war and then served in an experimental advisory capacity in the Pacific. His last mission in the Solomons was on 9 June and although he now went to New Guinea to fly combat in P-38s, his association with the Corsair was not yet over. One of the Corsair's problems at this time was its limited bomb load capability which, due to the short, rudimentary airstrips in the Marshalls, dictated that loads seldom exceeded 1,500lb. The problem became Lindbergh's to solve. Soon after his arrival at Roi-Namur, Kwajalein Atoll in the Marshalls, early in September, Lindbergh worked mainly with Colonel Calvin B. Freeman and ordnance personnel of MAG 31, progressively raising the bomb load available to Corsairs, until finally, the F4U was capable of hauling loads of 4,000lb of bombs. This was achieved by successfully mounting a 2,000lb bomb under the centre section and rigging a 1,000lb one under each wing. Operating under conditions of strict secrecy, on 12 September, Lindbergh carried three 1,000lb bombs on his F4U-1D (one 1,000lb bomb had to be removed because a 14-knot crosswind was gusting at take-off time) while raiding an enemy radio station at Wotje Atoll. Lindbergh successfully dropped his bomb-load on the enemy target from 1,600 feet. Next day, after working on a new belly bomb rack, he returned to Wotje with 4,000lb of bombs – a 2,000 pounder on the centre-line rack and a 1,000lb bomb under each wing – to drop the first 2,000lb bomb ever carried on a Corsair. Lindbergh approached his target, a small concrete blockhouse, at 8,000 feet and dived at 65 degrees, but he miscalculated, overshot and dropped his bombs on the beach, where they blew a naval shore battery to smithereens. Lindbergh, who had spent six months in the Pacific, having flown fifty combat missions lasting 178 hours, left for Hawaii later in the day, his work completed.

The Corsair was assured of future employment in both the ground-attack and dive-bombing roles, actions that would continue long after the Second World War had ended. Moreover, there were men like Jack Hospers, the Vought Service Rep, and men in high places in the Navy, who believed that the use of Corsairs at sea aboard its carriers was long overdue. Among them was Captain John Pearson, Fighter Design Officer at the Bureau of Aeronautics, and Captain Hugh S. Duckworth USN. There were some, however, who still firmly believed that the Corsair was only suitable for operations from land bases. The Chief of Naval

Operational Training at NAS Jacksonville was one who believed that the Corsair's carrier deck landing characteristics were still too dangerous and that the accident rate, especially with new pilots, remained unacceptably high. In March 1944 he drafted a letter condemning the Corsair's ability to fly from carriers, but his letter was pigeonholed. By now, support for the Corsair to operate at sea was too great and 'Program Dog' was carried out immediately by Vought engineers to get the bent-winged bird ready for carrier operation.

In just ten days Vought modified the oleo legs with a longer-stroke landing gear oleo shock strut and eliminated the 'built-in bounce'. Commander T.K. 'Kip' Wright USN and Lieutenant Colonel John Dobbins USMC, conducted successful flight-tests at Jacksonville NAS and proved that the Corsair was safe for carrier operations. During April VF-301, a training squadron on the West Coast, carried out carrier trials with the newly-modified Corsairs aboard the escort carrier *Gambier Bay* and, after 113 landings without incident, declared their support for the Corsair to operate at sea. The move was rubber-stamped on 16 May when, after a series of comparative tests between the F4U-1D and the F6F-3 Hellcat, a Navy Evaluation Board concluded that the Corsair was the best all-round Navy fighter available and a suitable carrier aircraft. It was recommended that carrier and fighter-bomber units be converted to the F4U type. In May the new landing-gear oleo struts were installed on production Corsairs and new strut-filling procedures were introduced. F4Us no longer had to be 'de-bounced' by using field modifications. Later, in August 1944, a high level meeting of Marine and Navy officials at Pearl Harbor decided that Marine air squadrons would be assigned to escort carriers (CVEs).

Chapter 5

Night Nuisance Interceptors

His prop wash foamed the water. Consequently I had to depress my nose in order to hit the target. Anyhow, he finally went down after I had used 950 rounds.

Lieutenant Commander Richard E. 'Chick' Harmer

On 3 December 1943 the USS *Intrepid*, also known as 'The Fighting I,' sailed from Naval Station Norfolk for San Francisco, then to Hawaii. She arrived at Pearl Harbor and prepared for the invasion of the Marshall Islands, the next objective in the Navy's island-hopping campaign. In January 1944 four F4U-2s of VF(N)-101 were embarked aboard the USS *Enterprise* and a few were loaded aboard the USS *Intrepid* to be used for fleet defence during the Pacific battles On 16 January *Intrepid* left Pearl Harbor with the carriers *Cabot* and *Essex*. Starting on 29 January 1944, as part of Task Group 58.2, *Intrepid* raided islands in the north-eastern corner of the Kwajalein Atoll. By 31 January this group's carrier aircraft had destroyed or put out of commission all eighty-three Japanese aircraft stationed on Roi-Namur. The first landings were made on adjacent islets. That morning, *Intrepid*'s aircraft strafed Ennuebing Island until ten minutes before the first Marines reached the beaches. Thirty minutes later, the islet – which protected Roi's south-western flank and controlled the North Pass into the Kwajalein Lagoon – was secured, enabling Marines to set up artillery to support their assault on Roi. On 2 February *Intrepid* headed for Truk, the Japanese naval base in the centre of Micronesia. On 16 February the *Intrepid*, as part of Task Force 58, began airstrikes against Truk atoll as part of Operation Hailstone. The Japanese lost several warships and merchant vessels, alongside several hundred aircraft. The carrier raid demonstrated Truk's vulnerability and thereby greatly curtailed its usefulness to the Japanese as a base.

J. Martin, a Corsair Radar Officer on the carrier recalled: 'Our first operation was the invasion of Kwajalein Atoll's Roi and Namur islands.

The carrier's planes bombed the islands heavily and then battleships stood offshore and lobbed large shells onto them. Finally, Marines went ashore and secured the islands. The fleet retired to Majuro Atoll. Its circular reef was large enough to hold all our ships and had only one entrance. It seemed quite safe from Japanese submarines. For medicinal purposes, the ship's surgeon issued a two-ounce bottle of Navy brandy to each man on the carrier. This was much appreciated by all hands. When we left Majuro, someone pointed out a battleship I had not noticed before. It was flying an admiral's flag and the scuttlebutt was that Admiral Raymond Spruance was now in charge. We were headed for the Truk Islands. Some B-24 reconnaissance planes had recently flown over Truk, but it was cloud covered and they could not get usable photos of this important Japanese naval base. Thus, our pilots had no recent photos to use for planning. The air group from the *Intrepid* and planes from the other carriers attacked Truk during the day.'

On the night of 17/18 February the *Intrepid* was struck by a torpedo from a Japanese aircraft. Continues J. Martin: 'At sunset we put one of our F4U night fighters onto the catapult; the engineering officer (Herb Wade) ran up the engine and I tested the Corsair's radar and radio. All checked out okay and one of the pilots strapped himself into the seat. The ship's radar had picked up several planes coming from Truk. This was the event we were trained for and we were anxious to get our pilot into the air. However, we were told that Admiral Spruance's permission was needed to launch aircraft. Rumour had it that he was at dinner and could not be disturbed. I always considered that unlikely but, in any event, we did not get permission. And the Japanese planes got closer and closer and closer. Herb checked out the plane's engine again and I checked out its radar and radio and the pilot, still strapped into the seat, got more and more anxious. Finally the enemy planes reached us. Our ships started firing at them and they dropped torpedoes. Our carrier was hit in the stern while in a hard turn to port. Our rudder was jammed and couldn't be moved. I think about thirty men were lost who had been at anti-aircraft guns outboard of the flight deck, near the stern.'

The torpedo struck *Intrepid*'s starboard quarter, fifteen feet below her waterline, flooding several compartments, distorting her rudder and killing eleven crewmen. By running her port engines at full power and stopping her starboard engines or running them at one-third ahead,

Captain Sprague kept her roughly on course. Her crew moved all the aircraft on deck forward to increase her headsail to further aid in control. Some imperfect steering could be done by running the port engines at full speed and idling the starboard engines. 'Our night-fighter Corsair was still on the catapult when we were hit,' continues J. Martin, 'We never did get permission to take off. Could this have been a case of the battleship Navy not believing in the merits of the carrier Navy? The *Intrepid* could not conduct flight operations because of the steering problems and she limped back to Pearl Harbor.

On 19 February strong winds overpowered the improvised steering and left *Intrepid* with her bow pointed towards Tokyo. Admiral Sprague later confessed, 'Right then I wasn't interested in going in that direction.' At this point the crew made a jury-rig sail of wood, cargo nets and canvas to further increase her headsail, allowing *Intrepid* to hold her course. *Intrepid* arrived at Pearl Harbor for temporary repairs on 24 February and departed for the West Coast on 16 March. On 22 March she arrived at Hunter's Point, California. In June *Intrepid* moved to Pearl Harbor for two months of operations in the Marshall Islands. She was then sent to San Francisco for repairs. When the carrier got back to Hawaii, their part of VF(N)-101 was put ashore and sent to the Naval Air Station at Barbers Point on the south-west corner of Oahu.

VF(N)-101 was commanded by Lieutenant Commander Richard E. 'Chick' Harmer. A veteran combat pilot of the 1942 Solomons fighting, Harmer was credited with several kills while flying an F4F Wildcat against Japanese bombers and Zeros. During one mission he was wounded in the legs and nearly shot down, but he lost his attacker in clouds and crash-landed his F4F back on the *Saratoga*. While in the South Pacific, Harmer received orders assigning him to top-secret Project 'Affirm'; he was to report for duty at Quonset Point Naval Air Station, Rhode Island, in early 1943. Harmer was astounded to learn that his new job was to 'help develop night-fighter tactics and the CICs [combat information centres] aboard carriers and everything else necessary to handle, control and develop night fighters themselves.' He admitted: 'We got no instrument training at all at Pensacola. When the weather was bad they cancelled the flights. We graduated without an instrument ticket … Yet I was supposed to be able to fly in all types of weather at night, land on carriers at night. I never did any of that stuff!'

In the spring of 1943 'Chick' Harmer's unit was commissioned as VF(N)-75 under the command of Lieutenant Commander William J. 'Gus' Widhelm. In August, however, the squadron was divided. The navy sent Widhelm and five other experienced pilots along with new radar-equipped F4U-2s to operate from land bases in the Pacific; Harmer was given command of the rest, thirteen 'pretty green ensigns fresh from Pensacola'. While waiting for replacement F4U-2s, they practised flying and gunnery in F4U-1s. Although each man accumulated 125 to 150 hours of flight time, the training included only six practice radar interceptions and ten hours of night flying. During the project, Harmer helped solve practical aeronautical engineering problems and performed innovative experimental flying at night. Initially, his main concern was overcoming his deficiencies in instrument flying, which he accomplished by learning to rely on the needle and ball, gyrocompass and level horizon. 'You could do anything in the world – anything you wanted, any manoeuvre,' he remembered, 'and those instruments would bring you right back to level flight. That's when I really learned to fly at night.'

In December the unit received ten F4U-2s and orders to report to Hawaii for deployment on aircraft carriers. Except for the commander, however, none of the pilots was prepared for night carrier landings and Harmer was worried. By the time the unit reached Hawaii, it was down to eight planes: one crash-landed en route, the other was damaged while being unloaded at Pearl Harbor. Commissioned VF(N)-101 on 1 January 1944, the squadron practised day and night landings at Barbers Point Naval Air Station for two weeks and each pilot had ten day landings on the *Enterprise* followed by two night landings on the *Essex*. That was all the preparation the squadron received for what lay ahead.

The Navy had commissioned Vought to study a night-fighter version of the F4U-1 prior to the first flight of the XF4U-1. Working with the Sperry Company and the MIT Radiation Laboratory, the necessary radar equipment needed to accomplish the mission was developed and the necessary engineering design modifications determined for conversion of the F4U-1 to the night-fighter version. Instead of calling it the 'F4U-1N', a method the Navy used on all succeeding models, the dash one was transformed into the F4U-2 by removing the outermost Browning .50 calibre gun from the starboard wing to help balance the additional weight and the number of rounds for the remaining five guns was reduced from 450 to 250. There were no tracers loaded so as not to blind the pilot when firing. Considerable changes in cockpit instrumentation were made to accommodate the radar scope, control panel, scanner selector and associated switches. The radio bay in the fuselage was modified to accept the 'XAIA' ('Experimental Airborne Intercept A' radar) which was hand-built. With only a range of between three and four miles, the radar was quite primitive. The pilot used a small scope that generated two blips, one giving direction and distance to the target and the other giving the height. After radar installation, the aircraft weighed 235lb less than the standard dash one. The radio was placed beneath the pilot's seat. The radar antenna was placed in a radome two-thirds of the way along the starboard wing. The exhaust stubs were modified to hide as much of the exhaust flame as possible. The F4U-2 was also fitted with a radio-altimeter and an autopilot. There were other slight modifications, such as bore-sighting the guns to converge fire at 250 yards and angling them slightly upward so the pilot could fire without bouncing around in the target's slipstream. The engine was fitted with exhaust flame dampers.

The initial engineering design of the F4U-2 was complete at the time of the Japanese attack on Pearl Harbor and a mock-up was ready for review on 28 January 1942. Because Vought was heavily committed to meet schedules on other programmes, arrangements were made with the Naval Aircraft Factory at Philadelphia, Pennsylvania, to convert production F4U-1s to the F4U-2 configuration. Thirty-four F4U-1s were converted into night fighters (thirty-two being produced by the Naval Aircraft Factory and two converted by VMF(N)-532 at Rio Island, Kwajalein Atoll) and given the F4U-2 designation.

On 15 January 1944 VF(N)-101 became the Navy's first Corsair squadron embarked on an aircraft carrier, as well as one of the service's first carrier-based night-fighter squadrons. That day, Harmer took a detachment of six ensigns and four Corsairs on board the *Enterprise*. The rest of the squadron, led by Lieutenant Cecil 'Swede' Kullberg, went on board the *Intrepid*. Technicians were divided between the two detachments, but Ensign Frank Burgess, the principal radar controller, stayed with Harmer. The next day, the *Enterprise* joined Task Group 58.1 to begin a six-month cruise that would include strikes against Japanese forces in the Truk, Palau, Marshall and Mariana islands.

Once at sea Harmer quickly discovered that his enthusiasm for night-fighters was not shared by many officers outside VF(N)-101. In fact, the squadron was less than welcomed by the *Enterprise*'s flight operations staff. At his first briefing the air group commander, Commander Roscoe L. Newman, stated that night-fighters, if used at all, would fly routine day strikes. Harmer was horrified. As he wrote in his diary: 'Our planes are so much more vulnerable than normal F4Us and the kids just aren't ready for day action. I believe I was sincere in recommending against it on the grounds that we may be too valuable to waste in day actions for which we are not well suited.'

The Navy was sceptical of the Corsair's suitability for carrier operations, owing mainly to poor forward visibility from the cockpit because of the F4U's long nose and the plane's dangerous bounciness when landing. As it turned out, Commander Harmer and his pilots would be the guinea pigs.

The 'Big E's air officer, Commander Thomas J. Hamilton, also had his own ideas about if and/or when VF(N)-101 would fly and refused to allow Harmer's planes off his flight deck. Communication between the two men collapsed. 'The air department had about an eighteen-hour day,' Harmer remembered: 'and if they had to launch night-fighters it turned out to be a twenty-four-hour day. They hated us. The air officer on the *Enterprise* couldn't stand the sight of me. He would sneak into a corner and get physically ill when he saw me approaching. So I had a miserable first half of the tour.'

Daily, Harmer volunteered for combat air patrol (CAP) or rescue escort duty-anything that would get his planes airborne. In his view, the extreme hazards involved in night flying required 'the greatest of flying skill and ceaseless practice'. To be proficient in making night interceptions, his pilots not only had to be good in their normal carrier aviation abilities but also had to possess 'a definite desire and liking for this type of work'.

One evening after four frustrating weeks at sea Lieutenant Commander 'Chick' Harmer walked across the flight deck of the *Enterprise* toward his F4U-2. Like previous nights on standby, No. 15 was spotted on the catapult, fully-armed and ready to launch. But Harmer had yet to fly a single sortie. Approaching his plane, he was astonished to see freshly shellacked on the engine cowling an image of a half-naked redhead in a sarong seductively gazing down on him. Underneath were the words

Impatient Virgin. Apparently that afternoon his crew chief had taken the liberty of personalizing the skipper's plane. Smiling, Harmer climbed into the cockpit and strapped in. But for the next three hours he sat there without being 'squirted off the catapult'. Writing in his diary that night, he noted, 'It is appropriate – the "impatient" refers to me and the "virgin" to the plane."[1]

Eventually, Harmer secured some daytime rescue and CAP duties for his squadron. On one occasion, during a strike against Guam, Harmer took off to fly a rescue combat air patrol for two OS2U Kingfishers that were picking up downed pilots. Arriving over them, he ended up 'right in the middle' of a flight of Zeros returning from attacking the American fleet. While Harmer chased them away from one of the seaplanes, his inexperienced wingman, flying an F6F Hellcat, broke off to follow a Zero that was heading for the other OS2U on the water several miles away. Two Zeros pounced on the Hellcat, shooting it down, but Harmer and the OS2U he was protecting got back to the fleet safely.

Despite the daytime flights Harmer was getting in, his frustration at being barred from night operations finally compelled him to approach the task group's commander, Rear Admiral John W. 'Black Jack' Reeves Jr. 'I've got to be launched at night in order to prove this gear,' he told Reeves, who replied, 'We've got night-fighters – we'll use 'em.' Harmer recalled the admiral said: 'He wouldn't have any confidence in us unless he saw us work. And that's what made the cruise for me … When the *Intrepid* had the night duty and a bogey appeared on the radar screen, Reeves would call on the TBS and ask if they were going to launch and the answer was always "No," so he would say "OK, I'll launch mine". So that's how we got used.'

Subsequently, Harmer got more co-operation from Commander Hamilton and VF(N)-101 passed another milestone: night practice. Typically, one Corsair would launch around 0430, before day operations commenced. Night landings were a constant worry for Harmer and his pilots who did not become competent at it were returned to Pearl Harbor. Those who remained, three pilots in addition to their commander, became adept at launching and landing with few reference lights. The air officer,

---

1. *The Big E's Impatient Virgins* by Dr Randolph Bartlett, retired professor of history at Cape Cod Community College (US Naval Institute).

however, routinely over-lit the flight deck. As Harmer recounted: 'Too many lights rather than not enough was our problem on landing. By that I mean it was felt we needed some types of lights when we actually didn't. When the carrier and several other ships were showing lights the danger to the fleet was increased, but our landings were not made easier. After we had convinced the fleet that we could land with a minimum of lights, we became of greater value because we could be used under more conditions without endangering the fleet'.

Gradually, Harmer slipped Burgess into the *Enterprise*'s CIC for practice interceptions. This was usually brief, because when the carrier's radar operators arrived they 'chased Frank away from the scope and used it to work the day fighters'. As Harmer recorded in his journal, 'Day fighters still come first on this ship (as perhaps they should), but I don't think they know what they have in these night-fighters.'

Harmer's first night contact, much to his dismay, resulted in only a 'probable'. The 18/19 February encounter could have been a 'kill,' except that everything went wrong. For starters, Burgess brought Harmer's Corsair in above the bogey, a Betty medium bomber, and he overshot the target. Eventually, he made visual contact and fired a short burst into the enemy plane's right engine, which began to burn. Although the Betty was going down in a steep spiral, Harmer lost sight of it and was unable to confirm that it had crashed.

In early April off Truk Harmer was in the ready room at sunset when he got a call that a downed pilot was off the southern end of the islands. It was turning dark and Hamilton reluctantly scrambled two F4U-2s. 'They didn't want to launch us,' Harmer remembered, 'but they did. We got lucky and found his life raft – I happened to fly right over him and he shot a Very pistol [flare] up at me. I circled until a submarine picked him up.'[2]

On the night of 13/14 April a detachment of VMF(N)-532 at Engebi Island made the Marines' first and only successful night interception using F4U-2s fitted with SCR-270 radar when Lieutenant Edward A. Sovik and Captain Howard W. Bollmann each shot down a Betty bomber. Lieutenant Joel E. Bonner Jr claimed a probable before his tail was damaged so badly that he had to bale out. He was picked up by a destroyer the following day.

---

2. *The Big E's Impatient Virgins* by Dr Randolph Bartlett.

Lieutenant Donald Spatz became lost and was never found. Such was the effect on the attackers though that the nine remaining Bettys dropped their bombs harmlessly in the sea and fled. On 17 April Marine Corps Corsairs supported US landings in the Malabang-Parang area of Mindanao in the Philippines. In June the Engebi detachment started making night raids against Wotje. On 12 July VMF(N)-532's twelve F4U-2s were flown off a carrier to Saipan. In May 1944 VMF(N)-533 conducted their final training on the Grumman F6F-5N Hellcat, equipped with the APS-6 radar, at Marine Corps Air Station Ewa, Hawaii, and then headed for Eniwetok. On 12 June they relieved VMF(N)-532 and assumed night defence responsibilities for the area. VMF(N)-532 were later pulled back to Guam and the squadron returned to the United States on 25 October, remaining there in training until the end of the war.

On the night of 24 April, meanwhile, off Hollandia in New Guinea, 'Chick' Harmer shot down his first bogey and narrowly missed becoming the Navy's first night-fighter ace – all in one evening. That night he was catapulted to intercept a 'snooper'. After several radical vector changes he established contact with the enemy plane on his cockpit radar screen at a range of two miles. The commander quickly closed and visually identified the intruder as a Betty. At 250 yards the bomber's gunners opened fire. Harmer executed an 'S-turn' to reduce speed, closed to 150 yards and fired a long burst. By then the Japanese plane was flying at an altitude of less than 100 feet, with Harmer's Corsair close behind. 'He was flying so low,' Harmer remembered, 'that his prop wash foamed the water. Consequently I had to depress my nose in order to hit the target. Anyhow, he finally went down after I had used 950 rounds.' A few minutes later, he 'ran into the chance of a lifetime' – five Japanese bombers flying in formation. Because he was low on ammunition, however, his guns started to jam. Harmer frantically managed to get off only a few rounds he fired at two of them: 'The plane I fired at dropped his left wing and flashed a row of vari-coloured lights along the upper surface of each wing. The other two planes followed suit. I got one gun working but as soon as I had fired three rounds it stopped. The plane I fired on turned on his vari-coloured lights and the whole formation again followed suit. I never did figure out what those lights were for unless they thought I was a friendly plane trying to join up on them and they were trying to identify themselves. I believe that the plane I knocked down was their 'snooper' and they thought I was he trying to return to the formation.'[3]

Initially, tracer ammunition was not recommended; however, after two sorties Harmer would find that one inboard gun loaded with one tracer every fifteen rounds 'helped considerably in correcting point of aim.'

On 15 June more night action followed when Harmer and Lieutenant (j.g.) Robert F. Holden Jr, attacked a formation of Sallys and Tojo fighters. On 20 June during the Battle of the Philippine Sea, the largest carrier aircraft battle in history, Harmer would again fly a night-rescue mission, this time to help guide home planes returning in the dark from Rear Admiral Marc A. Mitscher's famous late-afternoon strike against the Japanese fleet. The US warships 'turned the lights on for them,' Harmer recalled. 'It was just like a daylight landing for those who didn't run out of fuel [and] crash land in the sea.'

Enterprise and *Lexington, San Jacinto* and *Princeton* of Task Group 58.3 under the command of Rear Admiral John W. Reeves formed one of four carrier groups used in the battle.[4] For over eight hours, airmen of the United States and Imperial Japanese navies fought in the skies over TF 58 and the Marianas. Over the course of two days, six American ships were damaged and 130 planes and a total of seventy-six pilots and aircrew were lost. The aerial part of the battle was nicknamed the 'Great Marianas Turkey Shoot' by American aviators for the severely disproportional loss ratio inflicted upon Japanese aircraft by American pilots and anti-aircraft gunners. During a debriefing after the first two air battles a pilot from *Lexington* remarked, 'Why, hell, it was just like an old-time turkey shoot down home!' American carrier aircraft and US submarines sank three Japanese carriers (*Hiyō, Shōkaku* and *Taihō*) and destroyed 426 carrier aircraft, losses from which Japanese naval aviation would never recover.

On the night of 27 June, responding to a radar contact, an F4U-2 piloted by Robert Holden was catapulted from the *Enterprise*. Holden established visual contact with a Sally at 10,000 feet and then shot it down. The flaming plane crashed in the midst of the fleet. 'That put us

---

3. *The Big E's Impatient Virgins* by Dr Randolph Bartlett.
4. Task Group 58.4 consisted of one fleet carrier (*Essex*) and two light carriers (*Langley* and *Cowpens*); Task Group 58.1 of *Hornet, Yorktown, Belleau Wood* and *Bataan* and Task Group 58.2 of *Bunker Hill, Wasp, Cabot* and *Monterey*.

back in the good graces of everyone and set the stage for the next night, when we had a record evening,' Harmer recalled. Again, Holden was sent up. He found a Betty three miles away at 1,000 feet and closed until he made a visual 200 feet astern of it. When he fired a short burst into the starboard wing, the bomber blew up. The Corsair flew right through the ball of heat, flames and debris. Shortly thereafter Holden shot down another low-flying bogey and Harmer one.

More action followed and, as VF(N)-101 got increased exposure to Japanese tactics, its pilots honed their skills. A Betty bomber shadowing the fleet often preceded an enemy raid. Harmer learned that the safest and most efficient direction to approach the bomber was from directly astern. Because of the F4U's superior speed, overrunning the target was a frequent problem. He solved it by using his dive brakes when behind the slower aircraft. Harmer and his pilots also took advantage of the moon: 'If the moon's phase and position were of possible assistance, we preferred an approach out to the side so as to get the bogey directly up-moon from us.' That gave the fighter the advantage of making a visual before being spotted, allowing a positive identification and the time to drop behind and below the bomber before opening fire. Harmer's men found that the Corsair's canopy reduced visibility, so for interceptions it was important to open it, regardless of wind and noise. That permitted a clear view of the enemy plane's engines, which had excellent flame dampeners and were tricky to focus fire on.

One night Harmer joined Holden to practise some radar interceptions, which went smoothly. As the two fliers were returning to the *Enterprise*, Ensign Burgess, manning radar equipment in the carrier's CIC, informed them that an extra plane was in their formation. Assisted by Burgess, Harmer closed on the bogey who descended to 500 feet and side-slipped to the down-moon side of the target. At 400 feet the commander made visual contact: 'After slowing down, I pulled up to the target and sent a half- to one-second burst into the port wing root. The plane exploded immediately and hit the water.'

Only once did Harmer encounter bombers with fighter escorts. It happened 'just at dusk after the day CAP had been landed' and it didn't go well. Harmer and Holden ran into 'twelve to fifteen bombers, Bettys, or possibly "Franceses" escorted by Tojo fighters.' As the Corsairs made a pass at the enemy formation, they 'were jumped by four Tojos'. Holden,

Harmer recalled: 'knocked one off my tail and it disappeared from view at 1500 feet, headed down in a tight spin. It was rated as another probable. We were lucky to have some clouds around in which to hide, particularly after a 20-mm [round] shorted my formation lights and I couldn't get them to turn off. The bombers reached the fleet and anti-aircraft fire shot down eight of them.'[5]

By July, when the night-fighting Corsairs were withdrawn from 'The Big E', Harmer and Holden between them had accounted for five confirmed night victories, a probable and four damaged.

And so the 'Impatient Virgins' got to fly, after all. By the time the *Enterprise* returned to Pearl Harbor in July VF(N)-101 had demonstrated to Navy sceptics that night fighters had a place on aircraft carriers. The squadron recorded five kills, two 'probables' and two damaged. Harmer earned the respect of his men, a grudging air operations officer and the farsighted Admiral Reeves. 'While we did not shoot down all of our opportunities,' he stated in his final report to the Navy, 'we are very proud of the fact that no ship under our protection was damaged in a night raid.'

Chick Harmer finished his tour convinced of the bright future of Navy night-fighters. He foresaw a need for all pilots to be skilled in night operations and able to perform a variety of missions against air, sea, or land targets. In his report he recommended two-seater night-fighters armed with air-to-air rockets and predicted the future use of radar-equipped airborne-command planes that would eventually control multiple night-fighter interceptions. It would take many years for technology to catch up to Harmer's ideas but, by the time this visionary officer retired in the late 1960s as a captain, they would all be standard operating procedure for naval aviation.[6]

The Pacific War moved on. In August 1944 MAG-21 comprising F4U-s of VMF-216 'Wild Hares', VMF-217 'Bulldogs' and Marine Fighting Squadron 225, as well as Hellcat night-fighters arrived on Guam immediately after the island's capture and for several months MAG-21 carried out attacks on Rota and Pagan. On 26 September the 'Death Dealer' Corsairs of VMF-114 joined in providing close air support in the eleven-day-old battle for Peleliu in the Palaus group, about 500 miles

---

5. *The Big E's Impatient Virgins* by Dr Randolph Bartlett.
6. ibid.

east of the Philippines. In October the Corsairs of VMF-121 and VM-122, both of which were on their second deployment to the Pacific, with MAG-11, arrived at Peleliu from Espíritu Santo. From then until the end of the war these two squadrons were flying CAP and carrying out strikes against Yap, Babelthuap and Koror.

During October the USMC Corsair pilots began training for shipboard duty aboard escort carriers. Their presence was due in no small part to the lack of Navy carrier pilots available. Each MAG would now consist of one squadron of eighteen F4Us and one of twelve TBF Avenger bombers. Unfortunately, or luckily, depending on which way one wants to look at it, the move to carriers coincided, in October, with the start of the Japanese kamikaze offensive by Japan's 205th Air Group. The Japanese credo was 'One plane for one warship, one boat for one ship, one man for ten enemy and one man for one tank'. The waves of kamikazes or 'Divine Wind' suicide attacks would at least be met by an increasing number of Corsairs. In all, ten USMC F4U fighter squadrons were authorized for carrier qualification and preparations were quickly carried out to put two F4U-1D aircraft on each of five fleet carriers.

On the morning of 25 October, nine Zekes, five of which were 'human bombs' flown by suicide pilots, each wearing the traditional Samurai *hachimaki* scarf wrapped around their heads, took off from Mabalcat airfield and headed for the four escort carriers in the US invasion fleet off Leyte. As the alarm was sounded and the pilots of the Corsairs ran to their aircraft, the Zekes began diving on their targets. Japanese Lieutenant Seik picked out the carrier *St Lô* and deliberately crashed into the escort carrier, whose ruptured fuel tanks began burning and then exploded sending flames 1,000 feet into the air. The *St Lô* took two more hits and began sinking. The Zekes struck three more escort carriers. The suicide attacks alarmed the US chiefs and more and more Corsairs would obviously be needed to intercept the suicide planes at low level and destroy as many of them as possible before the enemy could sink more ships. On 26 November a Navy conference in San Francisco finalized the decision to put a 73 fighter-per-carrier complement on fleet aircraft carriers and to put Marine fighters aboard.

Meanwhile, many of the fixed-wing FG-1A Corsairs, which could not be used aboard carriers, were operated by USMC Corsair squadrons from land bases. On 3 and 4 December 1944 seventy-five fixed-wing

FG-1As, F4U-1s and F4U-1Ds of MAG-12 arrived at Tacloban airfield in Leyte from Emirau ready for combat from the muddy crowded field. On 5 December four of VMF-115's Corsairs on CAP over an American convoy off Leyte intercepted two Zekes and shot one down into the ocean. Next day twelve Corsair fighter-bombers of VMF-211 led by the CO, Major Stanley J. Witonski, attacked a Japanese convoy of seven ships heading for Ormoc Bay protected by a mass of Zekes high above them. One of the enemy destroyers was damaged by a bomb blast. Flak and fighters shot down three Corsairs and one pilot was lost. Major Stan Witonski, one of those shot down, was picked up safe and sound after ditching in the sea. Next day, 7 December, near San Isidro, twenty-one Corsair fighter-bombers of VMF-211, 218 and 313, supported by Army P-40s, made attacks on Japanese destroyers and transports trying to reinforce Leyte. Four of the vessels, including a transport which was hit by four bombs dropped by VMF-218, were sunk with 1,000lb and 500lb bombs dropped by the F4Us and P-40s.

Four days later, on 11 December, the F4U-s and FG-1As of VMF-115, VMF-211, VMF-218 and VMF-313 made a further two strikes on a ten-ship Japanese convoy in the area. In the morning, twenty-seven Corsairs attacked the enemy shipping forty miles east of Panay Island and in the afternoon, forty Corsairs and sixteen AAC P-40 Warhawks attacked again near Palompom on the west coast of Leyte. When the smoke had cleared two cargo ships had been sunk. Four FG-1As of VMF-313 which were flying cover for the US re-supply convoy heading for the Ormoc, Leyte beachhead, intercepted sixteen Zeke fighter-bombers and the combined firepower from the surface ships and the Corsairs shot down four of the Zeros. One of the Zekes got through and hit the destroyer *Reid*, which exploded and sank. VMF-313 bagged five more Zekes, bringing the total of enemy aircraft destroyed on the 11th to nineteen. MAG-12 lost six Corsairs and three pilots killed to fighters and enemy anti-aircraft fire and seven more F4Us were so badly damaged that they had to be written off.

On 13 December thirty-five Corsairs of MAG-12 helped provide close air support for US landings on Mindoro Island. Fierce fighting was made worse by the appearance in the Mindoro beachhead area of kamikazes, several of which were shot down by the Corsairs of VMF-211, which destroyed five Zekes on 14 December, and by the Hellcats of VMF(N)-541. In January 1945 the Japanese still showed no signs of ending the long drawn-out war which involved the Americans having to take one island after another. Fighting was dogged and bloody and the enemy gave no quarter. Most of the island-hopping was the province of the 'Grunts', supported by Corsairs and other land and ship-based aircraft.

Later that month the three Corsair squadrons in MAG-12 moved out of Tacloban and transferred to Leyte. On 6 January fifteen F4U-s of MAG-12 assisted Army aircraft in softening up enemy positions prior to the invasion of Lingayen by destroying key bridges in the area. The Corsairs continued with ground support missions throughout January for the loss of fifteen pilots. In January 1945 Marines from Green Island moved into Guiuan, Samar, and MAG-14 moved with them. First to arrive were twenty-two F4U-1s of VMO (Marine Observation Squadron)-251, on the 2nd to fly combat patrol the next day. VMO-251, which was redesignated VMF-251 on 31 January 1945, was followed at Samar by F4U-1s and F4U-4s of VMF-212 on 8 January and shortly thereafter they were joined by VMF-222 and, on the 14th, by the F4U-4s of VMF-223. MAG-14 movement was finally complete by 24 January. MAG-14's stay on Samar was marred by the loss of twenty Corsairs in crashes over a period of thirty days, the worst on 24 January when the crash on take off of a VMF-222 resulted in the deaths of thirteen men and more than fifty injured. On 23 February 1945 four Corsairs of VMF-115 'Joe's Jokers' claimed to have destroyed a Japanese midget submarine at Cebu City while skip-bombing with 1,000lb bombs.

On 10 March Corsairs of MAG-14 flew ground-attack missions at Zamboanga near Mindanao prior to the landings by US troops while the Corsairs of MAG-12 flew top cover. Four days later F4Us of VMF-115 landed at San Rogue airfield and flew two missions the next day. The airfield was renamed Moret Field and eventually many aircraft of various types were based there including ninety-six Corsairs. On 18 March Marine Corsairs flew air cover for the landings by the US 40th Division at Panay. Corsairs took part in the attacks on 26 March during the landings at Cebu and, on 29 March, for the unopposed landings at Negros. Support missions continued to be flown during April as the ground forces fought the Japanese on Cebu and Negros. Operating from the island and from Zamboanga Island, MAG-12 conducted operations throughout the Philippines until the end of the Pacific war. On 17

April American troops landed on Mindanao and on 2 May Davao fell. On 12 July the last American landing in the Philippines took place at Sarangani Bay and the last resistance on Mindanao was finally overcome. Meanwhile, from 22 May to June 1945, MAG-14's VMF 212, 222 and 223, moved to Okinawa to take part in the final battles of the Second World War.

The F4U-2 did not become the primary carrier-based night-fighter as the Navy preferred the Hellcat but it did contribute significantly to clearing the type for general carrier operations. The night-fighters did not destroy a vast number of Japanese aircraft but so effective was their mission that the Japanese soon ceased night-bombing raids altogether. They accomplished their objective in combat as well as pioneering the night-fighter mission. The F4U-2 experience served as a sound basis for the F4U-5N which later served with distinction in the Korean conflict.

Chapter 6

For King and Country

Not for nothing was it called the bent-wing bastard from Connecticut.

Norman Hanson, No. 1833 Squadron Corsair pilot[1]

Norman Hanson was a 26-year-old civil servant at the beginning of the Second World War. As he was in a reserved occupation, he had great difficulty in joining the forces. However, in 1941 he was allowed to volunteer for the Fleet Air Arm and was selected to commence pilot training at the US Naval Air Station Pensacola, Florida. There he learned to fly the N3N-3 biplane trainer and the more advanced Brewster Buffalo and was still at Pensacola when the Japanese attacked Pearl Harbor on 7 December 1941. Back in the UK in early 1942, after practising ADDLs (assisted dummy deck landings) at RNAS Yeovilton, Hanson made his first deck landing in a Fairey Fulmar on HMS *Argus*. After a period flying abroad he was posted to US Naval Air Station Quonset Point, Rhode Island, as Senior Pilot of 1833 Squadron equipping with the Chance Vought Corsair (F4U) fighter-bomber.

On 1 April 1943 personnel for 1830 Squadron commanded by 26-year-old Lieutenant Commander Donald Brian Milner Fiddes DSO RN assembled at Lee-on-Solent. On 7 May representatives from the squadron disembarked to Quonset Point for a five-month conversion training course in earnest to prepare for active service on the Corsair after familiarisation with the aircraft and equipment. The squadron was officially formed on 1 June. Initial equipment was ten Corsair Is. They were soon joined at Quonset Point by the nucleus of 1831 Naval Air Squadron, which initially formed on 1 July, and 1833 and 1834 Squadrons. No. 1834 Squadron personnel had assembled at RNAS Donibristle and Fleet Air Arm Transit Camp Townhill, Dunfermline, on 15 June for

---

1. *Carrier Pilot: An Unforgettable True Story of Wartime Flying* by Norman Hanson, by kind permission of Patrick Stephens (PSL) 1979.

passage to the USA. It officially formed at Quonset Point on 15 July. No. 1831 Squadron was commanded by Lieutenant Commander Peter Allingham DSC RNVR. No. 1833 Squadron was commanded by Lieutenant Commander H.A. 'Eric' Monk DSM* and 1834 was commanded by Lieutenant Commander (Acting) Alan Michael Tritton DSC** RNVR These personnel left Liverpool in June aboard the RMS *Empress of Scotland*. The ship, which was also taking 1,300 Afrika Korps prisoners to America as well as several hundred naval ratings to train on landing craft for D-Day, dropped anchor at Newport News, Virginia. Rommel's desert troops were destined for PoW camps in Canada, while the Royal Navy representatives travelled to Quonset Point, after an enforced two-week stopover in New York, to join the nucleus of 1830 and 1831 Squadrons there. (Four more FAA Corsair squadrons were to be formed by the end of 1943, bringing the total number of British Corsair squadrons to eight.)

The Corsair's fearsome reputation had first come to the attention of the FAA squadron pilots during their sojourn in New York. While it flew beautifully, it was a beast to land – in the United States Navy, after the first deck landings it had been nicknamed the 'Ensign Eliminator'. Norman Hanson wrote: 'For some months, Corsairs were decidedly tricky aircraft to handle. For one thing, they were damnably big fighters for their day. They had a vast length of fuselage between the cockpit and the propeller which, together with a rather low sitting position and a not-too-clever hood (both of which were modified and greatly improved in the Mark II version), made for very poor visibility when taxiing and landing. It was pretty long-legged in the undercarriage department in order to give clearance to the great propeller, said to be the biggest ever fitted to a single-engined fighter. To increase the clearance, which undercarriage alone could never have achieved, the wings were of "inverted-gull" format, dipping downwards for about four feet from the wing root at the fuselage, then rising sharply to the wingtip. Not for nothing was it called the "bent-wing bastard from Connecticut".

'Its armament consisted of six .5-inch Browning machine guns, hydraulically charged and electrically fired. The radial engine was a Pratt and Whitney R2800, developing 2,000hp from eighteen cylinders arranged in two banks of nine. Fuel was supplied to the engine through a Stromberg injection carburettor, which precluded "cutting-out" on the top of a loop – a disconcerting feature to which aircraft fitted with the normal carburettor were prone. A two-stage supercharger was fitted. The first stage was engaged at 10,000 feet and the second at 19,000 feet. The aircraft was capable of producing a genuine speed of over 400 mph at its rated altitude of around 22,000 feet.

'The Corsair was a rugged machine which could take any amount of punishment on the flight-deck and appeared to make light of it. Everything about it was high-class and great attention to detail proclaimed itself wherever one looked. The cockpit was meticulously arranged with all dials readily visible and every lever and switch comfortably and conveniently to hand, without any need to search or grope. (Infinitely superior, I may say, to the cockpits of British aircraft of that time which suggested, by comparison, that they had been designed by the administrative office charwoman.)

'The aircraft had two built-in safety devices which were worth their weight in gold if hydraulic trouble arose. Both undercarriage and arrestor hook were hydraulically actuated. Should hydraulic pressure be lost, the hook fell automatically, ready for a deck landing. The use of the undercarriage, too, was protected. One simply had to select "down" on the undercarriage lever and then open a CO_2 bottle which effectively "blew down" the wheels into the "landing-locked" position.

'Rumour had it that the prototypes had been equipped with "spin chutes" in their tails, to effect recovery from that deadly enemy the spin. Whether it was true or not, the Pilots' Handling Notes were emphatic on the point that spins should not be deliberately undertaken, for recovery was dubious if not downright impossible.

'The fighter had originally been ordered by the US Navy for carrier use to replace the Grumman F4F, the Wildcat (Martlet to the Royal Navy); but it had proved to be such a handful in Fleet trials – particularly in deck-landing – that the new Grumman F6F – the Hellcat – had been adopted instead. The F4U could now go to the shore-based squadrons of the US Marine Air Corps and to the Royal Navy, if they wanted it. The Royal Navy accepted it willingly. The only alternatives in sight were the Seafire and Sea Hurricane – RAF production models fitted with arrestor hooks – and these just weren't carrier material.

'Each morning we heard dreadful tidings of pilots being killed in Corsairs. Then, suddenly, when I felt there couldn't be any Corsairs left for us to fly, we found ourselves at Quonset Point. After supper on the first evening, the CO came across to me.

'"Feel like a stroll, Hans?"

'We walked up to the hangar that had been allocated to us. There was an armed sentry on guard, but Eric told him to open up and turn on the lights. For some reason or other we headed up a flight of stairs leading on to a balcony running the length of the hangar. Just then the lights came on – and there they were. Corsairs filled the hangar floor and I must say that, of all the aircraft I had seen, these were the most wicked-looking bastards. They looked truly vicious and it took little imagination to realise why so many American boys had found it difficult, if not well-nigh impossible, to master them, especially in deck-landing. We stared at them and hadn't a word to say.

'It was certainly no aircraft for a sprog pilot. It made no concessions to inexperience or nervousness and reacted viciously to the slightest hamfistedness on the controls. Its very size was enough to daunt the bravest and its engine power was staggering in comparison with those machines which even our experienced pilots had coped with so far in their careers. It carried a lot of "gubbins" which were all new to us – a cockpit full of switches, levers, dials and gadgets which demanded one's undivided attention. When that attention lapsed or wandered, things happened – and happened very quickly.

'Somehow or other the Royal Navy would see to it that the Corsair could be deck-landed.'

The Royal Navy's gruelling familiarization training flights at Quonset Point did not proceed without a few setbacks. Pilots practised low flying out to sea, formation flying in both close and open 'patrol' formation and numerous circuits as well as practice-firing and dummy deck landings. It had become obvious almost from the outset that the standard method of landing a fighter aircraft onboard an aircraft carrier would have to be re-thought. In 1943 the standard method was to fly the downwind leg abeam the length of the carrier opposite to the vessel's course, turn base leg perpendicular to the carrier's course, turn again to set up the final approach and then head straight for the deck. The FAA Corsair pilots were unaccustomed to the F4U-1's uneven wing stalling and landing bounce. It resulted in a number of fatal accidents until pilots realised that they could not carry out a standard carrier approach in the Corsair and instead began landing them on in a stalling turn all the way on to the deck.

Late in September 1943 1830 Squadron and the first of the FAA Corsair pilots, who, though they had made numerous ADDLs had yet to make any actual F4U deck-landings, flew their aircraft to the US Navy airfield at Norfolk, Virginia. There their aircraft were hoisted aboard the escort carrier HMS *Slinger* and they and their crews were shipped home to Britain. During October the remaining Corsair pilots continued training in Brunswick, before they too returned to Britain, aboard the newly commissioned escort carrier HMS *Trumpeter*. During further training in December on the River Clyde in Scotland deck landings were carried out on a full-sized deck for the first time in the Firth of Forth aboard HMS *Illustrious* prior to going to sea again.

Upon arriving home, 1830 and 1833 Squadrons, which formed 15th Naval Fighter Wing commanded by Lieutenant Commander Richard John 'Dicky' Cork DSO DSC were to go to sea on *Illustrious*, together with two Fairey Barracuda squadrons, Nos. 810 and 847. Born in London on 4 April 1917, Cork was promoted sub-lieutenant in March 1940. From 21 April until 11 June 1940 he served with Nos. 759 and 760 Squadrons flying Skuas and Gladiators and, on 11 June, he was graded as an above-average pilot. A shortage of fighter pilots during the Battle of Britain led to the Fleet Air Arm asking for volunteers to serve with the Royal Air Force. On 1 July 1940 Cork and two other naval pilots joined the Hawker Hurricane-equipped 242 Squadron under the command of Squadron Leader Douglas Bader; Cork was assigned to become Bader's wingman. On 30 August he was involved in his first combat action with 242 Squadron. The unit claimed twelve aircraft destroyed and Cork was credited with a Messerschmitt Bf 110 destroyed and a share in a second. By 13 September he had shot down five aircraft and become a fighter ace. For his exploits he was awarded the DFC on 18 October, which at the insistence of the Admiralty was exchanged for a DSC. Cork returned to the Fleet Air Arm after the battle and was posted to 880 Naval Air Squadron. The unit was equipped with Grumman Martlets, which were exchanged for Hawker Sea Hurricanes by mid-1941. The squadron then joined HMS *Furious* for attacks on Petsamo and Kirkenes in Arctic Norway. Cork flew two missions but did not come into contact with the German defenders. After this attack, 880 Squadron joined the newly-built fleet carrier HMS *Indomitable* in October 1941 and Cork was promoted to lieutenant the following month. One of the squadron's first operations with *Indomitable* involved the attack on Vichy French gun positions during the landings at Diego Suarez, Madagascar, on 6 May 1942. During these operations Cork claimed three Morane-Saulnier M.S.406s and four Potez 63s, all destroyed on the ground. On 12 August 1942, during Operation Pedestal, he became the only Royal Navy pilot to shoot down five aircraft in one day, for which he was awarded the DSO on 10 November 1942. Flying a Sea Hurricane, his first success was at 12:30 hours when he shot down a Savoia-Marchetti SM.79 over the convoy. Then, flying off the coast of Tunisia, he shot down a Junkers Ju 88 and shared in the destruction of another. Later in the day he shot down a Messerschmitt Bf 110 and another Savoia-Marchetti SM.79. The squadron leader, Lieutenant Commander F.E.C. Judd, was killed during these battles and Cork as the senior pilot was given command of 880 Squadron. In September 1942 he was promoted to acting lieutenant commander.

It had been decided to increase Corsair squadron complement to fourteen aircraft, so 1831 Squadron was disbanded and its pilots and Corsairs sent to bolster 1830 and 1833 Squadrons. These squadrons now came up with a new method of landing the troublesome Corsair on the carrier. It involved flying the F4U-1 just above stalling speed and, by judging the rate of descent exactly, by the time the carrier height had been reached, the carrier was directly underneath and the pilot could chop the throttle and drop the Corsair onto the flight deck. Unfortunately, not all the pilots were successful, and the Corsair could still prove more than a handful for even the more experienced pilot. One of the ensuing crashes resulted in the death of the 1830 Squadron CO, Lieutenant Commander Donald Fiddes. Despite his experience (his award of the DSO in November 1942 was for bravery and outstanding resolution during Operation Pedestal when an important convoy was fought through to Malta in face of attacks by day and night from enemy submarines, aircraft and surface forces) Fiddes made a bad approach to the deck. In trying to take a last minute wave off from the batsman – the Deck Landing Control Officer or DLCO, invariably an ex-pilot, who stood at the end and to one side of the runway, waving extra-large 'table tennis bats' covered with fluorescent fabric. Fiddes clipped his port wingtip on the flight deck. His Corsair toppled over the port side of the carrier and Fiddes drowned before he could be rescued.

Lieutenant Commander Alan Michael Tritton transferred from 1834 Squadron to take command of 1830 Squadron. Born at Sunningdale, Berkshire, on 6 July 1919, the son of a banker, he was educated at Eton, where he was a 'wet bob', rowing in the VIII. After leaving school in 1938 he worked on a tobacco farm in South Africa where he learned to fly. As soon as war broke out he returned to England. Like most wartime volunteer reserve naval pilots he had to start as a naval rating. Having gained his 'wings' on No. 8 Naval Pilots' Course Tritton was commissioned acting sub-lieutenant (Air) RNVR in July 1940. His first appointment was to 800 Squadron in the carrier *Ark Royal*, flying the Blackburn Skua, a poorly performing aircraft, which earned the description 'too big, too slow and too late'. In September 1940 *Ark Royal* took part in an assault on the French Navy at Dakar, North Africa, and while covering a Mediterranean convoy in late November, her planes attacked Italian battleships, though without making any hits. By April 1941 Tritton was flying the Fairey Fulmar, inferior to the modern single-seater fighters, but a reliable, sturdy aircraft with long range which at last provided the Navy with a monoplane fighter. He now took part in escorting the first of eleven convoys, which included carriers ferrying fighter aircraft to Malta; Tritton was in the carrier *Furious*. Having completed this task, he was based with his flight, 800X, on Malta for the next six months. From Hal Far, Tritton flew nearly every night for the next six months, in an anti-intruder role, until 800X Flight was disbanded. He was awarded the first of his DSCs for general operations in the Mediterranean from *Furious* and from Malta. Tritton's experience in night-fighting was seen as invaluable and, in order to pass on his skills to younger pilots, he was given command of the newly formed 784 Squadron. In July 1943 Tritton – who was promoted from naval airman second class to lieutenant commander in just three years – was sent to command 1834 Squadron. Tritton and his squadron successfully completed a series of trials both ashore and on board the American aircraft carrier *Charger*, even if one pilot remembered sheltering in the hangar during the early trials as shards of broken propeller scythed across the airfield.[2]

---

2. In November 1943 the squadron sailed home in the British carrier *Khedive*, subsequently embarking in the carrier *Victorious* for Operation Tungsten, the dive-bomb attack in April 1944 which put out of action the German battleship *Tirpitz*, which was hiding in Kaafjord,

While *Illustrious* waited to go to sea with its two new Corsair squadrons and two Fairey Barracuda squadrons, further Corsair deck-landing training and, in particular, approach pattern flying, was deemed essential by Captain Cunliffe, captain of the *Illustrious*. This continued aboard the escort carrier HMS *Ravager*, one of the thinly plated 'Woolworth' carriers built in the USA on merchant-ship hulls. *Ravager* was much smaller than a fleet carrier and was equipped with the smallest flight deck upon which the Corsair could land. No. 1833 Squadron, too, was brought up to speed on ADDLS at Stretton with the expert assistance of the *Illustrious* batsman, Johnny Hastings, an ex-fighter pilot. When *Illustrious* sailed for the Indian Ocean on 30 December 1943 the Corsair Is of 1830 and 1833 Squadrons went with them. It would not be until another nine months before the US Navy began Corsair operations from the decks of its aircraft carriers. During that time the Corsairs of the British Eastern Fleet and those aboard carriers of the Home Fleet in the Arctic would see action, proving once and for all the viability of the aircraft for successful fleet operation.

While the British Eastern Fleet had been preparing for action on the other side of the world, in Britain two other Corsair Squadrons, 1834 and 1836, had been embarked aboard *Victorious* on 12 February and 8 March

---

in the north of Norway. Although many of the men he had trained were involved in this action, Tritton himself missed it, having been sent to the carrier *Illustrious* in the Indian Ocean, where he took command of 15 Naval Fighter Wing in April 1944. His men were deeply affected by the death in a flying accident of their previous leader, the air ace Lt Cdr Dickie Cork. Tritton rebuilt the morale of the squadron's young pilots, earning their admiration and respect and he led them on a number of attacks on Japanese-held shore installations at Sabang and at Sourbaya, during which his Corsairs shot down four aircraft. These were the first combat successes by carrier-based Corsairs, even though the type had by then been in service with the US Navy and Marine Corps for seventeen months. For his part in the actions Tritton was awarded a bar to his DSC. In January 1945 Tritton's 15 Naval Fighter Wing, still embarked in *Illustrious*, took part in Operation Meridian, a series of raids on the oil-refining complex at Palembang, Indonesia, a vitally important installation in the Japanese war effort. The strike, on 24 January, was a complete success. Heavy damage was inflicted on the refinery at Pladjoe, reducing output by a half. The attack on the refinery at Serongei Gerong on 29 January encountered strong opposition from Japanese fighters and heavy anti-aircraft fire. But it was pressed home so accurately that production was stopped for two months; at least eleven enemy aircraft were shot down and more than thirty destroyed on the ground. For this Tritton was awarded the second bar to his DSC. However, on April 9 1945, *Illustrious* was damaged by a kamikaze attack and, after temporary repairs at Leyte, returned to Britain.

1944 respectively. The *Victorious*, together with *Furious* and four escort carriers, formed the main component of a huge Royal Naval strike force, which was tasked to sink the *Tirpitz*. This 42,000-ton German battleship, which had proved a constant thorn in the side of the British war effort, had been holed up in Altenfjord in Norwegian waters after being damaged in an attack by British midget submarines in September 1943. It would only be a matter of months before the *Tirpitz* would be seaworthy again and it had to be put out of commission permanently before then because of the threat that it posed to convoys operating in the Atlantic or en route to Russia through the Arctic.

The strike, code-named Tungsten was to be carried out by torpedo-bomber-reconnaissance wings comprising four squadrons of Fairey Barracuda dive-bombers. Top cover would be provided by twenty-eight Corsairs, fourteen each from 1834 Squadron, which was commanded by Lieutenant Commander P. Noel Charlton RN (who was known as 'Fearless Freddie', likely due to a 1943 incident at Macrihanish, Scotland, when he suffered burns pulling a pilot and observer from their Swordfish after it crashed and burst into flames) and 1836 Squadron, which was commanded by Lieutenant Commander Chris Tomkinson RNVR. Fighters to act as close escort to the dive-bombers and to carry out flak suppression would be the responsibility of sixty aircraft from four squadrons of Martlets and two of Hellcats. *Tirpitz* was armed with a main battery of eight 15-inch guns, each capable of firing 1,750lb shells, twelve 5.9-inch guns in its secondary batteries and sixteen 4-inch heavy anti-aircraft guns. Additionally, nine single and nine quadruple 20mm flak guns had recently been installed on top of the existing gun turrets. Each gun was capable of about 8,500 rounds per minute. *Tirpitz* was also very well protected with 12½-inch thick side armour plating. Anti-submarine patrols would be undertaken by eight Martlets and twelve Swordfish from the carrier *Fencer*, while two squadrons of Seafires would carry out CAP to protect the fleet.

After a full dress rehearsal on 28 March the strike force sailed from Scapa Flow in the Orkneys in two formations, joining up on the afternoon of 2 April about 220 nautical miles to the north-west of Altenfjord. From there the force sailed to the flying-off position, 120 miles north-west of Kåfjord, eighty miles from the main entrance to Altenfjord. On 3 April between 0415 and 0423 hours eleven Corsairs and twelve Barracudas of 827 Squadron took off from the *Victorious* and were joined by nine

Barracudas off *Furious*. Despite the difference in speed the Corsairs formed up with the Barracudas without difficulty.

Commander Anthony Kimmins'[3] account to the BBC after the raid: 'There was little sleep in those carriers the night before the attack, for we were now in the danger period as we steamed close into enemy waters. Lookouts and guns' crews, only their eyes visible through their scarves and balaclava helmets, were constantly on the job. Supply and Damage Control parties never left their posts. Down in the huge hangars there was feverish activity. On one side were the long lines of Merlin-engined Fairey Barracudas – the new Fleet Air Arm torpedo-bombers which were being tried out in action for the first time. With their wings folded back over their bodies they looked rather like enormous beetles. And on the other side were the American Corsairs with their wings folded vertically and almost touching overhead at the tips. While mechanics swarmed over their aircraft making final adjustments, great yellow bombs were being wheeled down the narrow gangways, loaded up and fused.

'At first light, at exactly the pre-arranged minute, Commander Flying shouted the welcome order "Start up!" The words were hardly out of his mouth before there was a roar of engines. By now the carriers and the escorting ships were all heeling over and swinging into wind. A final nod from the Captain, a signal from Commander Flying, the Flight Deck officer raised his green flag, the engines started to rev up, the flag dropped and the first aircraft was roaring away over the bow. One after the other they followed in rapid succession and nearby you could see the same thing going on. More Barracudas, Seafires, Corsairs, Wildcats and Hellcats. In a few minutes the sky was full of them and as the sun started to rise and the clouds turned pink at the edges, they formed up in their squadrons.

'It wasn't long before the mountains in the coastline showed up ahead. As they gained height and crossed the coast the sun was rising to their left, shining across the snow-covered mountains, throwing shadows in the gorges and against the snow-covered trees in the valleys and lighting up the deep blue of the clam fjord. Down to the left were two or three enemy ships, but these took no visible interest in the proceedings. Everything

---

3. Anthony Martin Kimmins, born in Harrow, London, on 10 November 1901, served in the Royal Navy and upon leaving the navy he became an actor, director, playwright, screenwriter and producer.

seemed calm and peaceful, but I'll bet that down below the wires were humming and that up at the far end of the fjord alarm bells were ringing, fat-headed Huns were falling out of bed, rubbing their eyes and cursing the British as they threw on some clothes and stumbled out to their cold action stations.'

Though visibility was 'excellent', 9/10ths snow cover on the ground made it difficult to see the aircraft below. After sixty-five minutes' flying, the Corsairs' long-range tanks were jettisoned between Altafjord and Langfjord (literally 'The Long Fjord'). As the target came into view a German smokescreen was beginning to form and as the bombers began their dives from 8,000 feet, the Corsairs ranged over Langfjord and Kåfjord, while the close-escort Martlets and Hellcats attacked the flak guns. The *Tirpitz* seemed to be caught unawares and the Barracudas scored several hits on the battleship. At 0600, about half an hour after the first wave attack, the Corsairs set course for *Victorious*. All the strike aircraft, except for one Barracuda, which was shot down, were safely recovered aboard the carriers. The longest of the Corsair sorties lasted two hours thirty minutes.

'By now the strike was passing its next landmark, a huge glacier on the top of a mountain,' recalled Kimmins. 'Soon they were crossing the final ridge and sighted a flak ship on the far side of the fjord. She immediately opened up, but raggedly and without great effect. And then, as they crossed over the final ridge, they had a thrill which none of those aircrews will ever forget. There, nestling under the sheer mountains in a fjord not much wider than the Thames at London lay one of the largest battleships in the world – the *Tirpitz*. A motor-boat alongside raced off at full speed and I don't blame him. Up till then the strike had kept dead radio silence, but now as they arrived in position everyone gave an instinctive start as a sudden rasping noise hit them in the ears. The leader had switched on. And then a shout – "All fighters anti-flak – leader over." And with that shout things really happened. Hellcats and Wildcats literally fell out of the sky. As the Barracudas hurtled down they could see the fighters strafing the surrounding gun positions and whistling across the *Tirpitz*, with the tracers from their bullets bouncing off her deck. Green and red tracer came shooting up, but the fighters had entirely disorganized her AA fire and the Barracudas were able to take perfect aim. Down they went with their eyes glued to her funnel – 6,000 – 5,000 – 4,000 feet. They went down so fast that anything loose shot up to the roof of the cockpits.

'Now the leader was at the right height and he let go. The first three bombs went whistling down, exploding bang on the bridge, the nerve-centre of the ship. The other pilots – diving from either side – were close on his tail. One extra large bomb, bursting through the armour-plate amidships, went off with a terrific explosion between decks. The huge ship shuddered, her stern whipping up and down and sending waves across the fjord. It was only 60 seconds – one minute – from the first bomb to the last. There was no sign of life from the hutments close to her berth. No doubt these housed many of the repair workers. Six months' work was going west in sixty seconds.

'And now, as the first strike weaved away and made off down the valleys with fires raging in the *Tirpitz* and the artificial smoke cover belching out from all around her, they saw above them the second strike – which had been ranged in the carriers the moment the first had taken off – now coming in from the sea.

'This second strike had, if anything, a more difficult task than the first. Admittedly the artificial smoke and the smoke from the first strike's explosions helped to guide them to the target, but by the time they got over the whole fjord was almost completely obscured with a strong box barrage above the smoke. But luckily – at the critical moment – the smoke cleared over the *Tirpitz* and with a shout of joy they roared down, carrying out similar tactics. Again there were many hits; one heavy bomb in particular was seen to crash from the upper deck and explode with a sheet of flame that reached above the topmast. By the time the last pilot dived the AA fire had ceased. And so a few hectic minutes over the target and the brilliant dash of those Fleet Air Arm crews had been the highlight in a naval operation which had left the *Tirpitz* crippled.'

Between 0515 and 1520 hours *Victorious* sent off ten Corsairs and they were followed at 0525-0535 hours by eleven Barracudas of the second wave attack force. *Furious* despatched its nine Barracudas and they joined with the others to head for the target, climbing to 15,000 feet. Hellcats and Martlets, meanwhile, made their attacks on the battleship's gun crews and flak defences ashore. The second wave attack had gradually reduced height to 10,000 feet and the dive-bombers made their final dive from 7,500 feet. They also scored hits on the *Tirpitz*, for the loss of one

Barracuda, which crashed into a hillside after releasing its bomb load. Another was shot down in flames as it pulled out of its dive. *Furious* and *Victorious* each put up two CAP Corsairs over the fleet when the second wave aircraft returned. One of the returning Corsairs missed the arrestor wire on *Victorious* and crashed on its nose about twenty-five to thirty feet beyond the second barrier. Incredibly, no one was hurt. Altogether, the Barracudas were believed to have hit the *Tirpitz* with three 1,600lb armour-piercing, eight 500lb semi-armour piercing, five 500lb MC and one 600lb anti-submarine bombs. The two wave attacks killed 122 sailors and wounded 316 more, while the FAA had lost three Barracudas and one Hellcat, whose pilot was saved. Ten direct hits on the *Tirpitz* were from heights insufficient to penetrate the decks but *Tirpitz* was put out of action for three months during which the weather and enemy interception prevented any more attacks on the battleship. On 14 May an FAA strike force of twenty-seven Barracudas and twenty-eight Corsair escorts with four Seafires and four Martlets was flown from *Victorious* and *Furious* but 10/10ths cloud at 1,000 feet in the target area forced a recall while the aircraft were en route.

Operation Mascot was mounted on 17 July using the fleet carriers *Indefatigable* (twenty-four Barracudas, twelve Fireflies and six Swordfish), *Formidable* (twenty-four Barracudas and eighteen Corsairs of 1841 Squadron, which officially formed under Lieutenant Commander R.L. Bigg-Wither DSC* RN at Brunswick in March 1944 with eighteen Corsair Is, IIs and IIIs, embarking in June 1944 with Corsair IIs on HMS *Smiter* for the UK) and *Furious* (twelve Seafires, twenty Hellcats and three Swordfish). Forty-eight fighters, including the eighteen Corsairs of 1841 Squadron from *Formidable*, escorted forty-four Barracudas to the target. Twelve of the Corsairs carried cameras to photograph the bombing attacks and the other six were to be used in flak-suppression duties, providing no enemy fighters were encountered. The attack was detected early on German radar and the defenders were able to fill Kåfjord with smoke, obscuring the *Tirpitz*. None of the Barracudas' bombs hit the battleship and a second strike was cancelled when fog threatened. One Corsair was shot down, its pilot being captured by the Germans.[4]

---

4. The senior pilot Lieutenant H. S. Mattholie RN was lost with the Wing Leader Lieutenant Commander R. S. Baker-Falkner RN of No 8 TBR Barracuda Wing.

In August the FAA carried out four more attacks on the *Tirpitz* under the code name Operation Goodwood. All three fleet carriers were involved and the Navy, worried by the possibility of heavy fighter opposition, added two escort carriers, *Trumpeter* (with eight Avengers and six Martlets) and *Nabob* (with twelve Avengers and four Martlets). *Indefatigable* carried twelve Barracudas, twelve Fireflies, twelve Hellcats and sixteen Seafires, *Formidable* twenty-four Barracudas, plus 1841 and 1842 Squadrons respectively with eighteen and twelve Corsairs, mainly for top-cover escort duty, but also for dive-bombing if needed, while *Furious* carried twelve Barracudas and twenty-four Seafires. Under the command of Lieutenant Commander Tony McDonald Garland RNVR, 1842 Squadron had officially formed at Brunswick in April with eighteen Corsair IIIs. 'We spent two months working up the squadron,' recalled one of the pilots, 21-year-old Christopher Cartledge, 'and by June we were ready to complete our preparations by a trip down to Norfolk, Virginia where we achieved the standard three successful landings on a US carrier. This new and powerful fighter aircraft was immediately distinguishable by its cranked "gull" wings. From head on, with its radial engine, it had an aggressive appearance, but was fast and nimble, its long and horizontal nose giving it an unmistakable profile. It was faster than the Hurricane on which I had trained and was very responsive and manoeuvrable, with formidable fire power. For a crisis it could go into water-injection mode for those extra knots, the water tank giving ten minutes of boost. It was particularly tricky to deck-land due to its long, straight nose, which blotted out the pilot's vision ahead when the aircraft was adopting the landing position with flaps down. The final approach had to be made while still turning in order to keep the deck and batsman in sight, straightening out at the last moment before touchdown. Of the eighteen pilots in the squadron photo at Brunswick only nine would survive the war. Total squadron losses were fourteen. Tragically, half these losses were non-operational and could to some extent have been caused by the Corsair's long, level nose, which restricted the pilot's view ahead.

'In June coming back to the UK on HMS *Rajah* we were based briefly at RNAS Eglinton (where we lost Sub-Lieutenant William Derek Wheway who dived out of cloud vertically into the ground at Doungbrewer Farm, a mile west of the airfield) before being embarked from Stretton on to HMS *Formidable* (Captain Philip Ruck-Keene RN) in the Irish Sea in August. We were on our way to the Arctic to attack the German battleship *Tirpitz*, which was sheltering in the Altenfjord. Little did we know that some of us were to be used as dive-bombers. Corsair Squadrons 1841and 1842 were on board, plus 848 Avenger Squadron. Stopping briefly at Scapa Flow, we sailed northwards carrying out flying exercises whenever weather permitted. Those who had volunteered for dive-bombing, of which I was one, were given practice on towed targets. We lost another pilot in an air collision, the younger brother of our own ship's surgeon. As we neared the Arctic, we ran into the roughest seas I had so far experienced. There was no possibility of flying. The huge seas were throwing the ship in all directions and breaking over the flight deck, drenching the lashed-down aircraft with salty water. As we drew nearer the target the weather improved, enabling four strikes [codenamed Operation Goodwood] to be carried out on 22, 23, 24 and 29 August, involving Barracudas, Hellcats, Corsairs, Avengers and Seafires. [On the 22nd conditions were still marginal and they prevented the participation of the Avengers. A strike force of thirty-one Barracudas and their twenty-four Corsair escorts was forced to turn back fifteen miles short of the Norwegian coast.] These included some daredevil attacks led by Lieutenant Commander Archibald Richardson RNZVR [a 27-year-old Hellcat pilot][5] and Major V.B.G. Cheesman, Royal Marines [a Firefly pilot], who screamed low over the *Tirpitz*, attempting to lob their bombs down the funnels.[6] We simultaneously supported diversionary attacks on

---

5. Born in Gisborne, Archibald 'Arch' Richardson like other New Zealanders, opted for service with the Fleet Air Arm during the Second World War. In 1944 he was a fighter pilot with 1840 Squadron flying Hellcats. In August he was posted with his squadron to the carrier HMS *Indefatigable* for an operation to attack the *Tirpitz*. Within the strongly escorted carrier attack force, which included HMSs *Victorious, Furious, Emperor, Searcher, Fencer* and *Pursuer* there were about sixty New Zealanders, including Barracuda aircrew of Nos. 827 and 830 Squadrons and Hellcat pilots of 1840 Squadron. During the series of strikes, which were diving massed attacks from high altitude, the *Tirpitz* was initially caught by surprise. Eight direct hits and five probable hits were scored, mostly by armour-piercing bombs, before the German smokescreen was set up. One bomb hit just forward of the bridge and penetrated two decks, but failed to explode.

6. Vernon Beauclerk George Cheesman, known throughout the Navy as 'Cheese', was born on 8 January 1917 and went to Cheltenham College. He was commissioned in the Royal Marines in January 1936 and served in the battleship *Royal Sovereign* before beginning flying training and getting his wings in 1939. In February 1944 Cheesman took command of 1770 Squadron, the first to be equipped with the new Fairey Firefly fighter-reconnaissance aircraft. The squadron embarked in the carrier *Indefatigable* in May and in July and August took part in the Fleet Air Arm strikes against the *Tirpitz*.

related coastal targets. These left a trail of damaged or destroyed tankers, airfields, radio stations and three Narvik-class destroyers near the islands and neighbouring fjords. In one attack Richardson, having run out of ammunition, lowered his arrestor hook and tore away the station's radio mast and aerials from almost zero feet.

'The Corsairs of 1841 and 1842 Squadrons from *Formidable* did not take part in Goodwood II, which was left to a handful of Hellcats and Fireflies to make attacks on the *Tirpitz*. Goodwood III went ahead on 24 August after fog had prevented a strike the previous day. Twenty-four Corsairs of 1841 and 1842 Squadrons from *Formidable* escorted thirty-three Barracudas all the way to the target. Two Hellcats and three Corsairs were shot down by anti-aircraft fire as the F4Us traversed Kåfjord to strafe the 88mm flak-gun positions and a fourth Corsair ditched close to *Formidable* on the return flight. Later, a Barracuda pilot, Sub-Lieutenant Fulton praised the Corsair pilots for their 'sheer cold-blooded gallantry'.

Goodwood IV, which went ahead on 29 August also met with little success. This time two Corsairs in *Formidable*, each carrying a 1,000lb bomb apiece and three Hellcat fighter-bombers joined twenty-six Barracudas. Fifteen more Corsairs and ten Fireflies flying as close escort were used on flak suppression as Christopher Cartledge in 1842 Squadron recalled: 'The "dive-bombers" were told that a 1,000lb bomb would be fastened under the port wing, the central fuselage position being taken up by the extra fuel tank. We were advised to trim the aircraft to give maximum lift to the port wing in the hope that this would compensate for the bomb. We would only find out when the aircraft left the flight deck on take-off! It was a fine and beautiful morning and we approached the islands and main coastline as low as possible to avoid radar detection knowing the Germans would operate a smokescreen as soon as they received warning. We climbed as we hit the coast and gained height for the dive-bombing.

'The view over the mountains and fjords on this brilliant morning was breathtaking and I could see the whole party of Avengers and the escorting Corsairs of 1841 and 1842 Squadrons. As we approached the *Tirpitz*, the white puffs of AA shells started to burst around us and I lost my No. 2, Sub Lieutenant French RNZVR. The smoke screen was already across the fjord, but leaving the huge outline of the *Tirpitz* just visible through it. I turned and, as I dived, saw one bomb explode close to the outline of the battleship. I released my bomb and pulled away hard, partially blacking out. There was a lot of flak blazing away in all directions. I turned and fired into one of the gunnery positions, then broke away at low level along the fjord. Cruising along just above the water I was admiring the scenery when bullets kicked up the water just in front of me. My Corsair responded well to some violent turns and twists and I escaped. Several pilots did not return, however, two of whom were from 1842 Squadron. Whilst waiting his turn to land, one pilot ran out of fuel and ditched alongside the fleet. He was quickly picked up from the icy water. Very few of our aircraft returned unscathed, causing the maintenance crews a busy time patching up the bullet holes. Although immediate observation was made impossible by the smoke, we learned as we withdrew southwards that the *Tirpitz*, such a menace to Atlantic shipping, was disabled but not sunk. At least it was put out of action until it could be finished off by RAF Lancasters operating from Russia.

It had been a gallant operation and had served its purpose of preventing the German battleship from sailing out of the fjord on further deadly missions. Major Cheesman was awarded a DSO[7] and, later, Lieutenant Commander Richardson a posthumous MiD for their exceptional bravery and determination in the attacks.[8] There were also twelve DSCs and a DSM awarded to other squadron commanders and flight leaders, of which I was privileged to be one, which I took as recognition of the gallantry of all the aircrew involved.'

Of the fifty-two tons of bombs dropped, several near misses and just two hits were claimed. One Corsair and a Firefly were lost over Kåfjord and later two Barracudas had to be pushed over the side of their carrier after crash landings.

In the wake of Goodwood, the results were analysed. They made for pretty grim reading. It had been the most costly Fleet Air Arm operation

---

7. 1770 Squadron's role was to escort the Barracuda bombers to the target, then fly ahead and suppress flak batteries. He worked closely with the operation's Strike Leader Lieutenant Commander R.S. Baker-Falkner RN to ensure that the first operational involvement of the Firefly was a success. They flew at sea level before climbing to 8,000 feet to cross the mountains. Cheesman led four strikes in all and successfully strafed flak batteries around *Tirpitz*, but the bombers were hampered by cloud and smokescreens covering the target. No serious damage was done to *Tirpitz* and one Firefly was lost. Cheesman was awarded the DSO for the determined way he led his squadron.

8. 'Arch' Richardson died when 'a hail of flak and shell' disintegrated his aircraft. He was considered for the posthumous award of the Victoria Cross for his part in the attack, but eventually received a Mention in Despatches.

of the war. One of the 1,000 AP bombs that had 'possibly' hit the *Tirpitz* had been dropped by one of the Corsair fighter-bombers. It was mooted that future carrier attacks on *Tirpitz* should be carried out either by 'Mosquitoes, or as many Hellcats and Corsair fighter-bombers as possible with suitable anti-flak support provided these can be adapted to carry 1,600lb bombs'. In fact, *Tirpitz* was later moved south to Tromsø for repairs and it was there, on 12 November 1944, that the battleship was capsized by 12,000lb 'Tallboy' bombs dropped by Lancasters of Nos. 9 and 617 Squadrons.

After Goodwood *Victorious* and *Formidable* headed for Scapa Flow and later they both left home waters to join the British Eastern Fleet. 'After three months delay at Gibraltar waiting for a new gear wheel to be sent out from the UK,' recalled Christopher Cartledge, 'we sailed through the Med and on to Colombo, losing three pilots in flying accidents off Alexandria, Lieutenant Dunkley RNVR, Sub Lieutenants Chipperfield and Railton RNVR. We finally arrived in Sydney early in June 1945 and from there we headed north stopping in the Philippines for provisions and briefing. We were to join the British Pacific Fleet operating on the right of the line of the US fleet. On the way we carried out regular sorties in pairs, attacking targets on the Sakishima Gunto, a chain of islands between Formosa and Okinawa. Here we lost our squadron commander Lieutenant Commander Tony Garland DSC, who did not return from one such sortie. It was a shattering blow to lose Tony, who had been such an inspiring and efficient commander since the squadron's formation. He was replaced by Lieutenant Commander Douglas Parker RN.'

Meanwhile, on 5 January 1944 *Illustrious* had reached the Straits of Gibraltar without incident but the first Corsair was lost off Alexandria one evening shortly after when the standby Corsair flight was scrambled to intercept a high-flying Ju 88 reconnaissance aircraft. The Corsair, piloted by Sub Lieutenant D. Monteith on 1833 Squadron, crashed on take off when the pilot tried to take off without locking his wings properly in the 'spread' position. When he retracted his undercarriage as he passed over the destroyer screen his wings folded and the Corsair plunged into the Mediterranean without trace. *Illustrious* continued its passage, through Port Said, the Suez Canal and Port Tewfik, into the Red Sea. The carrier refuelled at Aden and headed across the Indian Ocean to China Bay, Ceylon, where the Corsairs were moved to Trincomalee airfield and further pilot training. On 22 February *Illustrious* put to sea to intercept a possible German blockade-runner sailing between the Cocos Islands and the Sunda Strait. The Corsairs and Barracudas flew exercises for two days before bad weather halted proceedings. *Illustrious* returned to Ceylon on 3 March and, five days later, made another 'Calcutta sweep' after a Japanese cruiser force ventured into the India Ocean from Singapore and sank two ships, but again it was to no avail. Accidents continued to happen and two Corsairs and one pilot were lost during further training.

'Hans' Hanson reflected that he had always maintained that carrier life: 'infinitely happy and enjoyable though it was, did nothing to make it easier for us. As a member of a shore-based squadron, one could at least go off to the nearest town and see a film; or find a few civvies with whom to have a drink and forget "shop" for a while. One could take out one's wife or girlfriend. But in a carrier we were *there*. There was no escape from it all. Your Corsair was in the hangar, one deck up. The flight-deck, that torrid arena of the grim game of life and death, was only two short ladders beyond that. Life was lived, utterly and completely, within a space of something like 10,000 square yards. Within that area we ate, slept, drank, chatted with our friends, attended church, watched films, took our exercise and flew, landed or crashed our aircraft. Friendships became, if anything, too close and the hurt was all the more painful for that very reason.'

The Royal Navy planned to carry out strikes in Sumatra but not before *Illustrious* could be supported by the arrival of a second carrier, HMS *Victorious*. To fill the gap the USN agreed to lend one of its carriers and, on 2 April, *Illustrious* was joined by the arrival from Espíritu Santo in New Britain of the USS *Saratoga* and her air fleet, Air Group 12. Hans Hanson wrote: 'The great *Saratoga*, the last big carrier of the US Navy's old guard, made an impressive sight as she and her three attendant destroyers climbed out of the southern horizon to meet us. They had run into a typhoon whilst crossing the Great Australian Bight and had taken some punishment, but *Saratoga*'s menace and power were there for all to see. On the day following our rendezvous she proceeded to show her teeth. Her complete air group – Air Group 12, said to be one of the most efficient striking forces in their navy – disappeared over the horizon. An hour later they returned to deliver a devastating simulated attack on their own vessels. Dive-bombers (Douglas Dauntless), fighters (Grumman

Hellcats) and torpedo-bombers (Grumman Avengers), all at the very peak of efficiency, gave a display which took our breath away.'[9]

For two weeks the two carriers worked up their routine prior to putting to sea and the Corsairs continued to be upgraded. Sadly, during this time, on 14 August, Lieutenant Commander 'Dicky' Cork was killed in a flying accident at China Bay airfield. In the half-light of dawn during night flying governed by light signals in the absence of radio communications he crashed into another aircraft which was on the runway about to take off. The RAF controller had given him a red on his Aldis, since he had just given permission for a young pilot to taxi down the runway for take off. Cork accordingly tucked up his undercarriage and did another circuit. He now made another approach but he ignored another red on the Aldis and a red Very light. Her pressed on with his approach and landed on top of the other Corsair who, by this time, had reached the middle of the runway. Both men were burnt beyond recognition. Hans Hanson was a long time getting over that one: 'Silently, I swore like a trooper to think that someone like Dicky, who had already gone through hell and high water, should throw his life away so contemptuously. He deserved a better fate. Sad, yes, but they would both have been proud and happy to see the full *Saratoga* air group lined up with our own as a guard of honour as we slow-marched them to their final landing.'

Cork is buried at Trincomalee War Cemetery. His final score was nine destroyed, two shared, one probable, four damaged and seven destroyed on the ground. He was fifth on the table of Royal Navy Second World War aces.

During their time in Ceylon, the Corsair Is were exchanged for the improved Corsair II version with the water-injected engine and improved cockpit hood and undercarriage. The Corsair IIs were shipped by sea in crates from the USA to Cochin, south-west India, and re-assembled at the Royal Naval Air Repair Yard at Coimbatore where they were test flown before being issued to the carrier squadrons. The Corsair Is were flown to Coimbatore and the pilots returned to Ceylon, flying back in the Corsair IIs. By mid-April all was ready for Cockpit, which would see the first Corsair fleet action of the war.

---

9 *Carrier Pilot: An Unforgettable True Story of Wartime Flying* by Norman Hanson, by kind permission of Patrick Stephens (PSL) 1979.

On 16 April the Eastern Fleet put to sea in two groups for an attack on Sabang, a small island off the north-east tip of Sumatra. The harbour was used by shipping servicing the Japanese armies in Burma and this, together with a large airfield at the back of the town, was a target worthy of the fleet's attention. Task Force 69 was composed of the battleships *Queen Elizabeth*, *Valiant* and *Richelieu* and the cruisers *Newcastle*, *Nigeria*, *Ceylon*, *Gambia* and *Tromp*, with nine escorting destroyers. Task Force 70 comprised the carriers *Illustrious* and *Saratoga* accompanied by the cruiser *London*, six destroyers and an air-sea rescue submarine. Before dawn on 19 April the carriers arrived at their flying-off position 100 miles south-west of Sabang Island. At 0650 hours, first light, thirteen Corsairs of 1830 and 1833 Squadrons and seventeen Barracudas of Nos. 810 and 847 Squadrons from *Illustrious* and fifty-three SBD Dauntless, Hellcats and Avengers from *Saratoga* took off and headed for Sabang Harbour. Hans Hanson's first sight of enemy territory was of, 'a luscious green island, basking in the early morning sunshine. It was all so very beautiful that when red flashes burst from the deep, verdant green, I felt considerably put out. "Good God! It's enemy fire!" Why I was surprised I can't imagine. I can only suppose that I was appalled that some vandal should set fire to Paradise. We dived down ahead of the Barracudas, firing enthusiastically at warehouses and quays and suddenly found ourselves at the far end of the harbour, unscathed. We were still green and hadn't yet learned about targets of opportunity. So we milled around like a lot of schoolgirls and left it to the Barracudas, who made a splendid attack on the harbour and oil installations. The Corsair boys returned to China Bay with a feeling of anti-climax. We had been to the enemy and had found no opportunity to cover ourselves with glory. But we would learn.'[10]

The strafing and dive-bombing attacks on the harbour facilities, radar stations and military installations were, however, quite impressive. In a preemptive strike on the airfield, the Corsairs and Hellcats destroyed twenty-four Japanese aircraft on the ground. A considerable amount of surprise had been achieved, the port was heavily damaged, two small merchant ships were destroyed and the oil storage tanks destroyed. None of the Corsairs was lost but one Hellcat failed to return, the pilot being picked

---

10. *Carrier Pilot: An Unforgettable True Story of Wartime Flying* by Norman Hanson, by kind permission of Patrick Stephens (PSL) 1979.

up by a rescue submarine. During recovery aboard *Illustrious* four of 1833 Squadron's Corsair IIs, which were flying CAP, intercepted a Mitsubishi Ki-21 Sally reconnaissance bomber and shot it down in flames into the sea.

On return to Ceylon, *Saratoga* was ordered back to America for re-fitting and it was decided that en route home the American carrier would take part in Operation Transcom, a joint RN-USN strike against the big aviation fuel dump at Sourabaya, Java. On 15 May the two task forces, 65 and 66, comprising the two carriers, three battleships, five cruisers and fourteen destroyers, departed Ceylon and headed for Exmouth Bay, Northern Australia, before heading north for Java. Onboard *Illustrious* longer-ranging Avengers replaced the Barracudas of Nos. 810 and 847 Squadrons because the strike aircraft would be required to fly across the breadth of Java. The Corsairs and Hellcats would fly top cover for the torpedo- and dive-bombers and fly on in two waves to the north to make strafing attacks on Sourabaya town and industrial areas, the harbour and the Wonokromo oil refinery and the Bratt engineering works south of the city. 'We sailed with our full fleet and *Saratoga* and her destroyers,' wrote Hans Hanson. 'We edged our way slowly into Exmouth Gulf, on the north-western corner of Australia. A more desolate place cannot be imagined. This great bay, surrounded only by sand, scrub and pitifully stunted trees, shimmered in a suffocating heat. The air was lifeless, as indeed was everything else. The only signs of activity were aboard the oil-tankers, preparing to refuel us. We sailed again the same evening, heading north and going fast. We were aiming for Java.

'At 0705 next morning we took off and thanks to assiduous practice over the past few weeks, we joined up in quick time – from *Saratoga*, twenty-four Hellcats, twelve Avengers and eighteen Dauntlesses; from *Illustrious*, sixteen Avengers and sixteen Corsairs. We had two accidents. One of the Avengers literally fell over the round-down into the sea and another ditched soon afterwards through total loss of power. All six crewmen were saved.

'This time we knew what we were about. We flew seventy miles to the coast and quickly crossed the island to attack Sourabaya on the north coast. Our targets were the Wonokromo oil refinery and the Bratt engineering works, both to the south of the city, and the big harbour. All went well. I had two flights to escort our Avengers and *Saratoga*'s Dauntless dive-bombers attacking both the southern targets and we successfully saturated the anti-aircraft defences without suffering any losses. Hathorn, the Dauntless squadron CO, made a classic attack on the oil refinery which severely damaged the three retorts. Our new Avenger bombers attacked the engineering works with bombs especially long-fused for low-level work, which they delivered with letter-box precision. [Surprise was achieved and fighter attacks on Malang airfield succeeded in destroying about a dozen enemy aircraft and airfield buildings, but the oil refinery was only slightly damaged and only one small ship was sunk.] One or two aircraft which sought to interfere – though not in our part of the sky – were readily shot down. Our only casualty was one of *Saratoga's* Avengers. Her squadron was busily engaged in torpedoing ships in the harbour when Rowbottom, their CO, was badly hit. With commendable airmanship he managed to coax his dying Avenger out into the bay, where he finally ditched. Fortunately he and his crewmen, although captured, survived the war. The hearts of my own flight fluttered briefly but excitingly when, in the middle of shooting up a coaster heading up the bay towards Sourabaya we found ourselves surrounded by crossfire from a flight of Hellcats, hell-bent on doing the same thing. The moment passed.

'On the way home I took up my position as stern cover. My first realisation that the American strike leader was leading us through the wrong pass in the mountains came when I saw a flight of Hellcats diving below us, obviously heading at a rate of knots for the surface of Java. There, far beneath us, was a great airfield with a welcoming spread of parked aircraft. I thought quickly. All the fighters had used a lot of ammunition, and four aircraft wouldn't be carrying sufficient to deal with the great array of tempting targets below us. If I waited for permission to attack the element of surprise would be gone. I prayed hard and took my flight down in a great sweeping dive to the airfield. This was Malang, an important Japanese Army Air Corps base and we had them on toast.

'I was breaking the rules. My job was to provide stern escort for the bomber force and now I was gallivanting on a private jolly (for which I was later censured and rightly so – by Captain Cunliffe). Nevertheless, here I was; and for the first time I realised the power and majesty of the Corsair. At over 300 knots, with my three boys well spaced out in line abreast, my aircraft slid into the airfield.

'Closing quickly into firing range, my first impression was one of bodies rushing like ants all over the field. Some were heading for AA emplacements, others dashing for the hangars, presumably to taxi out aircraft from the fires which the Hellcats had already started. As I flattened out at about 30 feet, heading for a row of parked fighters, my first burst blew to hell a machine into which a pilot was climbing. Tracer ricochets were flying in all directions in front of me and my six guns were thudding away with a healthy, dull thump, a bass *Te Deum* to the painstaking work put in by my armourer. I flashed across the airfield boundary, went into a screaming low turn, pulling streamers from my wingtips. Then I was firing again, the .5-inch shells banging into a group of three two-engined aircraft. There seemed to be no gunfire from the field. Fires were raging all over – hangars, aircraft and living quarters. We made another run at a small group of fighters and then there was nothing left to hit. We climbed away, joining into formation again, grinning hugely at one another through the Perspex of our cockpit hoods.

'Johnny Baker had a yearning to blow up a railway locomotive and I agreed to loiter over Malang town while he and his wingman went down to the station, probably to consult the timetables to see what was due to arrive. Whilst Brynildsen and I circled lazily over the town at about 8,000 feet, I became intrigued by a large black building in the town centre. What on earth was it? One sure way to find out. Telling Neil to stay put and to cover me, I dropped my port wing and fell quickly to around 2,000 feet, then headed down, straight for the mystery building and delivered a two-second burst through the roof. The result couldn't have been more dramatic. Doors on all sides burst open to disgorge hordes of people into the streets, milling back and forth like a disturbed nest of ants. Then I got it. I had frightened the living daylights out of a cinema show – or a cockfight, to which I believe the Javanese are more than partial. For a moment I felt myself to be the biggest heel of all time. Then I thought again and decided they should have more to think about at ten in the morning!'[11]

Next day *Saratoga* bade farewell and headed for Pearl Harbor while *Illustrious* and the rest of the task force returned to Ceylon for replenishment.

---

11. *Carrier Pilot: An Unforgettable True Story of Wartime Flying* by Norman Hanson, by kind permission of Patrick Stephens (PSL) 1979.

An opportunity to put *Illustrious'* air wing to the test once again arose during 10/13 June. The US Navy had requested a diversionary operation to help mask the opening stages of the attack on Saipan in the Marianas. This diversion would be labelled Operation Councillor. It would involve *Illustrious* and the escort carrier HMS *Atheling*. *Atheling* had been in the Indian Ocean as a trade-protection carrier since May. She carried ten Seafire F.IIIs of 889 Squadron and ten Wildcat Vs of 890 Squadron. In this mission, *Atheling's* role was secondary – though necessary. With her full wing in the air, a serious risk was posed during *Illustrious'* recovery operations. A series of severe deck crashes could result in most of her aircraft running out of fuel and being forced to ditch. The escort carrier was therefore present to operate as a 'spare deck', as well as a source of supporting CAP. The submarine HMS *Surf* took up position 300 miles west of Sabang, transmitting false signals designed to give the impression that an RN carrier group was about to launch an attack. *Illustrious* deployed CAP fighters and air patrols, watching her radar for any Japanese response. She was acting as bait. No strike was planned. No Japanese response emerged. Nevertheless, the exercise provided a valuable lesson: at 12 knots slower than a fleet carrier, combined operations with escort carriers had proven not to be viable for fleet-scale operations.

After Operation Councillor, *Illustrious* underwent an air-group shake-up and a third Corsair squadron was embarked to improve fleet defence. To make room for the extra fighters, her two Barracuda squadrons were cut back: 1830 Squadron, fourteen Corsair IIs; 1833 Squadron, fourteen Corsair IIs; 1837 Squadron, fourteen Corsair IIs; 810 Squadron, nine Barracuda IIs; 847 Squadron, six Barracuda IIs. With a total of fifty-seven aircraft aboard, *Illustrious* was operating at the edge of her capacity. Not only was there little space left in her hangars and on deck, there was next to nowhere for the extra crews and support personnel to sling their hammocks.

Illustrious' next action was Operation Pedal, 19-21 June, when her carrier group sailed for the Andaman Islands in the Bay of Bengal to attack the harbour and airfield at Port Blair. There was no American presence but the force comprised the cruisers *Renown, Richelieu, Ceylon, Nigeria, Gambia, Phoebe* and seven destroyers. At dawn on 21 June under a cloud cover of 1,500 feet, this force took up position about ninety-five miles west of Port Blair. *Illustrious*, without the 'spare deck' of HMS *Atheling*, launched a strike of fifteen Barracudas backed up by sixteen Corsairs. A CAP of eight Corsairs was established above the task force itself. The Barracudas were tasked with bombing harbour facilities. Half of the Corsairs were to strafe shipping, a seaplane base, a sawmill and a headquarters building. The other half were sent to two nearby airfields. The FAA aircraft met stiff anti-aircraft fire as they dived through scattered rainstorms over their targets. One Barracuda was shot down over Port Blair while a damaged Corsair managed to struggle back over the coast for its pilot to be rescued from the water. Four further damaged aircraft limped their way home towards *Illustrious*. At the height of the operation *Illustrious* had fifty-three of her fifty-seven aircraft airborne. It took an hour to recover all aircraft successfully. The mission was deemed a moderate success: two Barracudas had to return with engine failure before dropping their bombs. But there was an unacceptably high bomb arming and release failure rate among the Barracudas over target. No Japanese fighter opposition was encountered though the Corsairs claimed ten Japanese aircraft destroyed on the airfield and many buildings wrecked while a handful of small coastal vessels were also sunk. Overall, the operation, which was hampered by bad weather, was not a success. Shortly after Task Force 60 returned to Ceylon, *Victorious* and *Indomitable* pulled into Colombo to join *Illustrious* in the British Eastern Fleet.

After three weeks of lectures and demonstrations from *Illustrious'* pilots and flight crew, *Victorious* would be put to the test. She sailed with *Illustrious* as part of Task Force 62 in Operation Crimson to cover a bombardment of Sabang scheduled for 22 to 27 July by the heavy units of the Eastern Fleet.[12] *Victorious* was only carrying fighters: three Corsair squadrons (1834, 1836 and 1838), totalling just thirty-nine aircraft. The two fleet carriers were to provide CAP for themselves and the warships. *Indomitable* was not ready. Most of *Illustrious'* Barracudas were replaced by additional Corsairs of 1837 Squadron to help provide full defensive cover for the Barracuda dive-bombers to be used in the attack on the oil refinery. Two from *Illustrious* were allocated a radar/radio station.

---

12. The force comprised the battleships *Queen Elizabeth, Valiant, Richelieu* and the battlecruiser *Renown*; cruisers *Nigeria, Kenya, Gambia, Ceylon, Cumberland, Phoebe, Tromp*; destroyers *Relentless, Rotherham, Racehorse, Raider, Roebuck, Rocket, Rapid, Quilliam, Quality* and *Quickmatch* and ASR submarines *Templar* and *Tantalus*.

On 25 July the force arrived twelve miles off Sabang. The carriers took up position thirty-five miles north of Sabang before dawn at 0530. The attack was preceded by a terrific naval bombardment from the fleet of four battleships, five cruisers and five destroyers. To make recognition easier each battleship used a different coloured shell burst. *Illustrious* launched eighteen Corsairs, while *Victorious* sent up sixteen. Eight from each carrier were tasked with attacking the airfields of Sabang, Lho Nga and Kotaraji. Two Corsairs were allocated to each battleship to spot for the guns, reporting the accuracy of the fall of shot by R/T. The remainder were to form a CAP over the bombardment ships. The battleships began to move up to the coast at 0640. However, the carrier operations were not unfolding according to plan. The launch had been intended for thirty-three minutes before sunrise. But deck handlers did not have enough light or suitable equipment to carry out their duties in the dark. The launch, delayed by five minutes, was a fumbled affair in the gloom. Then the aircraft of the multi-carrier strike force simply took too long to form up, further delaying the operation; 1838 squadron's Corsairs went off course and stumbled about in the darkness attempting to locate its target through old maps.

Over 1,300 shells ranging from 4-inch to 15-inch were fired at Sabang, followed by a torpedo and shellfire attack on the harbour itself by four of the ships. Hans Hanson wrote: 'Fifteen-inch shells are the very devil for demolition work. The big warehouses along the sides of the quays were systematically pounded to rubble and I remember quite vividly seeing one actually burst. A tremor blurred the quayside; then a warehouse literally took off and rose towards us in one piece. At some height which it was impossible to judge the building then disintegrated and fell to the ground in a monstrous cloud of dust and smoke.

'The flak gunners were wide awake by now and were becoming more menacing and much too accurate. After a minute or two's search I found at least one battery which was giving the spotters a few headaches. Three guns were dug in on the crest of a hill on the southern end of the airfield and we did a quick flash over the position to see how the land lay. Back at 8,000 feet I summoned another flight and told them to attack low and fast from the southern side. I allowed a few seconds for the low-flying flight to get in their burst of fire, in the hope of unsettling the enemy by strafing him from an unexpected quarter; and then we were roaring downhill, frontally attacking the position. Once you are committed, nothing seems to matter. We saw the great muzzle flash as one of the guns was fired. I remember seeing the upturned faces of the gunners as they looked for a hit. Where the hell the shell ended up I don't know. We were past the point of no return and all that seemed to matter was that we should destroy them. And then we were within range. The Corsair shuddered as the six guns hammered away with their deep thud. Chunks flew off the gun mountings and bodies were hurled to the back of the gun emplacements. Then we were flattening out, our wingtips throwing off great streamers of vapour as we flashed over the gun position at 30 or 40 feet and out to sea.

'We had carried out our mission but as the big ships were still busy it seemed a pity to go back. I looked around for something else to hit and suddenly remembered a fat merchantman of two to three thousand tons apparently anchored in the middle of the harbour. It seemed to have escaped damage from the bombardment. We reformed quickly and dived down again in line astern, firing with armour-piercing bullets at the ship's water-line. We had long been assured that a close pattern of .5-inch ammunition could tear up the deck of a destroyer, so a cargo ship's hull should be vulnerable enough. Our attack must have perforated her, at least, for she lost no time in getting under way and heading for a quay – to avoid foundering, I hoped.

'And then it was time to go. The bombardment had lasted twenty minutes. Even the destroyers had enjoyed a field day, for some of them had come up to the harbour entrance to discharge their torpedoes at the wharves and jetties. This time the Japs were well and truly nettled.'[13]

Ten Japanese aircraft, which attempted to attack the fleet, were intercepted by combat air patrols, which destroyed seven of their number. Sub-Lieutenant Ben Heffer on 1837 Squadron recalled, 'was directed towards the enemy at 1645 hrs and sighted five aircraft. There was a large storm astern the fleet, but *Victorious* managed to vector me onto the enemy. A Japanese aircraft dived past me and I followed him down, hitting him on the port quarter with a long burst of fire. He was weaving, but flames were coming from his port wing. He disappeared into cloud

---

13. *Carrier Pilot: An Unforgettable True Story of Wartime Flying* by Norman Hanson, by kind permission of Patrick Stephens (PSL) 1979.

and, following him, I came out dead on his tail at a range of about 100 yards. After another long burst the aircraft went up in a sheet of flame.

'It was still dark as the Ramrod squadrons strafed the airfields. Anti-aircraft fire was intense and targets of opportunity almost invisible in the deep pre-dawn shadows. Two small ships were sunk, oil facilities were set alight and harbour infrastructure destroyed. But Japanese shore-battery fire was accurate: only *Quickmatch* would not be hit. Damage, fortunately, was slight. The fleet withdrew at 0930. One damaged Corsair limped over the coast and out to sea where the pilot was rescued. Two Japanese reconnaissance aircraft then closed on the task force in an effort to ascertain its strength. Both were shot down by the CAP. As the sun dipped towards the horizon, the fleet's radar detected a flight of what were judged to be ten A6M Zeros (though they were almost certainly Ki-43s) at a range of fifty miles. A force of thirteen Corsairs was sent against them, claiming four kills (some accounts say two kills, two damaged). *Illustrious'* Corsairs also claimed a Ki-21 Sally. These were the first kills by the Corsair while operating from an aircraft carrier. SEAC C-in-C, Lord Louis Mountbatten signalled 'The results will hearten all forces in South-East Asia'.

On 30 July *Illustrious* departed China Bay for the Simonstown dockyard at Durban, South Africa, for a boiler refit, arriving on 9 August. *Indomitable* had arrived in the Indian Ocean shortly before the departure of *Illustrious* for South Africa. During the last week of August Corsairs, Hellcats and Barracudas from *Indomitable* and *Victorious* took part in strikes against the port of Emmahaven and the cement works at Indaroeng on Sumatra. All the strike and fighter escorts returned without loss, the Corsairs and Hellcats encountering no fighter opposition. On 24 August Ronald Cuthbert Hay first led the 47th NFW into action when *Victorious* and *Indomitable* struck targets at Padang, Sumatra, in Operation Banquet. Hay was born on 4 October 1916 in Perth, Scotland, one of five children. He was educated at Ampleforth College in Yorkshire. Too old for a cadetship in the Royal Navy, Hay volunteered for the Royal Marines in 1935 and served a year at sea in the cruiser HMS *Devonshire*. In 1938 he volunteered for flying duties with the Fleet Air Arm and was posted to the recently reformed 801 Naval Air Squadron, assigned to the fleet carrier HMS *Ark Royal* and equipped with the two-seater Blackburn Skua and Blackburn Roc fighter aircraft. His first victory during operations over Norway was on 27 April 1940, when he shot down a Heinkel He 111 bomber. During the Battle of Britain, Hay flew Fairey Fulmars with 808 Squadron. He then joined the carrier *Ark Royal* and saw action on the Malta convoys and the attack on the German battleship *Bismarck*. After surviving the sinking of *Ark Royal* in November 1941, he was awarded a DSC for his actions in the Mediterranean. A spell ashore as a flying instructor was followed by command of 809 Squadron in the carrier *Victorious* during the Torch landings in North Africa. Hay then taught carrier air group tactics before flying out to Ceylon as an acting major. Promoted to acting captain in May 1942, he was given command of 809 Naval Air Squadron, which was assigned to the fleet carrier HMS *Victorious*. Hay's time in command of 809 Squadron did not last long as he was soon posted to Ceylon as an acting major in April 1943.

In the run-up to Banquet, both HMSs *Illustrious* and *Victorious* surrendered their third Corsair squadron. *Victorious* would now bring aboard a TBR squadron to form a balanced strike group of twenty-eight Corsairs in 1834 and 1836 Squadrons and twenty-one Barracudas. *Illustrious*, meanwhile, headed south-west for a long-overdue refit at Durban. It was the first attention she would receive for more than a year. Top of the priority list was to strip down and examine her centreline shaft. She would be off the front line until mid-October. The fleet left Trincomalee on 18 August. On 22 August the force refuelled from the Royal Fleet Auxiliary *Easedale*. By 0550 on 24 August the fleet was at its launch position. The sky was clear. The seas were slight. The wind was just six knots. The carriers had to race through the waters at 27 knots to generate enough wind-over deck to get their aircraft airborne. Each carrier launched ten Barracudas, each carrying 500lb bombs. Escorting this strike force were nineteen Corsairs from *Victorious*. A little more than an hour later, at 0710, a second strike wave was launched. This time it was made up of nine Barracudas from *Indomitable* and three from *Victorious*. The escort was twelve Corsairs, again from *Victorious*.

The strikes on Padang were considered a success. After the attack, the fighters roamed the area looking for the most impressive buildings in the area. 'These,' recorded Ronnie Hay, 'were then machine gunned in the hope that the Japanese overlords were in residence.' One Corsair was lost to light anti-aircraft fire. Hay expressed dissatisfaction in his report to *Victorious*' CO, Captain Michael Denny: 'The almost complete lack of opposition made the raid rather a "picnic" and so the soundness of the air organisation used was not verified. I consider this most important since not only has nothing been learnt as a result of this operation but the younger pilots may develop a casual attitude to flying over this part of Japanese occupied territory which will certainly stand them in no stead when they are called upon to perform more hazardous operations. In this connection it is hoped that future operations will be against increasingly more important objectives which, because they may be more hotly defended, will train the younger and more inexperienced pilots, who are greatly in the majority, the art of waging war successfully under battle conditions.'

Major Ronnie Hay now took over command of the 47th Naval Fighter Wing, which was composed of two squadrons of F4U Corsairs aboard HMS *Victorious*. The Eastern Fleet was now a force to be reckoned with, comprising as it did, two carriers, two to three battleships, a battlecruiser, eleven cruisers and thirty-two destroyers. From 16 to 20 September 1944 the two carriers, supported by ten other ships of the Eastern Fleet, carried out Operation Light, a strike on the railway junction at Sigli in northern Sumatra. The fleet arrived off Sumatra to find what some called the 'Elephant Monsoon' sitting over the top of the whole area; in other words thick cloud at low level and pouring, incessant rain with little wind. Results overall were poor, the main reason being the lack of target intelligence available to the attacking aircraft.

Victorious only carried nineteen Corsairs in 1834 Squadron and eighteen Corsairs in 1836 Squadron for this strike for a total of thirty-seven aircraft. Light A was to take place on 17 September and involve a fighter sweep over Japanese airfields in the area of Medan and Belawan Deli, as well as a photographic survey of Aru Bay. Much of this had to be abandoned, however, because the weather made it untenable, with heavy drenching rain. Light B, on 18 September, was an air strike on railway facilities at Sigli, Sumatra. It was a shambles. Both carriers turned into the 10-knot wind at 0600. Without *Illustrious'* experience, the *Indomitable* and *Victorious* continued to struggle. Form-up took forty minutes. Each carrier launched ten Barracudas. Escort was provided by eight Hellcats and sixteen Corsairs. Much of the delay was caused by *Indomitable* realising, at the last minute, that the wind was insufficient to allow all her strike aircraft to be launched in the one range. Some had to be hastily stowed back below in order to provide sufficient deck space for take off. One of *Indomitable*'s Barracudas ditched on take off. Three Corsairs quickly returned to *Victorious*. All had been part of the deck park and had had their engines drenched in the previous day's rains. *Indomitable*'s deck-park aircraft also suffered – with several becoming unserviceable as they were readied for launch. Bad weather lingered over the target. But anti-aircraft fire was light and no Japanese aircraft encountered. The Barracudas were hasty in their attack runs, hitting the main targets but missing several of the secondary objectives. The top-cover Corsairs had gone astray, abandoning their escort position to strafe ground targets. All the while several pilots had accidentally left their radio transmitters turned on, effectively jamming all communications with flight leaders and the carriers. Once again the fuel reserves of the Barracuda strike aircraft proved to be cause for concern. *Illustrious* and *Indomitable* let themselves get out of position during landing operations, causing the approach circuits for the carriers to overlap dangerously. This caused further delays, which the Barracuda could not afford. As a result, Rear Admiral Moody reported back to London that the torpedo-dive-bomber simply did not have a sufficient strike radius for operations in the Pacific. *Victorious* launched her afternoon CAP of Corsairs without long-range fuel tanks. When HMS *Howe*'s radar lit up with aircraft moving across the islands, though not towards the fleet, the fighters were simply not able to take advantage of the rare opportunity. Admirals Fraser and Moody were not impressed. As the fleet travelled home, they called together their staffs and instigated an intense training programme to begin the moment they returned to Trincomalee. FAA commanders, however, argued that intelligence about the targets had been virtually non-existent and their maps had been out of date. This had added considerably to the difficulty the pilots faced. Their objections were duly noted.

At the request of the US Navy, Eastern Fleet's next task was to provide diversionary support against the Nicobar Islands in the Bay of Bengal preparatory to the American invasion of Leyte Gulf in the Philippines. (The huge US fleet approached Leyte on 19 October for the landings and the landings went ahead during 20-26 October.) In an attempt to divert some of the Japanese forces away from the Leyte force and make the enemy believe that an invasion of the Nicobars was imminent, the Eastern Fleet carried out a three-day air assault, beginning on 17 October, on the Japanese defenders on Car Nicobar. Task Force 63 comprised the battlecruiser *Renown*, cruisers, *London, Cumberland* and *Suffolk*, destroyers *Relentless, Raider, Norman, Quilliam, Queenborough, Quiberon, Van Galen, Whelp, Wakeful, Wessex* and *Wager*. Both carriers retained their established air groups and operated in a sub-group with the anti-aircraft cruiser HMS *Phoebe* with the destroyers *Whelp, Wakeful, Wessex* and *Wager*.

'Operation Millet, as it was codenamed, was only partially successful, although the British fighters and dive-bombers were met in some strength. On 19 October Corsair IIs of 1834 Squadron from *Victorious* destroyed four Nakajima Ki.43 Oscars and two more were shot down by Hellcats. An attack by twelve Japanese torpedo-bombers on the fleet resulted in the loss of seven being shot down. On the British side, only two aircraft, a Barracuda and a Hellcat, were lost.'

'*Indomitable* launched ten Barracudas covered by eight Hellcats to hit Nancowry harbour on 17 October. Eight Corsairs from *Victorious* provided top cover. Another nineteen Corsairs flew off *Victorious* to suppress activity on nearby airfields and attack targets of opportunity. The Japanese were surprised, harbour facilities were demolished and a merchant vessel in the harbour sunk. Two Corsairs were shot down and another three damaged during their strafing run, made after the main attack had alerted defences. One of *Indomitable*'s Hellcats crashed on landing, killing its pilot. Operation Millet would prove to be the Barracuda's last active deployment from RN fleet carriers for the war. Following this strike, the longer-ranging Grumman Avengers permanently replaced the Barracudas.'

Task Force 63's heavy warships bombarded Car Nicobar, with Hellcats from *Indomitable* spotting. Unusually, the British task force would linger in the area. This was largely due to the bad weather; plans to strike Sabang were non-viable. However, the big guns of the task force would again bombard Car Nicobar targets during the morning of the 19th. As the fleet prepared to withdraw on the 19th, a Japanese twin-engined reconnaissance aircraft flew high over the bombardment force at 0840 without being intercepted. Two of *Indomitable*'s Hellcats, on spotting duty, attempted to climb, but were unable to close. *Victorious'* Corsairs finally managed to engage when the hostile force was just twelve miles north-east of the carrier formation. It was a formation of Ki 43 Oscar fighters from the 1st Reserve Flying Unit, nine flying at 7,000 feet with another three at 16,000 feet as top cover. The dogfight whirled over the fleet from 0950 to 1030. The bombardment force CAP Hellcats scrambled to join in. Seven Oscars were claimed to be shot down by the FAA. Japanese records reveal four to have been shot down and two force-landed and credit two of these pilots as diving their burning aircraft into British ships, which then sank. No such event occurred. However, two Corsairs of 1834 Squadron were lost by the FAA in this engagement, as was a Hellcat of 1844 Squadron.

Despite the losses, Major 'Ronnie' Hay aboard *Victorious* was impressed with the performance of the Corsair. He would write after Millet: 'The Corsair was just the right aircraft for that war. It was certainly better than anything we had and an improvement of the Hellcat. It was more robust and faster and although the Japanese could out-turn us in combat, we could out-climb, out-dive and out-gun him. By far the most healthy improvement was its endurance, as with about five hours' worth of fuel in your tanks you didn't have the agony of wondering whether or not you would make it back to the carrier.'

Hay described a fighter sweep serial over Ceylon on 10 November: 'A good rendezvous was effected over Puttalam with twelve Hellcats from *Indomitable* covered by six Corsairs from 47 Wing and a top cover consisting twelve Corsairs 1834 Squadron and twelve Corsairs 1836 Squadron. The sweep was made seawards over the Colombo-Katukurunda area and was intercepted by twelve Spitfires. The exercise was considered a failure owing to lack of cohesion between the two squadrons. The Spitfires waded into the bottom squadron and the battle was nearly over before the two fighter cover squadrons intervened. The top squadron never made the area at all and finished up at Nagombo eighteen miles north, while the battle was on at Colombo. However another valuable lesson was learned: i.e. it is no good having large height intervals if you are thereby going to lose contact with the force you are supposed to cover.'

Meanwhile, after its refitting in South Africa, *Illustrious* had sailed to Ceylon, arriving on 1 November, to join *Indomitable, Victorious* and the other ships of the British Fleet. In December the four fleet carriers, *Victorious, Illustrious, Indomitable* and *Indefatigable*, formed the First Aircraft Carrier Squadron, under Rear Admiral Sir Philip Vian as Flag Officer Commanding. Operation Outflank, the first operation under Vian's command, against the oil refinery at Pangkalan Brandan in north-eastern

Sumatra, about eight miles inland from the Malacca Straits, was planned for 20 December. Vian decided to use strike aircraft from the *Indomitable* and *Victorious*, which between them put up sixteen Hellcats, fourteen Corsairs and four Corsair fighter-bombers each carrying two 500lb bombs, and twenty-eight Avengers. Bad weather prevented the primary strike against Pangkalan Brandan, so the secondary target, Belawan Deli near Medan, an oil outlet port, was attacked instead. The Corsairs and Hellcats strafed an airfield at Medan and destroyed several enemy aircraft on the ground, but the port was obscured by low cloud and heavy rain squalls and the strike was largely ineffective. On the withdrawal flight to the north of Sumatra, the Corsairs and Hellcats attacked the airfields in the Sabang area, destroying more enemy aircraft on the ground.

At the end of November, the British Eastern Fleet was re-organised into the British East Indies Fleet and the British Pacific Fleet, the bigger and more powerful of the two, which included the carriers *Illustrious*, *Indomitable* and *Victorious*. On 17 December the First Aircraft Carrier Squadron, comprising *Indomitable* and *Victorious*, together with four cruisers and seven destroyers, mounted Operation Robson, the second strike on Belawan Deli. During Christmas 1944 the First Aircraft Carrier Squadron was further strengthened by the arrival in Ceylon, of *Indefatigable*, giving the British Pacific Fleet four carriers in all. *Indefatigable*, *Indomitable* and *Victorious* now provided the aircraft for Operation Lentil, a second attempt at bombing Pangkalan Brandan and the largest raid yet carried out in the theatre, involving ninety-two aircraft. Task Force 63 sailed from China Bay leaving *Illustrious* behind and, on 4 January 1945, the strike went ahead by *Indefatigable*'s Fairey Firefly fighter-bombers protected by Corsairs and Hellcats, which also made a sweep of the Japanese-held airfields before the bombing strike went in. The strike eventually formed up and headed to the target in extreme visibility and scattered clouds. They crossed the coast at 3,000 feet and after climbing over the mountainous terrain, approached the target at 11,000 feet. The Fireflies carried out a rocket attack to suppress flak, followed by the Avengers, whose attack 'was concentrated and the majority of the bombs were seen to fall on their targets'. As this transpired, Corsairs, including 1834's, attacked a cluster of airfields thirty miles to the south. Nonetheless, enemy fighters got airborne and began to wade in to the attack just as the Avengers finished their bomb runs.

Fleet Air Arm Corsair JT108 '7C' and '7A' of 1834 Squadron in 1943.

Lieutenant Commander Richard John 'Dicky' Cork DSO DSC (right) who on 14 August 1944 was killed in a flying accident at China Bay airfield.

Norman 'Hans' Hanson, No.1833 Squadron FAA Corsair pilot.

Lieutenant Commander Joseph C. 'Jumping Joe' Clifton and pilots of VF-12 'Peg Legs' in front of F4U-1 in 1943. In October 1942 VF-12, commanded by Clifton had became the first USN Corsair squadron to be formed but after navalised Corsairs had been declared unserviceable for use aboard carriers, VF-12 had received F6F Hellcats instead. In 1944 Clifton was named Commander of Air Group 12, which combined air groups from HMS *Illustrious* and USS *Saratoga*.

Damage to HMS *Formidable* caused by a Kamikaze that hit the carrier at the base of her island in the Battle of Sakishima on 4 May 1945.

Lieutenant Hampton Gray RCNVR who was killed leading four Corsair fighter-bombers from HMS *Formidable* in an attack on enemy shipping in Onagawa Harbour on 9 August 1945, the day on which an atomic bomb was dropped on Nagasaki. He was awarded a posthumous Victoria Cross, only the second such award made to an FAA airman in WW2.

Fires rage inside Soengi Gerong refinery after the Palembang 'Meridian II' strike in January 1945.

Crowds inspect the line up of 'R' Division planes to be entered in the Bendix Trophy race on 30 August 1946 at Metropolitan Airport, Van Nuys, California to Municipal Airport at Cleveland, Ohio. In the foreground is Joe DeBona's all-white Goodyear FG-1D Race #90 NX63382 'Joe'. The winning aircraft was the P-51C '46' flown by Paul Mantz with a top speed of 435.50 mph in a time of 4:43:14. DeBona's Corsair, flown by Thomas Call finished 15th. (*Acme Telephoto*)

1947 Bendix racer Goodyear F2G-1 NX5590N #94 Super Corsair.

Cook Cleland receives the 1949 Thompson Trophy from Fred Crawford.

Jesse Leroy Brown, born 13 October 1926 in Hattiesburg, Mississippi was the first Black-American commissioned Navy pilot.

Jesse Brown and fellow pilots walking the deck on the USS *Leyte*.

Thomas Jerome Hudner Jr. on VF-32 on the *Leyte* who received the Medal of Honor for his actions in trying to save the life of his wingman, Ensign Jesse L. Brown on 4 December 1950. These two pilots were among a group of pilots on patrol near the Chosin Reservoir when Brown's Corsair was struck by ground fire from Chinese troops and crashed. In an attempt to save Brown from his burning aircraft, Hudner intentionally crash-landed his own aircraft on a snowy mountain in freezing temperatures to help Brown. In spite of these efforts, Brown died of his injuries and Hudner was forced to evacuate, having also been injured in the landing.

F-4U-4B BuNo62934 of VF-113 gets the 'GO' signal from Lieutenant Hugh H. Dunkum Jr., Flight Deck Officer aboard the USS *Philippine Sea* while a second Corsair waits its turn to take off on 5 September 1950. On 9 June 1952, BuNo62934, now with VMF-323 'Death Rattlers', crashed and burned.

USMC F4U-5 on the *Coral Sea* in November 1950. The carrier returned to the Mediterranean for duty with the Sixth Fleet from 9 September 1950 to 1 February 1951.

Rocket-armed F4U-4B of VMF-214 'Swashbucklers' aboard *Sicily* off Korea in 1950 during the time that the 'Black Sheep' Squadron was embarked from 1 August to 13 November 1950. The carrier was on station off Korea from 4 July 1950 to 5 February 1951.

Naval Reserve Squadron F4U-4s of VF-884 'Bitter Birds' or VF-791 'Rebels' of Carrier Air Group 101 (CVG-101, composed of Navy Reserve squadrons from Dallas, Texas; Glenview, Illinois; Memphis, Tennessee and Olathe) returning from a combat mission over North Korea on 4 September 1951 circle the USS *Boxer* as they wait for planes in the next strike to be launched from her flight deck. CVG-101 began operations in Korea on 29 March 1951 and was the first in the Naval Reserve to launch strikes in Korea. Most of these missions were airstrikes against Chinese ground forces along the 38th parallel and this duty lasted until 24 October 1951.

Captain Bernard H. Williams of VMF-323 on the USS *Sicily* in 1951.

Lieutenant Guy P. Bordelon, the US Navy's only ace of the Korean War.

AU-1 Corsair in flight in 1952.

General Clifton B. Cates, commandant of the USMC, pins the Silver Star on Major J. Hunter Reinburg usmc, a WW2 pilot with VMF-121, scoring seven victories, for his achievements in the Korean War.

VF-653 pilots pose on the *Valley Forge* in July 1952 with 13 flight helmets for their fallen colleagues. Among the survivors are Cook Cleland (back row, middle), Ray Edinger VF-653's 34-year-old executive officer, (to his immediate left) and 'Bob' Balser (to Cleland's right). (*USN*)

'Bob' Balser, 26, one of VF-653's few bachelors and an illustrator for the *Pittsburgh Post-Gazette* was one of thousands of Naval Air Reservists or 'weekend warriors' who, by 1952 had flown 6,000 of the 8,000 sorties from US carriers on combat missions in Korea.

Ensign Owen W. Dykema a Corsair pilot in VF-192 'Golden Dragons' aboard the *Princeton* during the Korean War.

F4U-4 BuNo097385 in the VF-192 'The Golden Dragons' on the *Princeton*.

On 10 September 1952 the Corsair became the first and only US Navy propeller-driven aircraft to destroy a MiG in the air over Korea when Captain Jesse G. Folmar of VMFA-312 'Checkerboards' from the *Sicily* was credited with destroying a MiG-15. Folmar's remarkable victory was the sole Corsair MiG kill in the Korean War.

Corsairs of VF-713 'Vultures' among AD Skyraiders on the USS *Antietam* off Korea on 15 October 1951 during the carrier's first war cruise (8 September 1951-2 May 1952).

F4U-4 of VMF-312 'Checkerboards' getting unstuck in Korea in January 1952. Leaving the USS *Bataan* in June 1951, the 'Checkerboards' spent a short period of USMC ground based close air support operations before returning to sea, first with *Bairoko*, then with *Bataan* and later with *Sicily*.

1st Lieutenant Burcher V. L. Sheard of this VMF-323 'Death Rattlers' F4U-4B in mid-1951 had just landed on the USS *Sicily* when his fuel filler cap on the belly tank broke off. The remaining fuel in the tank splashed onto the hot exhaust pipes and burst into flame. Within days of this accident, pilots aboard the light carrier were ordered to empty the external tanks before landing. The 'Death Rattlers' operated from the *Sicily* from 5 June to 20 September 1951. (*USMC*)

F4U-7 BuNo 133727 of Flottille 12 patrolling the Suez Canal in 1956. In October that year Corsairs of Flotille 14 and Flotilla 15 took part in Operation 'Musketeer', the Anglo-French-Israeli seizure of the Suez Canal. They were tasked with destroying Egyptian Navy ships at Alexandria but the presence of US Navy vessels prevented the successful completion of the mission. On 3 November 16 F4U-7s attacked airfields in the Delta, with one Corsair shot down by anti-aircraft fire. Two more Corsairs were damaged when landing back on the carriers. The Corsairs engaged in 'Musketeer' dropped a total of 25 tons of bombs and fired more than 500 rockets and 16,000 20mm rounds.

Corsairs flew their final combat missions in 1969 during the so-called '100 Hour War' or 'Soccer War' between Honduras and El Salvador in service with both air forces. The conflict was allegedly triggered, though not really caused, by a disagreement over a football (soccer) match on 14 July 1969 when the Salvadoran military launched an attack against Honduras. A cease-fire was negotiated on the night of 18 July, which took full effect on 20 July. Salvadoran troops were withdrawn in early August. The Fuerza Aérea Salvadoreña (FAS) operated 25 F4U/FG-1Ds from 1957 to 1976. The Fuerza Aérea Honduras did not retire its fleet until 1979.

On Lentil Sub-Lieutenant Don Sheppard DSC, a Canadian Corsair pilot with 1836 Squadron aboard *Victorious*, had his first encounter with enemy aircraft. Born in Toronto on 21 January 1924, Don Sheppard volunteered for the Fleet Air Arm in December 1941, directly from school. He joined Pilot Course 38 at HMS *St Vincent* in May 1942 and on completion of basic training was selected for pilot training with the US Navy. After graduation in summer 1943 he was posted to 1835 Squadron in October. However, the squadron was disbanded in December and he was transferred to 1836 Squadron. This became a part of 47 Naval Fighter Wing, joining HMS *Victorious* in March 1944. From April to June he was involved in operations off the Norwegian coast, including the first successful strike on the battleship *Tirpitz* on 3 April. During this period he was transferred from the RNVR to the RCNVR, but remained with 1836 Squadron.

On 4 January Sheppard was flying Middle Cover with fourteen Corsairs from 1836, probably leading a two-plane section. He wrote: 'In this particular case the Japanese fighters came vertically down through the fighter cover in an attempt to shoot down the bombers, so I saw fighters coming straight down at high speed and then going straight up at high speed (or so it seemed at the time). My first kill appeared immediately below me and as I rolled down to attack he attempted to evade me by rolling over on his back and pulling through. However, about halfway through this manoeuvre, I fired a burst at him from a relatively short range and he baled out! I can't be sure that he left the aircraft because he was hit or because he was merely frightened.'

His victim was a Ki-43 Oscar and Sheppard later reported the pilot appeared to be dead when he hit the sea. Climbing back to rejoin the strike, Sheppard spotted another 'Oscar' below heading for his aerodrome at high speed. 'Since I had an altitude advantage I was able to despatch him quite quickly before he regained the sanctuary of his aerodrome.'

This time the weather was very good and the attack was deemed a great success. The Corsairs and Hellcats destroyed about a dozen enemy aircraft in air-to-air combat and a further twenty aircraft on the ground. 1836 Squadron's Corsairs from *Victorious* alone destroyed five Oscars, while 1834 Squadron shot down a Sally and a Mitsubishi Ki-46 Dinah. None of the Corsairs was lost and only one aircraft, an Avenger, whose crew was rescued. Heavy damage was caused to the refinery, which significantly reduced its output of oil.

At 1430 hours on 16 January the BPF, as Task Force 63, commanded by Rear Admiral Sir Philip L. Vian sailed from China Bay in the first stage of its planned deployment to the Pacific Theatre to Sydney, Australia. The force comprised the battleship *King George V*, four cruisers and six destroyers and the 1st Aircraft Carrier Squadron comprising the *Indomitable* (flag), *Illustrious, Indefatigable* and *Victorious*, with 220 strike aircraft in total. On board *Indomitable* were twenty-eight Hellcats and twenty-one Avengers, on *Illustrious* twenty-eight Corsairs of 1830 and 1833 Squadrons and twenty-one Avengers, on *Victorious*, twenty-eight Corsairs of 1834 and 1836 Squadrons and twenty-one Avengers, on *Indefatigable* forty Seafires, twelve Fireflies and twenty-one Avengers. On the way to Australia Vian planned to carry out a series of operations, the biggest ever by the FAA in the Second World War. Codenamed Meridian I, II and III, they were against the oil refineries at Pladjoe and Serongei Gerong, Palembang, South-East Sumatra. Pladjoe was the larger of the two and these refineries supplied a large part of Japan's aviation fuel. As well as dealing a severe blow to the Japanese war effort, the strikes would help convince the Americans that the British Pacific Fleet meant business. Before the force left Trincomalee, all four carrier-groups took part in a rehearsal attack on Colombo. An intensive mission briefing took place starting the day after Force 63 put to sea. The senior officers of the squadrons, after studying target models, then told their aircrews and worked out a plan of attack. They were told that there would be an attack on each refinery and, if necessary, a third to mop up anything that was left undamaged. (The BPF was incapable of mounting simultaneous strikes against both targets.)

Palembang town lies on the north side of the Musi river, some miles from its mouth, south of Singapore and opposite Borneo. The two refineries were on the south bank of the river on either side of the Komerine river where it joins the Musi. The Royal Dutch Oil Refinery at Pladjoe lay on the north bank of the Komerine, while the Standard Oil Refinery at Serongei Gerong was on the opposite bank. The confluence of the rivers, the town and the huge refineries, all within an area of five square miles, was to make spotting them easy. Force 63 was opposed by four fighter squadrons of the 9th Air Division of the Japanese 7th Area Army and by heavy AA batteries. Aircrews were warned that there would be stiff opposition from ack-ack and fighters. They would have, however, 'plenty of fighter cover from the Hellcats and Corsairs'. Aerial reconnaissance showed that there were no barrage balloons, but this was to prove false on the days of the attacks.

Meridian I, the first strike, against Pladjoe, was originally scheduled to take place on the 22nd. However, a prolonged tropical storm of high winds and driving rain on the night of 21/22 January and again on the night of the 22nd/23rd each time caused a twenty-four-hour delay. This did not do the aircrew's nerves, already strained with the thought of what might happen if they fell into the hands of this particular enemy, any good. The final approach was made on the night of Tuesday 23rd/Wednesday 24th. The low cloud lifted and the four carriers made another run into the flying position, about seventy miles east of Engano Island, for a take off. The wind had dropped and the rain stopped but there was low cloud over the fleet. At 0630 launching of forty-three Avenger bombers armed with 172 500lb bombs began. Twelve rocket-armed Fireflies from *Indefatigable* were detailed to strafe the balloons during their rocket dives. Top cover and fighter Ramrods (strafing attacks on enemy fighter opposition on the ground by groups of fighters) on three airfields in the area were to be the tasks of eighty-nine Corsairs and Hellcats. *Illustrious* and *Victorious* each contributed twelve Corsairs and *Indefatigable* her Seafires to create the Ramrods. In order to prevent the enemy fighters from reacting in strength, four Avengers and six Hellcats of the fighter escort were to attack Mana airfield on the west coast. Although a diversion, their main aim was to put out of action the runway and reconnaissance bombers which were known to be there.

Because of launching difficulties, the twelve Fireflies, which were detailed to provide low cover and then strafe the balloons ahead of the Avengers, left long after the main strike had disappeared towards the mountains of Sumatra and joined only at the tail end of the action. This left just eight Corsairs of 1833 Squadron to provide the whole of the low cover for the Avengers. In the words of Lieutenant Commander Norman S. Hanson, the squadron CO: 'We were too busy on the climb to take much interest in the rest of the escort. Once we levelled out on top, however, I was a bit shattered to find that our eight Corsairs constituted the whole of low cover. Where the hell were the Fireflies? I hadn't the faintest idea what had happened to them and at this stage was reluctant to break radio silence to find out. We positioned ourselves over the centre of the bomber force and hoped for miracles.

'Quite suddenly there was no more time to goof at the breathtaking scenery. Things began to happen. The Avengers opened the taps, pushed the stick over a little and cracked on more speed. Palembang appeared and away in the distance the Banka Strait gleamed in the sunshine with the river, glinting snakelike, winding through the flat country to join it. There, astride the river, lay the massive refinery, a town in itself. I was still taking in the spectacle when – "RATS!! Eleven o'clock up!"

'Top cover was shouting the odds and the battle was joined. The air became alive with warning shouts, orders to close up and all the natter that excitement generates. And then I could see them. Over to the north, pinpricks of black were hurtling downhill from a great height and contrails were streaming out across the unbelievably blue sky as our fighters pulled tight corners to get at them. The Avengers were now deploying for their bombing run and their line was lengthening. Christ! I could do with twenty Corsairs right now! Suddenly a Jap levelled out over the port side, going like smoke as he made his run to take the bombers on the beam.

'"Break left – GO!"

'The flight wheeled over on to its wingtips. We gave him a burst head-on and he ducked. Whether or not we hit him I don't know, but fire from twenty-four .5 guns is enough to make the bravest put his head down. I hadn't turned back to the Avengers before someone yelled, "RATS! Three o'clock up!"

There were two more, belting downhill at high speed. The other flight had already turned at one of them and we took the other. Someone must have been a damned good shot at three-quarters deflection, for bits and pieces flew off him as he dived down, down – he had forgotten all about the bombers now. We had given him something more to think about! Then we turned back again. The Avengers were now diving steeply on their run to the target. The bloody great balloons were still up, floating between us and the earth like some fat, green, obscene reptiles with red spots. And I cursed the Fireflies. They were the great destroyers who were going to clear these ugly sausages out of the way for us; and as far as I knew their crews were still sitting in their wardroom with their feet up, reading *Lady Chatterley's Lover*.

'Where the hell were they? We were searching ahead, weaving all the time like maniacs, when tracer tore past us, fired from astern. There in my mirror – he looked as though he were sitting on my elevators – was an Oscar, his guns flashing along his wings. I had time neither to shout nor to break before he dived beneath us, only to re-appear in a split second, pulling up in front of us, the length of two cricket pitches away. We all heaved back on our sticks and gave him the works; no need for gunsights. The silly bastard was half-stalled, sitting there like a broken-down whore. His port aileron took off and sailed over our heads. What looked like a section of flap fell away to our right. Someone must have hit his engine, for he fell, smoking, down on the port side and Matt Barbour must have nearly flown through him. God knows how he missed him. I yelled and did an aerobatic turn to port where a Tojo was boring in. Business was brisk and we were dashing about like frustrated virgins.

'Reggie Shaw and Matt Barbour – Numbers 3 and 4 – had vanished. I did a quick scan around the local sky – not a sign. When you lose a fast-flying formation, you can be two miles away before you realise it. Whatever the reason, Jimmy Clarke and I were alone. Our other flight had disappeared too. Perhaps they were already on their way to the rendezvous on the far side of the target area. So we pushed off in that direction, diving to get up some more speed.

'Quite suddenly, out of an empty space, rose a Nick – a sleek two-engined fighter. He came up like a rocket on our starboard side and obviously hadn't seen us. I saw quite clearly the two Japs sitting side by side in the greenhouse. Jimmy was the nearer of the two of us and turned to give him a quick squirt. I lifted and horsed the stick over, firing over the top of Jimmy's Corsair. The Jap fell away to starboard, with strikes evident on his port wing; and for one fleeting moment the idea of following him down entered my head. Then I remembered what my job was – it certainly wasn't that. A year before I had been reprimanded for forsaking the bombers to shoot up aircraft. I sucked my teeth and flew on to the rendezvous.'

Hanson crashed into the sea half-a-mile astern of his carrier but, although being carried below the surface, unconscious and still strapped in his cockpit, he recovered before his Corsair finally sank, escaped from the aircraft and was picked up by a destroyer thirty-five minutes later.[14]

---

14. *Carrier Pilot: An Unforgettable True Story of Wartime Flying* by Norman Hanson, by kind permission of Patrick Stephens (PSL) 1979. Norman Hanson died in 1980, aged sixty-six.

The fighter-sweep destroyed thirty-four enemy aircraft on the airfields, but was unable to prevent about twenty Japanese fighters from getting airborne. The escort accounted for fourteen enemy aircraft, for the loss of seven FAA aircraft from all causes. By 0940 the first planes started to land on the carriers and the fleet then withdrew to the south-west. In his report Ronnie Hay RM, now promoted acting lieutenant colonel, wrote: '*Victorious* group was flown off and formed up in twenty-five minutes. At this time (0645), all the groups appeared ready and the Strike Leader (*Indomitable*) should have commenced his circuit of the force, since time for departure was 0655. He was so long in coming that I flew over to *Indomitable*'s sector to see if there was any trouble. But their squadrons were all formed up and the additional circuit made was unnecessary and delayed departure at least five minutes. On future occasions I will break R/T silence if necessary, to prevent similar delays.

'Circuit of the force was commenced at 0650 and departure taken at 0704. The strike was thus nine minutes late, but it was just as well, since if they had been on time, the Fireflies (*Indefatigable*) would not have joined up before the strike reached the target. All went according to plan here except that the escort, instead of remaining at the same height as the bombers, as had been previously arranged took up their correct escort intervals. An accurate landfall was made at 0718 at 4,500 feet. The climb was continued to 7,000 feet in order to clear the mountains. This height was not lost again, as had been arranged and I am not clear why the Strike Leader had to alter this part of the plan. The weather was excellent for the strike. Thin 10/10th at about 20,000 feet which enabled pilots to look into the sun with ease; and very low 10/10th stratus covering large areas. Visibility was about sixty miles and the wind from the south-east.

'The formation of both the strike and escort was exceptionally good. For reasons unknown, one Avenger from *Indefatigable*'s squadron started to straggle. At 0738 we passed over Matapoera at 7,500 feet and observed three landing strips. Details of these have been reported separately. At 0803 the strike reached 12,000 feet. This was only twelve minutes before the attack and I do not consider soon enough. From the escort point of view, we want the strike at its top height a minimum of fifty miles from the target. This distance, allowing an average speed of 160 knots and a descent from 12,000 to 8,000 feet, would only take nineteen minutes.

'About twenty miles from the target the Strike Leader requested the Fireflies (*Indefatigable*) to go ahead and strafe the balloons which could be seen flying in the target area at about 3,000 feet. Unfortunately, owing to delays in the carrier, the aircraft still had not joined the main strike. I judged their time of joining to be 0806 and almost immediately afterwards they went ahead to strafe their special target. I do not think they heard the request for the balloons to be strafed.

'At about 0808 the enemy AA defences opened fire whilst the strike was still out of range, indicating that they had had warning of our approach. Almost immediately afterwards the escort was engaged by an estimated twenty-five Tojo fighters, although I myself only counted about twelve at the time. Their initial height was 13,000-15,000 feet.

'There seemed to be a rather long delay after the enemy had opened fire until the first bombs fell (about six minutes). When surprise has obviously not been achieved, as in this case, the time interval must be cut down to a minimum and the bombing become more concentrated.

'I did not see the Fireflies attack, but the first group of bombs to fall struck several oil tanks with the inevitable result; it seemed that all subsequent attacks had the same effect. The target of No. 1 Wing (*Indomitable* and *Victorious*) appeared well hit. No. 2 Wing (*Illustrious* and *Indefatigable*) appeared to have destroyed only half of theirs. During this period, when not engaged with enemy fighters or occupied in avoiding predicted flak, I was able to secure a series of oblique photographs of the bombing. When I finally left the target area (about 0823) the Avengers were just about to leave the rendezvous and I did not see them again.

'Throughout the attack the enemy had just sufficient fighters to saturate the escort. Enemy pilots showed as much contempt for Japanese heavy AA as we did and fights were raging all over the target area. It was almost funny to see the aircraft scrapping and all the while the AA bursting at all heights up to 15,000 feet. As far as I know no one was lost by this fire and very few damaged.

'The presence of three or four twin-engined aircraft seemed to indicate some air-ground control of AA or fighters. No noticeable difference was observed after three of these twin-engined aircraft had been shot down.

'R/T discipline during this air battle was good. No report was received from Force "X-Ray". An immense column of black smoke to the north-west of the target indicated their passage, but when I left they still had not arrived at Talangbetoetoe. Thus, although they achieved "very excellent results", they were too late to be of any material help to the strike.

'Once again the withdrawal was insufficiently protected by the escort. The Fireflies appeared to be the only aircraft there and they were unable to prevent several attacks by fighters taking place. There is no doubt more of the escort could have got there and discipline on this point must be tightened. At 0825 the enemy fighters appear to have been ordered off, as no further attacks developed after this time and the escort quickly formed up on the strike. In my attempt to rejoin the formation, my flight became engaged with four Tojos of which I shot down two and the remaining two in my flight damaged one each.

'Return was without incident. The top cover (*Victorious*) dispersed two Tojos which were attempting to shadow the formation. The fleet was several miles to the north of her advertised position. Attempts to home by beacon, as usual, failed. The reason for this continued failure of the beacon is not clearly understood. A very large number of aviators report failure each time with a lucky one or two reporting success. At any rate this matter needs most careful attention. At 0928 the group broke up for landing which was carried out speedily and with skill. I think this has been one of the better strikes the Fleet Air Arm has ever accomplished.'

Don Sheppard wrote that Hay's position as Air Co-ordinator meant that: 'he and his flight were given free rein to roam the skies at will. Because of this freedom, much of the time we were isolated and the Air Co-ordinator was exposed to attack by Japanese fighters prior to the strike, during the strike and after the strike when we circled the targets to take pictures of the damage. We were jumped from above and behind by an Oscar who fortunately missed us all with his initial burst and then made an error in judgement by breaking below us after his firing run and then pulling straight up in front of me to regain his original height advantage. When I spotted the error I reversed the turn, followed him up using water injection for additional power and hit with about my second burst. He then fell out of his climb and descended straight down towards the jungle.'

Sheppard was originally credited with a 'probable', but it was apparently later confirmed as his third victory. Hay shot down two others, a Nakajima Ki-43 and a Ki-44, recalling that two of the Tojos that jumped them 'went down in flames into the "ulu"'.

All told, Force 63 lost two Avengers, six Corsairs and a Hellcat in combat, while the pilots of a Corsair and a Seafire baled out over the fleet. Production at the Royal Dutch Refinery at Pladjoe was halved for three months and all its storage burnt out. A few merchant ships were attacked in the course of the strikes; at Pladjoe one of Japan's largest surviving tankers was damaged beyond repair.

There was to be a second attack, on 29 January, on the second largest refinery at the Standard Oil Refinery at Serongei Gerong, also in the Palembang vicinity. Meridian II benefited from the lessons of the earlier raid, but after Meridian I the Fleet had to withdraw for refuelling, and it was something of a shambles due to inexperience. To aircrews this was an awful waste of time and a five-day wait for the next attack was bad on the nerves. Meanwhile, the enemy, knowing that another attack was almost certainly imminent because the other refinery had been left untouched, strengthened their defences and brought down from the north some crack fighter squadrons to augment the local squadrons. This time the FAA fighter sweep would concentrate on the two major airfields. To cover Talangbetoetoe airfield *Victorious* despatched twelve Corsairs, while two Fireflies were sent up from *Indefatigable* to carry out an armed recce of Mana airfield.

Lieutenant Colonel Hay, who was awarded the DSO for his part in Meridian, reported on the strike against the oil refineries at Serongei Gerong, Palembang, on the morning of Monday, 29th January: 'In rather doubtful weather, carriers commenced flying off at 0640; about 0710 visibility improved sufficiently for all groups to be observed at the same time. At 0718 the Strike Leader commenced his left hand circuit of the fleet. All units were ready for him and joined up promptly. At 0729 the complete strike was all formed up and on the east side of the fleet, ready to take departure. Alas, the Strike-Leader once again, for no known reason, made a 360-degree orbit. I decided against breaking R/T silence, which was my error. Anyway, the flagship came up and ordered departure to be taken but it was too late and the strike departed at 0734 (four minutes late). Three Avenger squadrons were hopelessly out of position. The fighter escort was all jumbled up, which, with the poor weather conditions obtaining, made aviation in the area extremely hazardous. At 0740 the strike commenced climbing and the escort took up position. An accurate landfall was made at 0752 at 5,500 feet. Formations had by now all closed up and the escort was very tidily in position. I lost sight of the fleet at about ten miles owing to masses of low cumulus. But over the land, conditions were much improved. There was thin 10/10th at about 14,000 feet and over the eastern plain of Sumatra 10/10th cloud, 500 feet thick, covering large areas. In fact, the weather could not have been more ideal.

'On passing over Lake Ranau one Avenger commenced straggling and soon after turned for base. I reported this to *Indomitable* but got no reply. The climb was continued over the mountains to 7,500 feet. The formation of the strike and escort was very good. The weather, however, got worse and I had some doubts whether we would be able to see the target. As the top cover was being forced down by cloud, requests were passed to the Strike Leader to fly lower. But he continued to climb to 10,000 feet and caused embarrassment to the escort above him. The journey to the target was otherwise uneventful. At 0830 I shifted to R/T Channel "C" and heard Forces "X-Ray" and "Yoke" at work. They were on their targets about fifteen minutes before we struck and by the sound of things they were far too late. Most of their reports were of bandits airborne. At 0835 the vexed question of balloons cropped up and the escort leader, much to the relief of the bombers, decided to use the Fireflies for this work. At 0840 the target could be seen, fortunately quite clear of clouds. The balloons were [at] about 4,000 feet. All fires from the previous raid on Pladjoe were out. Shortly after, the Fireflies reported "Out Lights", the bombers deployed according to plan and I moved ahead to observe the target.

'Almost immediately, the heavy AA opened up on the Fireflies. Several groups of about ten rounds were observed extremely accurate for height and range but, fortunately, out for bearing. My flight also attracted the attentions of the gunners but they were completely unable to cope with gentle evasion. All this drew quite a bit of the AA away from the bombers. But, just after the deployment, several enemy fighters were seen diving down on them. I observed no reaction by the top or middle cover. The plan for guarding individual squadrons by sections of the escort appeared in most cases to be a failure. Both squadrons of No. 1 Wing received the unwelcome attentions of Jap fighters which did not cease until they commenced to bomb. During this period no protection was afforded by our own fighters. I believe No. 2 Wing were more fortunate. About three balloons were destroyed but I don't think they were worth the attention the Fireflies gave them.

'I commenced photographing at 0850 as the first bombs fell. From visual observation, some targets were severely hit and the photographs have confirmed this. Bombing by No. 1 Wing was truly impressive. By the time No. 2 Wing commenced bombing, it was getting a bit difficult to see. The first squadron of that wing (*Illustrious*) set off some oil tanks in the vicinity and certainly were very close to their target. Some of the last aircraft to bomb obviously could not observe their correct target and so, quite rightly, chose another. One stick was seen to burst along the wharves. It seemed a pity that so many aircraft were put on to one small target whilst Pladjoe was completely clear and could have been bombed accurately.

'About three minutes after the last aircraft bombed I finished photographing. I then climbed from 6,000 feet to 10,000 in order to take vertical line overlap photographs as the flak had died down. I soon had to change my mind as a Tojo was coming for us. In shooting this one down, we descended and attracted by the gunfire, an Oscar came along and by 0905 he, too, was dead.'

Both victories were shared with Don Sheppard, who recalled of the second Japanese fighter: 'This inquisitive fellow was an Oscar and obviously attracted by the smoke of the earlier victim, came to have a look. Hay ordered his flight of three aircraft to climb and not engage. This we did until we had a 1,500 feet height advantage and the leader and I then attacked. It was a vigorous dogfight and after a series of steep turns, the Jap settled down for a moment straight and level. My shells hit the pilot's cockpit which glowed with a dull red as the bullets slammed home and then he rolled over and crashed into the trees.'

Sheppard described the combat as 'a most exhilarating fight against a very competent and aggressive opponent'. In his logbook he simply wrote: 'Major Hay and self knocked down an Oscar and a Tojo between us.'

'During this time,' continues Hay, 'the radio was giving me an interesting picture of a long stream of Avengers dribbling out of the target area to the rendezvous, thirty miles away. It was evident some of them could not find it, nor could I from 7,000 feet even though I searched for some time. During this period there was quite a vicious air battle of which I can give no detail.

'The return was without opposition of any kind. There seemed to be a little confusion as to who was going to escort the stragglers. Formation on the return was good and the escort in position. I climbed to 10,000 feet and swept the area astern of the formation but no enemy aircraft attempted to shadow. After the strike had crossed the coast I examined Lake Ranau for any survivors but saw none. I then proceeded to the submarine rendezvous for the aircrews forced down and took oblique photographs of all the river mouths in the bay in question.

'R/T discipline up till now had been 100 per cent improved. But crossing the coast seemed to be the signal for complete radio chaos. Primarily the Avengers giving their damaged friends extracts from pilots' handling notes. It is about time everybody knew their emergency drill without having to talk about it. I found it extremely difficult to get a word in edgeways in order to report my return which was independent of the main strike and might have been mistaken for a raid. I could get no reply from *Indomitable* and eventually had to pass the message on Channel C to *Victorious*.

'In conclusion Meridian One and Two have been the most interesting and successful operations I know of. In both cases we succeeded in our object and I would like to praise the determination of the Avenger pilots who bombed so accurately in the face of maximum discouragement. The fighter escort proved itself against the most serious air opposition it has so far met.'

Meridian II proved even more successful than the 24 January strike but enemy fighters were up in force and there were continuous air battles all the way to the target when the heavy and accurate AA took over. The strike was pressed home and the Standard Oil Refinery at Serongei Gerong was put out of action for two months and when it did start again it was at greatly reduced capacity. In addition to thirty-eight enemy aircraft destroyed on the ground by the fighter sweep, over thirty were shot down by the escort.

In the early afternoon, the CAP shot down a group of eight aircraft that intelligence officers learned were from the 'Special Army Attack Corps', or kamikazes and more attacks were expected. Sheppard launched on CAP in the late afternoon and his flight was vectored onto a bogey but it escaped through poor fighter direction. All told, on 29 January, Sheppard was airborne for a little over six hours. Eleven Avengers and nineteen pilots or aircrew were lost. Crews complained about lack of adequate protection. Altogether, sixteen FAA aircraft were lost.

Force 63 was now due to carry out Meridian III next morning, 30 January, but how many planes would be ready by then was doubtful and the nerves of the pilots had worn thin. Many believed that the casualties would be appalling. Crews spent the morning of the 29th in a state of gloom but, at midday, the Tannoy blared out 'Meridian III has been cancelled'. The fuel situation would not allow more than one further attack. Crews felt 'as if a ton weight had been lifted from them'. The carriers and their consorts headed for Freemantle and Sydney, having inflicted enormous damage on the refineries, the effects of which would last for months. The air groups had cut the aviation gasoline output from Sumatra to 35 per cent of its normal level at a time when Japan was desperately short of oil in any form. Probably, the three strikes in January 1945 against Pangkalan Brandon, Pladjoe and Serongei Gerong were the British Pacific Fleet's greatest contribution to the ultimate victory. Sixty-eight Japanese aircraft were destroyed. British losses amounted to sixteen aircraft lost in battle, eleven ditched, fourteen destroyed in deck crashes – a total of forty-one aircraft from 378 sorties. Personnel losses amounted to thirty aircrew.

As they made their way towards Australia, Don Sheppard and his fellow aviators in HMS *Victorious* thought mostly of rest and recreation. After a brief layover at Freemantle and passage to Sydney, Sheppard and the other Corsair pilots eventually flew down to the naval air station at Nowra, south of bustling Sydney and not far from the picturesque white sand beaches at Jervis Bay where pilots spent most of the time relaxing. Lieutenant Robert H. 'Hammy' Gray RCNVR, senior pilot with *Formidable*'s 1841 Squadron, described his own carefree experience in Australia in a letter home: 'Now I am able to tell you about Sydney – Well it is a wonderful place indeed. There is no doubt that it is the most hospitable place of its size I have ever been to. We have a large number of ratings aboard and I do not think there is any of them which did not enjoy their stay here. The ratings who usually find very little to do in a strange port were given a full welcome and as far as I can see they nearly all got some home life with Australian families, which is something they do not usually get. I myself of course had a good time. I went with my CO and stayed with some people who gave us a very full welcome indeed and showed us everything. The swimming was by far the best I ever had and now I have a very beautiful tan.'

Born 2 November 1917 in Trail, British Columbia, Hammy Gray had enlisted on 18 July 1940 in Calgary, Alberta. His brother John 'Jack' Gray died on 27 February 1942 while serving with the Royal Canadian Air Force. Hammy Gray initially joined 757 Squadron at Winchester, England. He was then assigned to the African theatre, flying Hawker Hurricanes for shore-based squadrons, Nos. 795, 803 and 877, where he spent two years at Nairobi. He trained to fly the Corsair fighter and in 1944 he was assigned to 1841 Squadron in HMS *Formidable*. From 24 to 29 August he took part in a series of unsuccessful raids against the German battleship *Tirpitz* in Norway. On 29 August he was Mentioned in Despatches for his participation in an attack on three German destroyers, during which his plane's rudder was shot off. On 16 January 1945 he received a further Mention 'For undaunted courage, skill and determination in carrying out daring attacks on the German battleship *Tirpitz*'.

Don Sheppard recalled 'a very good shore leave', the highlight of which was meeting up with his older brother, Bob, who had also volunteered for the Fleet Air Arm and was flying Corsairs with 1845 Squadron in *Formidable*.[15] The two brothers had a great chance to catch up but, sadly, it was their final meeting. On 22 March 1945 when *Victorious* was staging for Iceberg at Ulithi and *Formidable* was working up off Australia, Bob Sheppard died in a flying accident. According to witnesses his Corsair appeared to clip a small protrusion at the forward edge of *Formidable*'s flight deck during a routine launch, stalled and plummeted into the sea. Strangely, a month passed before Don Sheppard learned of his brother's fate.

The British Pacific Fleet and the air group now began to grow into the new concept of a fast, efficient and hard-hitting task force, with, if necessary, continuous flying that was a feature of the American naval operations in the Pacific. The idea of the one set-piece strike was to

---

15. The squadron officially formed at Brunswick in June 1944 as a fighter squadron with 18 Corsair IIIs, embarking in August 1944 on HMS *Puncher* for the UK, the squadron then joining the 10th Naval Fighter Wing. In December the squadron re-equipped with twenty-four Corsair IVs and embarked on HMS *Slinger* for the Far East. One month was spent at Schofields, Australia, re-embarking on HMS *Slinger* in March 1945 to join the British Pacific Fleet.

give way to constant take offs and landings by smaller numbers of strike aircraft and continuous streams of fighters as circumstances demanded. Arriving at Sydney on 10 February 1945 the British Pacific Fleet worked hard to ready itself for action with the US Navy. Seventeen days later, the BPF departed to join Task Force 57, a part of the US 5th Fleet, which was destined for Operation Iceberg, the landings to capture Okinawa. After stopping at Manus Island in the Admiralty Islands the BPF sailed with TF57 for Ulithi Atoll in the Carolines.

By now the Royal Navy's Corsairs were certainly war-weary, as Lieutenant Colonel Ronnie Hay RM commanding No. 47 Wing on *Victorious* recalls: 'With the Corsair you felt like you were literally strapped into an armchair in your sitting room, the cockpit was that large. You honestly felt like a "king" sitting up there, with virtually unlimited visibility through the bubble canopy of the Mark II. We flew those aircraft very hard and just to illustrate this point, a little after the Sumatra show we ventured northward to Okinawa for Iceberg where I came across an airfield full of the latest spec F4U-4s in glossy sea blue at Manus, in the Admiralty Islands, awaiting shipment back to the US. I found the US Navy officer in charge of this operation and asked him what was occurring. He told me that they were being returned to the States for overhaul and repair, prior to being sent to the front line again. I enquired as to their individual service use per airframe and he replied that they had seen about 500 hours of flying each. I was astonished and replied that our Corsair IIs had accrued nearly 2,000 each and were no nearer an overhaul or deep service than the day they were built! I ventured a swap whereby I took one of his non-serviced machines in place of my old crate and he replied, "Sure bud, you can have any one you like. Any guy going up to the 'sharp end' can take anything he wants!" Sadly, I fear my admiral would have spotted the F4U-4's glossy blue scheme sat amongst the ranks of grey Corsair IIs on *Victorious*!'[16]

---

16. Hay was awarded a Bar to his DSC for his service leading the attacks on operations at the Sakishima Islands between March and June 1945, in support of the American invasion of Okinawa. At the end of the Second World War Hay, still on board *Victorious*, was involved in air strikes against the Japanese mainland until 11 August 1945 when *Victorious* was withdrawn to Sydney for a refit.

The British Pacific Fleet was to seal the six Japanese airfields on the Sakishima Gunto island group east of Formosa and south-west of Okinawa and the other Ryukyu Islands, whilst the Americans took Okinawa. TF 57 reached its flying-off position about 100 miles south of Sakishima Gunto on 26 March and the first strike went ahead using forty Avengers, twelve flak-suppression Fireflies and small formations of Corsairs and Hellcats. The air attacks were repeated on the 27th before the task force withdrew for replenishment. Bad weather prevented the resumption of air attacks until 31 March and, on 1 April, Japanese aircraft appeared over the invasion fleet in some strength. High-level bombers, followed by kamikaze aircraft, made their attacks but they were largely dealt with by the Corsairs and Hellcats. On 2 April, however, a Zeke made a strafing run over *Indomitable*, killing one rating and wounding two more. Another lone kamikaze made a strike on *Indefatigable* and hit the base of the island, killing four officers and ten ratings and wounding sixteen. The carrier was put out of commission for a time but, thanks to the armoured flight deck, no lasting damage was caused below. More kamikaze attacks occurred on 6 April and a Zero got through to hit the island on *Illustrious* with its wingtip before crashing into the sea. During this suicide attack the Corsairs of 1830 Squadron and the Hellcats of 1844 Squadron shot down five Aichi D4Y Judys and a Nakajima P1Y 'Frances'.

When not flying CAP the Corsairs and Hellcats were tasked with strafing the airfields, but the runways were made of crushed coral and could be easily and quickly repaired after the strikes. On 12 April air strikes switched to the northern part of Formosa, where it was believed that a number of kamikaze attacks were waiting to be launched against the 5th Fleet. The first strike, by forty-eight Avengers and forty Corsairs against the port of Kirun and airfields in the vicinity respectively, went ahead in bad weather. A few Corsairs found targets in the Shinchiku area and strafed aircraft on the ground. Later in the day a joint strike by Avengers and Corsairs succeeded in cratering airfield runways and destroying aircraft and buildings. Attacks on Formosa continued on the 12th when Corsairs of Nos. 1834 and 1836 Squadrons shot down three enemy fighters. Later in the day a CAP intercepted a kamikaze attack on the BPF carriers and four enemy aircraft were destroyed with six more damaged. Next day eight Japanese aircraft were shot down during air strikes on the BPF.

Having been at sea almost continuously for the past four years the crew of *Illustrious* and her two Corsair squadrons, 1830 and 1833, were long overdue for rest and recuperation. On 15 April *Illustrious* was withdrawn, to be replaced by *Formidable*, which entered the battle off Sakishima on 16 April. On board were two Corsair Squadrons, Nos. 1841 and 1842. On the night of 20 April the BPF withdrew for much needed replenishment at Leyte in the Philippines. Operations were resumed on 4 May with air attacks on Ishigaki. At 1100, shortly before the first strike force of Avengers returned to the carriers, the BPF was attacked by a wave of twenty kamikaze aircraft. All available Seafires, Hellcats and Corsairs intercepted the suicide aircraft and only two got through the screen. The Corsairs of 1834 and 1836 Squadrons shot down a Nakajima C6N 'Saiun' ('Painted Cloud') 'Myrt', a Yokosuka D4Y 'Suisei' ('Comet') Judy dive-bomber and two Zeros.

Don Sheppard, who on 12 March received news that he had been awarded the DSC, was credited with the Judy. Visibility was good, with about 3/10ths cloud at 20,000 feet, and as Sheppard climbed through 15,000 feet 'by sheer luck I spotted a small dot about five thousand feet above us'. As they continued to climb, the dot grew into an Aichi Judy with 'greenish brown camouflage'. In his combat report Sheppard wrote: 'I dropped my tank and gave full boost; climbed up and under enemy aircraft. At 300 yards aircraft started to turn to port, I fired a one-second burst at about 30° and he straightened out and must have dropped his flaps and cut his throttle as I began to gain on him rapidly. I cut my throttle and fishtailed and had time to give him a two-second burst from astern at about 100 yards. He blew up in a terrific flash of flame and at the same time the bombs or drop tanks dropped loose from the wings. The aircraft then descended in pieces and burned on hitting the water. A parachute made free from the aircraft while it descended and was strafed, but there was only the harness attached when I had a closer look.'

Sheppard was in too close to avoid the massive fireball, which he thought was sparked by the explosion of a long-range fuel tank in the Judy's bomb bay. That 'made a bit of a mess of my fabric rudder and elevators', but he was able to land safely on *Victorious*.

Intelligence officers concluded that the Judy was a so-called 'Gestapo' aircraft that co-ordinated kamikaze attacks making it an extremely valuable kill, both in terms of the mission that may have been thwarted and the personnel who went down in it. In a news report in July 1945 entitled *Toronto Airman Downs Fourth Jap*, Don Sheppard was described thus: 'A Toronto pilot of the Fleet Air Arm, Lieutenant Donald J. Sheppard, Weybourne Crescent, has shot down his fourth Japanese plane in the recent British Pacific Fleet attacks on the Ryukyu Islands in the Pacific. Lieutenant Sheppard, whose first operation with the Fleet Air Arm was in the attack on the German battleship *Tirpitz*, bagged the Japanese plane after a twenty-mile chase at 20,000 feet. The enemy plane blew up as Sheppard closed in and he was going so fast that he flew through the flames of the exploding plane, burning the elevators and tail of his Corsair.'

Later, Sheppard's claim for a 'probable' on 24 January was re-assessed as 'Confirmed' and so his victory on 4 May took his overall score to five.[17]

Despite the Corsair pilots' best efforts one of the suicide planes hit *Formidable* at the base of the island on the 4 May raid and destroyed eleven aircraft on deck. Christopher Cartledge recalled: 'As we came within striking distance of Japan, the *Formidable* suffered a direct hit on its flight deck from a kamikaze pilot, causing casualties around the control tower and killing one of our pilots, Sub-Lieutenant Bell RNVR. My flight was airborne at the time, but we never saw the Jap plane. We landed on the *Indefatigable* for a three-day stay while *Formidable*'s flight deck was repaired.

'Wally Stradwick, a 22-year-old pilot from Clapham, was flying his Corsair at 6,000 feet above *Formidable* when he saw a kamikaze pilot crash into its flight deck. In his diary he recalled, 'One of our carriers appeared to explode. I could only see the bows protruding from a colossal pall of black smoke in the centre of which was an ugly sheet of flame.'

---

17. On return of the fleet to Australia after these operations, Don Sheppard was posted back to Canada on leave, the war ending before he saw any further action. Subsequently he transferred to the RCN, serving in a number of air and sea appointments until promoted Commander in July 1958. He was commanding officer of a destroyer escort in the early 1960s and following a final appointment at NATO HQ, he retired from the service in January 1974. He then farmed in Nova Scotia and Ontario until 1984 when he settled in Aurora, Ontario.

Unlike the wooden flight decks of the American carriers, the British ships had four-inch armoured flight decks and the hole caused by the attack was simply filled with quick drying cement. *Formidable*'s captain grasped the arm of an American liaison officer standing alongside and shaking his fist, asked, 'What do you think of our bloody British flight decks now?'

'Sir,' came the reply, 'they're a honey.'

Remarkably, *Formidable* was fully operational again by the end of the day.

'As a terror weapon, these kamikazes have a quality of their own,' one officer in *Formidable* later wrote. 'There is [still] something unearthly about an approaching aeroplane whose pilot is hell bent on diving himself right into the ship. Wherever you are, he seems to be aiming straight for you personally.' Another sailor, from Portsmouth, said, 'I remember thinking, I've been through the Blitz; we've had bombs, we've had incendiaries, we've had landmines thrown at us, but it's the first time I've had the bloody plane thrown at me as well. You feel that it's aimed at you, especially when he looks around and you think: can he see me?'

Five days later, following the return of a strike, *Formidable* was again hit by a kamikaze. It struck the carrier and exploded among the full deck-park of aircraft destroying six Corsairs and one Avenger and another ten aircraft were damaged by fire but the bomb did not penetrate the flight deck. The fires were soon under control but burning petrol seeped into the hangar deck and caused the loss of four more Avengers and fourteen Corsairs. *Victorious* was also hit by two kamikazes, which killed three ratings and wounded nineteen, disabled the forward lift and destroyed four Corsairs on the deck.

'It's a dirty war; all war is dirty, this one particularly so,' wrote 22-year-old Chris Cartledge, in a letter home on 16 May: 'Judging by the fanatical methods of defence used by the Japs they do not intend to give in however hard pressed ... One cannot anticipate the reactions of a race so radically different from us. We can't apply our logic to them.'

Formidable left the battle area for Sydney on 22 May after an accidental hangar fire destroyed thirty of her aircraft. *Indomitable*, which needed a refit, was replaced later by *Implacable*, which had joined the BPF at Manus anchorage in the Admiralties in June and, on the 12th, had joined in attacks on Truk in the Caroline Islands. The air attacks on Sakishima Gunto continued until the 25th, by which time Okinawa had been taken.

During the attacks on the Sakishima Islands, the British Pacific Fleet flew 2,444 sorties, dropped 412 tons of bombs and fired 325 rockets, with the loss of forty-seven aircraft and twenty-nine aircrew. The Corsairs and Hellcats destroyed twenty-eight Japanese aircraft. In two months at sea TF-57 lost seventy-three aircraft in the kamikaze attacks and the fire aboard *Formidable*, a further sixty-one aircraft had been destroyed in accidents and twenty-six in combat with the Japanese.

In July 1945 the BPF, now re-titled Task Force 37, joined USN TF38 in attacks on Honshu, the largest of the Japanese home islands. It was the height of the typhoon season when attacks began on 17 July and the US Navy was forced to recall its first strikes. The FAA Corsairs and Fireflies, however, carried on and attacked airfields and railway marshalling yards in the northern part of the island. Christopher Cartledge on 1842 Squadron recalled:

'Early in the morning Douglas Parker led 1842 Squadron in the first British air attack against the Japanese mainland. We were to attack airfields and other targets at Matsushima, Sendai and Masuda on the east coast, north of Tokyo. We came in low through poor visibility, but the Japs were ready for us. As I came across Matsushima airfield targeting two planes on the ground, my aircraft was hit and its trimming went suddenly berserk as I zipped over the hangars. I had to apply full right rudder and pull hard on the stick in order to fly straight and level. I could not carry on with the others and radioed that I was returning to the fleet. I suspected my hydraulics were damaged, so I decided to bale out on my return, as deck landing without operative flaps and arrestor hook would almost certainly be disastrous, especially if I couldn't jettison the extra fuel tank! I climbed painfully to a safe bale-out height of 5,000 feet and was later relieved to see the fleet coming into sight. The drill for baling out is to eject the hood, for which there is a lever. I pulled it, but instead of ejecting the hood it jammed it shut! I would have to do a deck landing after all (I must have said a prayer or two). The fire appliances were all ready waiting for me should I crash the barrier.

'As I made my final approach the batsman waved me on and I received a radio message to wait while the fleet turned out of wind to regain its correct position. I circled the carrier, waiting for it to turn back into wind, at probably not more than 500 feet, trying to free the hood. At each effort I had to let go of the stick, continuously losing height.

'Then the miraculous happened. As I turned for another effort I flew into the sea. The next thing I knew I was floating, supported only by a Mae West, with the last piece of my Corsair's wing just disappearing into a wave about twenty yards away. The impact had knocked off the hood and thrown me out, breaking my safety straps and parachute harness, yet leaving me more or less unscathed. A friend watching from *Formidable*'s bridge said that my aircraft exploded on impact and he was amazed that I survived. I was picked up by a destroyer and was sent back to Australia for a rest and check-up.'

Next day, while the US Navy attacked the Yokosuka naval base, the largest in Japan, aircraft from the BPF were allocated targets to the northeast of Tokyo. Only the Corsairs were able to find their targets in the bad weather conditions prevailing and make their attacks. *Indefatigable* was delayed by mechanical problems and did not join the battle until 24 July, when airfields on Shikoku and coastal shipping in the Inland Sea were bombed and strafed. The airfield attacks were met by intense light flak and the shipping strikes were hampered by a low cloud base, but two Corsairs, six Avengers and two Fireflies carried out a successful attack on the Japanese escort carrier *Kaiyo*, leaving it crippled and burning. Further shipping strikes in the Inland Sea and against the naval base at Maizuru, on the northern coast of Honshu, were carried out during 28-30 July.

Operations early in August were cancelled because of bad weather and then, on 6 August, the first atomic bomb was dropped on Hiroshima, but Japan still refused to surrender. Attacks were resumed against Honshu on 9 August by aircraft from *Indefatigable*, *Victorious* (Corsairs of Nos. 1834 and 1836 Squadrons), *Formidable* (Corsairs of Nos. 1841 and 1842 Squadrons) and *Implacable* when the second atomic bomb destroyed Nagasaki. Shortly before sunrise four Corsair fighter-bombers of 1841 Squadron led by Lieutenant Robert Hampton Gray RCNVR were flown off *Formidable* for an attack on enemy shipping in Onagawa Wan harbour. On 18 July Gray had led a strafing mission against airfields in the Tokyo area. On 24 July Gray led another flight to the inland sea which damaged one merchant ship and damaged two seaplane bases and one airbase. Gray earned a DSC for aiding in sinking a Japanese destroyer in the area of Tokyo on 28 July. The award was not announced until 21 August 1945 when the notice appeared in the *London Gazette* with the citation, 'For determination and address in air attacks on targets in Japan'. When five Japanese destroyers and escorts were sighted Gray detailed two of the Corsairs to strafe anti-aircraft positions and a third to provide top cover while he dived on the escort sloop *Amakusa*. Gray's Corsair was hit repeatedly and it quickly burst into flames, but he continued his dive and his 1,000lb bomb sank the vessel.

Gray was awarded a posthumous Victoria Cross for his action. It was only the second such award made to a FAA airman during the war and the last Victoria Cross to be awarded for actions in the Second World War.

On 10 August more FAA strikes went ahead from dawn to dusk and more Japanese ships were sunk. On 15 August Japan surrendered unconditionally and the Pacific War was all but over. Christopher Cartledge, recovering in Sydney, heard the news of the atom bombs and the Japanese surrender and, early in September, from the Botanical Gardens overlooking Sydney Harbour, he watched the triumphant return of *Formidable*. 'Going on board I found many new faces but several old ones missing. 1842 Squadron had lost a further three pilots. These included Sub Lieutenant Jimmy Ross (Canadian), whose aircraft wings folded up on take-off.'

One last shock awaited the British Fleet. When the carriers *Venerable* (with Corsairs of 1851 Squadron onboard) and *Indomitable*, two of the four carriers based in Sydney preparing for operations in the East Indies and the Philippines, were tasked to re-occupy Hong Kong on 31 August and 1 September, they were attacked by suicide boats. Corsairs, Avengers and Hellcats dive-bombed and strafed the attackers and finished off the rest that were hidden in the bays on the north of Hong Kong Island. Next day, 2 September, the main British Pacific Fleet, now designated TF 38.5, was part of the Allied fleet assembled in Tokyo Bay to witness the Japanese surrender aboard the USS *Missouri*.

And what of the FAA Corsairs? Under the terms of Lend-Lease all aircraft that were left either had to be returned to the United States, or paid for. Most Corsairs, therefore, were pushed over the side of the carriers off Sydney Harbour and sank to the bottom of Davy Jones' locker. A few aircraft were retained but those squadrons were rapidly decommissioned and, by the end of 1945, only four Corsair squadrons remained in FAA service – Nos. 1831, 1846, 1850 and 1851 – and all were decommissioned in the summer of 1946. The last to disband were Nos. 1831 and 1851 Squadrons on 13 August 1946.

Chapter 7

'The Sweetheart of Okinawa'

There were parked aircraft lined up on the runway and with the red Jap meatball zeroed in on my gunsight, I blasted away. I was almost mesmerized watching the first plane explode in a violent ball of flame and the second one fly apart as my bullets struck home.

Lieutenant (j.g.) Roy D. 'Eric' Erickson USNR VBF-10[1]

On 28 December 1944 Corsairs finally went to sea aboard fleet carriers. VMF-124 'Checkerboards' and VMF-213 'Hellhawks' sailed from Ulithi Lagoon in the Carolines aboard the *Essex* for their second Pacific deployments. VMF-124 had left the Solomons on 7 September 1943 and had trained in California until 18 September 1944 when it had moved to Pearl Harbor. VMF-213 had returned to the United States on 9 December 1943 to reform at Mojave, California, before being declared ready for a second deployment and moving to Ulithi on 25 December to join VMF-124 aboard the *Essex*. The 'Checkerboards' had already qualified for carrier landings aboard the flat-tops *Saratoga*, *Makassar Strait* and *Bataan*. The voyage back to the Pacific War begun on 30 December when *Essex* slipped anchor at Pearl and headed west. The start of the voyage was marred by three fatal landing crashes during training. On the first day after his first take off, Lieutenant Thomas J. Campion's Corsair spun in off the starboard bow. He was killed when his Corsair burst into flames as it hit the flight deck.

Next day a second Corsair pilot spun in but he was picked up by a plane-guard destroyer. A short time later another F4U pilot lost power while recovering aboard and he, too, spun in and was drowned when the Corsair sank beneath the waves. Altogether the two USMC squadrons lost an unlucky thirteen F4U-1Ds and seven pilots before the *Essex* reached its destination. This was in part due to the Marine pilots' relative inexperience

---

1. All Eric Erickson quotes are from correspondence with the author.

in bad weather instrument-flying and navigation from a carrier at sea. Operating in the northern Philippines, in very limited visibility, three pilots took off on a mission and never returned. The other Corsairs lost were written off in water landings. Then, on 3 January, the Corsairs from *Essex* mounted their first strike – escorting bombers to Okinawa. They shot down one Japanese aircraft for the loss of one of their own.

After the seizure of the Philippines, most of the American fast-carrier task forces were deployed forward to the Western Pacific for the final assault on the Japanese home islands. The Pacific War reached another turning point on 12 January when the *Essex* entered the South China Sea with ten other carriers of Task Force 38 and its Corsairs escorted TBM Avenger bombers on a raid on the Saigon area in French Indo-China. The raid caused considerable damage to enemy airfields and fourteen warships and thirty-one merchant vessels were sunk. Corsair pilots claimed twelve enemy aircraft destroyed on the ground for the loss of one F4U to anti-aircraft fire. By 25 January VMF-124 and VMF-213 had destroyed ten enemy aircraft in the air and sixteen on the ground, as well as damaging several Japanese vessels, but seventeen F4U-1Ds and eight pilots were lost, the majority of them from operational accidents.

During December 1944 the *Bunker Hill* had received VF-84 'Wolf Gang', VMF-221 'Fighting Falcons' and VMF-451 'Blue Devils', part of CVG Carrier (Air Group)-84 and at the end of the month VMF-112 'Wolfpack' and VMF-123 'Eight-Balls', part of CVG-82, had gone to sea aboard the *Bennington*. During the first week of February 1945 the F4U-1Ds of VMF-216 'Wild Hares' and VMF-217 'Bulldogs', part of CVG-81, were taken aboard the *Wasp*. During March *Wasp* also received the F4U-1D Navy Corsairs of VBF (Bombing-Fighting Squadron)-86 'Bengal Bandits'. By February 1945 three more USN fleet carriers besides *Essex*, which in March also received the F4U-1D Navy Corsairs of VBF-83, had received Corsairs. Altogether, the eight Marine squadrons totalled 144 Corsairs, or 16 per cent of the fighter strength of the Fast Carrier Task Force. The United States were also supported by the addition of thirteen land-based RNZAF Corsair squadrons, where previously they had flown Curtiss Kittyhawks. Three of the RNZAF Corsair squadrons were based on Bougainville, one on Guadalcanal, two at Espíritu Santo, one on Emirou, two on Green Island, one on Los Negros in the Philippines and two in New Zealand.

Also on 3 February Marine Carrier Division 27 received the first of its four 'jeep' carriers for the final battles against Japan. *Block Island*, which received eight F4U-1Ds of VMF-511 and eight Hellcats on 20 March 1945, was assigned to MCVG (Marine Carrier Air Group)-1. *Gilbert Islands*, with the Corsairs of VMF-512 embarked, was assigned to MCVG-2. *Vella Gulf*, with VMF(N)-513 'Flying Nightmares' embarked on 17 June, was assigned to MCVG-3. *Cape Gloucester*, with F4U-1Ds and FG-1Ds of VMF-351 embarked, went into action off Okinawa in July. The *Gilbert Islands* flew support missions at Okinawa in May and carried out airfield suppression at Sakishima Retto during June before supporting the landings at Balikpapan, along with *Block Island*, which was off Formosa when the war ended. The *Vella Gulf* arrived at Saipan late in July and served briefly in August at Okinawa. Also in July, the *Cape Gloucester* provided support for minesweeping and air strikes in the East China Sea.

Meanwhile, the first stage in the final assault on the Japanese home islands had begun on 16 February. Extensive raids on enemy airfields in the Tokyo area were made from the carriers by 144 Corsairs and other fighters, while the invasion fleet moved to take Iwo Jima, a small island midway between Saipan and Tokyo. Launch began sixty miles off the coast of Honshu, 125 miles from the Imperial City. The nine squadrons of Corsairs – VMF-112 and 123 on *Bennington*, VMF-124 and 213 on *Essex*, VMF-221 and 451 and VF-84 on *Bunker Hill* and VMF-216 and 217 on *Wasp* – were credited with seventeen enemy planes destroyed in the air, for the loss of ten Corsairs and eight pilots. On the 17th, to inflict maximum damage on Japanese aircraft factories in the Tokyo area, a large strike group was formed from three aircraft carriers. Air Group Four (with twenty-two F6Fs, seven F4Us and thirteen TBMs) was joined by Air Group 84 (twelve F4Us, fifteen SB2Cs and fifteen TBMs) and Air Group 46 (eight F6Fs and nine TBMs). Captain Wilbur Jackson 'Gus' Thomas of VMF-213, who had eighteen-and-a-half victories thus far in the war, led a flight of seven F4Us escorting thirteen TBM3s of VT-4 into, over and back from Nakajima Tama aircraft engine plant on the north-western edge of Tokyo city. A total of twenty-four Tonys, Oscars and Tojos 'annoyed' the formation at times from shortly after the time they crossed the coast line south of Tokyo throughout their approach, their final bombing run and to their rendezvous point south and west of the city. Two were definitely shot down and two were observed to be badly smoking and burning about the engine. No American planes were lost. First to attack were four Zekes, reddish brown with big red meatballs. Making an opposite pass outside the fighter cover, they slow-rolled as they went by.

'Our flight was high cover, at about 17,000 feet and had just crossed the coast line,' Gus Thomas recalled. 'They made stab passes, possibly trying to force our cover off after them. Five Oscars then appeared above and at 10 o'clock and followed the planes into the target area, where two more appeared. Four Oscars followed the VT down, but could not get through the fighter cover. Dahl, guns frozen, found an Oscar on his tail and executed a 360-degree turn, with Goetz sticking by. The manoeuvre relieved Dahl's situation, but put the Japanese on Goetz's tail. Doing a wing-over, Dahl sliced toward the Oscar, relieving Goetz's tail position (the Japanese got one hit in his wing) and the section rejoined. Falling on the Oscar's tail, the old weave when he turned did the trick and Goetz got a burst in from 11 o'clock at the Japanese's engine, flaming it.'

Thomas saw it hit the deck in flames and the kill went to Goetz. Thomas and Reynolds found themselves attacked by four Oscars and, in the ensuing melee, Reynolds flamed one when he turned to get away from Thomas. A second Oscar made the mistake of getting in front of Thomas' guns for a brief instant and was last seen smoking around the engine nacelle. A fourth, intent on getting in a position to fire at Reynolds, came under Thomas' guns and fell away with flames and smoke visible about the engine. Credit, two 'probables' to Thomas, one destroyed for Reynolds.[2]

While proceeding to the rendezvous area, two Oscars came down astern of Kerceude's three-plane division above. The division immediately went into a defensive weave. A 20mm shell exploded in Deboeuf's cockpit. A piece of shrapnel entered his shoulder and minute fragments splattered into his face.

The bombs observed to hit seemed to fall directly into the target and smoke and fires could be seen emanating from the vital area of the plant. AA was intense, but not too accurate.

In addition to the main strike group to hit Tokyo the *Essex* launched several fighter sweeps. At 0708 hours a Marine Corsair group from VMF 124 attacked Teteyama airfield. At 0755 another VMF search group under

---

2. Gus Thomas, born 29 October 1920 at El Dorado, Butler County, Kansas, was killed on 28 January 1947 in an F7F-30 in bad weather at Old Saddleback Mountain, California.

Major Marshall attacked shipping along the coast and Second Lieutenant R.D. Greer destroyed a Judy. By the end of the day the Marines had been credited with seven kills and the VF-4 'Red Rippers' with eight confirmed kills.

On the 19th the air attack on Iwo Jima began. It was the first close air support mission of the war for an amphibious assault. As the troops hit the invasion beaches F4U and Hellcat pilots aboard *Bunker Hill, Wasp, Bennington* and *Essex* were told to 'go in and scrape your bellies on the beaches'. The Corsairs roared into action over the sands of Iwo Jima firing their 5-inch rockets and machine guns at gun positions just 200 yards ahead of the invading US troops and unleashed their deadly cargoes of bombs and napalm on the enemy emplacements inshore. *Bunker Hill, Wasp, Bennington* and *Essex* repeatedly launched Corsairs and Hellcats on strikes against over 640 enemy strongpoints and gun positions throughout the day. Air strikes on Iwo Jima continued for four days, until 22 February. The island citadel, dominated by Mount Suribachi at its southern end, finally fell on 23 March at a cost of 6,000 American and 22,000 Japanese lives. At Iwo Jima twenty-five suicide aircraft sank an American escort carrier, and damaged a large carrier and two smaller ships.

On 23 February aircraft from the Fast Carrier Task Force (58) made attacks on Chichi Jima before heading for Japanese home waters for another strike on Tokyo. The raid went ahead at 0800 on 25 February but the weather was bitterly cold and some of the F4Us' machine guns and gun cameras froze and pilots were unable to fire properly. Nine Corsairs of VMF-124 and VMF-213 from the *Essex* made strikes on Kamagaya and Matsuyama airfields north of Tokyo and duelled with fourteen Japanese fighters, shooting down five and damaging six. The *Essex* Corsairs completed their mission by strafing cargo ships off Inubo Point. Meanwhile, Corsairs from *Bennington* had also gone on shipping strikes, in Tokyo Bay. Two F4Us of VMF-123, including the CO, Major Everett Alward, were lost. Sixteen F4Us of VF-84 from *Bunker Hill* attacked Katori airfield with HVARs (high velocity rockets) and they shot down at least nine enemy fighters which tried to intercept the Corsairs. Two Franks and one Zeke were downed by 'Fighting 84's CO, Lieutenant Commander Roger R. Hedrick, to take his final tally to twelve confirmed victories. Bad weather cancelled all further operations during the afternoon.

The end of the war was in sight and Japan could not win. During the Battle for the Philippines the Japanese had lost an estimated 9,000 aircraft, including 4,000 in combat. Of these, the *tokko tai* (special attack) pilots, who sank sixteen US ships and damaged another 150, destroyed 650 in suicide attacks by hits or near misses. Okinawa, an island sixty miles long in the Ryukyu chain, only 350 miles from Kyushu, would see the supreme effort by the kamikazes. Experienced Japanese pilots were now few and far between and barely enough were trained to be able to hit shipping by conventional means. So a plan called Ten-Go (Heavenly Operation) was devised whereby aerial attacks known as *kikusui* or 'floating chrysanthemums', would be made on American shipping by the kamikazes. Even though the Japanese air force was outnumbered and outclassed by American airpower there would certainly be plenty of targets for the kamikazes to aim for. Some 1,457 US ships would be involved in the operation to take the heavily-fortified island.

On 1 March Task Force 58 carrier aircraft, including Corsairs, began strikes on Okinawa before heading south to Ulithi Lagoon in the Carolines. VMF-112 Wolfpack and VMF-123 Eight-Balls on *Bennington* were credited with shooting down twenty-three enemy aircraft in the air and destroying a further twenty-four on the ground for a loss of twenty-four Corsairs and nine pilots. In a five-week period aboard *Wasp* F4U-1Ds of VMF-216 and VMF-217 were credited with the destruction of nineteen Japanese aircraft, five of them in the air, and a Japanese destroyer, for the loss of nine Corsairs and five pilots. On 10 March VMF-124 and 213 left the carrier *Essex* and returned to the United States onboard the escort carrier *Long Island*. In a two-month period the Checkerboards and Hellhawks had shot down twenty-three Japanese aircraft in the air and destroyed sixty-four on the ground for the loss of twenty-four aircraft and nine pilots. On 13 March the pilots of VMF-216 and -217 from *Wasp* left for Pearl Harbor also. Some of their thirty-six F4U-1Ds and deck crews remained aboard to be used by the incoming VBF-86 Bengal Bandits of CVG-81 and, likewise, VMF-216 and 217's F4U-1s were retained aboard *Essex* for the incoming VBF-83, part of CVG-83. VMF-112 and 123 were on *Bennington*, VMF-221 and 451 and VF-84 on *Bunker Hill*, VBF-10 and VF-10 with thirty F4U-1D/4s on *Intrepid* and VBF-6 on *Hancock*. With the arrival on 18 March 1945 of the *Franklin* with the F4U-1Ds of VMF-214 (the old Black Sheep Squadron'with new pilots), VMF-

452 'Sky Raiders' and VBF-5's FG-1Ds, there were now thirteen Corsair squadrons in the task force, with seven being USN and six USMC.

On Sunday 18 March *Franklin*, *Bennington* and *Bunker Hill* sent off their air groups on raids on forty-five airfields on Kyushu. VBF-10's F4U-1D/4s from *Intrepid* were used on CAP and an inland strike but lost three Corsairs and two pilots, shooting down just one Judy in return. Ensign Roy D. 'Eric' Erickson recalled the events of that day: 'The rough sea sheared against the great steel hull of *Intrepid*. I looked up at the black ominous sky and found it next to impossible to discern the horizon from the cockpit of my F4U-ID. My plane captain, a man in his early thirties, was near tears and shaking as he came up onto the wing beside me and helped me into my shoulder harness. He seemed much older to me, though, as I inserted the plotting board into its slot and locked it in place. He told me they'd all heard a report that the sky was thick with Jap planes overhead and he feared for his life. I consoled him as best I could, but I had to be about my business.

'I flicked on the black light, illuminating my control panel and enabling me to adjust my trim tab settings. From the bridge the loudspeaker bellowed, "Erickson, turn off those Goddamn lights!" I complied in a flash. How the hell did they know it was me? With the absolute blackout, I couldn't understand how they could identify me in particular. Of course, the men up on the bridge had every plane and pilot's position carefully plotted on the deck.

'The deck of the carrier seemed to explode with smoke, fire and noise as we all started our planes. Like a blind man reading Braille, I went through the checklist, knowing the failure to follow one step could kill me. Tightening my shoulder straps, I followed the lighted wands of the deck officer and moved forward to the left catapult, lowering and locking my wings into place. The deck crew hooked my aircraft to the hydraulic-powered monster. The image of myself as a stone in some giant sling came to mind. As usual, the commander and his wingman were already in the air and Lieutenant (j.g.) G.R.H. "Windy" Hill, my section leader, had just been launched off the right catapult. I put my head back against the headrest and raised my arm to show the deck officer I was ready for launch. Lowering my arm, the catapult shot me into space!

'Tail-End Charlie was my position in the division of four aircraft led by [CAG] Commander [John J.] Hyland. Ensign Tessier was on the commander's wing and my section leader was Windy. Not only was the CAG's division the first to be launched from *Intrepid*, it was the first to land and the first to wait as well. We circled above and watched the other divisions launch and join up, grouping in a long waving tail before each division proceeded to their designated target.

'All the fighters and fighter-bombers were in the air and now the torpedo planes were taking off from *Intrepid*'s deck. The first TBM took off and sank out of sight below the deck. I watched as he re-appeared and saw him land in the water. Fortunately, the pilot had managed to ditch safely to one side of the oncoming carrier. The three crewmen scrambled from the still floating Avenger and managed to get into their lifeboat. No sooner had they gotten their feet out of the drink when the identical thing happened to the next TBM attempting a take off. They too had cleared the oncoming carrier and were safely getting into their lifeboat. As soon as the carrier and the destroyers had cleared the area, they were picked up by the trailing DD and transferred to *Intrepid* for the next day's strike. I thought to myself, does this happen every day? If it did, we sure didn't need the enemy to help us. We were doing just fine by ourselves and it wouldn't be long before we would be out of torpedo planes altogether! Later, I found out that there was too little wind over the deck that day to obtain enough air speed to get the two planes airborne with their heavy loads of torpedoes and fuel. I never again saw or heard of a similar experience.

'It was Commander Hyland's responsibility to co-ordinate all the attacking aircraft within the air group. He was also air co-ordinator for other great sweeps involving the aircraft from carriers operating with us. One of my duties was to protect his tail.

'The sun and mist were breaking over the horizon as we continued to the target over an endless sea. I was nervous with anticipation over what was in store. It was hard to realize that I was actually on my way to attack the home islands of Japan as my eyes kept searching the sky for enemy aircraft and the ocean below for enemy ships or any sign of life. I calculated the force of the wind from the size of the waves and kept track of our course on my plotting board. If we were to encounter enemy planes and I was to get lost in the melee, it would be my only tool to help me find my way home to the fleet.

'Flying wing is not like leading the pack. It is an unending juggling of the throttle and working diligently to stay close to your section leader, keeping a constant watch on any movements he might make. The last position in a formation was usually the first one that got picked off from an unknown assailant coming out of the sun and I was not about to let this happen. I was kept very busy.

'My mind started playing tricks on me when I thought I heard strange noises coming from the engine but a quick glance at my instruments told me everything was OK. My imagination kept conjuring up problems that didn't exist. Was I running out of fuel? Were the magnetos firing properly? Were my guns even working? I even practised grabbing the ring of my parachute just to be sure it was still there!

'An hour of monotonous searching and checking had passed when suddenly through the mist appeared our target – Saeki Naval Base, located on the shoreline of Kyushu. I forgot all the imaginary problems and concentrated on the target, arming my guns, bombs and setting my outboard rockets to fire. I checked all the instruments to make sure all was in working order. My adrenalin was really flowing as we pushed over in our attack. I went to the outside of the formation and a little behind Windy so that I could concentrate on the target. There were parked aircraft lined up on the runway and, with the red Jap meatball zeroed in on my gunsight, I blasted away. I was almost mesmerised watching the first plane explode in a violent ball of flame and the second one fly apart as my bullets struck home.

'As we cleared the field I saw a tanker cruising in the harbour. Re-setting my eight rockets, I fired them in salvo while strafing the tanker. The rockets all smashed into its deck and hull. As I looked around it was blowing and blazing and sailors were diving into the ocean; one less ship in the Jap Navy. We made a few more strafing runs over the airfield and then CAG gave us the thumbs up and turned for home. I had not yet learned to conserve fuel while flying Tail-End Charlie, which used much more gas than when flying lead. Pumping the throttle and flying wide in a turn would suck up your fuel all too quickly. The next day, I learned to conserve fuel by slipping under aircraft on a turn and by fine-tuning the richness of my fuel mixture until full rich was really needed. However, the four-and-one-half hour flight had nearly depleted all fuel tanks.

'Upon returning to the fleet, *Intrepid* was in the process of launching aircraft and was unable to land any planes. Many of us were running out of gas. The carrier *Enterprise*, the "Big E," had just cleared their decks and had turned into the wind and they were prepared to take me aboard. As my fuel gauge showed my tanks to be nearly empty, I knew I would have to make the first approach a good one or go for a swim. I made the standard approach down the right side of the carrier, lowering my flaps and landing gear and opening my cowl flaps. I lowered the tail hook, making sure my tail wheel wasn't locked, put the prop in full rpm and moved the mixture control to full-rich as I made my turn into the groove. Sighting the landing signal officer, I waited for his signals and corrections, but he stood there just as if he was cast in stone. While closing in on the fantail of the *Enterprise*, I kept watching the LSO. The *Enterprise*'s deck seemed much narrower and shorter than *Intrepid*, but I had never made such a perfect approach before and I began to wonder if the LSO was OK. He was still standing there with both arms extended in a "roger". As I came abreast of the fantail, he gave me a cut and I dropped onto the deck, grabbing the number-two wire. I raised my tail hook, folded my wings and crossed over the barriers. I was later told that I had five gallons of fuel left. Not enough to have taken a wave off, but then I knew that already.

'Crossing over the deck I went into the pilots' ready room and grabbed a cup of cocoa. As I sipped the hot concoction the LSO arrived, with a big smile on his face. Shaking my hand he said, "Congratulations, you're the first Corsair I've ever landed!" The "Big E" was flying F6Fs and this explained his statue-like stance as I made my final approach. He said he figured I knew more about the Corsair than he did and he decided to leave it all up to me!'[3]

Also on 18 March, VBF-83 from the *Essex* claimed seventeen Zekes and a Judy destroyed and nine more enemy aircraft probably destroyed. Three of the *Essex* Corsairs were shot down over Tomikaka airfield. The Marine Corps' Corsairs from *Bunker Hill* and *Bennington* were credited with the destruction of fourteen enemy planes for the loss of two Corsairs. *Franklin*'s contribution to the war against Japan, however, was all too brief. At 0708 hours the following day she was hit by two 550lb bombs dropped from 100 feet above the carrier by a Judy. The explosions ignited thirty-one fuelled and armed Corsairs, Helldivers and Avengers on her flight deck ready for launch. Only superhuman efforts managed to extinguish the blazing inferno, which resulted as bombs, fuel and rockets exploded,

---

3. Correspondence with the author.

but 724 men died and a further 265 were wounded. *Franklin* survived but she was out of action for the rest of the war. She limped away under her own power and headed for sanctuary at Ulithi Lagoon and ultimately made it to Pearl.

Ensign Eric Erickson of VBF-10 takes up the story again, on Monday 19 March: 'Japanese Air Group 343 was flying the new NIK2-J Shiden 21, codename 'George'. Derived from a Kawanishi 'Rex' floatplane, the aircraft had gone through many stages of development. Unlike the Zeros, the George had a special automatic flap system that enabled it to turn on a dime. It also had self-sealing gas tanks, armour plate to protect the pilot and two 20mm cannon in each wing. With a top speed of 369 mph at 18,370 feet, it was a formidable foe against the Corsair and the Hellcat. In the hands of a veteran pilot the George was probably one of the best fighters to come out of the Pacific theatre of war.

'Dawn was breaking above the mountains and what a sight it was, nearly overwhelming! Having studied art since the age of eight, I was familiar with Japanese prints. I had always thought Japanese artists had taken a very broad artistic licence when they showed their mountain peaks to be so sharply pointed, with clouds of mist and fog lying in milky layers at their base. But here, before my eyes, was the very embodiment of a Hiroshige print and with the rising sun no less, providing the luscious kind of theatrical lighting. The colours of the canvas before me literally produced tears of appreciation, but then my mind snapped back to reality. I gently rolled off to one side to test my guns. Hitting the charger-buttons with my feet, I pulled the trigger on the control stick and found to my satisfaction that all six fifties were in superb working order.

'We crossed the mountains and arrived over the inlet at 12,000 feet. As we approached the target, I could see a group of eight Japanese planes circling 6,000 feet above us at eleven o'clock. Little did any of us realize they were from Genda's 343 Air Group, led by Lieutenant Kanno from 301 Squadron. Excitedly, I radioed Hyland and told him of my sighting, but he informed me he'd already been watching them for the last few minutes. They were tail-chasing each other in a circle. One would do a snap roll, followed by another and then another. Whether they were trying to draw us away from the target, getting their courage up, or just plain showing off, I do not know. This was my first encounter with enemy fighters and, staring at the bright red meatballs on their wings and fuselages, it seemed as though I was watching a movie unreel before my eyes. We were indeed over Japan! I couldn't help thinking of an article that had been recently published in *Life* magazine. A full-page photo showed some downed B-24 pilots getting their heads chopped off in a town square by their Jap captors. The memory alone left me both angry and apprehensive as we flew deeper over the island.

'The commander led us across the bay, making a 180-degree turn, and we started our approach toward the oil storage tanks. At about 12,000 feet, we released our belly tanks and then armed our bombs in the dive. Our division began the attack followed closely by the other six planes. We were met with an absolutely ferocious barrage of anti-aircraft fire. Dropping our bombs, firing our rockets and strafing the target, we pulled out over the bay at 3,000 feet to avoid small-arms ground fire, which was as capable of killing us as anything else. Then a peculiar thing happened.

'I informed Commander Hyland that I'd sighted a Rufe floatplane taking off in front of us. Hyland went after the Rufe and Hill and I started to climb. I was confused – should I join Hyland or continue with Hill? In a split second I realized there really wasn't a decision to make. My duty was to fly wing on Windy and I stuck right with him. Hyland splashed that floatplane, a well-deserved first victory in his new squadron. My observation was that it was a Rufe, a basic Zero fighter with a float attachment. Hyland recorded it as a Rex floatplane, the forerunner of the George, which we would encounter shortly. Almost fifty years later I was proven right. The CAG's victim had indeed been in a Rufe! Lieutenant Shunji Yamada of the 951 Air Group survived the encounter, but his aircraft was destroyed.

'My three years of training were about to pay off. No longer did I have to think about a manoeuvre – it was as if my aircraft and I were one! Every fighter pilot aboard ship thought he was the best and knew he was. With a competitive nature and spirit of aggressiveness, he wouldn't allow for the possibility that he would be the one to get shot down. His ego wouldn't allow it. I myself had formed great confidence in two things, my ability to navigate accurately, but, most importantly, I could damn well hit whatever the hell I was aiming at.

'After we'd climbed to 3,000 feet I suddenly realized, as had Windy, that we were alone! I kept a very watchful eye on the circling enemy aircraft above us and, as we continued to climb, two of the Zekes did a snap roll and flew straight down towards us. As they came within range I pulled up into them, pulling back on the stick and greying out for a few seconds. Thank God I had my anti-blackout suit on, for I could still see the oncoming aircraft. Without the suit I would have blacked out completely. My vision was clear as I put my gunsight directly on the lead plane and fired. The Jap pilots were flying in such a tight section that I raked both planes with .50 calibre rounds. My plane shook as the tracers flowed and I could see them sparkle against the silver-grey under-bellies of the oncoming Zeros. As the lead plane passed over me he was already in flame, trailing thick black smoke. He was so close I could count the rivets in his wings. Windy was below me and wasn't able to confirm my kill, but now, out of formation, I wisely decided to form on Windy and not follow the plane that I'd lit up.

'Making a turn to join up, I saw another Zeke sitting on Windy's tail, guns flashing away! We started our weave and Hill shouted, "Shoot the son-of-a-bitch, Eric, shoot the son-of-a-bitch!" By now we were well into our first weave and I answered, "What the hell do you think I'm trying to do?"

'My first efforts to get him in my sights were fruitless and I quickly realized that we were weaving too tight. On the second weave, I went out far enough to make damn sure I had him sighted. All this time he had been hammering at Windy and I'm sure my partner's drawers were a bit moist. The Zeke suddenly broke away to the left of Windy and now flew directly in front of me! I could see Windy off to the right, still zigging and zagging, seemingly unaware that his pursuer had turned away. In a matter of seconds I had the unwary Jap pilot perfectly bracketed in my sights and then, with all my six guns blazing, the Zeke blew apart! The front part of his plane flew on straight and level, but the tail section sheared off behind the cockpit and spun crazily away. Gaining on him fast, I flew through all kind of flaming debris, instinctively ducking to avoid getting hit by all the fragments. There was no sign of anyone even trying to jump out of the enemy plane, so I assumed the pilot was dead. The time it took to make that assumption was all the thought I gave it.

'I was now high above and in front of Windy and I made a turn to join up on him. To my amazement he was already shooting at another Zero! I watched as his quarry burst into flame and the pilot scrambled out. He was wearing a full-length, dark-brown flight suit and an astonished expression. As his chute billowed I tried to get my sights on him, but to no avail. At the time I didn't think of shooting the parachute. Later I heard it might not be a good thing to do, as it didn't help the treatment given to our PoWs below. I had no moment to consider this either – I was at war.

'What neither of us realized was that Windy had just shot down the Japanese ace, Lieutenant Kanno, leader of Squadron 301 from Air Group 343! Joining up, we headed toward the sea. As we traversed the mountains and hills I saw another Zero directly below and heading in the opposite direction. I thought it would be a great opportunity for an overhead run, but since Windy didn't see him, I again thought it prudent to stick with my section leader.

'Cruising back over Shikoku Island, I looked over at Windy, who had positioned me a hundred yards to the side of him and I couldn't believe my eyes. There sat a Tojo on his tail and all four of the Jap's cannon were blinking his way! I shouted a warning to Windy and we immediately broke to weave, but I couldn't get my sights on the enemy with the proper lead. Not wanting to waste ammo, I didn't fire. Having learned my lessons well the first time around, I went further out than seemed necessary. Coming back on the second weave, I had a straight 90-degree deflection shot. I had to put my sights directly on Windy's head to get the proper lead on the enemy aircraft and it took real nerves of steel to pull the trigger. True to my training, the tracers seemed to bend directly into the Tojo! He went ablaze and slid to earth as if he was on a greased wire. In my mind, this was my third victory of the day!'

The Japanese bomber and kamikaze strikes against Task Force 58.2 caused heavy damage to the *Enterprise* – on 18 March – and *Wasp*, and also forced their withdrawal from battle, reducing the number of navy and USMC Corsair fighter squadrons to nine on six carriers. 'The Big E' returned to be hit again on 11 and 14 April. *Wasp* took a direct hit, which ignited aviation gasoline, wrecking the hangar deck and killing or injuring 370 personnel. Like *Franklin*, only the bravery and efficiency of her fire crews saved the carrier from extinction and *Wasp* was able to recover her aircraft returning from strikes inland.

Despite the losses, US pre-invasion strikes continued. On 21 March a new threat against the fleet manifested itself. In addition to the suicide bombers, Japan could also call upon about fifty single-seat Yokosuka MXY-7 Ohka ('Cherry Blossom') 16.5-foot-long piloted missiles. These 'special attack' aircraft were packed with 2,645lb of explosive and powered by three rocket motors. They were taken up from Kanoya by a Betty or 'Peggy' (Mitsubishi Hiryu Ki-67) mother aircraft and, once Allied shipping had been sighted, would be launched from 20,000 feet to make diving attacks on ships at over 400 mph. The Americans called them 'Bakas'. (*Baka* is Japanese for 'fool'.) Eighteen of the Bakas were inbound on the afternoon of the 21st, escorted by thirty Zekes but the Hellcats of TG.58.1 mainly dealt with the threat. On 23 March Okinawa was attacked again and Corsairs from VMF-112 and VMF–123, together with VF-82, destroyed twenty-six suicide boats and damaged military targets on Okinawa. On the 24th eight Corsairs from *Intrepid* used 'Tiny Tim' rockets for the first time, on caves at Okinawa. These rockets were considered inaccurate and unreliable and were later withdrawn from use. One of the Corsairs was struck by one of the rockets and had to make a forced landing on the *Yorktown*.

At first light on Easter Sunday, 1 April, CVG-84 including Corsairs of VMF-221 'Fighting Falcons' and VMF-451 'Blue Devils' on *Bunker Hill* and VMF-112 and 123 on *Bennington*, bombed and strafed beaches with napalm and gunfire before more than 200,000 men were landed on Okinawa. Two days later, kamikaze attacks off Okinawa threatened to disrupt the invasion and the American fighter shield was hard put to cope with the suicide planes. Twelve Corsairs of VMF-451 played their part, joining sixteen Hellcats on an attack mission over Amami-O-Shima and Kikai Jima. The Corsairs destroyed eleven of the kamikazes, while the Hellcats bagged the others. On the 6th and the 7th, the largest concentration of kamikazes so far appeared over the fleet. About 700 aircraft took off from Kyushu and, of these, 355 (230 navy and 125 army) were flown by suicide pilots bent on sinking a carrier or other shipping. More than 200 of the kamikazes were shot down by the fast carrier force and fifty more by the escort carriers but twenty-eight kamikazes got past the combined air and sea defences and each hit a US ship, sinking three of them. On the first day Corsairs of VMF-221 Fighting Falcons and VMF-451 Blue Devils from *Bunker Hill* splashed twelve of the suicide planes and, on the second day, Corsairs from *Bunker Hill* and *Bennington* claimed seventeen of them.

Some measure of retribution for the suicide attacks was achieved on 7 April, one of the biggest days in the history of VBF-10. Early in the morning two target CAPs from the *Intrepid* were launched over Okinawa.

Commander Hyland, who led one flight, succeeded in shooting down a Val over the target. His flight then proceeded to Tokuno, where they destroyed a twin-engine and a single-engine plane and damaged other grounded aircraft in revetments. During the day Ensign Raymond V. Lanthier Jr, flying a target CAP, shot down a Tojo and Lieutenant Moran, flying CAP, damaged a Myrt snooper.

Meanwhile, aboard the *Intrepid*, considerable excitement was created by the report, made at 0830 by an *Essex* search plane, of a Japanese task group in the East China Sea steaming south towards Okinawa. It was composed of the super-battleship *Yamato*, an Agano-class cruiser, an Oyodo-class cruiser and seven destroyers. The *Yamato*, a 64,170-ton beast with nine 18.1-inch guns, had put to sea with only enough fuel for a one-way kamikaze trip of her own. The Japanese task group was shadowed by two PBM Mariner flying boats, which held contact for five hours despite being shot at by their prey. At 0915 Admiral Mitscher sent off sixteen fighters to track the *Yamato* and, at 0100, Task Groups 58.1 and 58.3 began launching a 280-plane strike. Included in this group were ninety-eight torpedo-carrying Avengers. The *Hancock* was fifteen minutes late in sending off her fifty-three-plane contribution. TG 58.4 followed this main strike with 106 planes. Among them were twelve Corsairs of VBF-10, led by Lieutenant Commander Wilmer E. Rawie, a former Dauntless pilot, who was also leader of seventy-five planes of TG 58.4.

One of the VBF-10 Corsairs was flown by Ensign Eric Erickson who recalls: 'It was 1030. I was resting in my sack, having served as the duty officer for the early morning 0600 flights, when suddenly over the squawk box I heard the message, "Ensign Erickson report to the ready room!" I put on my pants and shirt and slipped into a pair of loafers. In case I had to go for a swim, I wanted to get out of my shoes fast. I hurried down the corridor, through several hatches, crossing the hangar deck and up the ladder to the ready room. The duty officer said, "Get on deck." One of my buddies, Ensign Ecker, had injured his hand the day before and was unable to fly, so I took his place. They needed every available pilot. I didn't know whom I was flying with and was completely unaware of the urgent situation. Jotting down Point Option on my plotting board and putting on my flight gear, while noting the deck assignment for the aircraft, I left the ready room.

'Pilots were firing up their engines and many were already in the air. I crawled aboard my assigned plane and strapped myself in. The plane captain handed me a chocolate bar and a canteen of water. I said, "What the hell is this for?" Never had I been treated with so much attention. He said, "Haven't you heard? They have located the Jap fleet!" Suddenly, it dawned on me what the huge 1,000lb bomb was doing under my plane.

'I had never seen so much helter-skelter as the deck officer directed me forward. He rotated his flag violently and then pointed it down the deck. Pushing the throttle full forward, my plane rose from the deck. I joined up on a division that was missing a plane. I found myself flying wing on Wes Hays [Lieutenant (j.g.) Wesley M. Hays, was leading VBF-10's third division] from Texas. Lieutenant (j.g.) Hollister and Ensign Carlisse filled the other two slots. On the way to the target the sky became increasingly black due to rainsqualls and the heavy weather front the Japs were using as cover.

'Still groggy from this unexpected call to duty I cranked off the cap to the canteen and took a swallow of water. I grabbed the candy bar that I had stuffed in a trouser leg of my flight suit and I thought about how thoughtful the plane captain had been. It provided me with a new surge of energy as I slid under the lead plane. Now the rainsqualls were getting worse and visibility was lessening. Looking down at the water I could see white caps below and I estimated the wind to be around 25 knots, not a good day to make a water landing. No longer was the engine making imaginary noises as on my first combat flight, but was purring like a kitten. Checking all the instruments the plane seemed to be functioning properly. We had travelled for over two hours searching the sea through this muck looking for the elusive Japanese Fleet. I hadn't been present at the briefing so I had no way of knowing exactly where we were headed, but by plotting the time and course I knew we were somewhere south and west of Kyushu.

'At about 1330 my skipper, Lieutenant Commander Rawie ("Red One") was about ready to turn back. We were flying at 1,500 feet when, suddenly, through the scud, directly beneath me I saw a grey massive structure. I was the first in our group to see the biggest damn battleship in the world – the mammoth 64,000-ton *Yamato*! It had been hiding under rainsqualls and low clouds. I transmitted the message to Red One that the *Yamato* was directly below and Wes Hays signalled us to start our attack! We whipped into a fast 180-degree turn in an attempt to get on the *Yamato*. As we broke through the 1,500-foot ceiling, the *Yamato* appeared to be almost dead in the water, but still in a slow left turn. Smoking destroyers were all over the place and only two could be seen swiftly manoeuvring through the water. It was a navy pilot's dream with no enemy aircraft to repel our attacks.

'I had watched our task force shoot down kamikazes like they were ducks in a shooting gallery and I thought, "Oh my God! I'm now the sitting duck!" Now, I know how a kamikaze pilot must have felt as he was preparing to make his final assault. How could all those ships down there miss when they were armed with all that sophisticated radar? It was a true test of courage! Even the *Yamato's* 18.1 guns were shooting at the approaching aircraft, as they had in vain at the flying boats. In addition to her big guns, the Yamato was able to fire on us with her twenty-four 5-inch guns and about 150 25mm guns. The light cruisers and the destroyers joined in the crescendo.

'We tried to get our sights on the battleship, but we had started our run so low it was impossible. I could see men scrambling all over the deck in what looked like mass hysteria. Where were they all going? Diving and pouring on the juice we crossed over the *Yamato* and strafed the hell out of it. I could see bodies flying all over the place. In return the sky was bursting with thousands of brass wires as the Japs' guns zeroed in on us! Looking down I wondered why I wasn't getting hit; the tracers were so close you could smell the cordite. Black flak bursts were bouncing my plane violently from side to side and the sky was turning dark. I thought for sure that this was the day for me to meet my maker!

'I could read the wake of the light cruiser *Yahagia*, an Oyodo-class cruiser, as it turned around toward the *Yamato* to help protect it. This was my first time to wing Wes, but I knew he was heading directly toward the cruiser. I moved in closer and closer on him and concentrated on his aircraft as we dropped our bombs in unison. After releasing our ordnance, we headed for cloud cover and then, as if on a roller-coaster, we dived back down and skimmed along the ocean floor strafing the destroyer *Isokaze* that lay dead ahead. Flashes of bright light were blinding us as the destroyer tried to elude our attack. Suddenly the destroyer stopped firing as it went ablaze and dark black smoke poured from its deck. We passed over it and pulled up again into the low cloud cover. We thought we were out of range of enemy fire and, as we looked back, no longer were the cruiser and destroyer in view [the third division was credited with three direct hits and one near miss on the Oyodo-class cruiser]. We circled at 5,000 feet and five miles from the *Yamato*. The clouds started to clear and we could see the battleship and the rest of our group making their attack.

'While we were circling, I noticed great spouts of water rise from the ocean floor. My first thought was, some of us hadn't dropped our ordnance and were now doing so, but this was not the case. The damn *Yamato* was still shooting their big 18.1-inch guns at us – the largest guns in the world! Then, Air Group Ten's dive-bombers, torpedo-planes and fighter-bomber pilots completed their run and a terrific explosion took place. Great billows of black smoke were sent skyward over 6,000 feet – the end of the biggest battleship in the world!'

Lieutenant Commander Wilmer E. Rawie's own division had scored two hits and one near miss on the *Angano* cruiser. His second division, led by 24-year-old Texan Lieutenant Robert 'Hal' Jackson, went one better. Known as 'The Nightwatchman of the Wardroom', Jackson, who was attending law school when Pearl Harbor was attacked, achieved a completely bohemian existence amid the otherwise regimented life aboard ship. Never on the flight deck except to take off, the only way Hal knew whether it was night or day was by the activity in the wardroom. He led his flight of four VBF-10 Corsairs as high roving cover and carried out a roller-coaster type approach in order to avoid fire from the *Yamato's* gunners. He wrote: 'The four of us came in at the *Yamato* at low-level and delivered our bombs as we swept over the ship. The flak was very intense. Then we got the hell out of there as fast as we could, continuing our roller-coaster manoeuvring. One hit and several misses were observed on the ship. We circled the area below the overcast and shortly afterwards, there was a tremendous explosion.'

Hal's four Corsairs were the last aircraft to attack the *Yamato* and they were credited with a direct hit and two near misses on the battleship. They also strafed one of the destroyers, scoring many hits and starting a number of fires.

Ensign Eric Erickson concludes: 'The giant warship listed heavily to port and at 1423 disappeared underwater, followed by explosions of rupturing compartments and her magazines. It had taken ten torpedoes and five direct bomb hits to sink the *Yamato*. (Her sister ship *Masashi* had required eleven torpedoes and sixteen bombs to send her down in the Sibuyan Sea the previous October.) Two light cruisers in the *Yamato* force were sent to the ocean floor. One destroyer was sunk outright; three others were so severely damaged that they were scuttled. The four other destroyers were damaged to varying degrees. Only 269 men survived the *Yamato*; 2,498 including her captain and the force commander went down with her. Almost 1,200 more men were lost floundering in the sea. With the light cruiser and destroyers that were sunk, 3,700 lives were lost in the greatest kamikaze sortie of all. In an incredulous comparison, TF 58's carriers lost three fighters, four dive-bombers, three torpedo-planes and twelve fliers. One of the aircraft, a Corsair, was lost in a mid-air collision en route to the attack.

'Our air group rendezvoused all its planes and headed for home. Not one of our aircraft was shot down and only a few tail feathers were lost in this auspicious attack. Back in the ready room aboard *Intrepid*, five hours and fifty minutes later, our division was asked to identify who hit and who missed the cruiser we sank. The pictures taken by the photo planes showed three hits and one near miss. Of course, trying to identify your bomb from the others would be impossible. The four of us dropped our bombs together at the lead of our division leader and then, immediately pulled up through the low-lying clouds. One of the pilots however, said, 'I saw my bomb hit!' The remaining three of us were asked to draw cards to see who had dropped the bomb that nearly missed the cruiser; low card would receive that honour.

'The three of us walked over to the gaming table still set up in the pilots' ready room. We asked one of the pilots who were mulling around, to shuffle the cards. He placed the cards on the table and asked if we wished to cut. One of us cut the cards and he replaced the cut under the pack. I grabbed a section of cards, as did the others. Turning the cards over, I discovered I had drawn – the deuce of hearts! At the time I did not realize its importance and I thought, 'The whole damn war is like this, it's the luck of the draw!' A near miss in my mind might have done more damage than a direct hit. A bomb at the waterline could have blown open the seams and may have been the bomb that sank the ship. No one told us the low card would receive the DFC and the high cards would receive the Navy Cross. The Navy Cross was one of the most coveted awards the navy could bestow. A pilot can spend his entire career flying for the navy and never ever have the opportunity to receive such a distinction. The consequences of this draw continues to gnaw at me to this very day!'

Hal Jackson hoped the occult powers he demonstrated with cards aboard the *Intrepid* would aid him in studying and practising law in Denton, Texas, where his wife Barbara, waited for him. Hal, who finished the war with one Betty and three Zekes confirmed, was awarded the Silver Star for his role in sinking the *Yamato*. And when he went home in 1945, he finished his law studies and practised criminal law until retirement.

Next day, 8 April, Corsairs of VMF-224 destroyed three kamikazes trying to dive on destroyers on picket duty moored off Okinawa to give radar warning of approaching aircraft. More Corsairs arrived from Guadalcanal, Espíritu Santo and Manus Island on escort carriers during the first week of April to lend air support in the Battle of Okinawa. F4U-1Cs, F4U-1Ds and FG-1Ds of VMF-311 'Hell's Bells', VMF-312 'Day's Knights', VMF-322 'Fighting Cocks', VMF-323 'Death Rattlers' and MAG-14's VMF-224 'Fighting Wildcats' and VMF-441 'Black Jacks' were flown off the escort carriers, some during kamikaze attacks, to land at Yonton and Kadena airfields. On 7 April, while launching Corsairs of MAG-31 from the flight decks of the *Sitkoh Bay* and *Breton*, a Kawasaki Ki-48 Lily kamikaze bomber flying at 500 feet was engaged about ten miles from the carriers. The combined firepower of five of VMF-311's Corsairs blasted the kamikazes out of the sky just fifty yards short of its intended target, the *Sitkoh Bay*.

Based at Roi from January 1944, VMF-224 had taken part in strikes on the Marshalls before moving to Yontan on 7 April. VMF-441 had also operated from Roi and conducted strikes against Wotje and Maloelap before moving to Yontan with the Fighting Wildcats. The USMC squadrons entered the fray immediately. On 12 April the land-based USMC Corsairs shot down sixteen enemy aircraft, eight of them by Major Richard M. Day's VMF-312. (Day was KIA on 13 May 1945.) The four USMC Corsair squadrons from *Bennington* and *Bunker Hill* destroyed fifty-one other kamikazes. Five of them fell to the guns of Major Archie G. Donahue, CO of VMF-451, to take his personal score to fourteen confirmed victories. VF-84 from *Bunker Hill* waded in with eight victories while VBF-83 from *Essex* destroyed seven kamikaze bombers. VBF-10 from *Intrepid* claimed twenty-six kamikazes for the loss of three Corsairs, whose pilots were saved. Despite the Corsairs' best efforts, fourteen US ships were damaged during the mass suicide attacks on 12/13 April by an estimated 185 aircraft. On 14 April six F4U-1D pilots of VMF-112 flying over Iheya Shima destroyed nine kamikazes. As Lieutenant Dennis' target burst into flames, the pilot was thrown out and he struck the bulletproof windshield before bouncing off to the side and away. Later, Dennis found the remains of kamikaze silk flying clothes on his aircraft.

On 16 April a massive air battle took place off Okinawa as the enemy put up masses of kamikaze aircraft and Ohka piloted missiles. The land-based Corsair squadrons downed thirty-six kamikazes, with seventeen kills being awarded to twelve Corsairs of Major R.O. White's VMF-441, which succeeded in breaking up an attack by twenty-five Bettys, Vals and Zeros on the destroyer *Laffey*. In his first aerial combat Second Lieutenant William Eldridge shot down four enemy aircraft in four minutes. Three F4Us were lost and one pilot was killed. The carrier-borne Combat Air Patrol fighters destroyed twenty-nine enemy aircraft without loss. Pride of place went to VF-10 'Grim Reapers' from the *Intrepid*, which destroyed twenty kamikazes over northern Okinawa. One VF-10 F4U-1D pilot, Ensign (later Lieutenant (j.g.) Alfred Lerch, shot down six Nakajima Ki-27 Nates and a Val north-west of Okinawa. Two kamikazes put his carrier out of action with the loss of twenty fighters destroyed, ten men killed and almost 100 more injured. *Intrepid* was forced to leave the area for repairs at Alameda. (On 21 April the carrier *Shangri La* with VBF-85 'Sky Pirates' in Air Group 85 embarked, left Ulithi for the first of three sorties, remaining at sea the until 14 May, conducting operations in support of the Okinawa campaign). *Intrepid* took no further part in the Pacific War and VF-10 was decommissioned on 26 November 1945.

On 22 April the CAP was increased to thirty-two Corsairs and other fighters over the task force and twelve USMC Corsairs were held on ground alert. No enemy attacks were encountered during the day but, at about 1800 hours, the dusk USMC CAP was vectored towards the destroyers on the radar picket line where eighty-plus kamikazes had appeared. Ground-based Marine Corsairs were credited with the destruction of thirty-three-and-three-quarters enemy aircraft who tried desperately to attack and sink them. Of these, twenty-four-and-three-quarters were credited to VMF-323 which waded in fifty miles north of Aguni Shima. Major Jefferson D. Dorroh, the Death Rattlers' executive officer, shot down six

Vals in the space of twenty minutes. He was also awarded two 'probables'. Major George C. Axtell Jr, the CO, destroyed five of the Vals in fifteen minutes and received credit for three more damaged. First Lieutenant Jeremiah 'Jerry' J. O'Keefe also bagged five Vals, including one which tried to ram him after being set on fire. VMF-224 and VMF-441 destroyed five and three kamikazes respectively. VMF-323 would finish the Okinawa campaign with 124½ victories without loss. Corsairs of VMF-224 Fighting Wildcats and VMF-441 Black Jacks were credited with eight victories on 22 April. On 27 and 28 April the land-based Corsairs had another field day, being credited with another thirty-five-and-a-half aerial victories. On the 28th VMF-221 were credited with shooting down fourteen enemy aircraft and sixteen Corsairs of VF-84 destroyed eighteen out of twenty-eight kamikazes trying to get to the fleet.

The American forces were opposed by waves of kamikazes, which worked in conjunction with the Japanese ground forces. Kamikazes were formed into *Kikusuis*, 'floating chrysanthemums' of two to three hundred freshly-recruited, poorly-trained pilots. Between 1 April and 9 May, five *Kikusuis* attacked the American fleet. The Japanese used photo-reconnaissance, which played two roles. With a twelve-hour delay, it informed the Japanese ground force commander of army and Marine Corps movements. It also allowed the assignment of kamikaze pilots to individual ships. A reconnaissance pilot would make two complete circling photo missions around the island and the fleet. It had been their routine for several days in a row, where they would take photos back and the kamikazes could plan their suicide runs on choice targets. Interception of the reconnaissance missions was not an easy task. The kamikaze flew above the range of the largest gun of any battleship. The stripped and souped-up Nick, Kawasaki Ki-45 'Toryu' ('dragon-slayer') flew above the service ceiling, or the range, of the American fighter pilots. During 6 May two F4Us from VMF-312 had to discontinue a high-speed chase of a Mitsubishi Ki-46 Dinah. The lead Corsair's blower cut out and his wingman's engine froze. Only the flight leader, Second Lieutenant Merlin O'Neal, returned to base.

While combat air patrol and anti-aircraft fire could destroy 70 to 80 per cent of the kamikazes, the damage inflected by the remainder was horrific. On 4 May the first operational cannon-armed F4U-4s to reach Okinawa went into action, being credited with the destruction of sixty-and-three-quarters Japanese aircraft, most of them kamikaze, the second highest single day total for the USMC in the war. Six days later, on 10 May, the escort carrier *Block Island*, with VMF-511's eight F4U-1Ds, eight F6F-5Ns and six F6F-5Ps, went into action off Okinawa.

The same day, in anticipation of the reconnaissance flight, Captain Ken Reusser led his VMF-312 flight to 13,000 feet, an altitude 3,000 feet above the usual combat air patrol flight zone. For this flight Reusser was 'Ruby 1'. 'Ruby 2' was First Lieutenant Robert 'Bob' Klingman, one of nine children from Binger, Oklahoma, who, during four years as a marine, sent his pay to his mother, most of his cash coming from winning at poker. Captain Jim Cox was 'Ruby 3' and Second Lieutenant Frank Watson was 'Ruby 4':

'"Ruby 6, this is Handyman, over", the Air Control Centre called out.'

Bob Klingman listened to the voice of his flight lead in his helmet. '"Handyman, Ruby 6, go ahead."'

'"Ruby 6, Handyman … We have a bogey approaching on course one eight zero, angels two-five. Climb to angels two-five, steer 270, buster (full speed), over."'

'"Handyman, roger," Reusser responded. "Course 270 (directly West), angels two-five, out."'

At Reusser's command, they dropped their belly tanks containing reserve fuel and started to climb toward a lone Nick. When they reached 20,000 feet, Reusser ordered the flight to fire off some of their .50 calibre ammunition to reduce weight. Klingman fired off 2,000 rounds, lightening his Corsair by 687lb. When Ruby 3 and 4 started to experience engine trouble, Reusser ordered them back to CAP over the fleet. The Nick was completing a second leisurely pass when Reusser decided to take a desperation shot. Thus warned, the Nick took off at full speed.

Reusser and Klingman went to 'wartime emergency power'. Klingman recalled: 'My plane was faster than Ken's, so I went ahead of him at max speed. I remember watching the cylinder-head temperature where it was pegged in the red. I felt that when it got that hot, it would probably blow up. So, I found by easing back on the low pitch, I could get a little more speed out of my plane.'

At approximately 38,000 feet, 3,000 feet above the Corsair's rated service ceiling, Bob Klingman took position directly behind the Nick. He discovered the cold at the extreme altitude had rendered his guns inoperative. Reusser later told a reporter that Bob didn't think he had enough fuel to make it back to base and was not about to end an hour-and-a-half chase by letting the Nick get away. He quoted Klingman as saying, 'I'm going to hit him with my plane.'

Hitting the Nick was not easy. The slipstream prevented Klingman from closing with its tail. Reusser pulled up to the Nick's right side. To get above the air compression caused by the Nick's propellers and immediately behind the Nick, Klingman pulled back to come down on the tail from above.

Finally aware of the Americans, the Nick's rear gunner opened the cover of his cockpit just as Klingman was starting his descent. Bullets ripped through the right wing of the Corsair. Undaunted, Klingman continued his dive and chopped off part of the Nick's rudder with his propeller.

As he climbed for a second strike, the rear gunner turned his attention to Reusser. Klingman heard Reusser call on the radio, 'The way he is beating on that gun, he must think he's going to get it working again.' One clip was all the gunner could get off before the altitude also froze his weapon. Unaware of that, Reusser later admitted. 'I was calling to Klingman to hurry up. I wasn't comfortable looking down that gun barrel.'

On his second strike, Klingman's propeller flung the Japanese machine gun and its gunner into empty sky. Still the Nick continued level flight. Klingman's third strike severed the Nick's tail, putting both of their planes into an uncontrolled spin. The Nick broke apart but, after falling 1,000 feet, Klingman was able to regain control but the Corsair was shaking so badly he could not read his instruments. At one point he was afraid the shaking would dislodge the engine. Reusser stuck with Klingman, used his own compass to get him on a course back to Kadena and stood by as Klingman found an engine speed that reduced the shaking. Klingman remembered, 'About 10,000 feet, I ran out of fuel, but thought I could still make the field. I remember Ken said he thought I had better bale out. I felt I was in good enough shape that a wheels-up landing was not necessary. This was almost a costly mistake as I was surprised at the loss of altitude when I put my gear and flaps down.'

Reusser raced ahead and landed in time to watch Bob come in. Out of gas but not out of luck, Klingman's Corsair hit the ground and bounced onto the runway. Officers and enlisted crowded around the F4U. They saw a plane with pieces of the Nick stuck in the engine cowling, bullet holes in one wing and six inches of one propeller blade missing. The other two blades were bent back almost to the cowling. Those gathered recalled Klingman slowly climbing out of the cockpit, standing on the wing and saying in his Oklahoma drawl, 'It's a hell of a way to earn a buck.'

A few days later Bob Klingman did have to bale. His Corsair had one wheel which refused to descend. He was flying toward the fleet, he baled out. Instead of crashing, the Corsair started a slowly descending circle coming ever closer to the US ships. He received quite a bit of ribbing that his plane had to be shot down. Klingman was allowed to keep the parachute, which Jackie Cochran, his girlfriend, turned into her wedding dress when he returned to San Diego. Robert Klingman went on to serve in Korea as a forward air traffic controller with 1st Marine Division. Recipient of the Navy Cross and the Air Medal with Gold Star, for his actions on 10 May 1945, he had been awarded the DFC. He retired in 1966 at the rank of lieutenant colonel.[4] Ken Reusser would go on to become the USMC's most decorated aviator and is the only pilot to survive being shot down in every conflict from the Second World War to Vietnam. In addition to a slew of Navy Crosses and Purple Hearts, he held eighteen Air Medals.

On 11 May 135 Val kamikazes took off from Kokobu airfield's Airstrip 2 and headed for TF-58 again. They sighted two destroyers and over fifty orbited before diving down on the *Evans* and the *Hugh W. Hadley*. In a battle without pause lasting an hour and a half, the destroyers claimed thirty-eight of the suiciders and the USMC Corsairs from Yontan and Kadena finished off another nineteen before running low on ammunition. When the Hadley called for more from the marine Corsairs the squadron leader replied, 'I'm out of ammunition but I'm sticking with you.' He and the rest of his Corsairs did just that, flying straight into a formation of ten kamikazes heading fore and aft towards the destroyer and breaking them up amid ack-ack fire from the ships. The two destroyers suffered four kamikaze hits apiece but, thanks to the intervention of the Corsairs, they survived. Commander Mullaney of *Hadley* wrote, 'I am willing to take my ship to the shores of Japan if I could have these marines with me.'

Meanwhile, eight pilots of VF-84 'Wolf Gang' bounced about thirty kamikazes over Kikai and in two passes they destroyed eleven of them

4. See *Story of Bob; Drummer, Pilot, Legend* by Roger Klingman.

before returning to *Bunker Hill*. Just as Admiral Marc Mitscher's flag carrier was recovering some of her fighters, she was hit by a Zeke kamikaze piloted by Ensign Kiyoshi Ogawa and Lieutenant Junior Grade Seizō Yasunori. It crashed into the flight deck aft of the number 3 elevator and almost immediately the carrier suffered a second strike when a Judy crashed into the flight deck at the base of the island. The Zeke released its delayed-action bomb as it hit, then skidded along the flight deck to set rows of aircraft on fire. The Judy pilot released his bomb just before impact. It went through the flight deck and exploded on the gallery deck. The kamikaze penetrated the flight deck at the base of the island and poured aviation fuel into the galley and hangar decks, which were soon on fire at all three levels. It took fire crews five and a half hours to put out the fires that engulfed the flight and hangar decks and 389 personnel were killed or missing and 264 wounded from a crew of 2,600. *Bunker Hill* was finished as a fighting ship and VMF-221 and VMF-451 were effectively out of the war too, although fifteen Corsairs of VMF-221 were still airborne during the tragedy. They shot down four kamikazes in the attack and the surviving F4Us landed on the *Enterprise*.

VMF(N)-543 aboard ship off Okinawa was hit badly when a kamikaze exploded on deck wounding five men and destroying equipment. VMF-322 aboard LST 599 was also hit. All 424 tons of vehicles and cargo and gear were lost. Seven men were wounded. Four days later the *Enterprise* was hit by kamikazes. A Zeke successfully hit the forward elevator and exploded five decks below. Thirteen men were killed and sixty-eight wounded. Though badly damaged, *Enterprise* managed to remain in action for several more hours, shooting down two more diving Zekes before the 'Big E', too, was out of the battle. *Enterprise* limped away from the battle zone and headed for safer waters at Ulithi.

On 21 May Corsairs of MAG-22, VMF-113, 314 and 422, began arriving at Ie Shima from Engebi, but three F4Us were lost in bad weather en route. Four days later 165 kamikazes launched themselves against the fleet near Ie Jima, sinking two ships and damaging nine others. Four F4Us of VMF-312 intercepted and destroyed twelve out of a formation of twenty kamikazes north of Kadena airfield. One of Day's Knights' victorious pilots was Captain Herbert J. Valentine, who became the ninth and last Corsair pilot in the Second World War to become an ace in a day when he destroyed six enemy aircraft. Valentine was credited with two Zekes, two Tojos and a Val and the joint destruction of two Vals (one with First Lieutenant William Farrell, who was credited with four other kills and a probable), plus a Zeke probable. VMF-422 scored six out of twelve and the Marines shot down a total of thirty-nine Japanese planes this day. On 27 May Japanese suicide planes made fifty-six raids of two to four planes each throughout the day on the fleet off Okinawa. USMC Corsairs accounted for thirty-two kamikazes on this and the next day and Army Air Force P-47 Thunderbolts shot down seventeen more.

At the start of June the only Corsairs left on the fast carriers belonged to VBF-83 on *Essex* and VBF-85 'Sky Pirates' in Air Group 85 on the carrier *Shangri La*. They were joined by the end of June by VBF-6, en route to Okinawa onboard the *Hancock*, Air Group 88 with thirty-seven F4U-1Ds of VBF-88 on *Yorktown* and F4U-4s of VBF-94 on *Lexington*. VBF-83 had been commissioned on 2 January 1945 and during its only tour its F4U-1Ds scored ninety-one aerial victories. VBF-85, which operated F4U-1C, F4U-1Ds and F6F-5N and -5P aircraft, were credited with the destruction of forty enemy aircraft. VBF-6 flew FG-1Ds in combat from 18 March to 8 April and F4U-4s from 20 June to 15 August. It scored seventeen victories for the loss of six Corsairs and three pilots killed on operations and six Corsairs and their pilots lost in operational accidents. VBF-88 destroyed five enemy aircraft. VBF-94 lost one pilot during training, seven in action and four killed in operational accidents.

Four Corsair squadrons were still operating on *Block Island* (VMF-511 with eight F4U-1Ds), *Gilbert Islands* (VMF-512), *Cape Gloucester* (VMF-351 with eight FG-1Ds) and *Vella Gulf* (VMF(N)-513 'Flying Nightmares'). MCVG-1 and VMF-511 were used to support the landings at Balikpappen. After being used in support of operations against Okinawa in May, MCVG-2 and VMF-512 were used on airfield-suppression missions at Sakishima Retto during June, before supporting the landings at Balikpappen. In July MCVG-4 and VMF-351's Corsairs were used to provide support for minesweeping and strikes in the East China Sea, while MCVG-3 and the Flying Nightmares arrived at Saipan late in July and in August served briefly at Okinawa.

On 8 June the last two Marine Corsair squadrons aboard a big carrier, VMF-112 Wolfpack and VMF-123 Eight-Balls on *Bennington*, carried out a final strike mission, bombing Kadena airfield on Kyushu with special 500lb bombs. After this, *Bennington* sailed south for Leyte Gulf and home. The two squadrons lost thirty-one aircraft in combat and seventeen in operational crashes, eighteen pilots killed, but fifteen others were rescued. *Bennington* was the only one of the original ten Essex-class carriers not to be hit by the kamikazes, although none of them were ever actually sunk. That same day the first flight of the F4U-4 model, from VMF-212, arrived at Kadena airfield on Okinawa by way of Clark Field. Two days later, the Wolfpack obtained their first victory.

On 14 June sixty-four land-based Corsairs rocketed, bombed and dropped napalm on the enemy entrenched in the hills on Okinawa, which was finally secured on 21 June. On 22 June MAG-14 F4U-4s scored their ninth and last victory and Captain Ken A. Walsh, now with VMF-222 as its Operations Officer, bagged a Zeke kamikaze fifteen miles north of Okinawa to take his final score to twenty-one enemy planes destroyed. The twelve USMC Corsair squadrons had by now shot down a total of 436 enemy aircraft, with VMF-323 getting the most, with 124 confirmed victories. Next came VMF-311 Hell's Bells with seventy-one, VMF-312 Day's Knights with sixty and a half destroyed - four damaged and seven probably destroyed and VMF-224 Fighting Wildcats with 55-3-0. Of the 1,900 kamikaze sorties during the battle for Okinawa, only 14.7 per cent were effective. Even so twenty-five US and RN ships were sunk, 157 were damaged by hits and ninety-seven others were damaged by near misses. Total USN casualties on board ships in the Okinawa campaign were 9,731, of whom 4,907 were killed. Most of them were attributed to the kamikazes.

On 30 June 1945 the Pacific Tactical Air Force numbered 288 F4U-s, thirty-six F6F-5Ns, 144 P-47s, twelve P-5Is, sixteen P-38s and two F6F-5Ps. During July the USN accepted 303 Corsairs from Vought, the highest of any month, and 180 from Goodyear and the remaining carrier-borne Corsairs in the Japanese home waters carried out strikes on Japan and against enemy warships. On 1 July Okinawa-based Corsairs escorted army B-25s in the first medium-bomber attack on Japan since the Doolittle raid and on 15 August two carrier plane strikes were sent against Tokyo, but were recalled when it was announced that Japan had finally and unconditionally surrendered. Lieutenant Commander Thomas H. Reidy, the acting CO of VBF-83, who had nine air-to-air victories to his name, shot down a Myrt to make his score ten before the recall. Probably it was the last enemy aircraft shot down in the Second World War. Reidy returned to the *Essex* but as he made his approach, he discovered that he could not get his flaps down.

He remained aloft while the rest of his squadron landed aboard and then came in for a safe landing. Reidy eased the throttle to taxi away from the landing area but there was no response from the engine and the prop just turned slower and slower until it finally stopped. Reidy remarked, 'I guess the airplane knew the war was over.'

Japan was still thought to have 10,700 operational aircraft left, half of them ready for suicide attacks. If the Japanese had carried on fighting and the Allies had been forced to invade Japan, the losses would have been incalculable. On 2 September 1945, VJ Day, there were nine F4U squadrons on seven carriers in the area of Japan. Three more carriers, *Intrepid* with CVG-10, including thirty-six F4U-1Ds of VFB-10, *Boxer*, with Air Group 93 and *Antietam*, with Air Group 89, including VF-89, were en route.

In the Pacific Corsairs were credited with the destruction of 2,140 enemy aircraft in aerial combat, for the loss of 189 F4U-s. Of these, USMC Corsairs claimed the lion's share, destroying 1,100 fighters and 300 bombers, for the loss of 141 F4Us. A further 349 USMC and USN F4Us were shot down by anti-aircraft fire, 230 were lost from other causes, 692 were written off on non-operational flights and 164 were destroyed in crashes on carriers or airfields. A dozen squadrons in the Solomon Islands-Rabaul area of operations gained 64 per cent of all the USMC victories. Some 903 of the victories were attributed to eight squadrons.[5] Land-based navy Corsairs shot down 162 Japanese aircraft for the loss of fourteen F4Us and destroyed another 578 at sea for the loss of thirty-four Corsairs in air-to-air combat. VF-17 Jolly Rogers, the most famous USN Corsair unit, destroyed 152 enemy aircraft in the Solomons during its first tour, 27 October to 1 December 1943, before it converted to Hellcats for its second tour of duty. Some 64,051 operational sorties (54,470 from land bases and 9,581 from aircraft carriers) were made by Corsairs from 13 February 1942 to the end of the war. During that time the Corsair's total victory tally of 2,140 Japanese aircraft destroyed for the loss of 189 F4Us gave a victory ratio of 11.3 to 1.

It must have seemed to the majority that September that propeller-driven aircraft such as the Corsair would no longer be needed now that peace, finally, had been achieved. By February 1945 Vought had delivered its 4,996th F4U. During September 1945 Corsair production was severely

---

5. VMF-122, 124, 211, 212, 213, 214, 215 and 221.

reduced, with the navy accepting only forty-one F4Us from Vought and sixty-eight from Goodyear and after that, the Goodyear Corsair production line was stopped. A contract for 2,500 FG-4s was reduced to twelve, then scrapped. Before VJ Day total Vought F4U-4 production stood at 1,912. Vought continued producing F4U-4s until April 1946, raising the total number of this model built to 2,357. The Corsair was kept in production with a further 397 F4U-5 models being built during 1946-47 and the last, of a batch of forty-five F4U-5N conversions, was delivered to the navy in September 1951. Corsair production ceased on Christmas Eve 1952 with the last of ninety-four F4U-7s rolling off the production lines. In one of the longest production runs of all time, a total of 12,571 Corsairs had been built.

Post-war, four months after demobilization, there were twenty-five navy and twenty-one USMC fighter squadrons flying Corsairs. The Japanese surrender in 1945 created a vacuum in China and the Communist and Nationalist forces took up opposing stances. The US tried to mediate between the two sides and USMC squadrons were used in sporadic operations in northern China as tensions boiled over and a number of US personnel were killed. Among the air units involved were F4U-4s of VMF-224 and VMF-311 in MAG-32, F4U-4s of VMF-323 and F4U-5N night-fighters of VMF-542 of MAG-12 and F4U-4s of VMF-115 and VMF-211 in MAG-24. VMF-224 and VMF-311 were withdrawn from China in June 1946 and VMF-323 and VMF-542 followed in September. VMF-115 and VMF-211 were among the last units to leave, in April 1947. In January 1949 the Nationalist Chinese set up a government in exile on the island of Formosa (Taiwan) and in May the last US units left China. Tension in the area remained and it was to spread to other parts of SE Asia. Despite the subsequent decommissioning of many of the Corsair units and the advent of the jet fighter, as the 1950s dawned several Corsair squadrons would once again be required to fight a major war in the east.

Chapter 8

War in the Land of the Morning Calm

Pucker up, push her over and salvo your load.
Firewall that old U-bird and let's hit the road.
The commies are firing and the flak is right black,
But we're all determined that we're going to get back.

In 1945 the Soviet Union took the surrender of Japanese forces in Korea north of the 38th parallel while the United States handled the enemy surrender south of the dividing line. For a while, everything was peaceful in the land of the morning calm. That calm was shattered, five years later, early on Sunday morning, 25 June 1950 when the North Korean Army, using the false pretext that the South had invaded the North, crossed the 38th parallel, completely wrong-footing the Republic of Korea (ROK) Army and its American advisers. On 27 June Martin Mariners of VP-47 at Iwakuni in Japan began patrols off the Korean coast, while VP-6, equipped with Lockheed P2V Neptunes, were ordered to Korea. The navy planes had their work cut out. The peninsula of Korea is 600 miles long, 135 miles wide with an area of 86,000 square miles. On 28 June the first US ground troops were ordered to Korea but they were not flown in until 2 July.

North Korean Air Force (NKAF) Yak-9P fighters and Il'yushin Il-10 Shtormovik attack aircraft bombed and strafed airfields near the capital Seoul and Kimpo and quickly established air superiority over the whole country. The NKAF entered the offensive with only about 162 aircraft, all of Soviet manufacture, and all of them piston-engined. Mostly the fighter and ground-attack regiments consisted of Yak-3 and Yak-9 fighters and Il-10s. On paper the NKAF had no chance against the UN forces. USAF aircraft available for war in Korea, however, were ill suited to operate in a close air support and interdiction campaign. They needed paved runways 6,000-feet long and these only existed in Japan, which meant that air operations over Korea were restricted to only a few minutes. For the most part, the British and Commonwealth carriers would operate off the west coast of Korea in the Yellow Sea, while the US carriers would operate off the east coast in the Sea of Japan. Flying from flat-tops, navy and Marine units could operate in the Sea of Japan and be sent off at a point about seventy miles from the coast of Korea; the shallow sea-bed off the east coast of Korea prevented them from getting any nearer. Fortunately for the men aboard the carriers, the North Koreans lacked the capability to strike back at the UN fleet off its coasts. They also had no jet aircraft that could take on the American front-line aircraft. The USN was in a state of transition with the first jet fighters joining the more numerous piston-engine aircraft aboard its carriers. American air superiority during 1950 meant that Korea was an ideal hunting ground for both the slower Corsair fighter-bombers and Skyraider attack aircraft in which to operate in the ground-attack and interdiction roles.

The 'Bent Winged Bird' was still in production and was one of several wartime types still in front-line service at the outbreak of the Korean War. In January 1950 a carrier's air group (CVG) composition had been changed from three fighter and two attack squadrons to four fighter (VF) (two F4U-4 and two Grumman F9F-3 Panther jets) and one attack (VA) squadron (AD-4 Skyraiders). Each group comprised ninety aircraft, or eighteen in each squadron. While jets were about 100mph faster than Corsairs or Skyraiders, the early jets could not haul as great a war load over a long distance and were slow to respond from when the throttle was advanced to the time the engine 'spooled up' sufficiently to accelerate the aircraft. This delay could prove fatal if a jet had to be waved off a landing at the last moment. Corsairs, with their huge variable-pitch propellers and Double-Wasps, permitted fast acceleration. They could also carry a more formidable war load than the Grumman F8F Bearcat, which, though it had replaced the F6F Hellcat in twenty-eight navy squadrons during 1945-49, did not serve in Korea.

The F4U-4's eight 5-inch High Velocity Aircraft Rockets (HVARs), two 1,000lb bombs, or two 11.75-inch rockets would be used to great effect to destroy road and rail bridges, fortified positions and airfields on land, while at sea strafing and bombing using napalm would prove equally effective. During the first ten months of fighting, Corsairs would fly more than four-fifths of all navy and USMC ground-support strikes in Korea. Later, their main role shifted to attacks on troop concentrations and supply lines. When it was realized that the more conventional rocket projectiles simply bounced off the Soviet-built T-34 tanks used by North

Korea, specially-developed ATAR (Anti-tank Aircraft Rocket) 'Ram rockets' with a 6.5-inch funnel-shaped charge attached to the standard HVAR were used to great effect.

TF-77, comprising *Valley Forge*, which had sailed from the Philippines and the light fleet carrier HMS *Triumph*, with two cruisers and eight destroyers, which were in position by 12 July, were the only UN ships in the Western Pacific to begin operations against North Korean targets. CVG-5, which was the carrier group embarked on the 'Happy Valley,' comprised VF-51 and VF-52 flying F9F-2 Panther jets, VF-53 and VF-54 flying F4U-4Bs, VA-55 flying AD-2 Skyraiders and VC-61 with F4U-5Ps. *Valley Forge* arrived on station on 3 July 1950 and, at 0600 hours, the first strike went ahead with sixteen of VF-53 and VF-54's F4U-4s and twelve AD Skyraiders of VA-55. CVG-5's Panthers became the first jet fighters in the US Navy to go into action when VF-51 provided top cover for the Corsairs and Skyraiders. The attack aircraft concentrated their strikes on North Korean lines of communications, bombing and rocketing railway bridges, railyards, airfields and roads near the North Korean capital Pyongyang, while F9Fs shot down NKAF Yak-9s that tried to intervene and destroyed others on the ground.

Aircraft from *Valley Forge* continued their strikes on North Korean targets on 18 July with strikes on Pyongyang and Onjong-ni and on the 19th they attacked Yonpo airfield. These two strikes resulted in the loss of thirty-two NKAF aircraft destroyed on the ground and another thirteen damaged. *Valley Forge* left Korean waters at the end of the month and sailed to Okinawa, Japan, for rest and replenishment. Its place was taken by the fast-attack Essex-class carrier *Philippine Sea*, with Air Group 11 (CVG-11), commanded by 35-year-old Commander Raymond W. 'Sully' Vogel Jr, a Naval Academy graduate and Second World War veteran. VF-111 and VF-112 were equipped with the F9F-2, VF-113 and VF-114, F4U-4s, VA-115 with AD-4B Skyraiders and detachments from Composite Squadron 3 (CV-3) equipped with F4U-5N night-fighters/photo-reconnaissance models. VC-11 with AD-4Bs, VC-61 with F4U-4s and VC-35 were also embarked. *Philippine Sea* joined TF-77 on 31 July 1950, arriving in Buckner Bay, Okinawa, on 1 August to begin work ups for attacks on Korea from the Sea of Japan.

Once again it was time to send for the 'Flying Leathernecks'. In July Marine Air Group 33 (MAG-33) and USMC ground troop reinforcements left for Korea. MAG-33 arrived at Kobe, Japan, on 31 July and proceeded to Itami for maintenance and testing. On 2 August 1950 the carrier *Sicily* arrived in Tsushima Strait with F4U-4Bs of VMF-214 Black Sheep and began rocket and incendiary attacks on Chinju near the south coast. *Sicily* was joined on 6 August by the *Badoeng Strait* with F4U-4Bs of VMF-323 Death Rattlers embarked. VMF(N)-513 Flying Nightmares remained at Itazuki, Japan, where its F4U-5Ns were assigned to the 5th Air Force for night defence duties. The Flying Nightmares moved to K-9 at Pusan, Korea and flew its first combat missions on 22 January 1951. In February they moved to K-3 at Pohang and then to K-1 at Pusan, where it absorbed the F7F-3Ns of VMF(N)-542. In the early morning hours of 1 July a Soviet-built Polikarpov PO-2 biplane was destroyed by a Tigercat. On 12 July a F4U-5N intercepted a Po-2 over Seoul and shot it down in flames. On 23 September another Po-2 night heckler was destroyed by a F7F-3N. In November 1951 the Flying Nightmares moved to K-18 (Kangnung) airfield, sharing the airfield with South Korean Air Force P-51D Mustangs. Normal operations included night-interdiction missions and combat air patrols over K-16 (Seoul). Normally the F4U-5Ns would take off in the late afternoon, fly a weather reconnaissance over K-16 and then land to take on fuel. During the night, a total of four Corsairs would rotate on CAP station over K-16 to protect the USAF F-80s and F-86s from NKAF night heckler Po-2s.

CVG 11 onboard *Philippine Sea* launched its first attacks on 3 August when Lieutenant Commander William T. Amen led VF-111 in attacks on airfields at Mokpo, Kwangju and Kusan while eight F9F Panthers of VF-112 and twelve Corsairs of VF-114 hit rail and road bridges in the Mokpo-Kwangju area. The F4U-4s destroyed a bridge and damaged two dams south of Iri before strafing warehouses, sampans and junks on the way home. The F4U-4s of VMF-214 flying off the *Sicily* bombed Chinju and Sinban-ni while VMF-323 from the *Badoeng Strait* flew close air support (CAS) missions for Eighth Army units, attacking vehicles, supply dumps, bridges and railway lines. VMF-214 and VMF-323 flew, on average, forty-five ground-attack sorties a day during the fierce UN counter-offensive around Pusan.

Between 7 and 13 August *Philippine Sea* supported the UN counter-offensive in the Masan sector as the North Koreans attempted to break through the Pusan Perimeter. On the first day, VF-113 lost two F4U-4s, which collided during a strafing run when fifteen miles south of Kunsan while providing close air support and interdiction of enemy supply lines. Ensign J.F. Kail was killed, while Ensign C.T. Farnsworth nursed his damaged Corsair out to sea where he ditched. Farnsworth was picked up that same afternoon. Next day, one VF-113 pilot pressed home his attack at such low altitude that his Corsair took major damage from his own bomb blast, but he made it back to the *Philippine Sea* and carried out a safe landing. On 9 August Commander 'Sully' Vogel, CAG 11, flew with VF-114, leading a strike against the Riken Metal Company factory in Seoul. Using 500lb bombs and rockets, Vogel's flight hit the target 'very effectively'. Later, during the day, the Corsairs of VF-114 and AD-4 Skyraiders of VA-115 teamed up to blast the marshalling yards and the Standard Oil Company warehouses in the capital, leaving the latter burning. They also accounted for several boxcars and a locomotive on tracks nearby. Meanwhile, Corsairs of VF-113 bombed, strafed and rocketed a factory at Inchon, setting it on fire. Vogel led another VF-114 strike on 13 August, this time against targets near Pyongyang.

On 16 August, after replenishing in Japan, *Philippine Sea* sent its aircraft over Korea again with strikes on key bridges near Seoul. Next day, VF-113's Corsairs caught a twenty-truck convoy with a cargo of artillery on the road south of Songjin and obliterated it. On the 19th, thirty-seven F4U-4s and AD Skyraiders from the *Philippine Sea* and *Valley Forge*, escorted by Panthers, made attacks on the bridges near Seoul again. Eight direct hits were scored on the large steel Han river railway bridge west of the capital which had withstood days of heavy bombing by B-29s of the 19th Bomb Group, including one strike which saw fifty-four tons of bombs explode around it. Eight of the Corsairs were from VF-114 on the *Philippine Sea* and were led by Sully Vogel. While the four-plane CAP element encountered no enemy aircraft, the four strike aircraft hit a bridge span with one 500-pounder on the first pass. Sully Vogel came round again for a second pass, but enemy anti-aircraft fire hit his Corsair and set it on fire. The Pacific combat veteran baled out of the burning Corsair and pilots saw his chute stream, but it did not open and his body hurtled to the ground. Vogel was a little under a month short of his 36th birthday. He left a widow and five children.

General George F. Stratemeyer, C-in-C, FEAF (Far East Air Force), had promised a case of Scotch whisky to the first crew to destroy the Han bridge. The spans of the bridge fell into the river that night before B-29s of the 19th Bomb Group could drop their special 2,000 and 4,000lb bombs the following morning, but honours were declared even, with the 19th and CVG-11 both receiving cases of whisky. *Philippine Sea* cleared Korean waters on 20 August and next day, as the CV-47 lay anchored at Sasebo, a memorial service was held for Commander Vogel and Ensign C.L. Smith of VF-112 who died when his Panther crashed and burned near Sariwon. *Philippine Sea* completed her replenishment at Sasebo on 25 August and returned to the east coast of Korea. On 27 August CVG-11 attacked shipping in Wonsan harbour, damaging what pilots claimed as a 'destroyer escort' with rockets and cannon fire and two 'gunboats', by strafing. Between 29 August and 4 September CVG-11 pilots claimed destruction of a 'fleet-type minelayer' and four patrol craft at Wonsan. They conducted emergency CAS in defence of the Pusan perimeter and destroyed key bridges along the North Korean lines of communication. *Philippine Sea*'s pilots also discovered the enemy's major staging base at Kangge and photographed Inchon prior to the amphibious landing there.

On 1 September the North Koreans made an all-out attempt to pierce the Pusan perimeter and the Corsairs of VMF-323 and Far East Air Force fighters and bombers were used to repel the attacks. At night the F4U-5Ns of the Flying Nightmares and USAF B-26s flew numerous night interdiction missions, while, at sea, squadrons from Task Force 77 added their striking power to the counter-offensive operation. All this activity attracted the attention of the Soviets, who had a naval air base at Port Arthur on the tip of the Liaotung peninsula. On 4 September 1950 a VF-53 Corsair from *Valley Forge* on CAP shot down a twin-engined Soviet aircraft which approached the task force. Next day the North Korean People's Army (NKPA) offensive had petered out and on 11 September the break-out from Pusan began.

On 10 September USMC Corsairs from *Sicily* and *Badoeng Strait* carried out a preliminary series of raids on targets in the Inchon area, the first against Wolmi-do Island and neighbouring Solmi-do. Three days later the pre-invasion sea bombardment began and then, on 15 September, General Douglas MacArthur launched Operation Chromite using amphibious landings behind the enemy lines at Inchon. During 12 to 14 September F4Us and Skyraiders provided the majority of the 'deep support' from *Valley Forge, Philippine Sea* and *Boxer. Boxer* had recently arrived on station with CVG-2 comprising sixty-four F4U-4Bs of VF-23, VF-24, VF-63 and VF-64 'Freelancers'. In addition, it also had AD-2s and AD-3s embarked, along with VC-3 (Detachment 'George') and VC-61 detachments of F4U-5Ns and F4U-4Ps respectively. US Navy and USMC fighter-bombers strafed and bombed positions along the Inchon waterfront prior to the main landing. The UN forces enjoyed total air superiority and, by midnight on the 15th, the 1st Marine Division had secured the port of Inchon and, with the army's 7th Infantry Division, moved on Seoul and Kimpo airfield, severing communist supply routes to the south. The North Koreans fell back in the face of the offensive and the navy pilots went in search of interdiction targets behind the Main Line of Resistance (MLR) and over North Korea. CVG-5 from the *Valley Forge* discovered a North Korean convoy of trucks in open terrain at Taejong six miles east of Inchon and destroyed no fewer than eighty-seven trucks.

On 17 September Kimpo airfield fell into American hands and prepared to receive MAG-33 aircraft. On the 19th Corsairs of VMF-212 'Devil Cats' and Tigercats of VMF(N)-542 arrived from Japan. On 20 September Corsairs of VMF-323, operating from the *Badoeng Strait*, provided CAS for the 1st Marine Division when the NKPA tried to take Hill 118. Late on 27 September Seoul was recaptured and when another American amphibious landing went ahead at Wonsan on the east coast of Korea on 10 October, the Marines were supported by aircraft from *Boxer*, *Leyte*, *Philippine Sea* and *Valley Forge*. Black-and-white-checker-boarded Corsairs of VMF-312 from Kimpo attacked a large column of North Korean trucks and troops thirty-nine miles south-east of Wonsan and the unit, which had become famous as Day's Knights in the Second World War, destroyed most of the vehicles in a series of merciless bombing and strafing runs. By 28 September the Communists were in full retreat. The North Koreans rejected a surrender ultimatum and MacArthur had no choice but to continue the war north of the 38th Parallel and march on the North Korean capital, Pyongyang.

On 13 October the Corsairs of VMF-214 and VMF-323 and the F4U-5N night-fighters of VMF(N)-513 commanded by wartime Corsair ace Major Hunter Reinburg, took up residence at the repaired Wonsan airfield. The F4U-5Ns flew daylight missions until runway lighting was installed at Wonsan, after which they resumed their night-intruder operations. VMF(N)-513, VMF-214 and VMF-323 supported the 1st Marine Division when it was finally able to go ashore at Wonsan on 24 October. By the end of the month the North Korean capital of Pyongyang had fallen. The war seemed to be won. The carriers of TF-77 were relieved and retired to Sasebo, Japan, while the USMC squadrons moved up to Yonpo airfield to carry on CAS missions for the ground troops pursuing the remnants of the NKPA to the Yalu river which bordered Communist China.

On 14 October MacArthur's intelligence staff had reported a total of thirty-eight Chinese divisions in Manchuria, but it was believed that none had entered North Korea. In fact six Chinese armies began storming across the border at night and by the end of October almost 300,000 Communist 'Chinese People's Volunteers' were deployed for battle with the UN forces. Only small groups of Chinese troops were identified and the majority remained virtually undetected. Again American forces were caught on the wrong foot. On 1 November American aircraft were confronted by the MiG-15 for the first time and an area 100-miles deep between Sinuiju on the Yalu and Sinanju on the Chongchon river would soon became known as 'MiG Alley'. On 6 November TF-77 was recalled to Korean waters. For three consecutive days, beginning 9 November, F4Us and AD-4s from *Valley Forge, Leyte* and *Philippine Sea* protected by F9Fs flying top cover hit bridges on the Yalu and supply concentrations in Hungnam, Songjin and Chongjin. Because of political considerations, the navy pilots were only permitted to bomb the southern end of the bridges. Skyraiders, flying in formations of eight, supported by eight to sixteen Corsairs on flak-suppression duty destroyed a road bridge at Sinuiju and two more at Hvesanjin, 200 miles upstream. Up above as many as sixteen Panther jets kept an eye on proceedings flying top cover for the bombers.

Though outclassed by the MiG, the superior experience of the Panther jet pilots gave them the edge. On 10 November a Panther from *Philippine Sea* was the first US Navy jet to down another jet aircraft when Lieutenant Commander William T. Amen, CO of VF-111 'Sundowners', destroyed a MiG-15 near Sinuiju. For the next nine days the Corsairs and Skyraiders continued their attacks on the bridges across the Yalu. On the 17th aircraft from *Philippine Sea* and *Leyte* dropped both bridges across the Yalu and Hyosanjin but, by using pontoons, the Chinese were able to cross the river. When in late November the Yalu froze over, the Chinese were able to cross almost at will. This build-up of its forces led to the first real confrontation on 28 November, when heavy fighting broke out between the Chinese forces in the Hagaru-ri and Yudam-ni areas and the 1st Marine Division. The 5th and 7th Marines became cut off from the rest of the Division and were forced to withdraw to the rugged terrain around the Chosin Reservoir.

All available land-based and carrier-borne aircraft were thrown into the battle and evacuation from Hungnam. *Valley Forge* had departed the area for a much-needed overhaul and the light carriers were involved in ferrying replacement aircraft to the USMC squadrons in the battle zone. Leading the way were USN and USMC close-air support Corsairs and Skyraiders, protected by USAF F-86 Sabres flying top cover. From Yonpo airfield came the Corsairs of VMF-214, VMF-323 and VMF(N)-513 and VMF-212 Devilcats and VMF(N)-542's Tigercats. At Kimpo there were the Corsairs of VMF-312 which, during the Chosin break-out, flew almost 2,000 hours in the air, losing four Corsairs and one pilot. By the time the USMC break-out of Chosin began on 1 December the fast carriers, *Leyte* and *Philippine Sea* were on station and they were soon supported by the *Bataan* and *Badoeng Strait*.

Lieutenant (j.g.) William H. Koenig, a Corsair pilot in VF-32, born Des Moines, Iowa, on 24 May 1926, recalled: 'Our missions more frequently became armed reconnaissance instead of close air support. We were now operating deep into North Korean territory. And I suppose it's possible that some flights may have come close to crossing the Manchurian border. Apparently, for this reason, we received a directive to cut off the area on our charts to the north of a line that was south of the Manchurian border. As the offensive moved to the Yalu river, we had to tape the top part of the charts together again. The deeper we operated into North Korea, the more intense the ground fire became. In the squadron organization, Ensign Jesse Brown, Thomas Hudner and I flew with the Squadron Executive Officer, Lieutenant Commander R.L. Cevoli. Tom was Dick Cevoli's wingman, "Jess" was the section leader and I was Jess's wingman. We kept this tactical organization for the Mediterranean deployment and during the Korean operation. I met Jesse Brown in the course of checking into the squadron. I was not surprised when we met, because I had seen a picture of Jesse in late-1949 edition of the *Naval Aviation News*. In physical appearance, Jesse was lean and athletic in build. He was quiet, a bit on the serious side, easy to talk with and pleasant to be in company with. His performance in the air and on the ground was that of a competent aviator and officer. The fact that he had become the first black naval aviator was almost overshadowed by the seeming ease with which he took his place in the squadron. This, to me, characterized the relationship between Jesse and his squadron mates. He often attended church and I would say that his daily life reflected the confidence of his belief.'

Jesse Leroy Brown, born 13 October 1926 in Hattiesburg, Mississippi, was the first Black American commissioned navy pilot. Hudner, born 31 August 1924 in Fall River, Massachusetts, a graduate of Annapolis in 1946, had been with the 'Fighting Swordsmen' since receiving his wings. He and Jesse Brown were good friends and Hudner thought that he was an inspiration to all blacks. At the age of thirteen, Brown took a job as a paperboy for the *Pittsburgh Courier*, a black press paper and developed a desire to pilot while reading in the newspaper about African-American aviators of the time. He also became an avid reader of *Popular Aviation* and the *Chicago Defender*, which he later said heavily influenced his desire to fly naval aircraft. In 1937 he wrote a letter to President Franklin D. Roosevelt in which he complained of the injustice of African-American pilots being kept out of the US Army Air Corps, to which the White House responded with a letter saying that it appreciated the viewpoint. During his second year in college, Brown learned of the V-5 Aviation Cadet Training 'Program' being conducted by the US Navy to commission naval aviation pilots. In spite of resistance from recruiters, Brown passed the entrance exams and enlisted in the US Naval Reserve on 8 July 1946 and was admitted to the aviation programme. By June 1948 Brown had begun training for carrier-based aircraft and hoped to fly either the F4U Corsair or F6F Hellcat. On 21 October he completed his training and was given his naval aviator badge. The *Associated Press* profiled him and his photograph appeared in *Life* magazine. Brown was commissioned as an ensign in the US Navy on 26 April 1949.

Bill Koenig recalled: 'En route to Japan, we spent much time picking the brains of those who had experienced [Second] World War … combat. Tom, Jess and I frequently talked about what we thought we would encounter. At one combat briefing, I remember that the squadron CO, D.T. Neill, strongly emphasized that if one of us was shot down, the others were to provide cover as best possible, but there was to be no Hollywood-type rescue attempt that might well result in an additional loss.

'On one flight, as the strike group broke out under the overcast, we immediately came under intense fire. One shell burst very close behind us and that was the first time that Jesse Brown or I had heard the noise of an exploding AA round meant for us. He immediately detached our section. We dived for the deck and went on our assigned reconnaissance route. In November, the air group made a number of co-ordinated strikes with the air force against the Yalu river bridges. The Chinese troops had come into the war and everything soon would be turned around. By the first of December, we were flying close air support for the Marines who were fighting their way south from the Chosin Reservoir.

'For the flight on 4 December I did not fly my usual position. Lieutenant George Hudson, our LSO, was flying Jesse's wing in my place. And I was leading another section with Ensign Ralph McQueen as my wingman.'

Lieutenant Commander Dick Cevoli, who had joined the navy a month after the attack on Pearl Harbor, and Tom Hudner completed the six-aircraft armed reconnaissance mission and the formation took off at 1338 KST. Brown had the call sign 'Iroquois 13'. The flight travelled 100 miles from the task force's location to the Chosin Reservoir, flying thirty-five to forty minutes through very harsh wintry conditions to the vicinity of the villages of Yudam-ni and Hagaru-ri. The flight began searching for targets along the west side of the reservoir, decreasing their altitude to 700 feet. The mission was a three-hour search-and-destroy flight as well as an attempt to probe Chinese troop strength in the area. Hudner's flight group was covering the marines' escape, looking for more Communist forces advancing from the north.

Flying above the snow-covered mountains, they saw no sign of enemy troops but Jesse Brown's F4U-4 was struck by anti-aircraft fire and he reported that he was losing oil pressure. Bill Koenig was following astern of the Exec's division and as they flew up a valley he noticed a stream of vapour coming from Jesse's plane: 'By way of explanation, in the Corsair, when transferring fuel from an external tank, the automatic shut-off valve sometime would not close and fuel would be dumped overboard. I called Jess and told him that he was dumping fuel. As we pulled up to clear a ridge, he transmitted that he was losing power and going to have to put down. I didn't see him make the landing. The terrain was far from level and we were flying at a very low air speed; so he didn't have much time to set up for ground contact, but he made the best of a lousy set of conditions. We then set up a defensive orbit over the crash site.'

Brown put his Corsair down in a clearing on a heavily-wooded mountainside but such was the force of the impact that the engine broke off and the fuselage twisted at a forty-five-degree angle near the cockpit. The other Corsairs circled overhead and, on the second pass, they saw Brown open his canopy and wave but he did not get out. Bill Koenig recalled: 'At this latitude and in the month of December, darkness comes early. We could see signs of fire in the nose of Jesse's airplane. In the Corsair, the 230-gallon fuel tank is located just forward of the cockpit. It was painfully obvious that any successful rescue attempt would have to start now. I felt, as I'm sure others did, that the only immediate help for Jesse would have to come from one of us and one man made the decision.

When Tom Hudner saw smoke coming from the nose back toward the cockpit he realised that the F4U would catch fire at any moment and the trapped pilot would be burned alive, but he knew that by the time the helicopter arrived they would be too late. He radioed the others that he was going down to help Brown. Hudner released his rockets and auxiliary fuel tanks, selected his flaps and tried to put his Corsair down as close as he could to Brown's wrecked Corsair. Hudner hit the side of the mountain hard and skidded across the snow, but his Corsair was safely down. He leaped out and ran to Brown's wrecked F4U.

'He did a good a good job of putting his Corsair down,' said Bill Koenig. 'We watched him go to Jesse's plane and then go to his plane and radio to us that Jesse was pinned in the cockpit, that he was alive and "had all the faith in the world and that's what counts". As we orbited, watching for enemy troops and watching Tom's efforts to fight an incipient fire with snow, I recall my feeling that it would be like Tom to go down and help. For us, fuel was becoming a consideration and as daylight ended we left the site.'

Jesse Brown was trapped. The fuselage had broken at the cockpit, pinning his leg at the knee and he was in bad shape. He had taken off his helmet and removed his gloves to try to unbuckle his parachute harness but the freezing cold (the snow was two feet deep and it was 25 degrees below zero) had frozen his hands solid. Hudner rushed back to his Corsair to grab a wool hat and scarf he always kept for emergencies. He put them on Brown and tried to pull his friend free but the Corsair's cockpit was too high off the ground for him to reach. Hudner tried to climb up the F4U's inverted gull wing, but it was too slippery with snow and he just kept sliding off. Finally, Hudner grabbed the handholds in the side of the fuselage and pulled himself up to the cockpit where he tried in vain to reach down to lift Brown. It was hopeless. Finally, Hudner returned to his Corsair and radioed his flight leader, Lieutenant Commander Dick Cevoli, to send a rescue helicopter with fire extinguishers and an axe. As he waited, all Hudner could do was throw handfuls of snow onto the still-smoking nose, stopping now and again to talk to Brown to try and boost his spirits. Hudner suspected that Brown had internal injuries but the trapped pilot never once said that he was hurt and remained calm throughout the ordeal.

Finally, a USMC Sikorsky HO3S-1 helicopter of VMO-6, piloted by 1st Lieutenant Charles C. Ward arrived and landed on the mountainside at roughly 1500. For forty-five minutes Ward and Hudner used the helicopter's fire extinguisher and the rescue axe in a futile attempt to cut into the aircraft's skin to free Brown. They tried to get Brown out of the wrecked Corsair but were unable to make any headway. The axe made no impression on the tangled metal pinning Brown's knee and the tiny fire extinguisher had no effect on the smoke and flames. As the light began to fade so did Brown's spirits and his words became fewer and fainter. Ward knew that he and Hudner had to get out of the crash spot before dusk because the helicopter had no night-flying instruments and trying to fly among the mountains at night could be fatal. Realistically, Ward told Hudner, 'You can stay here if you want, but I can't see that either of us can do any good.' Hudner knew Ward was right. The only way they could have gotten Brown out was to chop off his leg at the knee with the axe but neither was about to do that because in Brown's state the shock would more than likely kill him. All they could do was return to base for better metal-cutting equipment but, privately, they knew that by the time they returned Brown would be dead. Hudner told Brown they were going to have to leave him and get help. Brown must have known that he was dying and he mumbled a last message to Hudner for his wife Daisy. Brown slipped into unconsciousness before Hudner and Ward left. The helicopter reached the marine base at Hagaru-ri airfield at nightfall and Hudner remained snowed in there for three days. Bill Koenig recalled: 'My wingman, Ralph McQueen and I landed at the Marine base at Yon

Po where we spent the night as guests of Marine Aviation. The next day, the Marines flew Tom to Yon Po and the two of us had a chance to talk briefly. In his usual quiet way, Tom expressed sadness and disappointment at the outcome and was a bit apprehensive as to how his decision to crash land would be received by his superiors.'[1]

When Hudner finally returned to his carrier, Thomas Sisson, the captain, called him to report to the bridge. Hudner relayed the events of 4 December and waited for the reprimand that he thought would surely come for acting without orders. Sisson, however, nominated Hudner for the Medal of Honor. President Truman duly decorated him at the White House on 13 April 1951. Hudner was the only Corsair pilot to receive the supreme award during the Korean War. Ensign Jesse Brown was the first Black naval officer to die in combat in an American war.

On 5 December the task force was strengthened still further by the arrival of the *Princeton* with CVG-19 consisting of two F4U-4 Corsair squadrons, VF-192 and 193, one F9F-2 squadron and one AD-4 squadron. On 7 December the *Sicily* arrived on station with VMF-214's Corsairs flown in from Yonpo. On 16 December the light carrier *Bataan* arrived with VMF-212 and next day the Corsairs covered the Hungnam evacuation. On 23 December the *Valley Forge* again took up station in the Sea of Japan after its much-needed overhaul. The Marines holed up in the Chosin Reservoir were protected by fighters and fighter-bombers on an around-the-clock basis, often flying in and around the treacherous mountainous passes in appalling weather conditions. Weather in the region is one of extremes. While the summers are hot (so hot that many pilots believed the conditions were worse than winter), Korean winters are freezing with sub-zero temperatures being the norm. The ten-mile-long Funchilin Pass was particularly dangerous, while some of the others were at around 4,000 feet where the temperatures dropped to over 32 degrees below zero.

After the successful completion of the Chosin break-out, achieved mainly due to the Navy and Marine air support, the USMC squadrons were evacuated from Yonpo beginning on 7 December. VMF-124

---

1. On 6 December an F4U Corsair from VF-32 returned to the crash site and observed Brown's body still inside the cockpit of his aircraft. On 7 December F4U Corsairs from VF-32 returned to the site and dropped napalm onto both aircraft to destroy them.

went aboard the *Sicily* and VMF-312 was embarked on the *Bataan* on 12 December. (The 'Checkerboards' were ordered to Bofu Air Base in southern Honshu.) Two days later VMF(N)-513 and VMF(N)-542 were moved to Japan. Completing their operations in the Chosin Reservoir area on Christmas Day 1950, *Philippine Sea* and *Leyte*, which had been on the line for fifty-two consecutive days, departed for rest and replenishment in Japan, arriving at Sasebo and Yokosuka on 26 and 28 December respectively. Their departure was followed, on 31 December, by a Chinese New Year offensive. On 5 January 1951 the Chinese recaptured Seoul and soon the UN forces were in headlong retreat.

On 8 January the *Sicily* and the *Philippine Sea*, together with *Valley Forge* were on station off Korea again. After days of concerted and unremitting attacks, the Chinese advance was finally stopped on 15 January. One of the most amazing actions of the Korean War occurred on 15 January. Ensign Edward J. Hofstra Jr, of VF-64 aboard *Valley Forge* was strafing coastal roads when his F4U-4 struck the ground in a flat attitude, shearing off his belly tank, napalm bomb and wing bombs. The engine was also stopped when the propeller made contact with the ground. Following impact, the Corsair bounced back into the air. The remaining inertia carried the aircraft about 1,000 yards, 500 yards out to sea. Hofstra was able to ditch the F4U-4 and get into his life-raft. He was rescued by a Sunderland flying boat about three hours later.

Aircraft from the *Philippine Sea* attacked enemy positions until 1 February, when the carrier replenished again in Japan and from 12 February to 13 March. Four days later *Philippine Sea* and *Valley Forge* returned to Yokosuka and an exchange of air groups began. CVG-11 disembarked and three Corsair squadrons, VF-24, 63 and 64, and VA-63 with AD Skyraiders and the usual Composite Squadron detachments were embarked from CVG-2 aboard *Valley Forge*. *Philippine Sea* rejoined TF-77 on 4 April and her Corsairs and Skyraiders resumed operations in the Sea of Japan until the 8th, when she and her screen sailed for Formosa to counter Red Chinese threats against the island. After a show of force off the Chinese coast and over the northern part of Formosa between 11 and 13 April, *Philippine Sea* returned north, giving support to UN ground forces between 16 April and 3 May and returning to Yokosuka on 6 May. The North Korean spring offensive, however, soon pulled the *Philippine Sea* back to the line and during 17 to 30 May

1951 she furnished close air support for the hard-pressed UN forces. She detached from TF-77 and departed for California on 2 June 1951 for a complete overhaul.

Other Corsair units off the west coast of Korea at this time included VMF-212 Devilcats aboard the *Bataan*, now assigned to TF-77. On land in February 1951, USMC squadrons returned to bases in Korea, with VMF-214, 311, 312, 323 and VMF(N)-513 being deployed to K-3 airfield near Pohang. Night-interdiction missions against troop and truck convoys entered a new phase with the navy F4U-5N/NLs detached by VF-3 and VC-4 and F4U-4P post-strike reconnaissance Corsairs detached by VC-61 and VC-62. Additionally, land-based F4U-5Ns operated alongside the F7F-3N Tigercats in VMF(N)-513 and VMF(N)–542 'Flying Nightmares'. The first USMC Corsair night victory occurred on 12 July 1951 when Captain D. Fenton, of VMF(N)-513 flying an F4U-5N, shot down a Polikarpov Po-2 biplane 'night heckler' over Seoul. On 7 June 1952 First Lieutenant J.W. Andre, also of VMF(N)-513, flying a F4U-5NL, shot down a Yak-9. The squadron's eight night victories after this were all in F3D-2 Skyknights.

In all 468 F4U-5s were built. Of these, 351 were F4U-5s, forty-five were F4U-5Ns and seventy-two were F4U-5NLs. The twelve F4U-4Ps built served with VC-61 and VC-62 before they were replaced aboard the carriers by the Grumman F9F-2P jet. The F4U-4P was fitted with a 90-degree lens prism, which enabled the pilot to fire rockets, strafe, or drop bombs and then activate the camera during pull out to record the damage done by his and previous attacking aircraft. VC-61 had F4U-4P detachments aboard *Valley Forge* from 31 July to 23 November 1950, on *Boxer* from 24 August to 11 November 1950 and on *Philippine Sea* from 1 August 1950 to 28 March 1951. VC-62 flew F4U-5Ps from *Leyte* from 9 October 1950 to 19 January 1951. At night, the navy and USMC Corsairs were used on 'Firefly' missions in conjunction with flare-dropping aircraft, such as the PB4Y-2 Privateer, which would orbit and illuminate a target area for the Corsair pilots to bomb and strafe with their deadly fusillades of rockets, bombs and napalm. Night fighting in Corsairs in this manner was particularly dangerous work for the pilots because the flares not only illuminated ground targets, they also lit up the strafing Corsairs for the Communist anti-aircraft gunners.

On 13 February 1951 Lieutenant (j.g.) David A. McCoskrie of VC-3 was shot down and killed flying a F4U-5N near Yontee-ri. Seven nights later Lieutenant Bernard F. McDermott of VC-61, flying an F4U-4P, took a light AA shell hit in his oil cooler while on a low-level reconnaissance mission near Wonsan Harbor. The F4U-4P was not fitted with an oil-cooler shut off and McDermott quickly lost oil pressure as he tried to nurse his Corsair back to the coast. The engine quit over Wonsan Harbour and he had to ditch. McDermott was immediately picked up by a small craft launched from a destroyer. On 21 March 1951 Major Scott G. Gier of VMF-212, who was flying an F4U-5, was brought down by enemy AA fire during a close-air-support mission. He made a successful crash-landing but was killed later that day by Communist ground troops. In April Second Lieutenant Alan Beers of VMF-212 was killed on a close-air-support mission over Korea on the 7th. Six days later, Captain John E. Van Housen of VMF(N)-513 was lost in a F4U-5NL near Pyongyang. This unit's losses continued to mount during 1951. On 20 May 1951 Captain William Lesage was shot down flying an F4U-5NL on a 'Firefly' mission near Yang-gu. Seven days later Captain Arthur Wagner was killed flying a F4U-5N near Mayhon-ni Kunwha. On 13 July First Lieutenants William K. Garmany and Arnold Olson were killed during napalm-dropping missions at Hanp'o'ri and Namchon-jom. By the end of the war about thirty night-fighting Corsairs had been lost and many more written off in landing accidents. The Flying Nightmares finally received F3D-2 Skyknights in June 1952 and these slowly replaced their F4U-5N Corsairs and Tigercats.

On 15 March 1951 Seoul was back in UN hands but the continued presence of Chinese troops in South Korea meant that reinforcements were needed and the wholesale re-activation of naval reservists began. By 27 March Air Group 101 embarked on *Boxer* was composed entirely of recalled reserve squadrons and included VF-884 (Olathe) and VF-791 (Memphis), equipped with F4U-4 Corsairs. From 5 March VMF-312 were deployed on the *Bataan* and, on 4 April, the CO, Major D.P. Frame, was killed in action. His replacement, Major Frank H. Presley, was wounded in action on 20 April but remained in command of the unit for the remainder of the tour, until 6 June 1951.

On 21 April the F4U-4s of VMF-312 flew forty-two sorties over Korea. Four of the Checkerboard Corsairs were led by the executive officer of VMF-312, Captain Phillip Cunliffe DeLong, born on 9 July 1919 in Jackson, Michigan, a Second World War F4U-1/-4 ace credited with 11 victories, a probable and two enemy planes damaged. This formation, flying in support of 1st Marine Division, had an eventful mission. The division split into two sections and at 0645 First Lieutenant Godbey in the second section was forced to bale out after suffering engine problems. He was rescued by South Korean forces and returned to the *Bataan* after being airlifted out by helicopter. Near Chinnampo on the Yellow Sea four NKAF Yak-9 fighters attacked the first section. DeLong's wingman was First Lieutenant Harold Daigh who spotted the enemy fighters first. He recalled, 'We were fully loaded. I had two 1,000lb bombs on board and a drop tank and five rockets.' At first, Daigh thought the Yaks were Mustangs due to a similar incident that occurred earlier but, after seeing the aircraft's markings, he and DeLong dropped their stores and Daigh called the break as DeLong's Corsair began taking hits. DeLong told Daigh to 'start shooting'. Daigh saw 'big red balls large as baseballs' going over his wing and 'figured it was time to shoot'. DeLong took evasive action and Daigh scored hits on one of the Yaks, which started down in flames. DeLong destroyed two more Yaks, while Daigh got hits on the fourth fighter, which left the scene smoking and was credited as probably destroyed. Captain (later Colonel) DeLong flew a total of 125 combat missions in Korea and was awarded the Silver Star, an Air Medal, a strike/flight DFC and eight strike/flight Air Medals. Daigh eventually flew 118 missions before departing Korea in December 1951. He was to recall, 'We had very little air to air combat in Korea because the air force took care of the MiGs up and around the Yalu and we simply never got up there.' After he returned from Korea, Daigh joined VMF-124 at El Toro flying F9F-5s before leaving the USMC in 1954.

Next day, 22 April, the Chinese launched a major offensive in the Hwachon Reservoir area and on the morning of the 23rd VMF-323 and VMF-214 launched all their available Corsairs for a counter-strike. Altogether, the Flying Leathernecks flew 205 sorties in support of the ground forces, 153 of them being close air support along the Main Line of Resistance (MLR). That night the Chinese attacked the Marines at Horseshoe Ridge in force but the 'grunts' held out and, at daylight on 24 April, the CAS aircraft returned to strafe and bomb the Communists as the troops withdrew. Corsairs were proving one of the most successful aircraft in the Korean conflict. Despite the privations of climate, enemy action and constant operational use on a number of different missions, serviceability remained high. Some of the F4Us were 'retreads', previously used in the war in the Pacific in 1945.

The only use of aerial torpedoes during the Korean War occurred on 1 May 1951 when eight Skyraiders and twelve Corsair escorts from *Princeton* attacked the Hwachon dam. The ADs breached the dam, releasing a flood of water into the Pulchan river, which prevented the Communist forces from making an easy crossing. Attack and counter-attack continued for weeks until, on 31 May, Operation Strangle, an air-interdiction campaign using 5th Air Force, 1st Marine Air Wing and Task Force 77, was mounted against road and rail routes and bridges in north-east Korea. To enable more effective close air support (CAS) MAG-12's forward echelon moved from K-16 airfield outside Seoul to K-46 at Hoengsong about fifteen minutes flying time from the MLR. Known as the 'Kansas Line', it ran from Panmunjon north-east to Chorwon and Kumhwa, then east to the 'Punchbowl' and finally north-east to the Chado-ri area of the Korean coast. With reaction time much improved and the air support as near to the ground troops as possible, Corsairs of VMF-214 and VMF-323 were able to carry out the first of many CAS mission from Hoengsong with great success. Late in July MAG-12 moved even further forward to better improve the reaction times for CAS missions and increase their longevity, relocating to K-18 on the east coast near Kangnung. The move also brought interdiction targets in North Korea closer and permitted longer armed reconnaissance missions to be flown.

Late in the afternoon of 3 July 1951 Captain James V. Wilkins, a Corsair pilot in VMF-312 in the USS *Sicily* was hit by enemy fire during an armed reconnaissance mission about thirty-five miles south-west of Wonsan. Wilkins parachuted from his burning F4U at low altitude and survived, despite being severely burned about the legs. Despite approaching darkness, worsening weather and enemy ground fire, Lieutenant John Kelvin Koelsch of Helicopter Squadron 2 (HU-2) on Q-009, a helicopter support ship for pilot-rescue duty located the downed aviator in the Anbyon Valley and began his pick-up. (On 22 June Koelsch, a Second World War torpedo-bomber pilot, rescued a naval aviator from the waters of Wonsan Harbour, south-east of Yo Do Island.) Thick fog prevented the air cover from protecting the unarmed Sikorsky HO3S-1. Wilkins heard Koelsch's helicopter approaching and moved back down the mountain toward his parachute. He saw the Sikorsky flying at about 50 feet below a layer of clouds. The helicopter was receiving heavy ground fire from the North Korean soldiers along the road. The Sikorsky was hit and Koelsch turned away, but quickly returned. Koelsch located Wilkins and brought the HO3S-1 to a hover while rescue crewman AM3 George M. Neal lowered a 'horse-collar' harness on a hoist cable. Neal then lifted the fighter pilot up to the helicopter. The helicopter continued to be targeted by ground fire and was finally shot down, crashing on the mountainside and rolling upside down. Koelsch and Neal were unhurt and, carrying Wilkins, they moved away from the enemy forces and headed toward the coast but, after evading the enemy for nine days, were captured. During his captivity, though beaten and abused, Koelsch refused to aid his captors or submit to interrogation. His fortitude and personal bravery inspired his fellow prisoners. On 16 October 1951, while a prisoner of war, John Koelsch died of malnutrition and dysentery. On 3 August 1955 he was posthumously awarded the Medal of Honor for his actions in Korea. George Neal received the Navy Cross.

In August 1951 the *Essex* arrived on station with CVG-5 to join TF-77. On board were F4U-4/-4Bs of VF-53 and a VC-3 F4U-5NL Detachment, as well as two squadrons of F9F-2s and one of F2H-2 Banshees and Skyraider units of various types. On 18 August aircraft from the task force attacked twenty-seven bridges and rail lines running to the east coast. Samdong-ni to Kowon was soon christened 'Death Valley' by navy aviators, who grew to respect the enemy AA fire in the area.

During 1951 the aircraft in TF-77 flew 29,000 interdiction missions over Korea. Their contribution to the war effort was immense. One of the most important contributions was that of the USN and USMC Corsairs, which were never far from the front-line action. VF-63, for instance, which operated from the *Boxer* and the *Valley Forge* from 15 September 1950 to 2 June 1951, flew over 1,000 sorties and were credited with the destruction of over 2,000 enemy troops killed, fifty-seven vehicles and twenty-seven gun positions destroyed or damaged and one tank destroyed. Added to this they also accounted for eighteen supply and fuel dumps, 1,156 troop shelters, 4,590 buildings, one locomotive, 1,246 rail cars, forty-five bridges, sixteen warehouses, 114 oxen and horses and five junks! Late in 1951 the navy made several far reaching changes to the composition of its carrier forces. On 15 October CVG-15, the second all-reserve air group, arrived in the Sea of Japan aboard the *Antietam*, with five reserve and four regular navy units. Four of the five reserve units – VF-713 (Denver), VF-653 (Akron), VF-831 (New York) and VF-837 (New York), were equipped with Corsairs. VF-653 soon joined ATG-1, the navy's first Air Task Group, which was formed that month to bring together all the USN's experienced F9F-2, F4U-4 and AD squadrons from regular carrier groups. ATG-1 was embarked on *Valley Forge* and the Corsairs of VF-653 were joined by VC-3 (Detachment 'George') flying the F4U-5N.

Several Naval Air Reserve squadrons volunteered en masse, the first being VF-781 from Los Alamitos and VF- 791 from Memphis. Many squadrons were flying obsolete aircraft, but mobilization brought newer, more modern types like the AD Skyraider and F9F Panther. Only those units flying the F4U Corsair needed little or no transition training. VF-653's pilots, typically, consisted of fathers and senior lieutenants with at least some Second World War flight experience. Nearly all lived in Ohio or western Pennsylvania. A few were still in school on the GI Bill, but most were white- or blue-collar workers. VF-653 was skippered by a hotshot navy aviator named Cook Cleland, born on Christmas Eve 1916 who, during the Pacific War, had flown Vought SB2U Vindicators and Douglas Dauntless SBD dive-bombers from the decks of the carriers *Wasp* and *Lexington*, providing close air support for the initial Guadalcanal landings. Cleland was on the *Wasp* when she was sunk in September 1942, spending over four hours in the water, waiting for rescue. He was then assigned to the USS *Lexington*. During his service on board the 'Gray Ghost' he became an air ace, shooting down five Japanese aircraft, unusual for a dive-bomber pilot. He and his wingman were also credited with severely crippling the Japanese aircraft carrier *Junyō* during the Battle of the Philippine Sea in June 1943. For his valour in action, he received the Navy Cross and many commendations. After returning to the United States, he evaluated captured enemy aircraft as a navy test pilot.

VF-653's 34-year-old executive officer, Ray Edinger, was a General Motors service representative. Bob Balser, 26, one of the squadron's few bachelors, was an illustrator for the *Pittsburgh Post-Gazette*. For each of these 'weekend warriors' the call to duty brought business and family routines to an abrupt halt. On 23 November 1951, on his way to fight in Korea, Navy Reserve Lieutenant Joe Sanko in VF-653, one of ten children in a tight-knit Polish-American family and a coal miner, whose occasional weekend aloft contrasted with long weekday shifts below ground, confessed his fear to his elder brother, Pete, a Jesuit, working as a cook at the St Andrew-on-Hudson seminary in Hyde Park, New York: 'To date we haven't lost a single life,' he wrote, '[but] we are going to lose some and perhaps quite a few.' The pilots had been briefed; they knew what awaited them. Sanko's son Dan was 3 years old when his dad left for the war and wife Millie was expecting their second child. Joe had fought in the Pacific in the Second World War. He wrote to his brother that his chances of being shot down would be 'much greater than in the war with Japan'. Surviving a hit would be much harder. If aviators ditched at sea, Sanko explained, they would be in waters where 'temp gets so low that a pilot can survive only five to eight minutes without a submersion suit'. He added, 'I've got a real fight on my hands this winter.'

Len DeFranco a 22-year-old squadron mechanic who later became part of Cleland's racing team recalled one mission, when Cleland's aircraft, 'Fighting 301', sustained damage: 'It was a low-level hop and Cook's plane hit a high-tension wire that chewed up the nose cone, prop and starboard wing. We had to replace just that one wing, but the only spares available were wings from newer Corsairs equipped with 20mm cannon, not .50-calibre machine guns. So a half-dozen of us worked all night to replace both wings and Cook was right there with us lending a hand.'

VF-653 lost its first Corsair pilots on 9 December, even before entering combat. One was Don London, Sanko's roommate and a close friend; the other was Jim Porterfield. Both were family men: London was a new father and Porterfield's wife was expecting their first child in March. 'What really hurts,' Sanko wrote, was that 'they weren't shot down. They were up practising some tactics, had a mid-air collision and hit the water without a chance of getting out.'

By 1952 naval air reservists had flown 6,000 of the 8,000 sorties from US carriers and, including other NAR units in the total – USNR ashore and Marine Corps Air Reserve shore-based squadrons –by the ceasefire in July 1953 the NAR had flown one-third of the combat missions in Korea. While on duty, each carrier rotated through four-day cycles, three days of air strikes followed by a day of rest. By Sanko's reckoning, he and the other aviators could anticipate flying roughly sixty combat missions over the course of four operational periods. Soon enough, the combat began taking its toll in pilots and aeroplanes. After completing his fourteenth mission, Sanko wrote in early January 1952, 'We came here with twenty-eight pilots and in one month have lost four ... so our wives are just about ready to give up by now.' He also betrayed a combat pilot's fatalism: 'If you have faith in that engine, you feel safe and secure (until the black puffs start rocking you around). If you get hit badly, it's usually a sudden death. If you don't get it, it's just another flight over enemy territory.'

Valley Forge's first tour ended on 19 January. Despite challenging winter conditions, ATG-1's 129 airmen and seventy-nine aircraft, which included Douglas A-1 Skyraiders and Grumman F9F Panthers, as well as Corsairs, had racked up more than a thousand combat sorties. Ten airmen had been killed or were missing. During deployment, a carrier and its air group usually operated, along with one or two sister carriers, plus a screen of cruisers and destroyers, for thirty days at a time. After that came a ten-day rest break in Japan. ATG-1 returned to duty on 1 February but this second tour was shorter – just twenty days – and, on two of them, foul weather shut down flight operations. There were fewer than 500 combat sorties, but the seventy flown on 8 February were especially gruelling. Many were Rescue Combat Air Patrol (RESCAP) flights in support of efforts to extract two VF-194 Skyraider pilots, downed behind enemy lines. Both rescues failed and two rescue helicopters crashed, one at each site. To make matters worse, a Corsair pilot from an ATG-1 night-flying detachment was killed, while five other RESCAP aircraft suffered crippling flak damage. VF-653's Ray Edinger flew one of the damaged Corsairs, which had lost hydraulics and was dangerously low on fuel. When his Corsair touched down on *Valley Forge*, its wheel struts collapsed. Then, as the F4U skidded along the deck, a hung rocket on the port wing was jettisoned and tumbled forward. Flight-deck crews raced for cover, but the rocket did not explode. Edinger managed to climb from the cockpit, shaken but unhurt.

Sanko, who had flown one of the RESCAP sorties, described it in a letter the next day. His flight had strafed and bombed a hill to keep North Korean troops from reaching the rescue site. Flying low, he'd destroyed a hidden anti-aircraft gun. His Corsair, he wrote, 'just quivered as near misses went by. I didn't care, as we wanted so hard to give those poor guys on the ground some help.'[2] Novelist James Michener, who after spending time on several navy carriers in Task Force 77, described the day's events in a newspaper despatch titled *An Epic in Failure*. In an article in the July 1952 issue of *Reader's Digest*, Michener recounted that the pilots had told him, 'We don't desert our men'. The experience inspired the fictional drama of downed aircraft and helicopter pilots that concludes Michener's 1953 novel *The Bridges at Toko-Ri*, the story of Harry Brubaker, a recalled naval air reservist and civilian lawyer from Denver. Published in 1953, the book was adapted a year later into a Hollywood film.

Throughout the winter of 1951-52 the war in Korea reached stalemate on the ground. In the air the navy and USMC squadrons continued their interdiction and close-air-support strikes against North Korean targets. At sea Task Force 77 could afford to rotate its carriers on a fairly regular basis. Eight carriers took their turn in the Sea of Japan and normally four US carriers were on station at any one time.[3] In March 1952 Operation Saturate, a sustained offensive aimed at short sections of railway line to deny their use to the enemy was launched. TF-77 and its aircraft groups and the Marine squadrons ashore were part of this offensive. During March-June 1952 the Marine Corps changed its VMF designation to VMA to reflect the Corsair's true attack role that had been a feature of operations ever since the war in Korea had started. By April the USMC had six Corsair day-fighter squadrons in Korea with VMF-115, 311 and 121 based at K-3 Pohang and VMF-212 and VMF-323 'Death Rattlers' at K-6 Pyeongtaek, while VMA-312 operated aboard *Bataan*.

On the eve of this fourth combat stretch, Joe Sanko's 13 April letter to his brother Pete expressed joy at the birth of daughter, Kathy, but also

2. David Sears, author of *Such Men as These: The Story of the Navy Pilots Who Flew the Deadly Skies*, writing in *Air & Space Magazine* January 2013.
3. After an overhaul *Philippine Sea* rejoined TF-77 on 3 February with CVG-11 including the Corsairs of VF-113 and VF-114. *Essex, Antietam, Boxer* (with CVG-2, -VF-24/63/64/65 and three detachments), *Princeton* (with CVG-19 -VF-191/192/193/195 and four detachments), *Bataan* (with VMA-312's Corsairs embarked), *Valley Forge* (with ATG-1 -VF-52/111/194/653 and four detachments) and *Barioko*), were the other carriers. The AU-1 ground attack version of the Corsair now began to be delivered almost exclusively to the USMC beginning with VMA-323 at K-6, Pyongtaek and VMA-312 at K-3, Pohang. During February-October 1952, the Marines received 110 AU-1s. Although heavily armoured, sixteen AU-1s were lost to enemy ground fire during the Korean War. VMF(N)-513 continued to operate a mix of F4U-5N Corsairs and Tigercats until total replacement by Skyknights.

contained dispiriting news: *Valley Forge*'s deployment had been extended. 'I'm afraid we have one more [tour] to face. We won't get back to the States until July.' By May Sanko had logged his forty-eighth combat mission. 'Not many more hops left now,' he wrote Millie on 10 May: 'Most of the people aboard ship are telling us to take it easy and play it safe. Kinda hard to do. A job is a job and I always try to do my best. At present I have about 180 hours over enemy territory. At most I have about thirty to go.'

Joe's last letter home was on 11 May: 'Received the letters I was looking forward to and one of them had the pictures in it. I'm so happy with them that I just had to answer right away. She sure is a little doll.' The letter arrived after a hand-delivered telegram to the home of his mother, Anna, in New Salem, Pennsylvania telling of her son's 13 May loss to anti-aircraft fire. Dan Sanko, though 'pretty small' at the time remembers the event: his mother's and his Aunt Mary's immediate distress and his grandmother stoically continuing to wash dishes in the kitchen. 'I think I was told later on that my grandmother had a premonition about my dad's death. So she wasn't surprised when the telegram arrived.' Though Joe was initially listed as missing in action, hopes for his safe return were dashed by a 17 May letter to Millie from his wingman, Eddie Kearns. Kearns recounted that a formation led by Cleland was in a bombing and strafing run. Sanko had dived on an anti-aircraft gun position, with Kearns following. 'I was in a straight dive when I saw Joe's plane hit by anti-aircraft fire,' Kearns wrote. The right wing of Sanko's Corsair was nearly severed. Kearns then saw 'a flaming mass of wreckage burning on the ground'. 'Millie, I want to be very honest with you. [I]t would just about be impossible for him to have gotten out of his plane. I am sure it was over very quickly.'

Joe Sanko was one of three ATG-1 airmen lost in combat during *Valley Forge*'s fourth tour. During the group's fifth and final tour, four more were lost, including two from VF-653. The squadron, having lost a total of eleven, was assigned for its final missions to less hazardous coastal hops.[4]

---

4. On 10 June, ATG-1's last day of combat operations, Cleland was still pushing. "He was shot up pretty good by flak," Len DeFranco recalls. "He ditched in Wonsan Harbor and was picked up by a helicopter." The airplane Cleland lost that day was not *Fighting 301*, which made it through the war. VF-653's Korean War losses – thirteen pilots missing, killed, or severely injured, about 46 percent of the number first deployed - represented almost half of those sustained by ATG-1. As measured by total sorties flown, the results are equally stark: ATG-1's airmen flew a combined 7,113; VF-653's rate of losses per missions flown was twice as high as the air group's overall rate.' David Sears writing in *Air & Space Magazine,* January 2013.

On 2 May 1952 23-year-old Ensign Owen W. Dykema a Corsair pilot in VF-192 aboard *Princeton*, flew his first combat mission of the war. He recalls, 'I was in the third division of the "Golden Dragons". After VF-192 appeared in the movie *The Bridges at Toko-Ri*, doing all the flying, we began to call ourselves "The World Famous Golden Dragons". We elected to have a special division patch made up to commemorate the farcical Police Action in which we were involved. We were the "Keystone Kops" of the UN Police Department'.

Dykema wrote a letter home to his wife Enid describing the day's mission: 'Speak to me softly, gal and watch what you say, I'm a ruff, tuff Korean veteran now. I had my first hop over war-torn Korea today. What a farce, there wasn't a thing moving, anywhere, not a soul in sight, even in the villages. We peacefully went in, dropped our bombs around a railroad – probably didn't hit it – flew all over looking for targets, shot up some ox carts and small boats and left. In all that time we didn't see a single return shot and only one person.

'Some guy was running with his ox cart down a street of a town. So, Dineen made a run at him, to warn him away from his cart. But he kept going, so we all strafed him, except Struce and I. Nobody hit him and the last we saw he was still going. A couple other ox carts that were sitting along a road we did hit, though. I got a long burst right into one of them. I probably used a hundred dollars' worth of ammo to destroy a ten-dollar cart. Well, that's this war. We also sank a sampan that was floating in a little bay. I put about fifty rounds right through the bottom.

'If this hop is any indication of how this war is going to be, it'll be long, dull and hard work. My bombing is lousy, now. I only saw one of my drops hit and it made a big blast in the middle of an empty field, about a hundred yards from the railroad! My butt was so sore when I got back I could hardly walk and my head feels like it is overloaded, or something. There's no relaxing on these flights, you're constantly in a deceptive weave.

'We more or less followed a group from the *Valley Forge* on the rail strike so they could show us how it was done. We circled and observed. Alongside the track there was a small hill and a relatively heavy AA installation. One of the *Valley*'s divisions went after the hill to silence the gun. They strafed and dropped "grass cutters". These were bombs with a radar fuse, set to explode just a few feet off the ground. They were specially constructed to shatter into zillions of little, bullet-sized fragments, to sweep the surrounding area. They literally "mowed the grass".

'Of course, the AA crew had reinforced tunnels to hide in. As soon as the bombs stopped going off they leaped out and fired at the planes going away. In the midst of all this one of the *Valley's* pilots came on the air and matter-of-factly announced: "Red One, this is Red Four, Red Three was hit on that last run and went straight in. No chance of survival." Despite all the destruction on the hill the AA team got him. A healthy, reasonably happy naval aviator, probably with a wife and kids, just like my own And there he was just smashed into small pieces on the side of a little hill halfway around the world from his family. What a way to start an eight-month tour of such nonsense.'[5]

On 6 May Ensign Owen Dykema flew on an early morning strike from *Princeton*: 'The skipper went on the pre-dawn "heckler" hop with VC-3 (the night-fighters) and we launched just after dawn. When we reached the coast the skipper and the three VC boys had a convoy of seventeen trucks cornered on a winding mountain road. We asked permission from the strike controller to direct our strike to the trucks. There we were, only ten-fifteen miles from the first really worthwhile targets we've seen since we got here, loaded down with a couple tons of high explosives and ammo apiece. We could have spent a couple hours destroying $20-30,000 worth of vehicles and supplies. But the controller said nix, bomb rails and sent three miserable jets over there with 200lb of bombs apiece. They only got one truck and a bulldozer. By the time we bombed the tracks and hustled over there to strafe there wasn't a truck or person in sight, except the one the jets hit. It was sitting off the road covered with green foliage for camouflage. We strafed it like mad but couldn't set it afire. The skipper had hit near one, knocked it off the road and rolled it down into the valley.

'Actually (of course) the strike controller's decision was probably correct. The best weapon against trucks on a winding road was strafing with explosive (20mm) ammo, which the jets had and we didn't. We just had solid 50-calibre chunks of metal. As we saw, we could pour those rounds into the trucks forever and perhaps damage them severely (we had a hard time telling), but usually we couldn't set them afire like the

---

5. Owen W. Dykema kindly gave permission to quote freely from *From The Bird Barge* (Dykema Publishing Co. 1997).

exploding 20mm could. Once on fire the whole truck would go – cargo and all.'

In all, Ensign Owen Dykema flew six missions in the two weeks before R&R in Japan. The one on 12 May was a 'Special hop': 'You bet it was special. It seemed that our intelligence guys had a direct observer of some sort involved in a big meeting of all the North Korean and Chinese intelligence community. It was being held in a small town well up the coast from the bomb line (the front), in a big building like a resort hotel in this small town. They even professed to know the exact rooms where the intelligence big-wigs were billeted and the exact schedule for breakfast. Our job was to surprise them just after first light and before they got up to go to breakfast, probably just when they were in the head for their morning "ablutions" and blast them all.

'In the briefing for the strike we were shown good pictures of the building, a large two-storey job and each of us was assigned a window. We were supposed to throw our napalm right in our assigned window. We didn't think it would make much difference if we hit the window or not because at 250-300 knots that napalm was going to go through the wall no matter where it hit.

'We took just two divisions (8) and we launched in the darkness just before dawn. We flew in to the beach right on the water, at 50 feet altitude or so, to avoid radar detection. Navigation was tricky because we were supposed to aim right at the beach, pull up at the coast, pop over the mountain range and find ourselves boring right down on the building. Any mistakes and we would give them time to get out of the building and into the bomb shelters.

'In the event, our navigation was flawless. We did the pull up and pop over thing and there was the building! The sun was just up and shining from behind us on the side of the building. I could easily identify my personal window and it looked exactly as briefed. We strung out a little bit to avoid conflicting with one another and went straight on in. I was number six in and I could see the leaders' napalm going right into and directly around those windows. By the time I got up close I had just about lost sight of my window in the smoke and flames from the earlier hits. Nevertheless, I think I got mine right in there. I cleared the roof of the building by only about 20 feet and got a clear, close-up view of the whole thing.

'Our surprise was apparently complete. Nothing was stirring in the town and no AA responded. On circling back we could see that the building was totally engulfed in flames. If all of our info was as correct as it seemed to be, the North Korean and Chinese intelligence community probably suffered its largest single loss in history. From the time we cleared the mountaintops and headed in until the first napalm hit was probably less than one minute. One pass, surprise was gone, so back home we went.

Princeton was back on station in the Sea of Japan on 2 June and The Golden Dragons recommenced strikes on North Korea. Ensign Owen Dykema flew his seventh mission on 5 June, against rail targets near Wonsan and on the 8th VF-192 launched twenty-three Corsairs under a 200-feet overcast for a strike on Hungnam. He recalls:

'Hungnam was considered by the "air farce"'to be the hottest place in Korea. They refused to go near it because of the intense concentration of flak. Flak – shmak, we made three-four runs apiece, each plane on an individual target all across the city. I was sixth in, so things hadn't deteriorated too much when I slid into place. However, we already were stepped down off the leader by about 50 feet, about 150 feet off the water. After that I just sucked in right to my leader (Struce) and tried to occupy as little space as possible and out of the corner of my eye watched the rest come in.

'At one point there were two Corsairs coming in too steeply, one slightly behind the other. They were both in pretty steep banks and pulling "G"s and both were trying to avoid crashing into (1) each other, (2) the already assembled formation (us) and (3) the weather. It was an exciting scene all right, even powerfully beautiful! The clouds were black and angry, with scud occasionally hanging down to a hundred feet or so off the weather and rain falling in some areas. The sea was a dark blue-grey with waves reaching 10-20 feet in the air. And there were the two dark blue Corsairs, seen nearly head on, showing the prominent inverted gull wings and the monster spinning twelve-foot props, coming at us at about 200 knots.

'The beautiful twin cities of Hamhung and Hungnam were not far ahead and they were clear of clouds. Time to get ready for the attack. We were just beginning to approach Hungnam when the long-range flak began to appear. It was apparent that the defences would be, as expected, fairly heavy. As a result, we planned to drop all of our ordnance in a single pass and then get the hell out of there. While setting up for and during the attack, the flak, of all kinds, was pretty heavy and Struce absorbed what seemed then to be a minor hit in the engine area.

'I set all my ordnance on "salvo", rolled into my dive (adrenalin pumping freely) and lined up on my two tiny buildings, firing all guns as I went. All the way down, the orange balls were floating up and the black puffs of smoke were magically appearing on all sides. At 25,000 feet I released my whole load and hauled out of there. No wonder I didn't see (or care) if I hit or not, I was already gone and clawing for ever-more distance and altitude by the time my load hit the ground. Once again, miraculously, everyone survived the attack and got joined up. I jockeyed around and looked over Struce's plane pretty carefully, but other than a possible thin haze of smoke or oil streaming back from his engine, everything seemed okay. I don't know for sure if I knocked my targets out – a pair of storage buildings – because we didn't go back to look, but I tried. They were such tiny buildings! Then we had to let down through the soup again, to return to the ship. Made it okay though'.

On 16 June 1952 aircraft from TF-77 pasted Kowon, supported by an effective rope chaff cloud to 'snow' enemy radar-controlled AA guns. Two days later VF-192 from *Princeton* struck at rail targets again, as Ensign Owen Dykema remembers:

'We went way up north and bombed the devil out of another little railroad town. We used napalm for the first time. Some of the guys had 2,000lb bombs. They tried to drop them right on the railroad ties stacked along the right of way. I guess the idea was to run them out of useable ties do they couldn't repair the rail cuts so fast. The big bombs would fragment them and our napalm would burn up the fragments. I saw some of the biggies hit and, man, was that impressive! It was a fairly humid day and the big bombs set up a shock wave that you could clearly see, a whitish circle rapidly expanding away from the hit. The pile of ties basically disappeared. I wonder what the economic trade off was – a 2,000lb bomb for 100 railroad ties?

'There were so many fires we couldn't assess the damage for the smoke. I guess we clobbered it good, though. Just like we got Puckchoni the day before, big mass strikes of thirty-forty planes. I heard rumours that the MiGs were down our way during the night also.'

TF-77 now prepared for strikes in concert with the US 5th Air Force on the North's four principal hydro-electric plants at Fusen, Kyosen, Chosin and Suiho on 23 June. The big generating plant at Suiho, the most dangerous target in MiG Alley, less than forty miles from Antung where 250 MiGs were based, would be attacked by fighter-bombers of TF-77 and Fifth Air Force. Meanwhile, Fifth Air Force Mustangs would bomb Nos. 3 and 4 plants at Fusen, while USMC Panther jets raided Chosin's Nos. 3 and 4 plants. A short time after, Skyraiders, Corsairs and Panthers from *Boxer, Princeton* and *Bon Homme Richard* would attack Fusen's Nos. 1 and 2 plants. Finally, when darkness fell, B-29s would hit the Nos. 1 and 2 plants at Chosin using radar-bombing techniques. For the initial strike on Suiho, thirty-five AD Skyraiders and thirty-five flak-suppression F9F Panthers from *Boxer, Princeton* and *Philippine Sea* with eighty-four USAF Sabres as top cover would be involved. A second strike consisting of seventy-nine F-84s and forty-five F-80s would go in an hour later.

Bad weather delayed the start of the operation, which went ahead at 1400 hours. Ensign Owen W. Dykema of the The Golden Dragons on *Princeton* recalls: 'The end of June 1952 was an exciting, even history-making, time in TF-77 in the Sea of Japan. As those of us in the trenches understood it, the UN allies had ruled out attacks on the electric power system and network in North Korea as long as there was a chance that we might have ended up taking it over. However, by June 1952 it had become amply clear that we were going to settle for some kind of armistice that left everything north of the 38th parallel to the Communists. So the high command decided that was an appropriate time to take out all generating capacity up there. The power plants were the only remaining targets of any significant, concentrated value in all of North Korea. As a result, as you might expect, they were heavily defended, with all sorts of anti-aircraft guns, of all types. Our hope was that, after a couple of years of ignoring them as targets, the North Koreans might have become complacent and might actually have diverted some of the idle defences elsewhere. The plan was to hit them all at once, throughout all of North Korea and knock them all out in a single massive strike. They got four carriers on the line on Sunday, the 22nd and that single massive strike went out on Monday the 23rd.

'Although they launched almost every available plane from the four carriers, I somehow failed to get on the schedule. In particular the guys who went way up north, to hit the Suiho plant on the Yalu river, had an exciting time. This plant was only about forty miles from the big MiG base at Antung, across the river in Manchuria. F9F-2 Panthers from VF-191 were flying high cover on that raid, but no one really expected that they would be capable of shooting down any MiGs. Air Force F-86s were up there for that. The surprise worked. The anti-aircraft defences were heavy but many were caught napping and it wasn't all that bad. Amazingly enough, no MiGs showed up. I don't believe there were any losses from those raids.

'The problem began, however, when damage reports late Monday began indicating that, while we had totally destroyed two of the plants, the Suiho and the Kyosen, and pretty well damaged a third, at the Fusen Reservoir, the fourth, the big hydro-electric plant at the (famous) Chosin Reservoir, was still operating. We all immediately began clamouring to launch a second massive strike as soon as possible, at least as early as possible Tuesday morning, to knock that plant out before they could beef up the defences. This was the last significant remaining source of electric power for all of North Korea and the element of surprise was gone. A child of six could predict that this remaining plant would soon be the most heavily defended site in the world. Since I was one of the few who had not flown on Monday's strike I was assured a place on this second strike.

'By nightfall we were all really upset. Word finally came through that we would indeed strike the Chosin plant the next day, first launch. Unfortunately, that still would give the Commies all night to prepare their best reception. And as luck would have it, I was indeed assigned to that strike. As the evening wore on we began getting reports from the night pilots who had been scouting the area that every road and railroad they could see had convoys of lights, all converging on Chosin. We fully expected that by Tuesday this would be the most strongly defended target we had hit to date. The ship's operations people were estimating 10% losses (acceptable). So I was looking at a 1-in-10 chance of getting killed the next day!

'I don't think I slept at all Monday night. Lying there in my sack, I was never so scared or lonely in my life. I kept thinking how this might be my last night, my last few hours on earth and I was spending it lying there alone in a bunk on a ship far from home in the Sea of Japan. The ship and the squadron were already fully anticipating the loss of several pilots tomorrow and they were not particularly concerned that one of these might be me. They were already geared up to perform the necessary notifications of next of kin, to adjust the squadron roster to fill in the empty spots (my place) and to go on operating as though I had never existed.

'As advertised, we were up very early Tuesday morning (who slept?). I really felt rotten and so did everyone else on the strike. Nobody talked about it, though, or shared their fears. As far as I could tell, I was the only one so scared. By 0430 we were in the cockpit and ready to go. Unfortunately, the weather over the target was poor so we were put on hold. For 3½ incredible hours we sat there, strapped in the cockpits, fidgeting, worrying, panicking (isn't the waiting always the worst?). I could just see hundreds of AA guns arriving at the plant, setting up, stockpiling the ready ammo, firing a few check-out rounds, getting ready for me (not us, me). Finally, around 0800, the word came: "Launch All Aircraft"! Sink or swim (survive or not), here we come!

'Due to a number of illnesses I ended up flying on the skipper's wing. The strike consisted of about forty planes, from all of the *Princeton* squadrons. Our skipper led the strike, so I was number two onto the target. We made the kind of attack where we all lined up generally in a circle around the target and peeled off into our dives like in an Esther Williams' movie. Everybody fired their guns at the defences on the way down, so the enemy gunners tended to keep their heads down, from the time the first guys (the skipper and I) started firing until the last "tail-end Charlie" pulled out of his dive. In addition, if they were firing back at us during our dives, they had to keep rotating their aim as we came in from all parts of the compass.

'The really sensitive parts of the attack were just before and after our defensive firing, just before the first plane went in, when everyone was close in and surrounding the target but no one was yet into their dive, and just after the last guy pulled out, when the ground defences could safely pop up out of their bunkers or tunnels and fire at everyone going away. Of course, gun emplacements off to the sides of the target area would be firing all the time.

'The skipper and I were exposed to the first sensitive period the longest, as we led everyone else into diving position around the target. The skipper was a real professional and I knew he would do it just right regardless of the danger. We were exposed to the ground fire at closer range and for a longer time than anyone else in the strike was. Who more appropriate than the skipper and I to number among the "acceptable" 10% losses?

'Nevertheless, I knew without a doubt that I would fly my wing position and do my best to hit the target regardless of the fear. With anything less, "cowardice in the face of the enemy", I would never have been able to live with the shame. I would never again have been able to look my fellow pilots, my friends or even my family in the eye. Perhaps most important, I realized I would not have been able to look myself in the eye, ever again. It was preferable to be killed in the strike than to demonstrate cowardice in the eyes of my own personal world. So I was between a rock and a hard place, which simply dictated that I go out and get killed, if that was to be my fate. There was no way out.

'The morning was bright and clear – cheery actually. I kept looking around to savour the view. As we approached the target the AA began appearing. In true form, the skipper flew up alongside the target, past it and began circling back, to line everyone up in the circle surrounding the target. Good tactics, the trouble was that the skipper and I (and a few others) were sitting up there like ducks in a shooting gallery, for what seemed like hours (just a few minutes). The AA was extremely heavy, with white and black (the heavy stuff) puffs appearing all around and orange tracers drifting by from all quadrants. At times the big stuff was close enough to hear the sharp "crack!" over the noise of the engine and the wind. That was probably within 50-100 feet of us.

'I was scrunched up into as small a ball as possible, there in the cockpit, looking over at the skipper and silently screaming at him to "Go, Man, Go!" He just kept calmly (unafraid? - hardly) flying around the target, looking over his shoulder to be sure everyone was in his proper position for the attack. So far there were no losses that I could see; though I failed to see why not. How could they have missed us in that shooting gallery? It was at this time that one of the ADs from VF-195 got his tail shot off. The pilot got out, though how or where I never found out.

'Finally the skipper seemed satisfied, waggled his wings and went in. I dutifully followed, with an enormous sigh of relief, at least to get moving and defending myself. We rolled into the dive and I began concentrating on the target, lining it up, putting the proper lead into it and firing all guns almost continuously. It's hard for me to believe that I was doing all this while racked with such fear. Apparently fear is not necessarily paralyzing. Finally I reached the proper altitude and everything seemed right on, so I dropped my bombs.

'Just then my windshield exploded into a million fragments of Plexiglass, blown back into the cockpit by a 400-mile-an-hour wind coming through a large hole. I thought, "So this is what it is to die!" However, I seemed to still be flying, though still hurtling earthward at a great rate. I paused a moment (a few milliseconds?) to thank God, first, that I was still (apparently) alive and in no pain and, second, that I had followed squadron doctrine and lowered my goggles as we approached the target. The shattered Plexiglass rained all over me and over my goggles, right in front of my eyes, but cut nothing!

'I even had the presence of mind to waggle the stick from side to side to see if I still had control and it seemed that I did. Next I had to find out if I was going to be able to pull out of the dive. I was already going down too fast and was too low to have much chance of baling out. But the nose came up nicely and I was soon past horizontal, climbing out of the target area and, especially, out of that shooting gallery. The plane seemed to be flying normally. Apparently I had only the hole in the windshield and no other significant damage.

'And that's what it turned out to be. What a relief! I was off the target, still alive and with nothing more than a scratch, a hole about eight inches in diameter in the windshield. Apparently something had gone through the outer, streamlined windshield and bounced off the flat plate of bullet-proof glass just behind it. It apparently had bounced up and over the cockpit and the plane, causing no further damage. What a relief to see that same fine morning and know that I again had a chance of seeing many more! I had this howling wind in the cockpit but that was no problem at all. Without further ado we flew back to the ship and I brought it aboard, hole and all, in a Roger pass (no signals required from the Landing Signal Officer). Just taxi that hog back into a convenient parking spot and get out. What a day! Despite it all, there I was, still alive and on the way back to Yokosuka for a few days of R&R. Did I need that R&R or what?'

The attacks on the hydro-electric plants were followed on 11 July by Operation Pressure Pump, the largest air attack so far, which saw massive UN strikes on thirty high-level targets in Pyongyang. CVG-19 onboard *Princeton* and CVG-7 aboard *Bon Homme Richard* combined with USAF and RN and Commonwealth squadrons to wreak havoc over the North Korean capital. Aboard *Princeton* Owen Dykema, who was grounded with ear trouble and finding life 'dull as a clipped wing bird', missed the strike. He recalled: 'Today the whole ship, except for three planes that were down, flew on a big combined raid on Pyongyang. Our planes had targets just 200 yards from a PoW camp and hit so well that not a single bomb fell outside the target area, much less near the camp. The weather was terrible around the ship so it was a bit hairy getting in and out.'

Some 1,254 sorties were flown beginning at 1000 hours on 11 July and ending next morning, for the loss of just three aircraft – a Corsair, a Panther and a Thunderjet. (On 29 August an even bigger force, including USMC Panthers and F4Us and navy Corsairs from *Boxer* and *Essex* returned to devastate the capital.) On 12 July *Philippine Sea* completed her second Korean deployment and sailed for San Diego and re-classification as an attack carrier. When she sailed for Japan on 15 December 1952, embarked aboard were CVG-9 from *Essex* with VF-91, 93 and 94, VA-95 and detachments from VC-3 (F4U-5N), 11, 35 and 61. During June First Lieutenant John W. Andre, a F4U-5N pilot, who had destroyed four enemy aircraft in the Second World War, became an ace when he despatched a Yak-9 to become the first Marine Corps ace in Korea.

Ensign Owen Dykema returned to flying on 23 July. He recalled: 'It was great to hear the roar of that engine again, to feel the thrust of power and to loft into the big blue. And to think they actually paid us to fly these planes! Struce and I ended up a hop pretty much alone, on road recce up north. He was again feeling pretty punk so he let me lead and just followed along behind. I spotted a very small railroad bridge, over a dry creek bed. It looked like it had never been touched by the war and there appeared to be no defenders around to shoot at me. So, I left Struce orbiting above the bridge and went down alone, to see if I could knock it out. The only ordnance we carried that would hurt a bridge was one 500lb bomb. (Nearly every hop we flew now they gave us a bunch of armour-piercing rockets, in place of bombs and they weren't worth "squat". All they were good for were tanks, locomotives, etc. The fragmentation and rockets were not designed for bridges.) I had only six armour-piercing rockets on the wings and 3,600 solid (non-explosive) 50-calibre machine-gun rounds, clearly not the best ordnance for bridge-busting. However, since there was no one in sight and no apparent ground fire of any kind, I elected to go right down into the streambed, below the level of the trees along the banks, to bore in close and fire one rocket at time. It should have virtually assured one or more hits, right? Wrong!'

'So "thar I wuz", on a quiet Friday afternoon, all alone (basically), zooming along at about 250mph just 20-30 feet above a dry creek bed way up inside North Korea, having the time of my life! (The trees were whipping by on either side, the bridge looming up in the distance. I set the gunsight pipper right on the middle of the span – a little elevation. Now it got bigger. This was about as close in as I should have gotten – Fire! Flash! Zoom! Through the trees nearby – bang out in the open field beyond! Back around again – down into the bed. There was the bridge coming up. I'd get it this time. Flash – Zoom, up and over the bridge and off into the distance! etc., etc., etc.)

'Half a dozen times I had that bridge lined up in my sights and waited till it nearly filled the windshield (maybe 100 yards out) before firing. Each time the rocket zoomed off in some kind of crazy "death spiral". One time it plunged into the bank nearby (too nearby). Another up into the air and over the bridge and once into the streambed not too far out in front of me – each time with the terrific bang of a hundred pounds of dynamite! (They said these rockets were stored horizontally since [1945] and the solid propellant may have imperceptibly packed down more tightly on one side or the other, giving it the asymmetrical thrust.) I should have fired from further out to minimise chances of picking up shrapnel, but then I might have missed the bridge! It's a wonder that one of the rockets didn't boomerang completely around and shoot me down from behind!

'Then I tried a run with just my six .50s. I hit the bridge all right but tracers were ricocheting all over the place and I had to pull up abruptly to avoid them. On closer inspection the 50-calibre slugs didn't seem to have affected the integrity of the bridge in any way. Score another eminently successful afternoon for #2 Keystone Kop of the UN Police Farce!

'We ended up expending our rockets at a bunch of small boats in a little cove. (An armour-piercing rocket was no good at all on small, wooden boats, either.) If I had managed to hit one of those boats the rocket fusing was such that, if it exploded at all, it was only after it has passed clear through the boat and out the other side. We conjectured that the military had whole warehouses full of these things and no enemy in sight had tanks to fire them at. I wonder if the steel strike was holding up bomb production? The real sad commentary, however, was that our country sent our boys in to fight and get killed and didn't give them adequate ammunition with which to do their job.'

On 1 August VF-192 was out again. One of the pilots was Ensign Owen Dykema: 'We hit another powerhouse today, way up in the mountains. All the buildings around the main powerhouse just disappeared and the main one was gutted too. We had four Corsairs and four ADs from the *Essex* along with us. When we got to the target we found that it was already so damaged that the Reds had basically given up defending it. There was just one heavy machine gun, probably a 20mm, a little off to the left of the bombing run. Our leader decided that, since it was so lightly defended, we would each make four (dive-bombing) runs, dropping one bomb each time. That way we could identify problems on the first drops (crosswind, etc.) and correct on the later runs. This was standard on lightly-defended targets and better assured that we really hit it before we were through.

'The trouble was that that one heavy gun was firing like there was no tomorrow and seemed reasonably accurate as well. I began fuming that if we took our deliberate time on this target and gave him forty-eight clay pigeons to shoot at, twelve planes in four runs each, he was going to hit one of us. So, I took it upon myself to drop all my bombs on my first run and to use the remaining three runs to duel with that gun. On my second run, then, I came around a little further and, in my dive, lined up on the gun. He had not been ducking down before because everyone else was ignoring him, so as I came down he was firing directly at me and I was firing all six 50-calibre guns back at him. His big orange balls of fire came floating up at me, passing over me and to the right about fifty feet and my smaller red balls streaked down at him. Near the end of my dive I walked my rounds right into his and he went a little wild and stopped firing.

'As I pulled out, though, I could see him firing again, at our next man. So, on my third run I started hitting him early, from way high up and held it in there pretty well. Part way down, however, I got a little miffed at him because he was still missing me pretty badly, above my right wing and still out about fifty feet. What the heck, isn't he any better than that? I remembered that I had colour film in my gun camera. (This hop was a good indication that I, at least, had been operating too long. I was getting blasé. There was a movie camera mounted on the right wing root of our planes. Every time we fired our guns the camera would capture all the action, usually in black and white. We used it to back up damage assessments and to diagnose aiming and firing problems.) It was getting this in living colour but he was too far off to make it especially dramatic.

So I adjusted my dive and flew up closer to his rising stream of orange fireballs until they were just passing over my right wing, just above my gun camera! What a shot! Cut! Take! Print!

'And I carried it lower than usual and poured my six 50s right into his bunker. To my satisfaction, the orange balls essentially went away. He did fire again but by the way he fired it looked like I hadn't killed him, I had just damaged his gun. He would fire off a few bursts, poorly aimed and stop a while, then fire off some more. The final run was anti-climactic. He didn't even challenge me. Lots of adventure. Lots of jackass gambling. For every one of his orange fireballs that I could see, there were five non-tracers that I couldn't see. Where were they going? Clearly I was getting jaded. I was an accident waiting to happen. I needed a rest.'

Princeton's Air Wing spent a break at Fujiya, but returned to the line again on 18 August. On 20 August the target was near Pyongyang and on the way back Dykema and his fellow pilots were 'exhausted and emotionally spent'. Next day VF-192 went after factories with bombs and rockets. After a break on the 22nd it was back to the war again on 23 August when VF-192 was ordered to strike supply targets south of Wonsan near the front lines. The weather, however, was so bad that the Corsairs were diverted further north, near Chongjin, to hit a lumber mill. Ensign Owen Dykema recalls: 'Oddly enough, we didn't set many fires, though we hit all the buildings. I guess it took incendiaries or napalm to get them going. Anyway, it was now a matchstick factory, or maybe toothpicks. We had a little different kind of excitement however. Several days before we had gotten word that MiGs had been coming down into our area and causing a little havoc. Generally, they were single planes. They would sit up there very high and watch us go back and forth to the beach. From time to time when we, they and the sun, were properly aligned they would swoop down and knock off one plane, usually our "tail-end Charlie". They would come from above and behind at high speed, fire at one guy and continue on down and away, back to Manchuria. We were so much slower and therefore could turn so much faster that if we could spot them coming they could never get us. Of course, neither could we get them. The key was in spotting them first.

'So, we were flying recce up the beach when we got an advisory from one of the ships that there were MiGs in the area. Our leader wisely noted that our time was just about up anyway so he started a turn out to sea.

Just as we got into the turn we spotted the MiG, coming down out of the sun. He had already been into his run on us before we started our turn, but even our relatively gentle turn was too steep for him to follow. When I saw him he was standing vertically on one wing, pulling vapour trails off the wingtips trying to turn with us and keep us in his sights. He was firing that big old cannon he has in his nose but the rounds were curving off behind us. If we hadn't started that turn when we did he could well have gotten one of us.

'However, as he passed underneath, "Tail-End Charlie", in this case an "Enswine" from 195 flying a big old AD, pulled up and over in a half-barrel roll and fired "from the hip", upside down, at him going away and nearly got him! Everybody applauded loudly in the cockpits. What a coup if he had shot him down (the duty "Enswine")! The rest of us slunk home quietly, with our tails between our legs.'

By 17 September Ensign Dykema's tour was over, or so he thought. He had flown forty-one missions. The skipper, Lieutenant (j.g.) Howard W. 'Wes' Westervelt Jr,[6] had completed a hundred and his successor, T.P. Butzen, 104. On 20 September *Princeton* docked in Japan but on 1 October the carrier left for the war zone once again. For Dykema it was the start of his fifth tour in Korean waters.

On 1 September 1952 TF-77 despatched the largest naval air strike of the war when twenty-nine aircraft from *Essex*, sixty-three from *Princeton* and fifty-two from *Boxer* destroyed the synthetic oil refinery at Aoji in north-eastern Korea. MiG-15s had never posed too much of a threat to USN or USMC fighter-bombers but, at this stage in the war, Chinese MiG-15s now began to harass CAS Corsairs and MAG-12 had to formulate tactics and brief its pilots on how to counteract the jet threat. Being much more manoeuvrable, Corsair pilots were urged to turn inside the faster, better-climbing MiGs and present them with less effective head-on passes. On 10 September the Corsair became the first and only US Navy propeller-driven aircraft to destroy a MiG in the air over Korea. Captain Jesse G. Folmar and his wingman, First Lieutenant Willie L. Daniels, both of VMFA-312 'Checkerboards', flew their F4U-4Bs off the *Sicily* and set course to attack a formation of 300

---

6. Westervelt was hit by AAA while on a strafing run in a valley running north to south on 13 September and crashed into a hillside.

enemy troops on the south shore of the Taedong river. Jesse Gregory Folmar, born on 13 October 1920 in Montgomery County, Alabama, joined the US Marines during the Second World War as an enlisted man. Jesse advanced in rank to captain and flew F4Us in combat in the Pacific. During the morning briefing on the USS *Sicily* prior to the day's mission, the MiG presence in the area was discussed and the plan was to turn head-on into an attacking MiG and fire away, since there was no way the Corsair could outrun a MiG-15.

As they neared their target, Folmar and Daniels were jumped by four MiG-15s, which attacked in pairs near the mouth of the river. The enemy jet pilots were evidently not as experienced as the two Corsair pilots, who immediately went into the well-rehearsed defensive weave, each pilot covering the tail of his wingman. After avoiding the first two MiGs, the two Corsair pilots were confronted by the second pair. The MiG pilots made a fatal error. As they flew a slow, climbing turn to the left, right in front of Folmar, he seized on the lapse to fire off a five-second burst of 20mm cannon shells into the enemy jets as they passed. One of the MiG-15s was hit and began trailing black smoke, pitched down and the pilot ejected. Four more MiGs appeared and with the odds stacked against them, Folmar and Daniels knew that it was time to leave. They dived for the safety of the sea. Daniels was able to chase one of the MiG-15s off Folmar's tail, but a second jet pumped 37mm cannon shells into the American's port wing. Folmar could no longer control the Corsair and he baled out near the US-held island of Sock-to. Daniels radioed air-sea rescue and circled while Folmar bobbed around in the water. The downed airman was soon rescued by a USAF SA-16 Albatross amphibian and taken to safety. Folmar's remarkable victory was the sole Corsair MiG kill in the Korean War.

On 4 October 1952 VF-192's Corsairs flew a close-air-support mission. Ensign Owen Dykema recalls: 'As usual we had to fly clear across Korea to the Yellow Sea, over near Seoul, Panmunjon, etc. We only had time left for one run on a small, beat-up hill infested with troops, mortars, guns, etc. Chazz put two of his rockets into an ammo bunker, with a spectacular display of fireworks resulting. Pieces of exploding shells went flaming into the air, trailing a dense white smoke. I put my bombs in the trenches but missed with my rockets. As long as I hit the area I aimed at I was satisfied, but coming aboard, after a couple weeks getting rusty, I got two wave-offs, as many as I'd gotten all cruise. I just couldn't get set up right commencing my turn. Third time around I made a long, wide, looping pass and got a "Roger" all the way! Good landing too.

'I flew a strike on 5 October on a little supply area. We hit the target and split into divisions to "recce" an area. All at once I was alone, with two guys following me wherever I went. Some feeling. Coming back the old clunker kept grunting, puffing smoke (a little) and throwing oil all over the windshield. When I got in the groove the sun was just so it glared on the water and the oil on the windshield so I couldn't see the LSO. So I made another "head out of the cockpit" pass and got aboard first try.

'Had a big strike on 7 October, on a very meagre target. A couple dozen of our planes and seventeen from the *Kearsage*. Boy, were those *Kearsage* planes ever fouled up! We all launched at the same time yet we had to circle just off the beach to wait for those crumbs, a smaller strike than we were. Then they were supposed to go in on their target ahead of us, while we hit one a couple miles north of theirs, after they were clear. They got started but drove ten miles right past the target and never saw it! Finally the skipper called up and told them where it was and that we would attack first, to mark the location. We made a run on the target and they followed us in, diving through our planes which were climbing out of the target and dropped their load in an empty streambed north of the target! All this time their jet cover mistook us for their planes and were busy covering us, although even that was screwed up and ineffectual. They'd been out here nearly a month, seem to think it's because we fight this war as professionals, not as a bunch of "flash-in-the-pan" amateurs or glory-seekers. We just operated efficiently, every day, hit our target good and kept it all orderly, safe and well-disciplined. I was proud to be a naval aviator, a member of Air Group 19 and a member of VF-192!

'This final tour on the line was expensive, though, because we lost "Connie Neville".[7] No chance of survival. He was on another close-air-support mission down around the bomb line. The way I heard it he was pulling out at the bottom of his run, just about horizontal and going at about 300mph, when a round of some kind of heavy AA caught him right in the wing root and blasted his whole wing off. With just one wing and going at that speed,

---

7. Ensign Conrad L. Neville was hit by AAA during a close air support mission on 7 October. No egress was reported. He was recovered during Operation Glory.

he spun like a top and went straight in. No chance that he could have gotten out, he was too low. He must have been glued in his seat by the centrifugal forces of that rapid spin anyway. One can only hope that the blast that got his wing (just 5-10 feet away from him) got him as well, rather than for him to have to endure those last few seconds of spinning terror.

'We had a twelve-Corsair strike on the 14th, on a bridge in the vital railroad junction at Kowon. There was a terrific wind, about 30mph, blowing right across the target so it was very difficult to bomb. Eric Schloer managed to get a hit on it by using an almost absurd wind correction. All I did was plough up the riverbed a bit. The skipper of 193 was leading the hop and for some fool reason wanted to approach the target at 15,000 feet (oxygen altitude), letting down to 12,000 feet at the "push over point" so we'd have lots of speed. We had speed all right, so much that three of 193's planes lost a big section of engine cowling. I had 375 knots, or well over 400mph, at the bottom of my run; so much speed, for a Corsair, it felt like it would fall apart. Speaking of VF-193, John Shaughnessey was also wiped out. I didn't hear any particulars but it apparently was another "no chance of survival" situation. Another combat loss, another ensign gone.[8]

Next day, 15 October 1952, Ensign Dykema flew his forty-seventh and final Corsair mission of the Korean War: 'All the wheels, even the captain, told us there was to be an amphibious landing near Wonsan. The night before, the skipper of the ship got on the PA system and gave a stirring speech about the upcoming amphibious assault. Just like in your best John Wayne movies: "The boys on the beach will have no defences but you, the planes and men of carrier aviation. Give it your all above and beyond the call. Clear the way for them. You can save hundreds of lives." I was touched and so were we all. As a result we all flew hard and took more than the average, more than sensible risks. We figured the lives of a bunch of doggies depended on our knocking out the guns on the beach, so we risked our butts and clobbered the area.

'For the past several nights the night-fighters had said they could see lights on the roads all over Korea, of supply columns and weapons carriers converging on the beach area just south of Wonsan (reminiscent of the Chosin Reservoir power-plant strike). We could see the beach defences

---

8. Ensign John Russell Shaughnessey was shot down by a MiG-15 near Hungnam on 7 October. He baled out over water but died shortly after being rescued by the USS *Boyd*.

being strengthened by the hour. Oh man, somebody was going to get clobbered. So we really went after them. That was about as aggressively as I flew throughout the whole cruise.

'And the defences on the beach were horrendous! Intelligence had warned us that the Reds had a new AA technique and this time they had the guns to do it. They would aim all their guns to cover a fixed cube of sky. Then as we flew into it, on command, everybody fired everything, all at once, into that cube. On my very last strike we made our very last run to the east intending to recover out over the ocean and be gone. I pulled out of my dive low and was climbing out heading out to sea as fast as I could get that old U-bird going. All of a sudden, as if by magic, the cube of sky right in front of me just suddenly blackened, with perhaps 100 bursts of AA, neatly filling out the cube. You could almost see the sharp edges and corners. They had fired at my buddies ahead of me but nevertheless I knew that if I flew into that cube there was a good chance that I would run into a lot of falling metal and not make it out the other side.

'So I rolled it over hard and pulled for all I was worth. I managed to get it turned away just in time, just before entering the cube. Then I found myself plummeting for the deck, with only a few hundred feet altitude remaining. So, once again, I rolled it hard, back to level and pulled for all I was worth. One more time, in the last few seconds of the whole cruise, I just managed to get it pulled out ending up just above the wave tops, high-tailing it for distance to seaward. My last flight in Korea and I came about as close as I did all summer to getting killed. What irony!

'Out to sea was the landing force, many, many ships of all sizes and descriptions. The ground-pounders were already in their landing craft, heading out for the beach. I saw myself as a witness to history, witness to the second major amphibious assault of the Korean War. But man, I had just gotten a clear view of what was waiting for them! We orbited out to sea a little way, waiting to see if we could assist anywhere. We were out of bombs and rockets but we still had lots of 50-calibre ammunition. The troops looked so defenceless in those little boats! Everybody was still ready to give their all to help them out.

'Then about 100 yards or so from the beach – I couldn't believe my eyes – in unison, all the landing craft made a 180-degree turn and headed back out to sea! Eventually, the troops all climbed back aboard the ships and the whole fleet disappeared over the horizon! Dumbfounded! Then when we got back aboard ship the powers that be actually had the gall to tell us it was all a very realistic exercise! Were they telling us that they were just acting, that the captain of the ship gave that emotional speech over the PA system as part of a "realistic exercise"? Or did the 'powers that be' above our "powers that be" run it as an exercise and not tell their troops that? I could see nothing but cynicism and/or duplicity in the whole operation. Man, I wished they had been in the cockpit with me as I squirmed to avoid getting shredded out of the sky! I thought once again that it was probably a very good thing that we had more or less decided not to make this our full-time career.

'I learned after the war that the whole operation had been planned and put in motion by General Matthew B. Ridgeway. He had observed that the Reds were getting very clever about keeping their troops and supplies out of sight during the day. His idea was to plan, but not execute, a major amphibious landing in order to draw the Reds out in the open, where we could strike them. I guess it worked but we lost a lot of guys, how much did they lose?'

Princeton sailed for Yokosuka to replenish and off-load her planes, before heading east to Hawaii and, finally, Alameda, on 3 November. On 16 October 144 pilots and about twenty crewmen received awards. Dykema received an Air Medal, a Gold Star for the Air Medal in lieu of a second award and the Navy Commendation Medal with the Combat device. A total of thirteen officers and three enlisted men, just about 10 per cent of the pilots in the air group, had been killed. Two days later *Princeton*'s remaining Corsairs were flown off to NAS Atsugi before the carrier docked. Ensign Owen Dykema recalls: 'So, I manned a Corsair for the last time and flew it off. I really felt funny taking off with no load. I was flying before I passed the island structure. And landing on a runway, the first time in 7½ months was really hairy! I hit hard on the wheels and bounced way back into the air. That last flight was actually kinda sad. It turned out to be the last flight I would ever make off a carrier, although not my last flight in a Corsair. After all the chaos, hard work, tension and fear the whole thing was over. No doubt about it, this cruise would forever remain the single most exciting, adventurous period of my life.'

In late 1952, the USS *Badoeng Strait*, a single escort carrier, barely half the size of the 900-foot-long Essex-class carriers off the east coast, along with one destroyer, fought a lonely war in the Yellow Sea and with China to the west. Every ten days, the little 507-foot-long American flat-top would head to Japan for re-supply, swapping places with a small British carrier and her escort. Lieutenant Colonel James L. Cooper was a pilot in Marine Corps Attack Squadron (VMA) 312 flying combat missions from the *Badoeng Strait*: 'While most were flown during daylight, a number were launched in the darkness before dawn – the "Early-Early" missions. Our little task unit of a single aircraft carrier and lone destroyer was appropriate for the size of the Yellow Sea. Only the *Badoeng Strait* operated in the sea's constricted waters about halfway up the west coast of Korea. Shortly after taking off, pilots could see the darkened landmass of the great Shandong Peninsula of mainland China to the west and the Haeju Peninsula of North Korea to the east, each less than a half-hour's flight away. On the day of this November 1952 "Early-Early" launch in the bitter cold off North Korea, the *Badoeng Strait* and her destroyer push through the sea's dark waters. The ships are blacked out. The icy sea is frosted with white-caps whipped up by a brisk wind. All night the carrier has been manoeuvring to place herself as near the target area as possible for the early-morning launch. On the hangar deck, one level below the flight deck, planes are serviced and repaired. In the frigid pre-dawn, crew members wearing heavy jackets are busy moving the F4U-4B fighter-bombers onto giant elevators up to the flight deck. Marine crewmen check the planes for readiness. Sailors, meanwhile, man their stations on a lonely watch. There is a clear division of labour on the carrier. The *Badoeng Strait* – nicknamed the "Bing-Ding" – has a navy crew, which operates the ship and launches and recovers aircraft. Combat missions and aircraft maintenance are conducted by the men of VMA-312 the Checkerboard Squadron.[9]

Armistice talks faltered in October 1952 and, despite attempts by new president Dwight D. Eisenhower to end the war, the conflict spilled over into 1953 with no end in sight. Bitter fighting took place during late March around a series of USMC outposts collectively known as the 'Nevada Cities' complex and only strong air support by Panther jets,

---

9. Lieutenant Colonel Cooper flew combat missions in the Second World War and the Korean War. Later, as a newsman in print, radio and television, he won numerous journalism awards, including two Emmys for news programmes. He ended his flight duties as VMA-312's executive officer. *Flying the Early-Early*, February 2009. Naval History Magazine Vol 23, No.1.

Tigercats, Skyraiders and the Corsair fighter-bombers of VMA-212 and 323 and VMF-115 and 311, retrieved the situation, albeit temporarily. Bitter fighting broke out along the MLR in May-June and the ADs and Corsairs of VMA-212 and VMA-323 were again called upon to dislodge enemy troops attacking Marine ground forces. Finally, the ground forces were forced to abandon the Marine outposts and the decision was made not to retake them. It would have cost too many lives to retake the outposts and the peace talks, which had resumed on 26 April after being recessed for 199 days, were by now progressing, albeit slowly. There was no let up as the communists tried to regain lost ground prior to a negotiated ceasefire agreement.

Princeton sortied from Yokosuka Harbor on 13 April to operate off Korea's eastern coast, in the icy Sea of Japan. They were 'on station' for just about thirty days, with three days at the start and end of the period in transit. Aboard were over 3,000 officers and enlisted men; 750 in the Air Group, of whom 129 were officers (mostly pilots). In this one month, seven pilots were killed. Weather permitting, they flew air missions three days out of four; on the fourth day the ship replenished fuel, ammunition, aviation gasoline and other supplies. In this one month, they replenished supplies on eight days, air operations were limited due to inclement weather on six days and they flew full air operations on sixteen days. On May 6, a typical day of full air ops, they flew 101 sorties, attacking a mining area and troop concentrations. Two strikes against the Komdok mining area destroyed a processing plant, several other buildings and started many fires. 'Cherokee' and close-air-support strikes effectively demolished supply shelters and frontline artillery positions. Two pilots were lost this day: Lieutenant L.R. Rickey was listed as missing following a strike south of Wonsan. His plane was believed to have been hit by AA. Ensign F.E. Painter was killed while ditching in the Sea of Japan. His plane was hit by anti-aircraft fire while on a strike north of Tanchon. The Corsair disintegrated upon impact and the pilot was not recovered.

During the last few weeks of the war most of the ground battles took place between the ROK army and the Communist forces, as the latter tried to land a final knockout blow. TF-77 was called upon to lend CAS and interdiction support for I and II Corps in the field. It proved to be the navy's last great all-out offensive of the war. For seven days during June 1953 aircraft from *Boxer*, *Philippine Sea*, *Princeton* and *Lake Champlain* flew round-the-clock missions in support of I ROK Corps' attacks to regain 'Anchor Hill'.

During this time the NKAF carried out some successful night 'heckling' missions against UN supply dumps. The North Korean 'Bed Check Charlie' pilots flew piston-engined Lavochkin La 9/-11s, Yak-18 trainers and Po-2 biplane aircraft that were too slow for USAF F-94 Starfires and USMC F3D Skyknight jet fighters to effectively intercept. An F-94 succeeded in shooting down a Po-2 by dropping its flaps and landing gear and throttling right back, but the Starfire stalled and crashed immediately afterwards. Even now, at this late date, the Corsair was once again required to take centre stage. On 17 June VC-3 onboard *Princeton*, the navy's only all-weather combat fighter squadron at that time, lent two of its F4U-5Ns under the command of 31-year-old Lieutenant Guy P. Bordelon, nicknamed 'Lucky Pierre', born in Ruston, Louisiana on 1 February 1922, to the Fifth Air Force at K-14 airfield near Seoul to intercept Communist night hecklers. The VC-3 detachment transferred to K-6, the big USMC airfield at Pyongtaek, thirty miles south of Seoul, which was better able to service the F4U-5Ns.

Guy Bordelon earned his wings as a naval aviator in 1943. He became a 'ploughback' instructor at Kingville, Texas, but not because he was a good pilot at that time. He barely squeaked through the navy's flight school, almost washing out. He later told his daughter, Michelle, 'Being kept back from going out to the fleet was the best thing that could have happened to me, because then I really learned how to fly.' He was training with an FM-2 Wildcat squadron when the war ended. He received a regular navy commission and stayed in the military. In 1951 he was assistant gunnery officer on the CA-75 *Helena*, in action off Korea. He was a thorough professional and did his job well, but was unhappy at the harassment he suffered under his 'black-shoe Navy' CO, who hated aviators. He was delighted to be ordered back to flight duty with Composite Squadron 3 (VC-3), an all-weather fighter squadron then at Moffet Field in California. This oversize squadron was equipped with F4U-5N night fighters; its pilots underwent specialized training; both planes and pilots were supported by specialist ground crews. VC-3 was then broken up into five-plane detachments, for assignment to individual carriers.

Bordelon joined *Princeton* for its second nine-month cruise of the Korean War. As night-fighters, Bordelon's unit had unique requirements that the naval bureaucracy had difficulty supporting, even down to the Corsairs' tail hooks. Starting in late October 1952, they began night-time strikes against North Korean road and rail targets. Like all ground-attack missions, these were very hazardous – low-level flying, exposed to intense flak and subject to vertigo in the dark compounded by the smoke of battle. On one occasion, while strafing a supply column of Chicom trucks on a mountain road, he noticed that his tracers were bouncing up and flying back over the top of his cockpit. He immediately pulled up, just barely missing flying into the side of a mountain.

Bordelon called *Princeton* a 'happy ship' but he was pleased to be detailed to the Seoul area in June 1953 to help the Bed Check Charlie raids which had just destroyed millions of gallons of aviation fuel and countless other valuable supplies. The air force jets flew too fast to counter the slow-moving, prop-driven Second World War-vintage planes used by the North Koreans for these harassment raids. Thus Bordelon's F4Us were called in and assigned to operate from a Marine base.[10]

At 2235 hours on 29 June Bordelon took off in F4U-5N BuNo124453, named *Annie Mo* for his wife, with another Corsair flown by Lieutenant (j.g.) Ralph Hopson, after the Marine radar operator at K-16 air base at Pyongtaek picked up a bogey in the Asan-Man area of Seoul. The other F4U-5N experienced problems with its radar but Bordelon had no such problems. Even though he carried radar, Bordelon's orders were to make a visual sighting before firing, just in case the bogey was a friendly aircraft. Luckily, it was a bright moonlit night so he stood a good chance of sighting the enemy aircraft's exhaust flames. Bordelon homed in on his prey and, when in visual range, correctly identified it as a Yak-18 two-seat trainer, powered by a 5-cylinder radial engine, capable of 140 knots top speed. Bordelon was ordered to fire and he did. Immediately the Yak-18 pilot banked hard right and his rear gunner returned fire wildly. These were futile acts of desperation. Bordelon locked on to the Yak and blasted it out of the night sky with a fusillade of fifty-sixty rounds of 20mm high-explosive incendiaries.

Shortly after, ground-control radar vectored Bordelon on to a second target, which he identified as another Yak-18. The American pilot closed

---

10. *Lt. Guy Bordelon Night-fighter Ace, US Navy F4U-5N Corsair pilot* by Stephen Sherman, March 2000. Updated 25 June 2011.

in from behind the fighter and at once the rear gunner opened fire on the Corsair, but he was firing in the wrong direction. Bordelon fired a long raking burst of 20mm cannon into the intruder and it caught fire. The wing came off and the plane exploded on the ground. 'Over so fast?' he thought. Bordelon returned to Pyongtaek at midnight and was credited with two night victories.

Bordelon took off again on the night of 30 June/1 July at 2130 hours in *Annie Mo* to chase more bandits that had been reported north of Seoul. North of Inchon, Bordelon was vectored by JOC (Joint Operations Center) on to an enemy aircraft. And when he was able to make visual contact he saw that there were not one but several bogeys, which he identified as Lavochin La-11 fighters. He turned on to the rear of a La-11 and shot it down before taking up the chase with another. By now he was over North Korea and was being fired on by enemy anti-aircraft. Undeterred, Bordelon pulled in closer. When the La-11 finally levelled out he gave him a long burst of cannon fire from not more than 200 yards and the plane exploded. Bordelon now needed one more confirmed air-to-air kill to make him the navy's only ace of the war.

For the next two weeks, the North Koreans didn't send down any 'Bed Check Charlies' but Bordelon was kept busy, being vectored onto friendly aeroplanes. Luckily, he didn't shoot at any of them. One night he closed in on two Tupolev Tu-2 bombers, but could not fire because of a disconnected wire in his direction-finder gear. Undeterred, he put on full throttle, pulled two miles ahead of the Tu-2s, turned directly at them, dropped his landing gear and turned on his landing light. He was almost on them when they panicked. One dived straight down, possibly into the ocean; the other just missed him and pulled straight up. He had broken up their bombing run on Inchon.

On the night of 16/17 July Bordelon was heading north to Seoul when one of his fellow pilots reported that he had a bogey. Shortly thereafter he reported that his radar had gone out. Bordelon was vectored in to take over. He picked up the target and gave chase until, finally, he got on his tail. Despite the Stygian darkness, Bordelon was able to pick up the enemy's exhaust pattern which identified it as a La-9 high-performance fighter. The wily Lavochkin pilot led Bordelon right over the anti-aircraft guns at Kaesong and they began firing, although their shells were exploding more to the rear of the La-9 rather than the Corsair so Bordelon pulled in closer to the enemy machine. Bordelon then pulled up and began firing at the fleeing Lavochkin. He pumped around 200 rounds into the machine, which turned to the right and exploded. The blast destroyed Bordelon's night vision and he had to reach up and switch on the auto-pilot, which he had pre-set so that it would come on easily. Bordelon was so overjoyed that he could have given the auto-pilot a kiss! He flew around until his night vision returned and saw the enemy plane burning on the ground. With that he headed back and landed on the *Princeton* in the early hours of 17 July. He was welcomed by the ship's band, banners, marine sideboys and a personal greeting by the Commanding Officer, Captain O.C. Gregg. *Princeton*'s official action report further noted, 'Movies and still pictures were taken'. *Annie Mo* did not fare as well; it was wrecked shortly afterwards in an accident while an air force reservist pilot was flying it. The air force officially confirmed all five of Bordelon's night victories. His actions earned him the Navy Cross. He was to say later, 'My top award was again to return to my family's arms.' His son Marc, daughters Marcia and Michele, to whom he creatively wrote letters through the guise of a 'little green lizard' that served as his co-pilot, and his wife, for whom he named his aircraft 'Annie-Mo', remained the loves of his life.[11]

Even with the signing of the armistice just days away the Communists continued their ground action right to the wire. On 27 July, the last day of the war, four of TF-77's carriers – *Lake Champlain, Boxer, Philippine Sea* and *Princeton* – were operating off the east coast while, off the west coast, *Bairoko* with Corsairs of VMA-312 and VMA-332 was on station. Altogether, 649 sorties were flown this day and the USMC squadrons, too, were active over Korea. Then, on 27 July, the Communists signed the Armistice and the thirty-eight month war was over. Peace reigned once again in the 'Land of the Morning Calm'.

Korea was the crowning glory for the Corsair. No fewer than seven USMC and twenty-eight navy squadrons flew Corsairs during the conflict.

---

11. Bordelon became an instructor after Korea and taught survival training to pilots during the Vietnam War. He was also chosen for the prestigious 'Top Gun' award. He made a career of the United States Navy, staying in for 27 years, until his retirement in 1969. Among his assignments, he was involved in recovery of the Apollo astronauts. Guy Bordelon retired as a commander, returning to his home town of Ruston, Louisiana. He died on 19 December 2002 at the age of 80 and was buried in the family plot in Greenwood Cemetery, in Ruston.

They were credited with ten air-to-air victories but, unquestionably, their most crucial contribution was the unstinting and unrelenting support given to the ground troops, often in the most appalling weather.

Korea was also the Corsair's swansong. Newer jet types gradually entered service and, by the end of 1953, only three USMC and seven USN squadrons were still equipped with F4Us. In 1954 only VC-3 and VC-4 were still equipped with Corsairs. VC-3's Corsairs onboard *Philippine Sea* were among the aircraft used during the 'Hainan Turkey Shoot' on 26 July 1954, following the shooting down three days earlier of a Cathay Pacific Airways C-54 Skymaster (VR-HEU) by fighter planes of the People's Republic of China off the coast of Hainan Island, when the plane was en route from Bangkok to Hong Kong, killing seven of the thirteen passengers. The crew was headed by British captain Phil Blown and included three female flight attendants. One flight crew member and two cabin crew members were killed in the attack and subsequent crash of the airliner. VF-54's AD Skyraiders destroyed a Chinese Lavochkin La-7 and a VC-3 Corsair flown by Lieutenant Commander E.B. Salsig and the ADs were credited with a second La-7.

VC-4 had the honour of being the last unit to fly the F4U in frontline service when it retired the last of its F4U-5Ns on 31 December 1955. Several Corsairs soldiered on in the USMC and USN reserves, the last being retired in mid-1957.

Chapter 9

War and Peace

He went past my P-51 like a freight train passing a bum.

**Mustang race pilot describing 'Super Corsair' pilot Cook Cleland's
winning streak in the 1947 Thompson Trophy Race**

Korea was not the only trouble spot where the Corsair operated in the
1950s. France was trying to re-assert its pre-Second World War colonial
influence in Indo-China, which during the war, had been overrun by the
Japanese. Indo-China was composed of the French colonies of Laos and
Cambodia and three provinces, Tonkin, Annam and Cochin China, which
made up Vietnam. After the war, France regained control of southern
Vietnam and was determined to 're-colonise' the remaining provinces.
Fighting against the Việt Minh started in 1946 and, by 1953, with the war
in Korea coming to a close France was fast losing control of Indo-China.
Now, in March 1954, with no land war to fight in Korea, Red China sent
a steady stream of munitions and materiel across 500 miles of jungle and
mountains to the battle front to enable the Việt Minh to sustain a major
offensive against the French. Just as in Korea, the supplies were moved by
night and French aircraft were unable to stop the flow of 16,400,000lb of
supplies and munitions reaching Dien Bien Phù in north-west Tongking,
170 miles from Hanoi, where French FFL and tirailleurs from North
Africa were surrounded.

French air support throughout the Indo-China conflict was composed
mainly of second-hand, ex-USN types, like the F6F Hellcat, and these
were used aboard three former US Navy carriers by the *Force Maritime
de l' Aéronautique Navale*. The only new aircraft in its inventory were 100
F8F Bearcats and ninety-four F4U-7s. The F4U-7, which first flew on
2 July 1952, was an ideal economical aircraft to be supplied to France
for fighter-bomber operations. The airframe was almost identical to the
AU-1 and the R-2800-43W engine used on the F4U-4 powered it. The
F4U-7s were obtained in 1952 by the US Navy and then transferred to

the *Aéronavale* as part of the United States' Military Assistance Program (MAP). *Aéronavale* pilots meanwhile began training on the F4U-7 at NAS Oceania, Virginia, in October. *Flotille 14* based at Karouba Air Base, Tunisia, was the first squadron to receive the new F4U-7 on 15 January 1953. When the last F4U-7 came off the production line at Dallas, Texas, on Christmas Eve 1952 no fewer than 981 major engineering changes had been made during the Corsair's thirteen-year production record which produced 12,582 aircraft.

Meanwhile, the situation in Indo-China was becoming ever more desperate and reinforcements of any kind were needed badly. In the spring of 1954 *Flottille 14* were airlifted to Tourane, later Da Nang, by USAF transport aircraft, while the *Saipan* delivered twenty-five AU-1 Corsairs from MAG-12 stock on Japan. On 26 April USMC pilots flew the AU-1s into Tourane and the Corsairs became operational at the *Armée de l'Air Française* base at Bạch Mai near Hanoi. On 30 April the French aircraft carrier *Arromanches* was relieved by the newly-arrived *Belleau Wood* which the United States had lent the French Navy for service in Indo-China and which was manned by a French crew. It brought from France *Flotille 14* commanded by Lieutenant Menettrier and eighteen F4U-7s. *Flotille 14* were to take over from the F6F Hellcats of *Flottille 11*, which unit had been decimated during four months of combat. Time was fast running out for the defenders at Dien Bien Phû, surrounded by almost 150 field pieces and at least thirty-six heavy flak guns among the numerous anti-aircraft batteries on the ridges around the mountainous outpost.

On 6 May the French were able to put up their largest single strike formation yet. Eighteen Corsairs, forty-seven B-26 bombers, twenty-six Bearcats, sixteen SB2C Helldivers and five Privateers carried out flak suppression at Dien Bien Phû as C-119s flown by American Civil Air Transport pilots attempted yet another supply drop. The Corsairs could only contribute limited support before the garrison surrendered the next day, 7 May, after fifty-six days of bitter resistance. By the end of the battle sixty-two aircraft had been shot down or badly damaged over Dien Bien Phû. The fighting in the rest of the country continued until 21 July 1954, when a negotiated withdrawal of French forces from Indo-China was agreed. At the Geneva Conference on Indo-China, the French agreed to partition Vietnam along the 17th Parallel and Ho Chi Minh assumed absolute power in the North. The Corsairs were returned to the US Navy in the Philippines, although some were refurbished and returned to the French for use in Algeria. In November 1953 *Flotille 14* personnel returned to North Africa, as fighting in French Algeria reached new heights.

Full scale war broke out in Algeria on 1 November 1954 when the *Front de Libération Nationale* (National Liberation Front, or FLN) began a series of attacks on French targets. The revolt was put down by February 1955 but a new FLN campaign began in 1956 and in 1958 the F4U-7s of *Flotilles* 15 and 17 flying from Karouba, Hyeres and, later, Telergma, Algeria, were used in the ground-attack role against villages near terrorist trouble spots. Algeria finally gained independence from France in July 1962.

Meanwhile, on 26 July 1956, France and the United Kingdom faced another major problem in Africa when President Gamal Abdel Nasser of Egypt nationalized the Suez Canal. Once again third world nationalism was making a challenge to the accepted post-war order. The canal was vital to Britain and France's economic interests in the Middle and Far East and Africa and beyond. The two European nations decided to invade Egypt and regain control of the important waterway and, in August 1956, French and British nationals were evacuated from the country. On 29 October Israel launched an attack on Egypt and on 1 November Britain committed her land-based air power from Cyprus and Malta. On 5 and 6 November the British and French naval forces went into action. Operation Musketeer (French: Opération Mousquetaire) involved Anglo-French landings in the Suez Canal Zone using five British and two French carriers, with airborne strike and helicopter assault operations being made against Egyptian airfields and military installations.

Onboard the French carrier *Arromanches*, previously HMS *Colossus* of the Royal Navy, were F4U-7s of *Flotille 14* and embarked on *La Fayette*, the loan Independence-class carrier USS *Langley*, were Corsairs of *Flotille 15*. Together, they formed a quarter of the carrier strike force and flew as many as four sorties a day during the two-day air campaign. On 1 November when the French cruiser *Georges Leygues* (C604) supported Israeli artillery at Rafah, French Corsairs took off from *La Fayette* to strike an Egyptian airfield but without success. A second strike took off and struck air bases at Alexandria. On 3 November eighteen F4Us from *Arromanches* and *La Fayette* bombed Egyptian airfields around Cairo. The *Aéronavale* attacked the bridge at Damietta and other targets of opportunity in the Suez and Port Said areas. The Corsairs, each painted with black and yellow recognition stripes on the wings and rear fuselage, flew close-air-support and air-defence sorties. Among their contribution they claimed to have sunk an Egyptian torpedo boat. In the afternoon of 6 November, 522 French paras of the *1er REP* (*Régiment Étranger Parachutiste* or 1st Foreign [Legion] Parachute Regiment) were dropped near Port Fouad. These were also constantly supported by the Corsairs of the *Aéronavale*, which flew very intensive operations: for example, although *La Fayette* developed catapult problems, no fewer than forty combat sorties were completed. Though the Egyptian Air Force numbered Soviet built MiG-15s and Il-28s, the Anglo-French forces quickly established total air superiority over the Canal Zone. Losses generally were light but two Corsairs, one of which was written off in an accident and the other, piloted by the CO of *Flotille 14*, which was shot down by AA fire over Cairo, were lost before a UN resolution brought the incursion to an abrupt end.

French Corsair squadrons also saw combat against Algerian guerrillas, starting in 1956, and limited action in Tunisia in 1961. The F4U-7 and AU-1 Corsairs remained in the *Aéronavale* inventory until 1964 when they were replaced by the Vought F-8E Crusader aboard its carriers. Others operated on ground-attack missions in Algeria up until the ceasefire in March 1962. A few F4U-7s went to technical schools in France while the rest were scrapped.

Three countries – Argentina, El Salvador and Honduras – received Corsairs under the Military Aid Sales Program (MAS) during the 1950s and 1960s. In May 1956 Argentina acquired ten F4U-5 and -5NL Corsairs for the *El Comando de la Aviación Naval de la Armada Argentina* (COAN). In 1957 a further sixteen F4U-5 and -5NL aircraft were received with a few additional non-flying Corsair airframes for spares. All Argentina's twenty-six Corsairs were operated aboard the carrier ARA *Independencia*, formerly HMS *Warrior* and at the shore-based Punta de Indio. All of Argentina's Corsairs were used solely for patrol duty and none saw combat action. However, the same could not be said about the Corsairs supplied to both Honduras and El Salvador! Under the terms of the Mutual Aid Program, the *Fuerza Aérea Hondureña* (FAH) received ten USN-surplus F4U-5/-5N/-5NLs early in 1956. Three years later ten more were received from the US warbird operator, the late Bob Bean, as trade-ins for five P-38 Lightnings and four Bell P-63 Kingcobras.

In 1957, meanwhile, the neighbouring El Salvadorian air force had acquired fifteen flyable Goodyear-built FG-1D Corsairs under the Military Aid Sales Program for service with the *Fuerza Aérea Salvadorena* (FAS). In October 1959 the government of El Salvador received five non-flyable condition F4U-4s to be used as spares. Ironically, US military mission advisors, concerned about the fragile balance of power in America, objected to the sale of fighter aircraft to the region but their objections were dismissed. Their worst fears were realised in the late 1960s when tensions between Honduras and El Salvador reached a new high. El Salvador's acute shortage of land resulted in an exodus by tens of thousands of landless peasants into Honduras and, by 1969, illegal immigrant refugees accounted for over 12 per cent of the Honduran population. The flow of refugees continued unchecked and matters reached a flashpoint in June 1969 when El Salvador and Honduras were drawn in a World Cup football qualifier. The first match was to be played in Tegucigalpa, Honduras, on 8 June, with the return game to be played on 15 June in San Salvador. Radio Honduras broadcast anti-El Salvador propaganda up to and after the first game, which the Honduran national team won 1-0. El Salvador claimed that its players had been poisoned. Tensions were further heightened when El Salvador emerged as the victors in the second game. With 'honours' even, the two teams then met in a decider in Mexico City, which the El Salvadorian side won. On 26 June Honduras and El Salvador broke off diplomatic relations and on 14 July 12,000 El Salvadorian troops invaded Honduras.

What became known as the 'Soccer War' lasted two weeks and, during that time, Corsairs were used against Corsairs over Honduras and El Salvador. *Fuerza Aérea Salvadorena* ground-attack Corsairs and their P-51D Mustang escorts attacked the *Fuerza Aérea Hondureña* main base at Tocontin near Tegucigalpa. Honduran Corsairs attacked an El Salvadorian oil refinery and set it on fire. On another occasion, an *FAH* Corsair pilot shot up an El Salvadorian C-47 Dakota while, in another incident, a pair of FAiH Corsairs from San Pedro Sula destroyed forty El Salvadorian buses filled with soldiers heading for the battle area. Early on 17 July *FAH* pilot Captain Fernando 'Sotillo' Soto, flying an F4U-5N, shot down an *FAS* Mustang. Later that same day he and his wingman, Captain Edgardo Acosta, were en route to bomb San Miguel, El Salvador, when they espied a pair of *FAS* FG-1Ds. Soto jettisoned his bombs and climbed to height to gain altitude advantage over the Salvadorian Corsairs before making his attack. He singled out one of the FG-1s and destroyed it with bursts of gunfire. The Corsair went down in flames, the *FAS* pilot parachuting to safety. Acosta had become embroiled with two other *FAS* fighters but, undeterred, Soto made a solo attack on the second *FAS* Corsair which exploded, killing the pilot. These three victories were the only aerial victories of the two-week Soccer War, which had cost the lives of 4,000 people, mostly civilians. Next day both sides accepted the Organization of American States' (OAS) peace plan, although fighting continued off and on until the mid-1980s. The *FAS* flew its last Corsair in the summer of 1971 while the *FAH* replaced their Corsairs with North American F-86 Sabres during the 1970s. The final air-to-air combat over America had flamboyantly brought the remarkable Corsair's long and distinguished record of war service to an end.

Ever since the end of the Second World War the Corsair has enjoyed a colourful career on the racing circuit and as an air show performer. With the end of the war, the famous pre-war National Air Races made their re-appearance as it was announced that the Bendix Trophy Race, a transcontinental speed dash from Van Nuys Airport, Los Angeles, to Cleveland, would take place on the 1946 Labor Day weekend, 28–30 August. Paul Mantz, flying a Mustang, won the event, which included an FG-1D among the twenty-two entrants. Mantz won again the following year. Although the Corsair could not compete with the Mustang in the Bendix races, it more than held its own in the Thompson Trophy Races, a 15-mile closed-course event which took place at Cleveland after the Bendix race. FG-1A BuNo13481 NX69900 *Lucky Gallon* flown by Cook Cleland, the Second World War SBD navy pilotm was one of a dozen aircraft which took part in the 2 September 1946 Thompson pylon racing meeting. P-39 *Cobra II*, flown by Tex Johnston, won with an average speed of 373.908mph. Cleland finished sixth in *Racer 92* with an average speed of 357.465mph.

Air racing by now was a serious business. Late in 1946 US navy pilot Cook Cleland bought three surplus Goodyear F2Gs for between $2,818 and $1,250 with the intention of modifying and racing them in the September 1947 Thompson Trophy speed-dash event. All three of Cleland's muscular 'Super Corsairs', powered by a 3,000-horsepower Pratt & Whitney R-4360 and painted in a vivid colour scheme, were ready in time. His personal racer, BuNo.88463 NX5577N (*Race 74*), was in overall dark blue with a white chequered cowling. BuNo88457 NX5588N (*Race 84*) was also finished in a dark blue scheme and would be flown by Tony Janazzo. BuNo14693 NX5590N (*Race 94*) was painted in a red-and-white scheme and would be flown by Richard M. Becker, a former navy ensign whom Cleland had met while assigned as a test pilot at Tactical Test, Naval Air Test Center, Patuxent River, Maryland. A fourth Corsair, BuNo14694 NX91092 (*Race 18*) *Miss Port Colombo*, owned and flown by Ron Puckett, was also entered in the twenty-lap race. Puckett, who paid just $1,250 on 19 March 1947 for the Corsair, could not get his R-4360 engine started, but he did eventually join the race, only to have to drop out in the nineteenth lap with a damaged engine. Of the thirteen racers, only seven finished. Joe Ziegler baled out of his XP-40Q after the engine exploded and a P-38 Lightning and three P-51 Mustangs had to make emergency landings during the contest. All of the pilots survived, but Tony Janazzo died when his F2G crashed into the ground near Pylon Two at full throttle and exploded in a ball of flame. A later accident investigation speculated that Janazzo had been overcome by carbon-monoxide fumes in the cockpit and had blacked out. (As a result, racing pilots began to wear oxygen masks during contests.) Cleland's team snatched a record-setting 396mph victory, Cook Cleland in NX5577N, with his throttle jammed fully forward, crossed the finish line with an average speed of 396.1mph. A P-51 race pilot later described him passing him 'like a freight train passing a bum'. Dick Becker came second in F2G NX5590N with a 390mph average.

Cook Cleland entered two of the Super Corsairs in the 1948 Thompson Trophy Race event. In an effort to increase the top speed of the aircraft, his personal machine, NX5590N (*Race 94*), had eighteen inches removed from each outer wing panel and the engine used a new type of fuel mixture. However, Cleland and Dick Becker's Super Corsairs, both of which used the new fuel, were forced to retire when engine combustion problems blew their improvised upper carburettor air-intake scoops loose as the Corsairs passed the 410mph mark. Cleland and Becker got their Corsairs down safely.

Not satisfied with the speed increase achieved by removing eighteen inches from each outer wing panel on NX5590N, Cleland removed an additional four and a half feet from each wing panel for the 1949 contest.

This, coupled with a fourteen-inch-diameter propeller, adversely affected stability to such an extent that he had to install wing-tip plates to help the roll rate. Cleland also fitted a hydrogen-peroxide injection system to the R-4360 to increase power to over 4,000hp at 2,800rpm. In all, four Super Corsairs including XF2G-1 N91092 *Miss Port Colombo* flown by Ron Puckett, were entered for the 1949 contest. Dick Becker was forced to withdraw *Race 74* after developing engine problems winning the qualifying heat (achieving a speed of 415mph). The rules did not permit an engine change. Altogether, ten racers started the fifteen-lap contest; Cleland, in *Race 94*, was the favourite, but Bill Odom in his highly-modified P-51C *Beguine* was expected to give him a run for his money. Ben McKillen's F2G-1 BuNo8854, *Race 57*, took an early lead but he was passed by Cleland and Puckett on the third and fourth lap. The three F2Gs came home in first, second and third place, Cleland winning with an average of 397.1mph and Puckett averaging 393.527mph.

Odom's highly-modified Mustang stalled around a pylon and the P-51C crashed into a house, killing Odom and two other people. This tragedy and the onset of the Korean War signalled the demise of air racing at Cleveland and it was not until 1964, when Reno began air racing again, that unlimited air racing was revived successfully. Corsairs competed against Bearcats, Mustangs and Sea Furies without much success but speeds increased with the advent of the highly-modified Air Museum's Planes of Fame 'Super' Corsair. This aircraft (M31518), an F4U-1, was modified to F2G configuration at Chino, California, in 1982 with a 3,000hp R-4360 engine replacing the R-2800 powerplant and a four-bladed propeller fitted. At Reno 1984 and 1985 five F4U-4/7FG-1Ds and a Super Corsair took part and, at the latter's Unlimited Gold Race, Steve Hinton set an average race speed record of 438.1286mph in the Super Corsair. The record stood for two years.

Index